# CHURCH FONTS

## Matthew Byrne

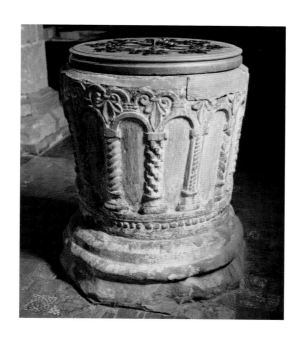

SHIRE PUBLICATIONS
Bloomsbury Publishing Plc
PO Box 883, Oxford, OX1 9PL, UK
1385 Broadway, 5th Floor, New York, NY 10018,
USA

E-mail: shire@bloomsbury.com

www.shirebooks.co.uk

SHIRE is a trademark of Osprey Publishing Ltd

First published in Great Britain in 2020

A catalogue record for this book is available from the
British Library.

ISBN:  PB 978 1 78442 391 9;
       eBook 978 1 78442 392 6;
       ePDF 978 1 78442 389 6;
       XML 978 1 78442 390 2

20 21 22 23 24   10 9 8 7 6 5 4 3 2 1

Typeset by PDQ Digital Media Solutions, Bungay, UK

Printed and bound in India by Replika Press Private Ltd.

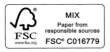

Shire Publications supports the Woodland Trust, the
UK's leading woodland conservation charity.

## COVER IMAGE
Front and back cover images: the Romanesque font at
St Wilfred's Church, Screveton, dating from c.1170,
and the water jug used for christenings
(J. Hannan-Briggs/CC BY-SA 2.0).

## TITLE PAGE IMAGE
The twelfth-century Norman font at Claverley
(Shropshire) has pretty colonettes supporting an
arcade.

## ACKNOWLEDGEMENTS
Like most people who visit and study English churches
and secular buildings I have always been accompanied
on my own visits by the appropriate county volume
of Nikolaus Pevsner's monumental *Buildings of
England* series, 1950–74, but now extensively revised
and expanded by subsequent writers. For breadth of
coverage, comprehensiveness of detail and scholarly
commentary these works are unique. Unless otherwise
stated all direct quotations have been taken from
this source. I am indebted also to the informative
guidebooks published by many churches.

## THE NATIONAL CHURCHES TRUST
The Trust is the charity for people who love church
buildings. There are around 41,000 churches, chapels
and meeting houses in the UK. Many of these are
some of the UK's most important historic buildings;
we want to make sure that they are there for future
generations to enjoy.

We do this by providing grants for urgent repairs
and community facilities, helping places of worship
keep their buildings in good repair through
our MaintenanceBooker service and on our
ExploreChurches website, making it easy for
everyone to discover the wonder of the UK's
sacred heritage.

Our Friends are a vital source of support.
If you love church buildings, please join
us today. You can find out more at
www.nationalchurchestrust.org/friends

## PICTURE CREDITS
Images are acknowledged as follows:

Matěj Baťha/CC BY-SA 3.0, page 57 (top); Marika
Bortolami/CC BY 2.0, page 6; Martin Brewster, page
56 (top right); Michael Garlick/CC BY-SA 2.0, pages
11 (top left), 11 (top right), 12, 13, 56 (top right); R.J.
Higginson/CC BY-SA 3.0, page 17; Hugh Llewelyn/
CC BY-SA 2.0, page 10; Nilfanion/CC BY-SA 3.0, page
60; Philip Pankhurst/CC BY-SA 2.0, page 45 (bottom);
Prioryman/CC BY-SA 4.0, page 43; Bill Strong, page 7;
Diego Torres/Pixabay, page 57 (bottom).

All other images are from the author's own collection.

# CONTENTS

# FOREWORD

The National Churches Trust is the UK's charity for church buildings. Our work helps to ensure that the nation's shared heritage of churches, chapels and meeting houses remains in good repair and open for worship and community activities.

We want to ensure that the priceless treasures inside churches, many of them pre-medieval, can continue to amaze us.

One of the most important architectural features inside a church is the font. This is where the life of a Christian begins: in the baptismal waters we see the reflection not just of today but of the life to come. It's not surprising, therefore, that the most highly skilled sculptors and stonemasons have worked on the creation of fonts.

For over forty years Dr Matthew Byrne, a Friend of the National Churches Trust, has been visiting the churches of the UK and photographing them in superb detail. We are delighted that in this book he has been able to share with a wider audience some of the best examples of his photographs of fonts and to tell the story of why they are so important.

The UK's church heritage is unrivalled anywhere in the world. It is important that we do everything we can to make sure that it remains there for future generations to enjoy. One way of doing that is by visiting churches and helping other people discover their glories. I hope that this book (and also our ExploreChurches website) will help you to do so.

Claire Walker, Chief Executive, National Churches Trust

# INTRODUCTION

Fonts for the rite of baptism, or christening, have been an important feature in Christian churches for nearly 2,000 years, ever since the time Christians were able to worship in public in the Roman Empire. The word baptism comes from the Greek *baptismos* meaning immersion, dipping or submersion. Just as water is the basic means of physical cleansing the Christian Church has used water in various rites as a symbol of spiritual cleansing. The symbolism pre-dates the Christian religion; it was used in the ancient religions of the Mediterranean world and the East. Before the time of Christ Judaism did not use the word 'baptism' but practised a rite of immersion as an act of moral cleansing and for the reception of proselytes. Thus in Ezekiel 36:25, Yahweh says, 'I shall pour clean water over you and you will be cleansed: I shall cleanse you of all your defilement and all your sins.' In the period immediately before the start of Christ's public ministry his cousin John the Baptist was preaching the imminence of the Messiah's arrival and performing baptisms of repentance in the River Jordan and elsewhere. Christ himself came to John and received baptism from him, and at this moment John recognised Jesus as the Messiah, when the Holy Spirit descended upon Him. Throughout three years of His public ministry Christ referred on several occasions to a time after His resurrection when people who came to believe in Him would receive a new rite, one resembling John's baptism but with an entirely new significance, not merely symbolic.

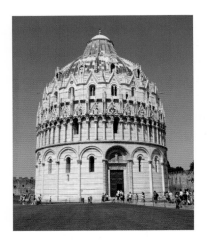

The twelfth-century baptistery at Pisa, the grandeur of which emphasises the importance given to the sacrament of baptism in the Christian Church.

The Christian sacrament of baptism would then bestow the Holy Spirit on the recipient and His gifts would enable them to live Christian lives. In John 3:5, Christ tells His listeners, 'I tell you most solemnly unless a man is born again of water and the Holy Spirit he cannot enter the Kingdom of Heaven.' In one of His final meetings with the apostles before His ascension into heaven, Jesus instructs them (Matthew 28:19): 'Go therefore and make disciples of all nations; baptise them in the name of the Father, the Son and the Holy Spirit and teach them to observe all the commandments I gave you'. And in Acts 2:38 the apostle Peter writes, 'Every one of you must be baptised in the name of Jesus Christ for the forgiveness of sins and you will receive the gift of the Holy Spirit'. It is because of this belief in God's gift at baptism that the Church has attached such importance to it.

The apostles and the first disciples baptised people by total submersion or partial immersion in natural waters, rivers, lakes or pools (Acts 8:27–39). It was only after the Emperor Constantine legalised Christianity by the Edict of Milan in 313 and later made it the official religion of the Roman Empire that Christian worship was centred in public churches, cathedrals and basilicas. In larger buildings so much importance was attached to the sacrament of baptism that special buildings – baptisteries – were built alongside them for the administration of the rite. With a wealthy patron these were massive structures designed by distinguished architects of the time, generally circular or polygonal and ornately decorated. Constantine built a baptistery for members of his family when he gave the bishops of Rome, the popes, their first cathedral of St John Lateran in 325. Such baptisteries, often larger than many churches, were built during the next 1,000 years. Outstanding Italian examples exist today at Parma (late twelfth century), Florence (late eleventh century, originally fifth century) and Pisa (twelfth century), the latter forming a splendid trio with the cathedral and leaning tower.

Initially the method of administering baptism in these places followed as far as possible that of earlier times in natural outdoor waters. Sunken pools about 2m square and 1m deep below floor level enabled total submersion of the recipients.

## THE FONTS

In the pre-Constantine era baptism was offered only to believing adults. But already by the time of the first baptisteries Christian parents had wanted their children to be baptised in infancy, taking the required affirmations of faith on their behalf. For this, smaller structures were needed and alongside the pools baptismal fonts were created (Latin *fons*, a fountain). In these fonts, baptismal water was received by affusion, i.e. pouring over the head only. The general form of these fonts has altered little over two millennia, with a small circular basin of stone, metal or ceramic mounted on a stand of convenient height. However, at least one church of the Reformation, the Baptist Church, held to the practice of baptism administered by submersion to faith-affirming adults and it has continued this to the present day. In the early twenty-first century the Archbishop of York has similarly performed baptisms of adults at Easter outside the main entrance to York Minster.

In England the detailed construction of fonts has followed an evolving pattern reflecting the architecture of the churches and this allows them to be dated with reasonable accuracy. Fonts are usually situated at the western end of a church, at the entrance, symbolising the entry of the recipient into the Church.

The full-immersion font at Cranbrook (Kent) was installed by a Georgian vicar in an unsuccessful attempt to attract Baptist Nonconformists back to the Anglican Church. It was only used once.

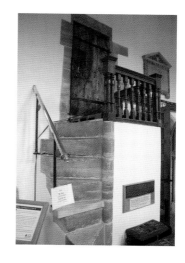

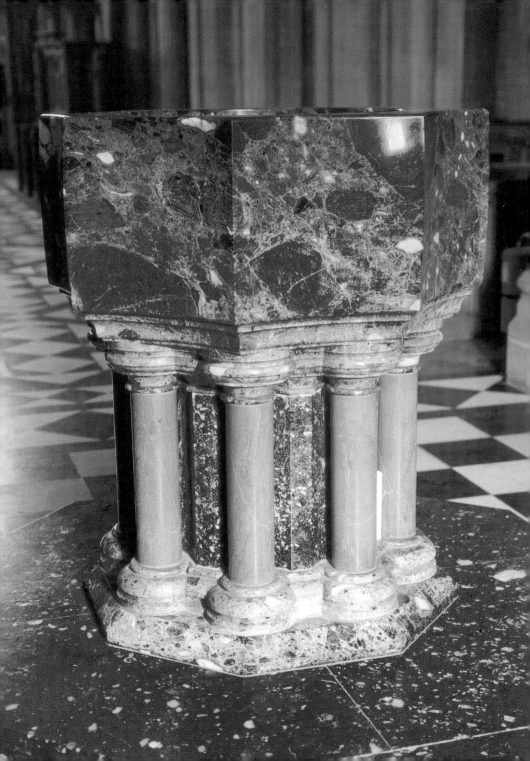

# FONT CONSTRUCTION AND MATERIALS

U NTIL THE SEVENTEENTH century the vast majority of fonts were built of stone, as of course were the churches themselves. The permanence and dignity of such a material are appropriate for items of church furnishings used in an essential rite of the Christian Church. The level of skill required to construct stone fonts varied. Some are simple circular tubs or squares or octagons with minimally adorned surfaces of the bowls or their supports (few are totally plain). These required a competent stonecutter but no more. The ornately decorated fonts, which feature predominantly in the following chapters and in the 'Places to Visit' section, required stone carvers and sculptors of considerable skill and artistic imagination. These specialists would be men who travelled through a particular region or further afield to accept commissions. They were the men who in the building of a church could carve the intricate tracery heads in the huge Gothic windows of the later medieval period that do so much to create the internal and external character of a church. Such men would also carve the decorative turrets, buttresses and finials outside and the capitals of the piers separating the nave and aisles inside, as well as the abundant statuary.

The stone used in the making of a font would generally be the same as used in the building around it. England is well endowed in good building stones and observing the variety of their colours and textures to identify them adds considerably to the pleasures of exploring a church. Apart from

OPPOSITE
Eccleston
(Cheshire).
The estate
village church
of 1897 was
the benefaction
of the Duke of
Westminster
whose wealth is
reflected in all
its furnishings
such as this font
in striking green
and pink marbles.
(See page 53)

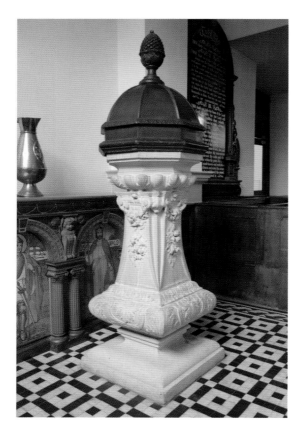

The font at Blandford Forum (Dorset) dates from the 1730s and is carved from the finest Portland stone.

the aesthetics of colour and texture an important practical property of a stone used in sculptural work is its hardness. This varies according to the very different chemical compositions of the English building stones as well as the environment and method under which they were formed in geological time. A very soft stone will crumble when carving is attempted (and when used externally would weather badly). On the other hand, a very hard stone will have excellent weather resistance outside but will be very difficult if not impossible to carve. An ideal stone for delicate intricate carving is one that lies between the two extremes.

The limestones (chemically mainly calcium carbonate) that form the underlying geology of much of England were laid down in periods separated by hundreds of millions of years. The earliest of those suitable for carving are of the Jurassic period, 190–225 million years ago. They vary in colour from pure white (Portland stone) through cream to a deep honey, depending on the concentration and composition of the iron oxides incorporated within them. They are the most widely used stone in font making. The older, steel-grey Carboniferous limestones laid down 280–350 million years ago mainly in the north of England are much harder to carve and allow only for plainer work.

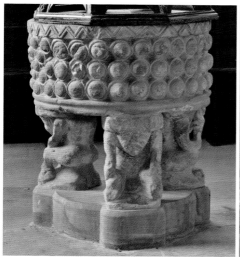 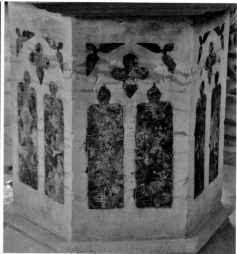

The sandstones (chemically quartz, a crystalline form of silica or silicon dioxide) are the other stones most widely used as building stones in England. The youngest, laid down in the Triassic period 190–225 million years ago, is often known as 'New Red' sandstone found mainly in the northwest and central west of England. Confusingly it is often buff-coloured, the variation in colour again depending on the nature of the iron oxides within it. It is a notoriously friable stone that weathers badly outside. Although this is not critical when used internally, it places limits on the degree of refinement that is possible in carving. Sandstone fonts are generally much plainer than the limestones further south. The 'Old Red' sandstones of southwest England are much harder. Chemically related to the sandstones but very different from them physically is flint, that most extraordinary of building stones used in England. Flint is an amorphous form of silica as opposed to the crystalline form of the sandstones. From the beginning it has been an important building material in eastern and central southern England, where it occurs not in coherent layered deposits that can be quarried but in small irregular pieces on

**ABOVE LEFT**
The sandstone font at St Margaret of Antioch, Crick (Northampton-shire), dates from 1160–70 and incorporates beading and three supporting animals.

**ABOVE RIGHT**
Highly skilled flint and stonework at Trunch (Norfolk).

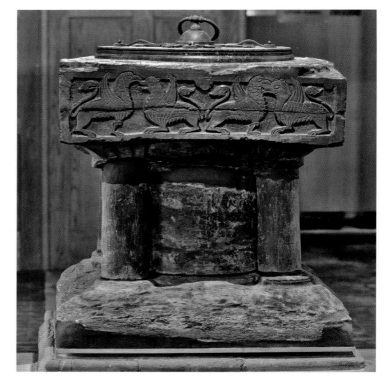

The twelfth-century Tournai marble font at St Lawrence, Thornton Curtis. (Lincolnshire) The pedestal is made of granite.

or just below the surface. It may be pure white, grey or even jet black but its important characteristic is its extreme hardness (hence its use for neolithic axe heads and arrow heads). It is not possible to cut the naturally occurring pieces into rectangular blocks as with other building stones so it is always used in conjunction with another stone in building work, invariably limestone, which is its geographical neighbour. In limestone fonts it is used by cutting small pieces (with great difficulty) into ornamental shapes such as quatrefoils and in-laying these into the surface of cut limestone blocks, a technique known as flushwork. This flushwork is seen widely in East Anglian fonts such as at Trunch, as well as in external walls where other effects can be created as well. The appearance in both situations can be very attractive.

A highly localised stone is granite, which occurs in Cumbria, Devon and Cornwall, where it is an important building material. It is a complex mixture of several minerals, mainly silica and silicates, and is therefore an extremely hard material, difficult to cut and even harder to carve. Nevertheless it has been widely used in Cornwall and Devon for church building where its weather-resistant properties have proved effective against the Atlantic winds and salt-laden spray. It has been equally widely used in font construction, particularly in the Norman period when church work was at its height in that region. Instead of trying to achieve intricate effects with figure carving or abstract designs, stone masons instead relied on miniature architectural features such as columns and arches.

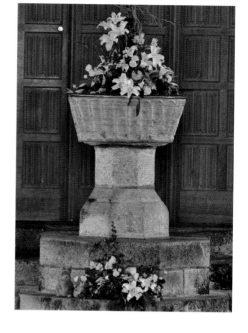

The simple Purbeck marble font at St Andrew's, Sampford Courtenay (Devon) (c.1100).

Clearly a local stone has always been preferred both for a church building and its furnishings, not just on the grounds of architectural harmony with its surroundings, but for ease of supply; this was particularly important in the Middle Ages when transport was much more difficult than today. Sometimes, however, if funds were available in wealthy parishes – or those with wealthy patrons – more decorative stones could be imported from other parts of England or abroad for use in various parts of the building or its furnishings. For a few prestigious fonts – just seven in all – the Normans imported Tournai marble, an almost black limestone from Belgium, hard enough to take a polish. In the twelfth and thirteenth centuries in the early Gothic period Purbeck marble from the Dorset coast was widely used throughout England. It too is a darkly striated limestone capable of taking a polish. It provides

This twelfth-century lead font at Gloucester Cathedral was originally installed at St James at Lancaut, now ruined.

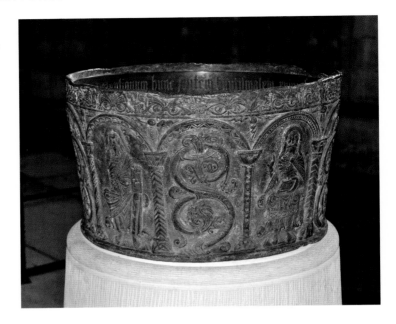

a pleasantly subdued contrast when used in conjunction with cream coloured limestone. Its use continues into the twenty-first century in the spectacularly designed font in Salisbury Cathedral (page 57). In the eighteenth century pure white marble imported from Italy and elsewhere became almost universally used for the huge monuments of the aristocracy, with life-sized figures erected in both medieval and contemporary churches. Its popularity extended to fonts although this was generally restricted, rightly, to churches of the time, not to replace earlier fonts. The Victorians liked highly polished surfaces in churches (and public buildings and houses) but their passion for bright colours led to the use of more spectacular polychromatic marbles from Europe, when a wealthy patron could provide the finance.

A description of the materials used in medieval fonts should not omit the lead fonts of the Norman period. (It is apparent how innovative they were in matters of architecture as well as in other fields.) The lead ore galena occurs in several places in England and the metal is readily extracted from this. The low melting point means that it is easily cast into complex compositions.

The crowning glory of medieval fonts is the free-standing wooden canopy; these are profusely ornate structures carved with foliage trails, flowers, birds and other motifs. Because of their cost they are extremely rare.

Fonts are nearly always mounted on a stone plinth for prominence. In the later Middle Ages this was often enlarged into a set of three steps leading to an octagonal platform so that the officiating priest could be seen more easily by a larger family group. It is a type most common in East Anglia. Subsequent centuries reverted to small single step.

With the exception of the relatively few lead fonts, stone has dominated the story of font making so far. However, in England in the late seventeenth century a school of woodcarvers of genius emerged who produced work of remarkably life-like, almost three-dimensional forms in which figures and foliage played a large part. The name of Grinling Gibbons stands foremost in this group. In the eighteenth century Robert Adam developed the art of woodcarving design (and other forms of decoration) into one of exquisite delicacy. It is not surprising that churchmen called upon the skills of these craftsmen for church furnishings, which apart from fonts included pulpits, reredoses, doorcases, benches and more. Few, of course, could afford them. Most notable are the late-seventeenth-century churches in the City of London and some parish churches associated with the aristocracy such as that at Croome d'Abitot (Worcestershire) (pages 46 and 48).

Turning now from materials to the subject matter of sculptural decoration, it is not surprising that this changed dramatically over the centuries, often quite suddenly according to the Zeitgeist or artistic spirit of the time. Font art ran in parallel with that seen elsewhere in churches: window tracery, arches, pier capitals, statues and screens. Decorative motifs in the Middle Ages were abstract patterns or various forms of figure sculpture. The latter could be lifelike human figures, sacred (Christ, the saints) or secular (knights, etc.) either singly or severally in enacted scenes. Animal figures were also widely used, wild or domestic, with or without humans, and they often had symbolic meanings. Apart from these natural figures the medieval imaginative mind was often filled with a taste for the grotesque in the form of distorted human features or more usually mythological monsters, often taken from the 'bestiary' books originating in classical antiquity, which were circulated among the educated at the time. These became less common in the later Middle Ages. The spirit of the fifteenth-century Italian Renaissance came late to England, a country cut off from mainland Europe by the English Reformation. The first signs appeared in the late sixteenth century and developed throughout the seventeenth and eighteenth centuries, when refined ornament based on the precedents of classical antiquity became the norm. Victorian fonts reflect the Gothic Revival of the time, often in an uninspiring way. Modern fonts are – with few exceptions – utilitarian rather than artistic; the font at Salisbury Cathedral is a rare outstanding exception.

Given the opportunity, dedicated church explorers will try to visit several churches in a county or area of a county. It sometimes becomes evident that a single sculptor or a small team of sculptors has been at work in the making of the fonts, as shown by the similarity of style and compositional ideas. It is not surprising that those responsible for making a much-admired font would then be commissioned by a neighbouring parish. The twelfth-century Herefordshire School of Romanesque Sculpture is an outstanding example, which actually extended to adjacent counties (pages 25–27). Also from the Norman period is a group in East Yorkshire centred on Driffield; one in Buckinghamshire centred on Aylesbury; and one in Cornwall centred on Bodmin. (One can see how widespread and prolific Norman work was.) In

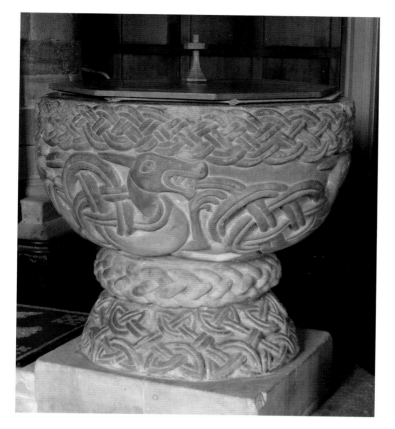

The Norman font at St Cassian's, Chaddesley Corbett (Worcestershire) is of the fine Hereford School of Romanesque Sculpture.

the later Gothic period, East Anglian fonts and font covers were the inspiration of one generation as were those in the Cotswolds. The fonts of Grinling Gibbons and his school in the seventeenth-century churches of Christopher Wren in the City of London, featuring cherubs, saints, garlands and swags, are perhaps the most notable group of all – two men of genius working together in the same spirit in the 'Square Mile'. (See 'Places to Visit' at the end of this book for details of these groups.)

The following chapters describe in more detail the fonts of the main 'periods' of English architectural history from Anglo-Saxon times to the twenty-first century.

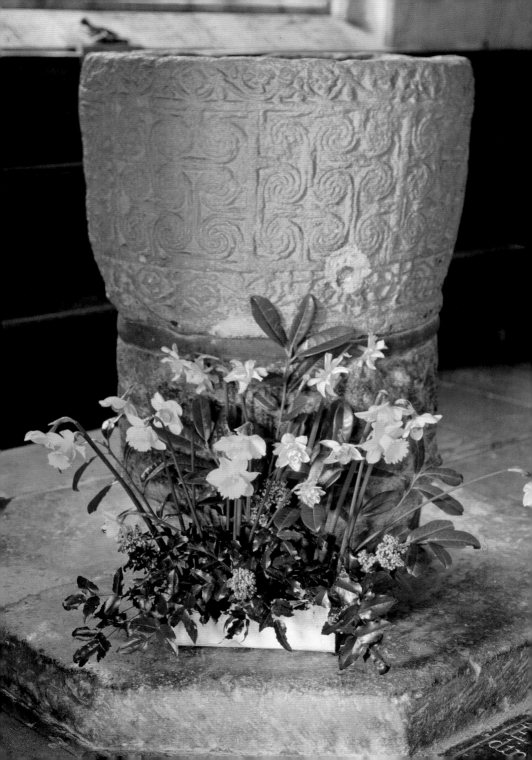

# THE ANGLO-SAXON CENTURIES, 800–1066

THE FIRST CONVERSIONS to Christianity of the Anglo-Saxon kingdoms, not then a united country, took place from the end of the sixth century. Two separate missionary campaigns were involved, one from the southeast led by St Augustine from Rome and the other by monks from the island of Iona into the far northwest. Successes and some failures led to the kingdoms being largely Christian by 800. There are today some 500 churches from the Saxon period, either wholly or in part, but fewer than a dozen of their fonts have survived. In the hamlet of Deerhurst (Gloucestershire), a few miles south of Tewkesbury close to the River Severn, the font stands within one of the largest, most complex and interesting Saxon churches in England. It is a cylindrical tub, the centre part of which is decorated with a double-spiral ornament. Above and below there are narrow bands of vine scroll. By comparison of these motifs with datable Saxon jewellery, the date of the font is probably late ninth century. Its survival is something of a miracle: at some unknown time it was removed from the church and used as a washing tub in a farmyard until found and recognised in 1844.

The history of old churches is littered with similar discoveries of statues, altar stones and other objects. In the mainly thirteenth-century church in the village of Potterne (Wiltshire), the font is again tub-shaped and plainer than the one at Deerhurst; along the rim is a Latin inscription taken from Psalm 42:1 which in translation reads: 'As a doe longs

OPPOSITE
Deerhurst
(Gloucestershire).
A late ninth-
century font with
typical Saxon
spiral and vine
scroll decoration.

Potterne
(Wiltshire),
c. ninth century.
A quotation in
Latin from Psalm
42 referring to
running water
encircles the rim.

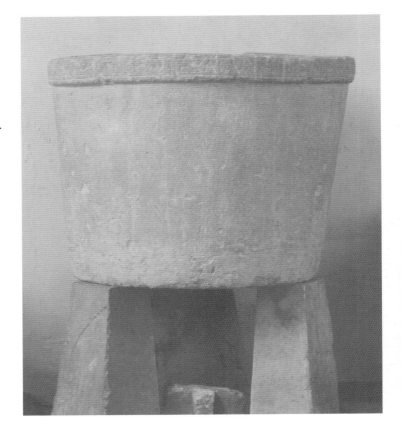

OPPOSITE
Melbury Bubb
(Dorset). Late
Saxon font with
strange 'barbaric'
decoration,
a mixture of
interlace and
small animals.

for running streams so longs my soul for you, my God'. The use of a Latin text that appeared in Saxon psalters of 750–900, and the way the letters are shaped, tells us that the font probably comes from the Saxon church discovered through archaeological excavations a short distance away. Interestingly, this church appears to have had a baptistery. The font at Melbury Bubb (Dorset) is a tapered cylinder with entangled strands or 'interlace', which is a characteristic form of Saxon decoration derived from antiquity. In addition there are animals placed upside down. In contrast to much Saxon sculpture, which is usually delicate and refined, this has what Pevsner describes as a decidedly 'barbaric' character.

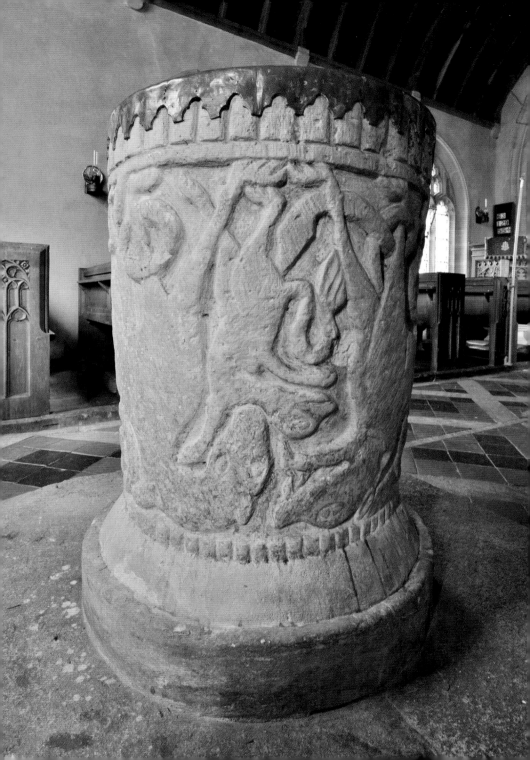

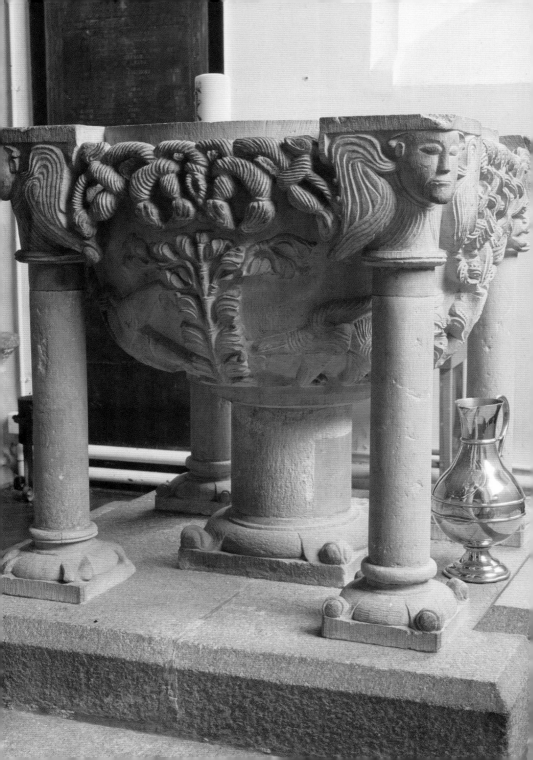

# THE NORMAN PERIOD, 1066–1200

AFTER THE CONQUEST of 1066 the Normans embarked on a prodigious building campaign of castles, cathedrals and churches, just as they had in Normandy. About 2,000 Norman churches are still in use, some largely in their original form, others modified or greatly extended. In contrast to the paucity of Saxon fonts there is a wealth of Norman work. In those churches that are still entirely or predominantly Norman in character it is not surprising to find the original fonts; what is surprising, however, is the large number of churches entirely rebuilt in later centuries in which a Norman font is the only evidence of the earlier church. It is as though in the re-buildings parishioners refused to replace an object in which their parents, grandparents and preceding generations had been baptised, at a time when families rarely left their ancestral villages.

The simplest (and earliest) Norman fonts have the same tub shapes as their Saxon predecessors. Wroxeter (Shropshire) is an example while that of Morwenstow (Cornwall) is similar but with a band of rope-moulding around the centre. More ornate examples with typical Norman motifs on the sides can be seen at Upton Cressett and Claverley (both in Shropshire), both of which have blank arcading. At Michaelchurch (Herefordshire) there is ornament not dissimilar to the Saxon font at Deerhurst, while at Laneast (Cornwall) there are rosettes on each side and faces at the corners. All these have a single central supporting column; more elaborate structures have four supporting outer

OPPOSITE
Bodmin
(Cornwall).
A complex
and interesting
late-Norman
work. The four
corner pillars
have human
heads and the
bowl has floral
decoration.

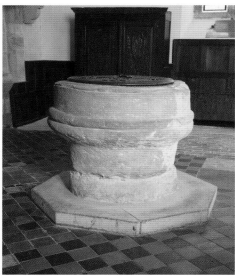

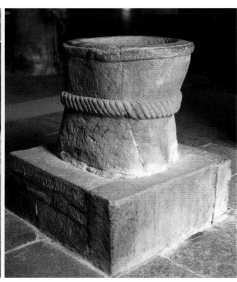

ABOVE LEFT Wroxeter (Shropshire). A plain early Norman tub font sits on a re-used Roman fort column.

ABOVE RIGHT Morwenstow (Cornwall). The early Norman bowl is decorated with a single band of rope moulding.

legs in addition with profuse ornament on the legs and the bowl. A particularly fine example occurs at Bodmin (Cornwall), where the legs have capitals with winged heads, while foliage and beasts can be found on the basin.

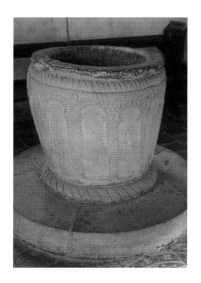

Upton Cressett (Shropshire). Later Norman, the bowl is decorated with shallow blank arcading with one moulding above and one below.

## LEAD FONTS

Several English counties are rich in galena, an ore of lead from which the metal has been relatively easily extracted from Roman to modern times. With a low melting point and soft, it is ideal for moulding into complex forms and as such was used for a number of Norman fonts. The one in Dorchester-on-Thames (Oxfordshire) has figures

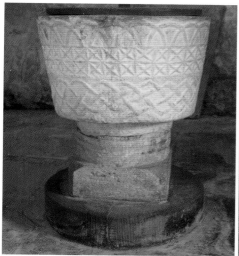

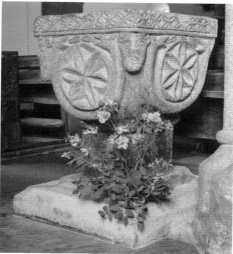

of the twelve apostles around the base. At Brookland (Kent) there is a surrounding frieze of the Signs of the Zodiac above (a strange motif in a Christian church but not uncommon), and below another showing the 'Labours of the Monthes', scenes from rural working life. All these compositions with so much detail would have been extremely difficult to carve in stone.

ABOVE LEFT
Michaelchurch (Herefordshire). The Norman sculptor has here been influenced by Saxon art.

## THE HEREFORDSHIRE SCHOOL OF ROMANESQUE SCULPTURE

A small number of churches associated with the castles built by the Marcher Lords appointed by the Norman kings to defend their border with the Welsh have fonts and other features such as doorways and chancel arches distinguished not only by their accomplished sculpture but by their subject matter, which shows a learned knowledge of scripture, theology and religious iconography drawing on sources as far afield as Italy and the Middle East. The hands of just two unknown sculptors have been identified, working 1120–60. The lords of the castles who commissioned this work were men of little learning and probably little piety but they employed as high-ranking

ABOVE RIGHT
Laneast (Cornwall). A bowl of local granite with rosettes on the sides and human heads at the corners.

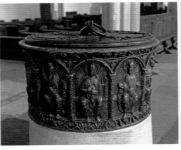 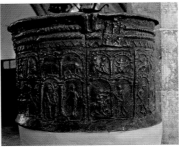

RIGHT
Dorchester-on-Thames (Oxfordshire). St John the Evangelist with his Gospel book is centre facing.

FAR RIGHT
Brookland (Kent), with its signs of the Zodiac and 'Labours of the Monthes'.

stewards men of education and ability who in turn were in regular contact with bishops and abbots throughout England and in Normandy. It is to these that we must look for the source of the work, which is notable by international European standards as well as English. Two of the most important examples are at Eardisley and Castle Frome.

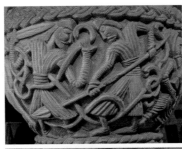 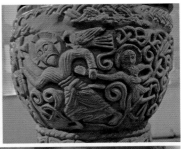

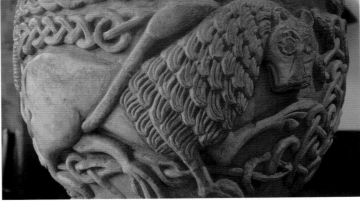

RIGHT
Three images of the font at Eardisley (Herefordshire): these two fighting men might represent the fight between good and evil, or commemorate an historic battle.

FAR RIGHT
The Harrowing of Hell: Christ rescues a redeemed soul from the underworld.

BOTTOM
A ferocious-looking lion.

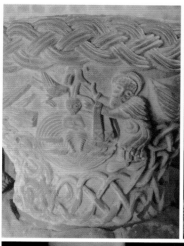
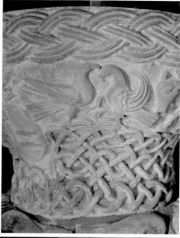
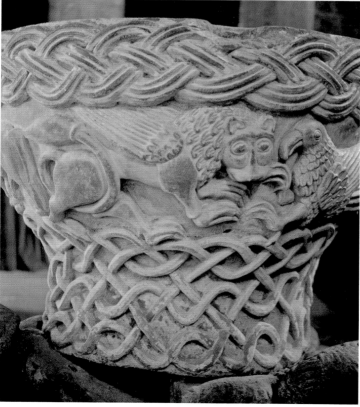

FAR LEFT
Three images from the equally splendid font at Castle Frome: this view depicts the baptism of Christ by John the Baptist in the River Jordan.

LEFT
Here two doves represent the Holy Spirit who confers His gifts in the sacrament of baptism.

BOTTOM
Another lion. This animal is a favourite subject of the two sculptors.

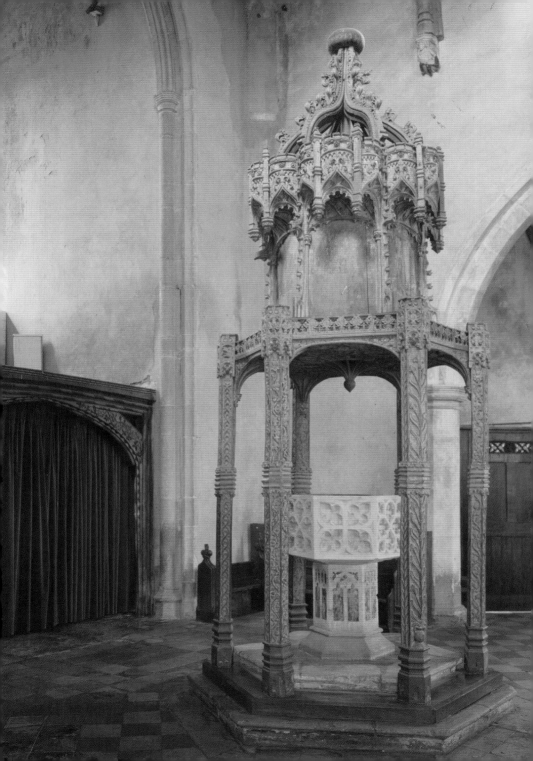

# THE LATER MIDDLE AGES, 1200–1500

AFTER THE EXUBERANCE, force and vitality of Norman sculpture, the fonts of the Gothic period settle down to calmer but nonetheless varied and interesting work, of which the associated superstructures are in a few cases the most spectacular. Architectural historians divide Gothic architecture into three periods: Early English (1190–1250), Decorated (1250–1330) and Perpendicular (1330–1550). The dates are approximate and are subject to overlap and variation in different parts of England. In terms of architecture the churches as buildings are readily distinguishable. In smaller structures such as fonts the styles are not always markedly different; it is the details that can provide dating – however, a font may be later or earlier than the church in which it sits.

At Eaton Bray (Berkshire) the splendidly carved 'stiff-leaf' capitals on the four corner pillars indicate a date 1220–40, the same as the church. At Stow (Lincolnshire), of the same Early English period, there are no fewer than eight supporting columns beneath a heavy octagonal basin, each side of which has a different carved decoration, none of which is specifically Christian. Visible on the left is a Green Man: a ubiquitous fertility symbol with leaves emanating from his mouth. At Elmley Castle (Worcestershire) the base but not the font is also early thirteenth century. The base is encircled by four lions. From the later Gothic period the font at Mellis has symbols of the four evangelists alternating with Tudor roses. At Grantham (Lincolnshire) the font is particularly richly carved overall.

OPPOSITE
Trunch (Norfolk). (page 34). A rare free-standing font canopy. It rises in stages, all richly carved with flowers and foliage between twisted branches.

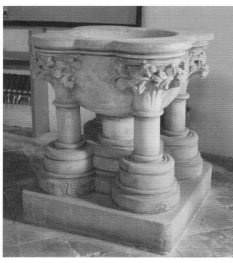 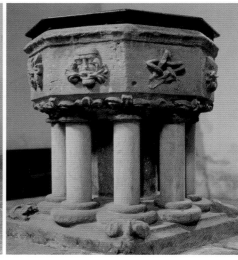

The basin has religious scenes including the Annunciation, the Nativity and the Baptism of Christ, all below miniature canopies. The stem has a circle of statuettes also under canopies. The length of time it must have taken a skilled craftsman to carve this is a sign of a very wealthy town parish.

## FONT COVERS AND FONT CANOPIES

From the beginning it was usual to provide fonts with covers, which were revetted into the basin and padlocked to it. The water used in baptism was blessed by a priest and it was common to leave this in the font. It would then be available for clergy or lay people for baptisms of infants in danger of death. The cover prevented contamination and the unauthorised removal of the water for medicinal or superstitious purposes. The covers could be simple: plain circular or octagonal cut to the shape of the font, but in the late-Gothic Perpendicular period, splendid ornamentation was added to the functional purpose – as it was in all aspects of church architecture and furnishings. Tall, tapering structures up to 4m (13ft) in height were sumptuously carved with tracery, buttresses and finials. These could be raised

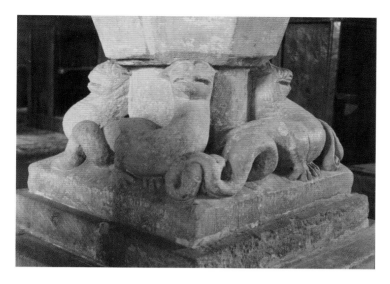

Elmley Castle (Worcestershire). The base of the early thirteenth-century bowl structure is enriched by fierce-looking dragons.

or lowered by counterpoised pulleys suspended from special font beams. East Anglia and Lincolnshire are rich in these covers as they are in other fine woodwork, such as rood screens and bench ends. They are relatively rare elsewhere. At Salle (Norfolk) the canopy is slender and relatively plain and the supporting beam for its pulley can be seen above it. At Freiston (Lincolnshire) the

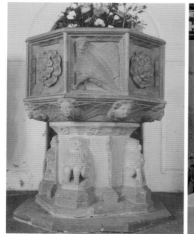

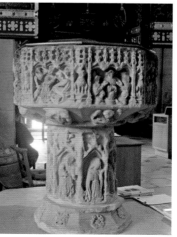

FAR LEFT
Mellis (Suffolk). The bowl of this late-Gothic Perpendicular font has Tudor roses as well as the symbols of the four evangelists. Facing centre is the eagle of St John.

LEFT
Grantham (Lincolnshire). The sides of the basin are richly decorated with religious scenes under canopies and the stem has a circle of statuettes.

# SLOLEY (NORFOLK)

The font at Sloley (Norfolk) is one example of a rare and special kind, the greatest glory of late-medieval fonts known as Seven Sacrament fonts. The pre-Reformation Roman Catholic Church recognised seven sacraments, just as it does today: baptism, confirmation, Eucharist, penance (confession), matrimony, holy orders (ordination) and extreme unction (anointing of the sick). The Thirty-nine Articles of the Anglican Church later recognised as sacraments only baptism and the Eucharist. In the fifteenth century parish churches with access to a skilled stone carver (and the necessary finance) realised that with a standard octagonal font it would be possible to depict the sacraments in sculpted scenes, one on each side, with an additional subject such as the crucifixion on the eighth side. Just forty of these fonts survive in England, concentrated in East Anglia, with twenty-five in Norfolk and thirteen in Suffolk. A great number were destroyed at the Reformation, while many of those that survived have been defaced. The one at Sloley is perhaps the finest remaining, with miniature figures in a series of charming vignettes.

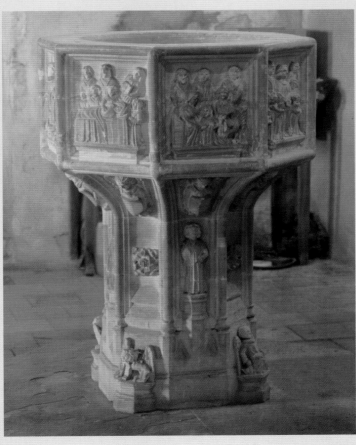

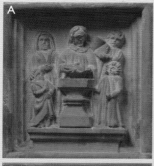

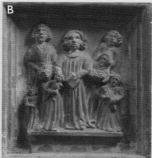

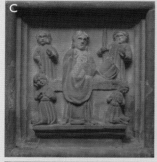

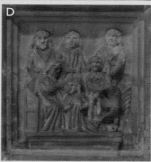

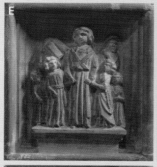

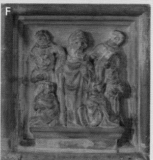

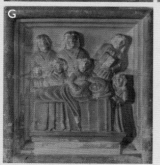

**A** Baptism. A priest appears to immerse a child fully while an assistant holds a service book and the family looks on.

**B** Confirmation. A bishop with a very young recipient.

**C** Eucharist. A priest celebrates Mass with boy altar servers and a bell-ringer.

**D** Penance or confession. On the left a seated priest and kneeling penitent. On the right an angel kicks away the devil shown as a dragon. The three 'eavesdroppers' behind may represent the three conditions for the sacrament: contrition, confession and absolution.

**E** Marriage. A priest with a very young groom and bride – commonplace in the Middle Ages.

**F** Ordination. Candidates kneel before a bishop with assistant clergy.

**G** Extreme unction or anointing of the sick. A priest with family at the bedside of the dying person.

Salle (Norfolk). The tall, slim font cover is typically East Anglian. It is raised and lowered by a pulley from the beam above.

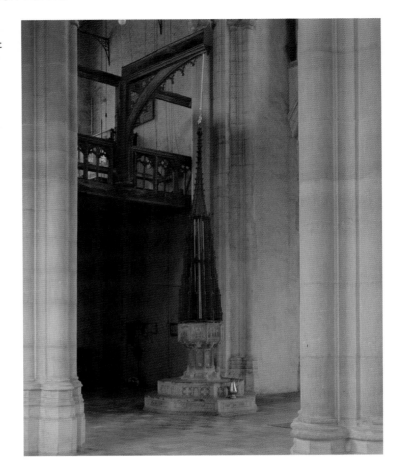

font itself is raised on three steps with delicate panelling on both stem and bowl. The cover rises about 3m (10ft) in tapering stages of open arches with buttresses, all finely carved.

Distinct from the font covers are the rare font canopies, of which there are only five in England: at Trunch (Norfolk, page 28); St Peter Mancroft (Norwich); St Mary's, Luton (Bedfordshire); Durham Cathedral; and Liverpool's Anglican cathedral. These structures are floor-standing, surrounding the font rather than sitting upon it, as do the covers. It is probable that their function was to draw attention to and emphasise

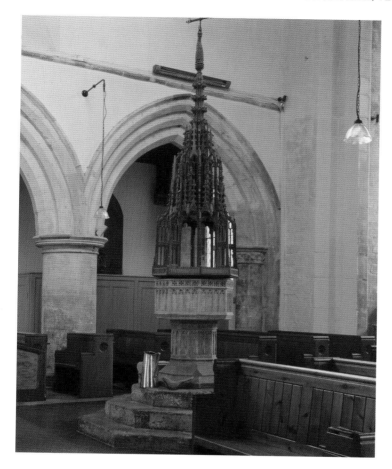

Frieston (Lincolnshire). The font cover is a series of tapering stages of open arches and buttresses finely carved all over.

the importance of the font, which might otherwise have been relatively inconspicuous. The canopy at Trunch surrounds a font that has a handsome stem and bowl with decorative flintwork panelling. The canopy itself is in two stages. The lower stage has six posts decorated with foliage trails of several species including vine, lily and thistle growing between twisted branches. This stage has its own vaulted roof. The upper stage has six heavy vaulted canopies, again all richly decorated. Above these there is yet more carving in the form of flying buttresses leading up to a finial.

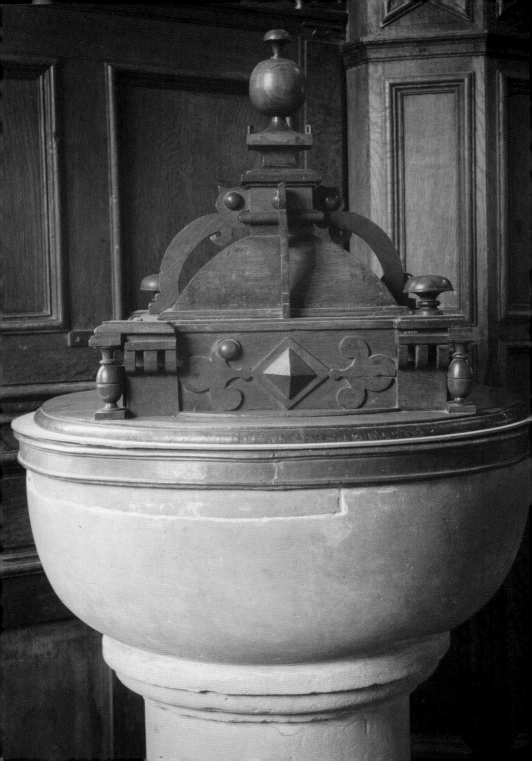

# THE SEVENTEENTH CENTURY

THE PROTESTANT REFORMATION in England in the sixteenth century did nothing to affect the rite of baptism, which was regarded as an essential sacrament for admission to both the Roman Catholic Church and the reformed Anglican Church. The ceremonies at the fonts did not change in essentials except that English replaced Latin. However, in the seventeenth and eighteenth centuries styles in architecture and architectural furnishings changed dramatically.

## THE CLASSICAL STYLE

In the early fifteenth century, Italy and later other European countries turned away from the Gothic style and in the Renaissance returned to the architecture of ancient Rome in terms of plans, elevations, decorative detail and furnishings in churches and secular buildings. This is what we know as the Classical style. England, isolated from this movement by reasons of geography, conservatism and later by the Protestant Reformation, was late to embrace the change. The sixteenth century saw the gradual adoption of elements of the Classical style in churches in smaller features such as monuments, screens and fonts, however, and this continued throughout the seventeenth century. It was not a time for the building of many new churches; these were rarely needed given the huge legacy of buildings from the medieval period. In the churches that were built, contemporary fonts were provided. Little Gidding (Cambridgeshire) is a small

OPPOSITE
Staunton Harold
(Leicestershire).
The font and
cover are both
mid-seventeenth
century. The
design of the
latter shows
Dutch influence.

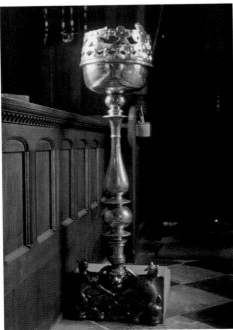

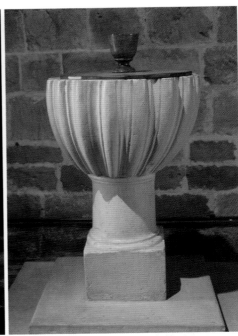

Classical church built by the Anglican scholar and churchman Nicholas Ferrer for his Little Gidding religious community, the subject of one of T.S. Eliot's 'Four Quartets'. The font has a slim brass baluster with a brass cover surmounted by a coronet. At Thornton-le-Moors (Cheshire), a font entirely in the Classical style was provided for the medieval church in the form of a big stone cup decorated with gadroons (lobed motifs).

## FONT COVERS

The most visible evidence of the seventeenth century in church fonts is in the large number of font covers that were added to older fonts. In the earlier part of the century these typically included a Dutch form of Classical motifs, demonstrating the influence of a near European country with which England had religious and trading links. The woodcarving had a

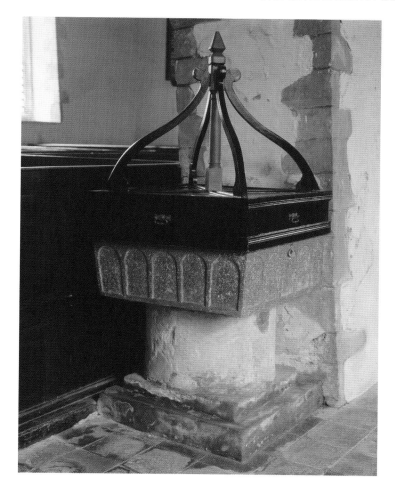

Fordwich (Kent). A Jacobean cover on a Norman font which is made of local Bethesden marble.

solid robustness rather than the delicacy associated with many medieval font covers. The wood now is dark in colour, either from staining or natural ageing. Fordwich (Kent) has a Norman font of local Bethesden marble. The cover is square with four radiating scrolls supporting a central finial. Staunton Harold (Leicestershire), where the church itself was built in the mid-seventeenth century, has a handsome restrained font and cover of the period. Mendlesham (Suffolk) has a much more elaborate and beautiful cover

Mendlesham (Suffolk), an example of an elaborate Jacobean font cover with its pendants and obelisks.

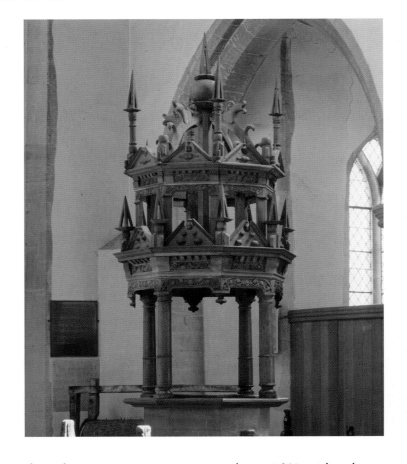

than the previous two; it was made in 1650 with a lower tier open between four tall columns and an upper tier with pendants and spiky obelisks. Wiggenhall St Mary (Norfolk) has a pretty cover on a medieval font. It has four columns and four pendants, and an octagonal pyramid roof with a pelican on top. The cover at Walpole St Peter (Norfolk) is a splendid piece, whose height is accentuated by the font's being raised on three steps. An octagon below has opening walls giving access to the font below. It has tapering pilasters in pairs, blank arches and arabesques (interlaced decorative motifs) with an octagonal spire above.

OPPOSITE
Wiggenhall St Mary (Norfolk). The highly decorative octagonal font cover is topped by a Pelican.

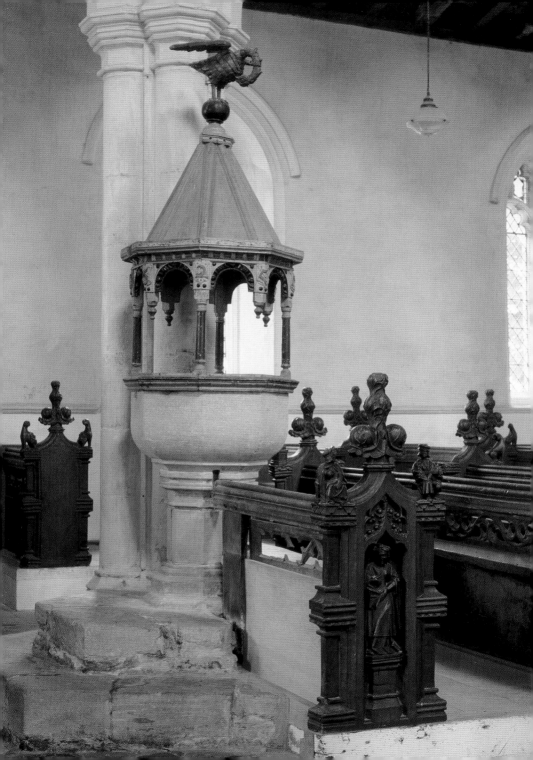

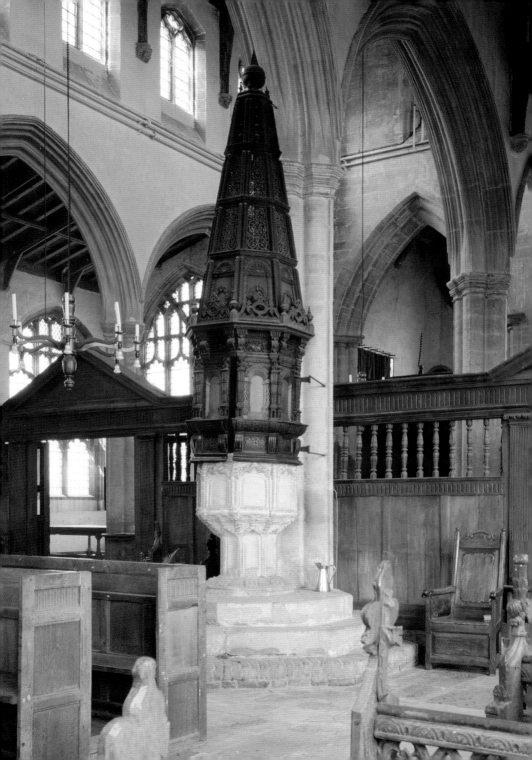

# THE BAROQUE STYLE

Towards the end of the seventeenth century a new influence from Italy affected most of the arts, including architecture, to create the Baroque style. A new spirit created buildings

OPPOSITE
Walpole St
Peter (Norfolk).
The tall, slender
cover has sliding
panels at the
base to give
access to the
bowl.

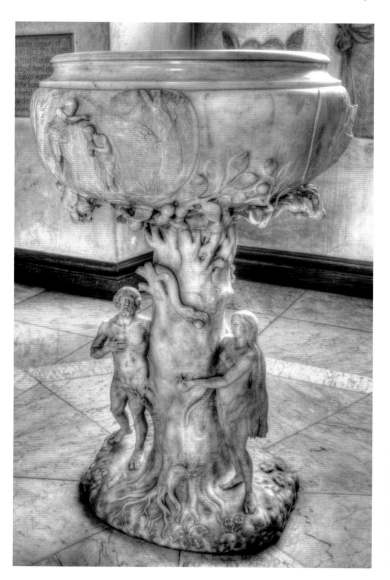

Grinling
Gibbons' font
at St James the
Great, Piccadilly,
unusually
executed in
stone rather
than his normal
medium of wood.

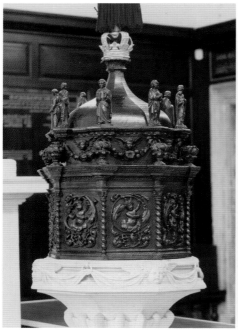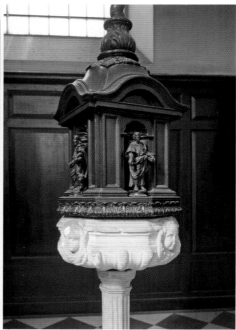

**ABOVE LEFT**
St Stephen Walbrook, City of London. The Baroque years of the late seventeenth century are characterised by exquisite figure sculpture in high relief.

**ABOVE RIGHT**
St Mary Abchurch, City of London. Another Baroque font with strong architectural elements.

of high drama, or melodrama, whose sinuous and complex forms extended to their sculptural embellishments and furnishings. Sir Christopher Wren (1632–1723), arguably England's greatest architect, pioneered the style in England but modified it to suit the more reserved native temperament. His work pervades the 'Square Mile' of the City of London in the churches he rebuilt after the Great Fire in 1666. To furnish these churches he employed carvers who raised their art to one of the high points in English woodwork. Chief among these was Grinling Gibbons (1648–1721) and the workers in or associated with his workshop. They created fonts, pulpits, reredoses, organ cases and galleries in sumptuous variety. English oak and other woods were carved with figures, foliage garlands, cherubs and other motifs of the Baroque style, all detailed in high relief.

The stone font at St Stephen Walbrook, the finest of Wren's City of London churches, was made in 1679. The tall wooden cover has lower panels carved with cherubs and fronds between twisted colonettes and above these a band of garlands. The domed top has seven small figures of The Virtues and a Christ of the twentieth century. The font cover at St Mary Abchurch is square and strongly architectural with statuettes of the four evangelists under curved pediments. Further afield the splendidly gilded font cover at St Martin-le-Grand in York has typical Baroque sinuosity. The all-stone font at Holme Lacy (Herefordshire) is carved with Baroque motifs including draperies. It sits in the eerily disused but well-kept church a mile from the village, surrounded by the monuments of the Viscounts Scudamore.

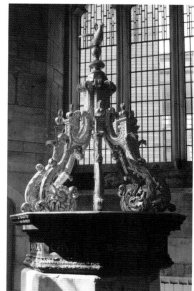

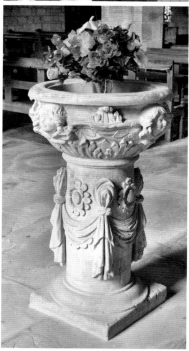

TOP
St Martin-le-Grand, York. The font cover has typical Baroque exuberance.

BOTTOM
Holme Lacy (Herefordshire). Bowl and stem are carved all over with favourite Baroque motifs such as cherubs and draperies.

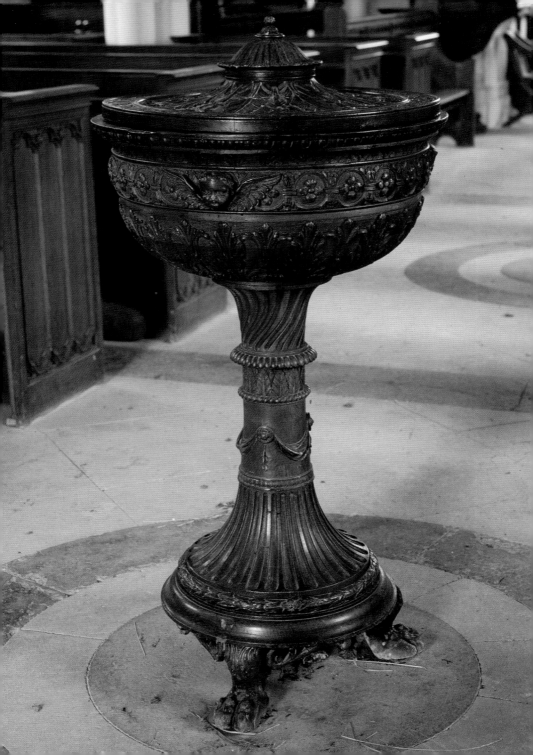

# THE EIGHTEENTH CENTURY

THE ENGLISH NEVER embraced Baroque architecture and decoration to the same extent as many countries in southern Europe. Its time here was limited to the decades around 1700. The eighteenth century saw a shift towards a more restrained and refined form of the Classical style, in keeping with the national feeling for moderation. A considerable number of new churches were built in cities, towns and villages, usually to replace dilapidated medieval churches whose Gothic architecture was now often despised as outdated and lacking the disciplined 'rules' of Classical architecture. So new styles of font were created in stone, now usually white marble or wood, which were smaller than their medieval predecessors and without the elaborate covers favoured in the seventeenth century. 'Chaste' is the adjective often used to describe these modestly sized and delicate creations. Most of those illustrated here are in eighteenth-century churches where they form part of an ensemble of contemporary furnishings,

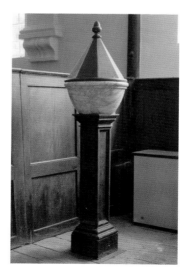

OPPOSITE
Croome d'Abitot (Worcestershire) (page 48). The font is a superb example of Robert Adam's style.

The 'pudding basin' font at Chiselhampton (Oxfordshire) takes simplicity to an extreme with a marble bowl and conical cover mounted on a panelled wooden pedestal.

Four examples of carved marble bowls with fluting and other eighteenth-century Classical motifs standing on baluster pedestals. Clockwise from top left: Wheatfield (Oxfordshire), 1730; Manchester, St Anne, 1709; Tunstall (Lancashire), 1750; North Runcton (Norfolk), 1713.

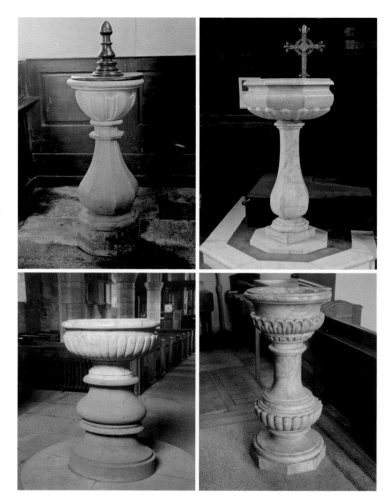

complete with box pews, pulpits, reredoses and galleries that, when preserved intact, are a joy to visit today.

The church at Croome d'Abitot in Worcestershire is an eighteenth-century 'Gothick' gem, standing as an eye-catcher on a hill in the park of Croome Court. It has perhaps the most exquisitely elegant wooden font in England carved in the style of the famous Robert Adam, 'exquisite in shape and exquisite in detail'.

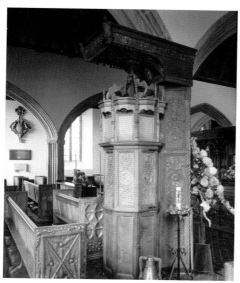 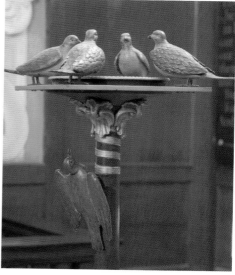

For the unusual, one may turn to Swimbridge (Devon), where the font is entirely encased in a three-stage wooden structure made up of Gothic and Renaissance forms. The font pedestal is within the lower stage and the lead bowl is in the middle stage, which opens out with folding doors. The upper section is a carved octagon rising to a finial. Behind and above is a tall canopy. If Swimbridge is unusual, the font at West Wycombe (Buckinghamshire) is strange to the point of bizarre, as is much in the landscape around the church, the epitome of eighteenth-century aristocratic eccentricity. The medieval church was rebuilt in 1775 by Sir Francis Dashwood. It sits on a hill as an eye-catcher for Dashwood's mansion and its park below. (The tunnels and chambers created inside the hill served as a meeting place for Dashwood's notorious Hellfire Club.) The font is perhaps the oddest in England. A clawed tripod base supports a shaft, up which climbs a serpent. Four doves surround a shallow tray for all the world like a garden bird-bath, whilst a fifth dove clings to the shaft. Here secular whimsy replaces religion.

**ABOVE LEFT**
Swimbridge (Devon).
An unusual eighteenth-century structure in which the bowl is enclosed in the shuttered mid-section topped by a canopy.

**ABOVE RIGHT**
West Wycombe (Buckinghamshire).
Four doves surround a shallow tray for the baptisms which resembles a garden bird-bath. A fifth bird clings to the stem.

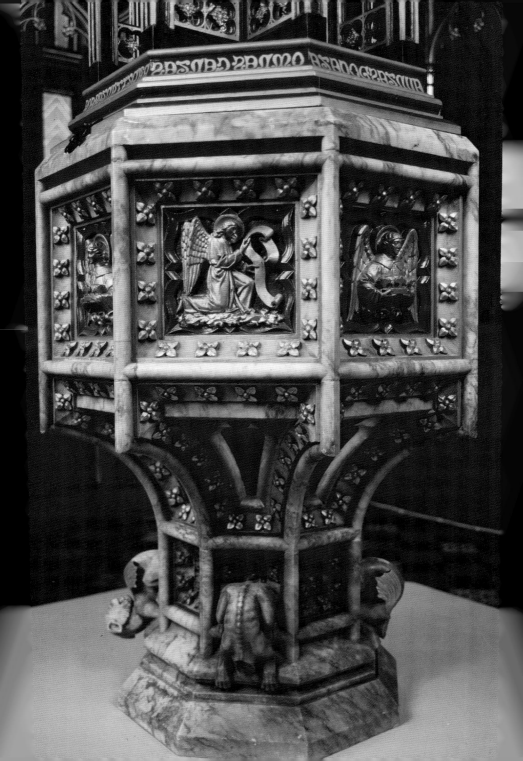

# THE VICTORIAN AGE

THE POPULATION AND wealth of England increased markedly during the reign of Queen Victoria (1837–1901). There was also a dramatic shift of the population from the countryside to the cities. In addition there was a considerable revival in religious belief and fervour promoted by both the evangelical and Anglo-Catholic wings of the Church of England. As a result about 6,000 new Anglican churches were built during Victoria's reign, about 100 for each year. In the Roman Catholic Church large-scale immigration from Ireland swelled its numbers considerably. Even before this period architectural taste had begun to turn full circle from the Classical back to medieval Gothic. The largest and finest churches were financed by wealthy patrons such as dukes, earls, rectors and rich widows commemorating their husbands, who commissioned the leading architects of the day to fulfil their own particular dreams. These architects included Augustus Welby Northmore Pugin (1812–52), the father of this Gothic Revival Movement, George Gilbert Scott (1811–78), George Frederick Bodley (1827–1907), George Edmund Street (1824–81) and John Loughborough Pearson (1817–97). No expense was spared in the furnishings, which were often designed by the architects themselves. For the fonts the limestones of the Middle Ages and the white marbles of the eighteenth century were usually replaced by imported polychromatic marbles – as they were in many other furnishings. The best of the Victorian churches were aglow with colour.

OPPOSITE Cheadle (Staffordshire). St Giles' Roman Catholic Church of 1846 is the greatest ecclesiastical achievement of A.W.N. Pugin. For the font, gilded marbles provide opulence while the angels provide religious feeling. The base of the tall canopy is visible above.

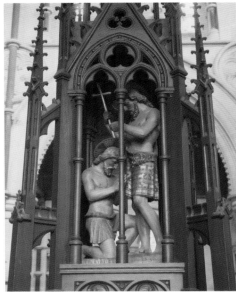
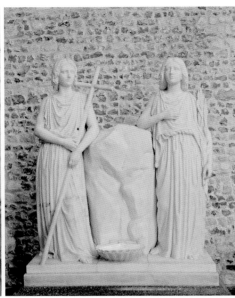

St Giles' Roman Catholic Church in Cheadle (Staffordshire) was among the earliest of these great churches. The church and all its furnishings were designed as one integral piece by A.W.N. Pugin for the immensely rich Catholic Earl of Shrewsbury in 1846. The sides of the font are are ablaze with gilded angels in various attitudes. In 1871 William Burges built the parkland church at Skelton-cum-Newby (North Yorkshire) for Lady Mary Vyner in memory of a son murdered in Greece. Here, too, the font is surmounted by a canopy, with several painted and gilded figures including that of the baptism of Christ by John.

Aristocratic eccentricity is occasionally seen in nineteenth-century fonts just as it was in the eighteenth century (see page 47). At Milton Abbas (Dorset) the former medieval abbey church was given a font by the Earl of Dorchester in 1880, where the bowl is a large shallow 'shell' placed between the feet of two angels, the whole creation being in gleaming white marble. For the use of polychromatic stones in fonts

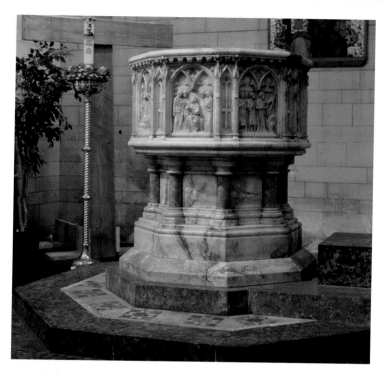

and other church furnishings we may look to the work of the leading architects in the closing years of the century. In the then-affluent Liverpool suburb of Sefton Park, J.L. Pearson built the cathedral-like church of St Agnes for the wealthy local stockbroker Douglas Horsfall in 1883. At the time Pearson was also engaged in building St Augustine's, Kilburn (London) and Truro Cathedral (Cornwall). The Liverpool font is carved in English alabaster with various religious scenes on the sides in the style of the medieval fonts. In 1897 the even wealthier Duke of Westminster commissioned G.F. Bodley, another prominent architect, to build a parish church for his estate village of Eccleston (Cheshire), situated at the edge of the vast estate surrounding his equally vast Eaton Hall. The combination of green and pink stones in the font here is particularly striking (page 8).

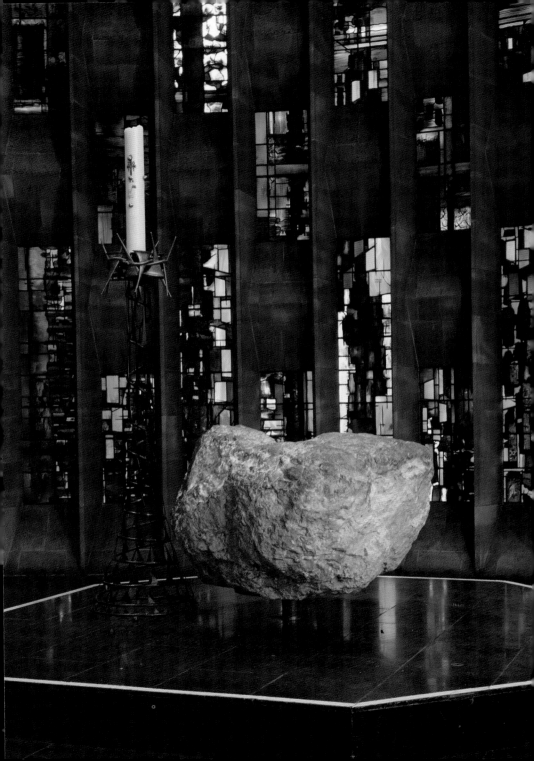

# THE LATE TWENTIETH AND EARLY TWENTY-FIRST CENTURIES

PARISH CHURCHES TODAY have neither the inclination nor the financial resources to continue building and furnishing churches to match the past either in size or opulence. This is no reflection on the sincerity or depth of their Christian faith. In parish churches modest, dignified fonts are typified by the one at St Helen's Church, Crosby, Liverpool. The situation is somewhat different in cathedral churches where deans and chapters can attract financial patronage from individuals and organisations.

The Liverpool Anglican cathedral has been described by Pevsner as 'the final flowering of the Gothic Revival as a vital creative movement … one of the great buildings of the twentieth century'. So it is not surprising that Giles Gilbert Scott should have designed a font ensemble to be worthy of it. The font itself is unexceptional but the cover and particularly the enormous freestanding canopy are a revival of the forms seen in the fifteenth century at Trunch (pages 28 and 34) and effectively make the southwest transept into a baptistery chapel.

The font at Basil Spence's 1962 cathedral at Coventry stands in front of an immense floor-to-ceiling stained glass window by John Piper and Patrick Reyntiens in what forms a baptistery area. It was the architect's imaginative idea to have the bowl cut out of a single raw boulder brought from the hills near Bethlehem. Frederick Gibberd's strikingly original centrally planned polygonal Roman Catholic cathedral in Liverpool was built shortly after Coventry

OPPOSITE
Coventry Cathedral (West Midlands). Sir Basil Spence's building of 1962 contains many strikingly original furnishings. The font is of limestone rock hewn from the hills near Bethlehem. It sits beneath the huge stained glass baptistery window of John Piper and Patrick Reyntiens.

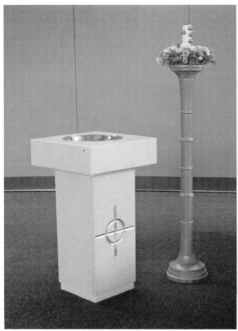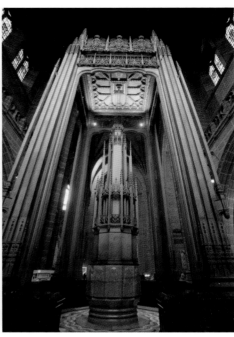

Cathedral, in 1962–67. It is ringed by chapels of various shapes and sizes. One of these was designed as a baptistery, an essay in pure white marble – walls, floors and font.

In 2008 in order to mark the 750th anniversary of Salisbury Cathedral the dean and chapter commissioned a new font to stand in the centre aisle of the nave near to its western entrance end. It is a singularly unusual and striking design by the water sculpture specialist William Pye. The font has a square or diamond-shaped bowl with cusped corner points, on a Purbeck marble base, reflecting the use of that limestone throughout the cathedral in the thirteenth century. Water rises up from beneath and fills the bowl from which it overflows through four corner spouts onto the floor of the cathedral, where it disappears through four bronze grilles. So there is the effect of a natural spring in the form of a man-made fountain, beautifully reflecting the origin of the word font.

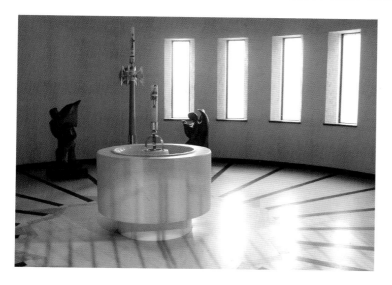

Liverpool's Roman Catholic cathedral. The entire baptistery chapel of 1967 is executed in white marble.

There is nothing unusual or strange about an ancient place of worship, cathedral or parish church introducing radically new ideas and structures into an existing building. For 1,300 years English churches have always added something to represent the spirit of their own age and it is right that the twenty-first century should continue to do so.

Salisbury Cathedral (Wiltshire). The font of 2008 celebrates the 750th anniversary of the building. Unique among English fonts, it features 'living water' rising from below and leaving the bowl through four corner spouts to a brass floor grille. The use of Purbeck marble reflects its use in the cathedral itself.

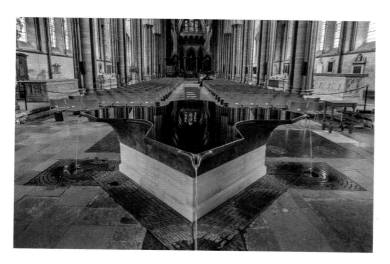

# FURTHER READING

Clifton-Taylor, Alec. *English Parish Churches as Works of Art.*
    Batsford, 1974.

Clifton-Taylor, Alec. *The Pattern of English Building.*
    Faber, 1987. Clifton-Taylor's knowledge and interest in
    English building materials based on extensive travelling is
    unsurpassed; an excellent complement to Pevsner.

Friar, Stephen. *The Companion Guide to the English Parish
    Church.* Chancellor Press, 2000. An A-to-Z encyclopaedia
    of church history, church people, architecture
    and furnishings.

Jones, Lawrence E. *The Beauty of English Churches.*
    Constable, 1978. A concise mini-encyclopaedia of
    church buildings in general and details of every aspect of
    their furnishings.

Murray, Peter and Linda. *The Oxford Companion
    to Christian Art and Architecture.* Oxford
    University Press, 1998.

Pevsner, Nikolaus. *The Buildings of England* (series).
    Yale University Press, first published 1951–74, and
    extensively revised and enlarged by other writers and
    editors. Pevsner was one of the most scholarly and widely
    travelled of architectural historians who visited and
    recorded almost every building of architectural interest,
    ecclesiastical, domestic, public and industrial in the
    cities, towns, villages and hamlets of England. These
    include tens of thousands of churches and chapels in
    which the exteriors, interiors and furnishings, including
    fonts are described in a concise and readable style. These
    books are indispensable travelling companions for all
    church explorers.

Thurlby, Malcolm. *The Herefordshire School of Romanesque Sculpture*. Logaston Press, 2013. A very readable, copiously illustrated book for the general reader, describing every aspect of the twelfth-century churches in Herefordshire and surrounding counties.

# PLACES TO VISIT

Some 20,000 Anglican and Roman Catholic churches contain many fonts of the highest historical and artistic interest and a small representative sample of these is described in this book. An extended list of a hundred fonts sadly not included in the book is given below but it has no claim to be comprehensive.

The detective work – historical, geological and artistic – that can be enjoyed in looking at church fonts is just a reflection of that in exploring English churches as a whole.

## ABBREVIATIONS

### PERIODS OF ARCHITECTURE
**(N)**     Norman, *c.*1080–1200
**(G)**     Gothic, *c.*1200–1600
**(C)**     Classical, *c.*1600–1800

### SCULPTURAL COMPOSITIONS
**H**       Human figures
**A**       Animal figures
**G**       Grotesque figures
**Ab**      Abstract patterns
**I**       Inscriptions
**HSRS**    Herefordshire School of Romanesque Sculpture
**TM**      Tournai marble fonts

## FONTS

### BEDFORDSHIRE
Eaton Bray (G), Ab; Studham (G), A

### BERKSHIRE
Avington (N), H

## BUCKINGHAMSHIRE
Aylesbury (N), Ab; Great Kimble (N), A; Stone (N), H, A, G; Weston Turville (N), Ab

## CORNWALL
Altarnun (N), H, G; Laneast (N), H, A; Lostwithiel (G), H, A, G; Roche (N), H, A, Ab; St Austell (N), H, G

## CUMBRIA
Bridekirk (N), H, G, I

## DERBYSHIRE
Ashover (N), H (lead)

## DEVON
Hartland (N), Ab; Luppitt (N), H, G; South Milton (N), G, A, Ab

## DORSET
Toller Fratrum (N), H, G

## GLOUCESTERSHIRE
Bisley (N), H; Southtop (N), A

## HAMPSHIRE
East Meon (N), H, A, G, TM; Winchester Cathedral (N), H, TM

## HEREFORDSHIRE
Orleton (N), HSRS, H; Shobdon (N), HSRS, A;

## HERTFORDSHIRE
Hitchin: St Mary (G), H; Ware (G), H

## KENT

Brookland (N), H (lead); Darenth (N), H, G; Shorne (G), H; Southfleet (G), H

## LINCOLNSHIRE

Barnetby: St Barnabas (N), Ab (lead); Huttoft (G), H; South Ormsby (G), H

## LONDON

*(Classical or Baroque fonts 1670–1750 in wood or stone by Grinling Gibbons, his studio or followers):* All Hallows Barking; St Benet Paul's Wharf; St Botolph Aldgate; St Edmund the King; St James Piccadilly; St Magnus the Martyr; St Margaret Lothbury; St Margaret Pattens; St Martin in the Fields; St Nicholas Cole Abbey; St Peter upon Cornhill; St Sepulchre; St Vedast Alias Foster

## NORFOLK

Acle (G), H, A, G, I; Breckles (N), H; Burnham Deepdale (N), H; Fincham (N), H; Happisburgh (G), H, G; Hemblington (G), H; Sculthorpe (N), H, A; Shernborne (N), G, Ab; South Wootton (N), G; Stalham (G), H, Ab; Surlingham (G), H, A; Toftrees (N), A, Ab; Upton (G), H, A
*Fifteenth-century Seven Sacrament fonts:*
Gresham; Great Witchingham; Little Walsingham; Walsoken

## NORTHAMPTONSHIRE

Harpole (N), G; Wansford (N), H; West Haddon (N), H

## NOTTINGHAMSHIRE

Lenton (N), H

## OXFORDSHIRE

Hook Norton (N), H; Shilton (G), H

## SHROPSHIRE
Holdgate (N), G, Ab; Stottesdon (N), HSRS

## SOMERSET
Locking (N), H, A; Lullington (N), H, A, Ab, I; Taunton:
St James (G), H

## STAFFORDSHIRE
Ilam (N), H, A; Stafford: St Mary (N), H, A, I

## SUFFOLK
Chediston (G), H, A; Saxmundham (G), H, A;
Snape (G), H, A, I
*Fifteenth-century Seven Sacrament fonts:*
Badingham; Cratfield; Laxfield; Westhall; Weston

## SUSSEX
Brighton: St Nicholas (N), H

## WARWICKSHIRE
Brailes (G), Ab; Coleshill (N), H, A; Stoneleigh (N), H;
Tysoe (G), H

## WILTSHIRE
Avebury (N), H, A; Stanton Fitzwarren (N), H

## WORCESTERSHIRE
Chaddesley Corbett (N), HSRS, A, Ab

## YORKSHIRE: EAST
Bessingby (N), A, Ab; Cowlam (N), H; Kirkburn (N),
H, A; Langtoft (N), H, G; North Grimston (N), H;
Reighton (N), Ab

## YORKSHIRE: WEST
Fishlake (G), H; Thorpe Salvin (N), H, Ab

# INDEX

# Tributes

## Volume 18

# Insolubles and Consequences

## Essays in Honour of Stephen Read

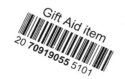

Tributes Series Editor
Dov Gabbay

dov.gabbay@kcl.ac.uk

# Insolubles and Consequences

## Essays in Honour of Stephen Read

Edited by

## Catarina Dutilh Novaes

and

## Ole Thomassen Hjortland

© Individual author and College Publications 2012. All rights reserved.

ISBN 978-1-84890-086-8

College Publications
Scientific Director: Dov Gabbay
Managing Director: Jane Spurr

http://www.collegepublications.co.uk

Cover produced by Laraine Welch
Printed by Lightning Source, Milton Keynes, UK

# CONTENTS

# FOREWORD

*Insolubles and Consequence* is a collection of essays written in honour of Stephen Read, Professor of History and Philosophy of Logic at the University of St Andrews. On the occasion of Stephen's retirement, friends, colleagues, and former students have contributed these essays to celebrate Stephen's work. The topics of the essays reflect Stephen's broad range of expertise, covering the philosophy of logic and language, metaphysics, and the history of logic. As a whole, the volume strives to live up to the quality of Stephen's own work.

In recent decades, Stephen has been a major figure in philosophy of logic, starting with his 'Scottish Plan' in *Relevant Logic* (OUP, 1988), and later with contributions to debates on paradoxes, logical inferentialism, the concept of logical consequence, and logical pluralism. His textbook *Thinking About Logic* (OUP, 1995) has been translated to four languages and is used in courses around the world. He also published numerous articles in some of the top journals of the discipline, such as *Synthese, Philosophical Studies, Journal of Philosophical Logic, Australasian Journal of Philosophy, Analysis, Mind* (among others). As the Principal Investigator of the three-year AHRC project *Foundations of Logical Consequence*, Stephen has (co-)organized a number of conferences and workshops, and maintained an international network of collaborators.

For others, Stephen is best known as a historian of logic, with a speciality in medieval logic. Stephen has edited and translated *Concepts, the treatises of Thomas of Cleves and Paul of Gelria* (Peeters, 2001, with E. P. Bos) and Thomas Bradwardine, *Insolubilia* (Peeters, 2010). In 2010 he received the Ivor Grattan-Guinness Best Paper Award, awarded to the best paper published in the journal *History and Philosophy of Logic* in that year. The paper, *Field's Paradox and Its Medieval Solution*, is just one example of Stephen's fruitful combination of historical insight and contemporary formal tools.

Stephen has also left a formidable mark in St Andrews as lecturer, supervisor, Head of School, Editor-in-chief of *Philosophical Quarterly*, and Professorial Fellow of the Arché Research Center. Friends and colleagues will remember him as a diligent, dedicated and loyal colleague, whose intellectual and professional integrity serves as an example to all.

Most of all, we look forward to the continuation of Stephen's work. Stephen's retirement from teaching and administrative duties will allow him to pursue his intellectual interests with even more gusto. Indeed, he is currently starting a new research project at Arché, named 'Models, Modality and Meaning', and has recently completed a new English translation with introduction of John Buridan's treatise on consequences.

A few words of thanks from the editors are in order. We wish to thank the contributors for their thought-provoking essays; their concentrated efforts allowed for the completion of this project within a very tight timeframe. Edgar Andrade-Lotero has provided his invaluable expertise for the preparation of the whole manuscript in LaTeX, and editorial assistance in general. But our final word of thanks should go to Stephen Read himself, for his crucial contribution to our respective philosophical upbringings. Stephen, we praise ourselves very lucky to have you as our intellectual mentor and collaborator.

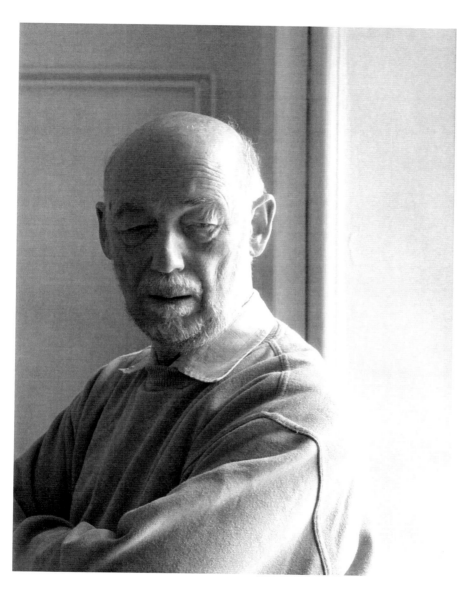

Photo by Julia Langkau

# Interview with Stephen Read[†]

ANDREW ABERDEIN[‡]

ANDREW ABERDEIN: What led you into logic in the first place?

STEPHEN READ: I actually wanted to do maths and English at university, but I went to Keele, because it was famous for cross-culturalization: there was a foundation year in which you studied every subject. That's when I discovered philosophy, and at the same time I discovered that English wasn't the right subject for me. So I concentrated on maths and philosophy. At Keele, there really wasn't any logic: they taught us the syllogism and not much more. In my last year Alan Treherne was appointed, and he ran a course on philosophy of mathematics. I took that, and a small part of that was interesting logic. So I decided to apply to do a masters in logic, and I went to Bristol maths department. Bristol was extraordinary at that time for they actually had nine mathematical logicians: eight full-time and Rod Laver, who was visiting for a year, so I was able to learn an awful lot of logic in that year at Bristol.

AJA: So when did you become interested in the history of logic?

SLR: When I went to Oxford, which is where one thought if you're going to do philosophy at graduate level you should go. Actually, there were two things that I was interested in when I was at Oxford, and Oxford had little of either.

One was the Chomsky boom. It was all the rage at the end of the sixties: 'Goodness me, there's all this stuff in transformational grammar and this is going to solve all our problems in philosophy of language!' I turned up at Oxford and said this is what I wanted to work on and they said, 'Oh, whoops. We don't know anything about that.' But then they appointed Pieter Seuren at Magdalen in January 1971 and I transferred to him as supervisor. He knew all the latest stuff about transformational grammar, and Chomsky, and so on, and tried to teach me some linguistics, and I think something rubbed off. The other thing that started to interest me then was history of logic. I had two years in Oxford, so I had one summer vacation, when I read the Kneales' *Development of Logic*. And, again, I turned up in Oxford, 'I'm interested in mediaeval logic, what is there in the way of mediaeval logic, or maybe even mediaeval philosophy?' And again, they said, 'Oh! We're not sure we do that. Well,' they said, 'there's a man called Lorenzo Minio-Paluello. But we don't really, sort of, recognize him. He's the only person whose office is in the Philosophy Subfaculty.' Having an office there meant you were a non-person, because you

[†]This is an edited version of the interview published in *The Reasoner* **5**(12), 2011.

[‡]Humanities and Communication, Florida Institute of Technology, 150 West University Blvd, Melbourne, Florida 32901-6975, U.S.A. Email: aberdein@fit.edu.

weren't part of the college system. The Philosophy Subfaculty building is just kind of a ...

AJA: A nice library?

SLR: A *small* library, a place where the Jowett Society could meet every week, and maybe a place for graduate students to mingle. *Plus* an office for Lorenzo Minio-Paluello, who had nowhere else to go, and no one else was interested in what he did: he was unappreciated. I mean here is a scholar of the first magnitude, the *Aristoteles Latinus* project that he developed is just extraordinary. So poor old Lorenzo had no one to talk to, apart from six graduate students, most of whom knew little or no Latin. But we had a fascinating reading group using Boehner's translations from Ockham. So he was the man who introduced me to mediaeval logic. Then I was appointed to a lectureship at St Andrews in 1972, and the next inspiration was when Graham Priest arrived in St Andrews in 1974.

Not many people know this, but Graham Priest was appointed to a temporary lectureship at St Andrews in the summer of 1974 and spent eighteen months there, and we ran some seminars together on medieval logic. Which led to one of my first two publications: a joint paper with Graham called ' The Formalization of Ockham's Theory of Supposition' in *Mind*.[1] We wrote two papers together, one of which, that was never published, arose out of working through Desmond Henry's *Mediaeval Logic and Metaphysics*, a very strange book that says the only way really to get an understanding of mediaeval logic is to formalize it using Leśniewski's Ontology.

But the two major things I have worked on in history of logic have both been on fourteenth century logic. All through the eighties I got into a big dispute with Geach, out of that stuff with Graham. Graham and I came up with the idea that there are only three modes of common personal supposition. There's the one that matches disjunctive descent, there's the one that matches conjunctive descent, and then there's a third one which is descent to disjunct terms. Geach said, 'Only logical idiots would think that!' Because of course, considerations of symmetry tell you that there's a descent to a conjunct term. Now Geach was very careful. If you actually look, he says you can descend to a conjunct term, he doesn't actually claim that there's a mode of supposition corresponding to it. So, over many years I was puzzled by this. I discovered a comment in a man called Eckius, Johann von Eck, whom the Catholic Church signed up to refute Luther, because he was such a clever man. But before that, he wrote some works on logic, and in one of those works on logic he says 'Thomas of Cleves, as I remember, was the first person to identify this fourth mode of supposition.'

AJA: Ah ha.

SLR: So I turned up at a conference in 1985, and asked a number of people including Professor de Rijk, who was the omniscient scholar of mediaeval logic, 'Who was Thomas of Cleves?' And it was when I discovered that even de Rijk had not heard of Thomas of Cleves, that I realised that there was a promising avenue of research to pursue. And so I rounded off my supposition theory time researching Thomas of Cleves.

[1] Priest and Read (1977).

In the meantime, George Hughes had published his translation of chapter eight of Buridan's *Sophismata* in '82, and I reviewed it in '84. I realised at the time that Buridan's theory was unsatisfactory, but I was dimly aware that there was a man called Thomas Bradwardine in the background, but very few people knew anything about Bradwardine then. It lay dormant with me for a long time, and it wasn't until about ten years ago that I started looking seriously at Bradwardine, and then I thought that Bradwardine had everything that was right about Buridan and answers to all the things that weren't satisfactory. So from thinking that this was a very interesting but *mistaken* account of paradoxes I had a road to Damascus moment when I suddenly thought, 'Hang on! This seems to work.'

What's interesting I think about this Bradwardine stuff, in the present context of what people are doing with the paradoxes, is that you make a very well-motivated revision of the truth principles, a revision which is not obviously inconsistent with what Tarski actually said, though it's inconsistent with how people now state what Tarski said, and you can solve the paradoxes without revising your logic. So, if you want to be a classical logician, you can actually do it in classical logic; if you want to revise your logic, as I do, it would be for entirely different reasons.

Very briefly, think of what Tarski actually says, rather than the way people remember him, about the so-called Convention T. For a theory of T to be a theory of truth every instance of '$S$ is true if and only if $p$' must be derivable, where what replaces $p$ is a translation into the metalanguage of the sentence a structural description of which replaces $S$. And the point about Bradwardine is that he points out that some sentences say more than at first appears. So to properly translate, for example the liar sentence, which you designate on the left hand side, so you've got $L$ is true, where $L$ is the liar sentence '$L$ is not true.' When you now replace $p$, you have to translate $L$ into the metalanguage. Now if $L$ is actually saying more than '$L$ is not true', you've got to say more than '$L$ is not true' on the right hand side, and Bradwardine has a proof that '$L$ is not true' not only says that '$L$ is not true' but also says that '$L$ is true.' So, the proper Tarskian instance of the T-schema is " '$L$ is true' if and only if $L$ is not true and $L$ is true." So there's no real disagreement with Tarski, but there's a new appreciation of what the T-schema is requiring, which then is a solution, because now the liar is simply a contradictory sentence which is just false.

AJA: I see, yes. Nice.

SLR: Paradox solved. The principle it all hinges on is a closure principle that says that signification, or meaning, or saying that, or whatever you call this semantic notion, is closed under consequence, so that a sentence signifies everything that follows from anything it signifies. I think that's exciting.

AJA: Um hm. Hmmm. Yes, there's a question I've been meaning to ask about that closure principle. Would it require, for example, that the Peano axioms 'mean' Goldbach's Conjecture (assuming it's true)? That struck me as rather startling. But have I got the wrong end of the stick?

SLR: Well, Gödel told us that the Peano axioms are incomplete, so perhaps Goldbach's Conjecture doesn't follow from them even if it's true (and remember that the Gödel sentence has the same form as Goldbach's Conjecture). But yes, Bradwardine does claim that a sentence means everything that follows from it, or from what it means. So if I say that the Peano axioms are true, and Goldbach's Conjecture follows from those axioms, then part of what I've said, what I've meant, is that Goldbach's Conjecture is true.

AJA: Golly. So logically equivalent claims, like, say, Zorn's Lemma and the Axiom of Choice, mean the same thing? (Well, strictly speaking Zorn's Lemma plus axioms of ZF means the same as the Axiom of Choice plus axioms of ZF.) And that seems odd—for instance, I am confident I could explain the Axiom of Choice to my students, but not confident I could explain Zorn's Lemma.

SLR: That logically equivalent sentences mean the same is not such an unusual claim. Anyone who identifies propositions with sets of possible worlds will have to accept that.

AJA: That's true.

SLR: Well, Zorn's lemma and AC are true in the same possible worlds. So on many other accounts, they express the same proposition, so have the same 'meaning' according to those accounts.

AJA: Indeed: that would be even worse. Which is why I wouldn't want to think about mathematical propositions that way—it's clearly at odds with mathematical practice.

But what's so extraordinary about all this is that it comes from the fourteenth century. Hasok Chang has this idea of philosophy of science as 'complementary science' (a rather unhappy term, as it sounds like complementary medicine). It's the idea that philosophers of science should go back to old, discarded paradigms and excavate them for bits that were missed. Your sort of history of logic strikes me as similar: you're going back and digging up things that were thrown away unnecessarily.

SLR: Yes, I think so. That was true of the supposition theory: it possibly has a solution to certain problems about intensionality, which don't have an easy solution given the Frege-Russell account of logic, and that seemed exciting. And Bradwardine was obviously an unbelievably brilliant mathematician, who is pretty famous in the history of science. He's famous in the history of theology for he became Archbishop of Canterbury, and then when he was a very, very young man, possibly in his early twenties, he has this brilliant idea about the semantic paradoxes. There is a sea change in reactions to the paradoxes in the 1320s: the rest of the fourteenth century is spent developing Bradwardine's ideas.

AJA: I also wanted to ask about the early years of relevance logic. You were not quite in the first generation of relevance logicians, but you overlapped with the second generation?

SLR: The first generation is Anderson and Belnap, the second generation is Meyer and Dunn and others, so I would be the third generation. I learnt from Dunn in particular about intensional bunching and suchlike. I've got a paper on 'Validity and the intensional sense of "and"' in 1981 and a paper about disjunction about the same time.[2] So I'm really the eighties generation.

---

[2] Read (1981) and Read (1982).

AJA: The impression I have is that at that point, in the seventies and early eighties, this was a philosophical topic that subsequently shifted away from philosophy. That interest in non-classical logics, interest in logic as a whole, became more emphasized in computer science.

SLR: It was philosophical right from the start, but then a lot of technical questions came up during the sixties, including in particular the one that's always talked about which is the Kripke revolution in modal logic. Modal logic had been a formal theory in search of a semantics in the fifties. People really seriously criticized modal logic. There might have been pretend semantics of various sorts, but there was no real semantics, and Kripke answered that. That's what everyone was waiting for: the world semantics suddenly became *intuitive* in a way that the algebra was completely unintuitive.

In the sixties, they then turned their guns on relevant logic, and said relevant logic is not really a logic because it doesn't have a proper semantics. And so lots of people, the second generation, come in: Dunn and Meyer, the Routleys, both Routleys of course, Maksimova and Urquhart. And Fine. And all of them produced, in various slightly different ways, semantics for relevant logic. But once again it was the Routley and Meyer semantics that took off.

AJA: The worlds again, yes... It's interesting, because it's the worlds that some people find most hard to stomach. But it's a very successful communication tool.

SLR: Right. Then we were left with two worries which have only recently been finally addressed, I think. There's this new paper with eleven authors... [3]

AJA: Yes, yes, I saw that.

SLR: ... in the *Journal of Philosophical Logic*. Well, that is finally answering a challenge which ought to be made, about what the semantics really means. Because relevant logics are paraconsistent, that means theories in them can be simply inconsistent without being trivial. That really was the original motivation, going right back to Ackermann, and the tweak that Anderson and Belnap made, dropping the rule gamma, was all to do with allowing theories to be inconsistent without being trivial. People often characterize paraconsistent logic as not containing the rule of explosion: From $A$ and not $A$ infer $B$. Now that is a consequence of allowing simply inconsistent theories without trivializing, it means you mustn't contain that rule. But, for example, you might not contain that rule, but the rule might nonetheless be admissible. In which case you wouldn't contain the triviality. So I think it's a bad definition. I think we ought to stick to 'simply inconsistent without trivialization' as the better account of what paraconsistent really means. The other thing that 'paraconsistency' is badly used to talk about is what we should call dialethic theories.

AJA: Yes. Things that are both true and false.

SLR: People often think that if one's a relevant logician, one is therefore ...

AJA: A dialetheist?

SLR: ... and therefore that there are true contradictions, yes. I am a relevant logician, I believe in paraconsistent logic, but I do not believe in the existence of true contradictions! It's actually an understandable consequence of the model theory, of the Routley-Meyer semantics, or the Routley star, more to the point,

---

[3]Beall et al. (2012).

because they need a world semantics which invalidates explosion. In the standard way of taking consequence, if we want to invalidate an inference, we have to find a world where the premises are true and the conclusion false: a world where $A$ and not $A$ are true and $B$ is false. That means we have to find a world where $A$ and not $A$ are true. And that seems to mean that we in some sense believe in the existence of worlds where $A$ and not $A$ can both be true, so we're dialetheists. So that's a bad inference, but I think an understandable one. And that's what my very first paper on the intensional sense of 'and' was really all about. It was saying that it all hangs on a bad account of consequence.

AJA: Is that where your version of relevance logic differs vis-à-vis its competitors?

SLR: I think that's right. My distinctive take was published in this book called *Relevant Logic*.[4] The title's no longer an issue, but there was a time when half the relevant logic community, or half the *relevance* logic community called it relevance logic—they tended to be in America—and the other half called it relevant logic, and they lived in Australia. What was the issue all about? Why did we get so agitated about such things in those days? I think really it was to do with the American Plan and the Australian Plan, wasn't it?

AJA: I always assumed that it was a question of whether or not you wanted to help yourself to a pun, about whether this is the stuff that's *relevant*, it speaks to having applications to natural discourse, rather than being the logic of relevance.

SLR: I think that's right too. We'd had *Entailment*, volume one, subtitled *The Logic of Relevance and Necessity*, that claimed that we avoided both fallacies of relevance and fallacies of necessity, which made a lot of people think that they could look at the turn to relevance logic, and they could find some account of relevance. I think it slowly dawned on people that that wasn't forthcoming. There is actually a paper of Bob Meyer's that sets out to establish that relevance logic is not the intersection of the analysis of relevance and the analysis of necessity. And I think that was quite a big thing, that may be the bigger thing that lay behind that change of name, as opposed to logic on the American Plan versus logic on the Australian Plan.

AJA: Yes, I remember you had a paper that was forthcoming for a while, 'The irrelevance of the concept of relevance to the concept of relevant consequence.' I thought that was a hell of title, but when it forthcame it was called something more mundane.

SLR: Much more mundane. It was 'Logical consequence as truth preservation'.[5] I wish it had come out with the original title. I'm not sure I remember quite why it lost that title. It was a bit long, but it had a certain *zing*.

For its first thirty years, the relevance logic programme didn't really have its own conception of consequence. Things were mostly done in terms of theses. This is not unusual. This is how logic was from Frege until the rediscovery of Gentzen in the eighties. We *eventually* realized—I'm sure that there were glimmerings of this before—that logic was really an analysis of logical consequence and not an analysis of logical truth. But for most of the twentieth century the

---

[4]Read (1988).
[5]Read (2003).

concentration seems to have been on logical truth, axiomatic systems, deriving theorems, not on the consequence relation. And that was true of relevance logic: mostly to do with theorems, very occasionally you would have single premiss consequence. So if you look at the semantics papers of Routley and Meyer, they often include a single premiss consequence relation, but they don't have a multiple premiss consequence relation. And if you look in Anderson and Belnap's book, they have a lot of discussions about things called the official deduction theorem, and so on, but don't really get clear in their own minds what's going on with a collection of premisses and don't clearly distinguish between a collection of premisses some of which could be irrelevant and a collection of premisses all of which are relevant. They talk about it, but they don't get very clear about it. So one of the main driving points about my book was to set relevance logic on a proper philosophical foundation. And that meant trying to be coherent: if one's talking about entailment or consequence, then set up a theory which has at its heart a consequence relation. Now the best way that I found to deal with that was to have a single conclusion consequence relation, with a special new object called a bunch of premisses.

AJA: Right, yes.

SLR: I owe that ultimately to Dunn, who developed this distinction between intensional bunching and extensional bunching, I think even back in his thesis, in the late sixties.

AJA: Do you have newer work I've missed on relevance logic?

SLR: I've moved on to talk about logical consequence in different guises. I can remember being required to say what my research interests were in a short paragraph for the department website, and saying something like, 'My central concern remains the notion of logical consequence in both modern and mediaeval logic.' Quite when that moves away from simply relevant logic I'm not sure. That's a continuity that goes right back to that paper in '81 on the intensional sense of 'and', which was saying that there must be an ambiguity in 'and' in order to diagnose the so-called Lewis argument. The short version of the Lewis argument is to say that it's impossible for $A$ and not-$A$ to be true and $B$ false, therefore $B$ follows from $A$ and not-$A$. So that second 'and' in there—'and $B$ false', right—if that's extensional 'and' and that argument's valid, then forget relevant logic; we have explosion straight away.

So what's going on here? Then you develop relevance logic, or you develop linear logic, and what happens is you move to substructural logics, which get identified by Schroeder-Heister and Došen in the early '90s, partly with the impact of linear logic. Once you restrict the use of structural rules, you appreciate that the connectives start to bifurcate. So that 'and' becomes additive and multiplicative conjunction, which alternatively gets called intensional and extensional conjunction. Similarly with disjunction; similarly with conditional. And, thought the other way, if you start off with these distinct connectives, you realise that by adding sufficiently many structural rules you can conflate them. So the particular ones are $W$ and $K$, contraction and weakening, and they would work to distinguish or conflate these connectives.

What I was saying is that having discovered that there's a *theory* of two conjunctions, can we put it to work in diagnosing problems? My idea in that paper in '81 was that having discovered that there's this distinct conjunction called 'fusion', then consequence is 'It's impossible for the premises to be true *fuse* the conclusion false.' And that's what led to that paper in 2003, 'Logical consequence as truth preservation.' Logical consequence really *is* truth preservation, but when truth preservation is properly understood using fusion.

Because if you don't do that, you're forced to say that logical consequence is not just truth preservation, but requires relevance preservation as well, and that in itself leads to paradox as I try to explain in that paper. The simple form of that paradox is to say, 'We know that it's impossible for the premises to be true and the conclusion false. So we know the argument is truth preserving. We know the premises are true. But you're not allowed to infer the conclusion because it's *not relevant*'! Even though you have to admit the conclusion is true because the argument is truth-preserving. And I think anyone who's saying that hasn't listened to what they've just said! That's the way most people I think had actually gone. So that's why I'm still interested in the subject.

AJA: I can see how that led to your current AHRC project on the Foundations of Logical Consequence.[6] How did that get started?

SLR: It's to do with the history of Arché. Arché had built up a reputation in logic over its first seven or eight years. You had the maths project, the *Grundgesetze* project, the modality project, the vagueness project. They all came to an end, and there were people still wanting to come to St Andrews to study logic, to visit, to talk about logic, and so on, and there were no logic projects.

Ole Hjortland and Walter Pedriali heard about this. They said, 'Well, would it be a good idea if Steve Read headed up this project?' And we also had Graham Priest and Stewart Shapiro as visiting professors and they're here 25%, so couldn't they be investigators on the project? And then Ole, Crispin Wright and I put a *huge* amount of time, and I suppose thereby effort, into identifying a series of questions and issues and telling a coherent story about how we could, you know, spend a three/four year project working on the foundations of logical consequence. And we put an application together in 2007, it was approved, and the project eventually started in January 2009. And we've had a very interesting, and I think successful, project on the Foundations of Logical Consequence. Funded very generously by the AHRC, I should record.

AJA: Yes. I keep seeing these very exciting conference announcements for times when I'm several thousand miles away! Epistemology of logic was something that caught my attention, because much of what I do is epistemology of mathematics.

SLR: I was wondering whether we could actually learn something from the philosophy of mathematics. Because normally I go to conferences, on the philosophy of logic and maths. People think they're *mates*, much like some people think philosophy and theology are natural mates.

AJA: Those guys both use symbols so let's throw them together?

SLR: Yeah. I mean philosophy of maths is epistemology or metaphysics, and

---

[6]See http://www.st-andrews.ac.uk/arche/projects/logic/.

the philosophy of logic is normally neither of those. But maybe we can learn something from philosophy of maths.

AJA: That's what Catarina Dutilh Novaes is doing, isn't it, with her idea of logical practice? The sort of stuff which my friends who work on mathematical practice do to mathematics, she wants to do to logic.

SLR: Right. She's keen for us to extend that to the practice-based side of epistemology, but there is a whole epistemology which isn't particularly interested in practice. There are two big names here: Peacocke and Williamson. Peacocke has this thing called the integration challenge—for any subject, but in particular there is an integration challenge for logic, which is, assuming that in the first three phases of the project we've worked out what logical consequence is, how does that square with its epistemology? How would one get a handle on the metaphysics given one's epistemological limitations? That's the integration challenge.

AJA: Right.

SLR: There's another interesting question that came up about all the Arché projects just about the time the FLC project started. That was how, or to what extent, or whether the principal investigator should direct the research of the other members of the project. So does the principal investigator say, 'Right, colleagues! You must now write a paper on...'

AJA: If you're doing physics or chemistry or the like this is part of the way the job works, but it's a novel problem for philosophers.

SLR: And there were people who thought that was the way it should work. Now, with the research students, there's a good chance that you actually can select your students to work on the published research. And to some extent that's true of the research fellows too, because you're picking people who have worked on this, but of course you can't ensure that their minds will continue to work on it. It's something which I think the humanities, or at least philosophy, hasn't really got to grips with.

You say that it's pretty much de rigueur in the sciences that you recruit people to a research project and tell them, 'Go and work on a particular project. Come up with answers to particular questions.' How does one do that in philosophy? My ideas and my experience were that this was a mistake. And to the small extent that I've actually practiced it, despite thinking it was a mistake, it's been a disaster! My answer to this challenge when it was first brought up, and I think it's the answer that other people in Arché wanted to give as well, was that you can only encourage people, you can't direct them. And one way of encouraging them is to organize events where you bring in outside researchers to, say, workshops, to give you talks, or maybe reading seminars, on this theme, and hope that by being exposed to enough of this, your colleagues on the project will suddenly start to have ideas about it, and then produce answers to these questions.

And the other side of it is that we end up producing things not directly within the anticipated phases, but nonetheless useful material, which would not have existed without this funding. And I think the Research Council is perfectly happy to hear that, provided that you have got worthwhile research.

AJA: Well, they certainly ought to be.

SLR: That's the way I've treated that particular issue. Given that there have been lots of workshops on the foundations of logical consequence, maybe, indirectly, other people, particularly graduate students, will have discovered, 'Oh! There's this interesting subject called philosophy of logic, and I can work on that.'

## BIBLIOGRAPHY

Beall, J., Brady, R., Dunn, M., Hazen, A., Mares, E., Stanley, J., Meyer, R., Priest, G., Restall, G., Ripley, D., and Sylvan, R. (2012). On the ternary relation and conditionality. *Journal of Philosophical Logic*, 41(3):595–612.

Priest, G. and Read, S. (1977). The formalization of Ockham's theory of supposition. *Mind*, 86(341):109–113.

Read, S. (1981). Validity and the intensional sense of 'and'. *Australasian Journal of Philosophy*, 59(3):301–307.

Read, S. (1982). Disjunction. *Journal of semantics*, 1(3–4):275–285.

Read, S. (1988). *Relevant Logic: A Philosophical Examination of Inference*. Basil Blackwell, Oxford.

Read, S. (2003). Logical consequence as truth-preservation. *Logique et Analyse*, 183:479–493.

# Nicholas of Amsterdam (†1437) on the Individual

E.P. Bos[†][‡]

## 1 Introduction

The German master Nicholaus Theoderici de Amsterdam (†1437) wrote a *Commentary (exercitium) on Porphyry*. In this contribution I present an introduction to and edition of question 12 of this work. The question is part of Nicholas' voluminous commentary on the Old logic, in which Nicholas comments on Porphyry's *Isagoge*, Aristotle's *Praedicamenta* and the *De Interpretatione* (it numbers about 120,000 words). The whole commentary has come down to us in a single manuscript, as far as we know, viz. ms Munich, *Bayerische Staatsbibliothek* CLM 500, ff. 146r–254v.

## 2 Nicholas of Amsterdam: his Life and Works

Our knowledge of Nicholas of Amsterdam's life and works is largely due to the investigations of Olaf Pluta.[1] Nicholas was a prominent master of arts in Germany during the fifteenth century.[2] He was active at the universities of Cologne, Erfurt and finally Rostock, where he became one of the leading masters in the formative years of this newly founded university.

The 1419 curriculum of the philosophical faculty of the University of Rostock is important for our understanding of the place of Nicholas' logical works in the history of philosophy.[3] As well as Aristotle's logical and physical works, students were required to study John Buridan's *Summulae logicales*, together with John Dorp's commentary during their first year. In the course of the year exercises were held on the other parts of Buridan's *Summulae*, viz. *De praedicamentis, de suppositionibus, de ampliationibus, de appellationibus, de restrictionibus*. Baccalaureate students were also required to take part in the following exercises: *vetus ars* (six months), *nova logica* (six months), physics (six months), *De anima* (three months), *Parva logicalia* (six months).

As well as the commentary on the old logic (labelled in the manuscript *exercitium veteris artis*) Nicholas also composed an *exercitium novae artis*.

---

[†]Institute of Philosophy, Leiden University, Leiden, The Netherlands.
Email: `egbertbos@kpnmail.nl`
[‡]Thanks are due to Dr. J.W. McAllister (Leiden) for his correction of my English.
[1]Pluta (2009).
[2]Pluta (2007, esp. p. 111, notes 10 and 11).
[3]Rostock, Universitätsarchiv, Statutenbuch 1419–1756 (Signature RIA1), pp. 73–76: Statuta facultatis artium.

Unfortunately this seems to have been lost. It was mentioned only in the
catalogue of the Benedictine Monastery of Saint Egidien in Nürnberg.[4]

It seems impossible to give an exact date for the composition of Nicholas of
Amsterdam's *Commentary on the ars vetus*. However, as Pluta says, we can
readily assume that this work was composed sometime during Nicholas' years
in Rostock, that is to say between 1422, when Nicholas was admitted into the
Arts Faculty, and 1437, when the University of Rostock moved to Greifswald.
In the text one finds two dates, viz. 1453 on f. 192r and 1447 on f. 230v. So
1447 seems to be the year in which the copying started.

From Nicholas' commentaries we learn how the doctrines of, especially, John
Buridan and Marsilius of Inghen were handed down in the Northern part of
Germany in the late Middle Ages. His tracts also show in what way a conceptualist like Nicholas criticized the great William of Ockham, and in what way a
conceptualist could incorporate the realist doctrines of the thirteenth-century
*antiqui*, Albert the Great and Thomas Aquinas.[5]

## 3   The Manuscript Munich, *Bayerische Staatsbibliothek* Clm 500.[6]

Here follows a description of the contents of the manuscript in which Nicholas'
Commentary on the old logic is found. The description in the Catalogue composed by Halm, Von Laubmann and Meyer is rather succinct.[7]

Manuscript: Format 4°, 286 fol. Liber Heinrici Schedelii.

On the flyleaf: Disputata Coloniae circa quaestiones veteris artis (secundum Porphyrium de V universalibus, Aristotelis Praedicamentorum et Perihermeneias etc. libros)

1. ff. 1r–143v: Anonymus, Expositio et Quaestiones in Artem veterem.
2. ff. 144v–145r: Anonymus, Quaestio de Principio individuationis
3. ff. 146r–254v: Nicolaus de Amsterdam, Exercitium veteris artis [8]

The text is written by a single hand. Two different hands add notes in the
margin. A fourth hand wrote running titles.

3.1. 147r–184v: Quaestiones in Porphyrium

*Inc.*: Circa nobile et multum utile necnon delectabile[9] exercitium veteris
artis venerabilis magistri Amsterdam etcetera.

---

[4]Information by Bos (2011, p. 237).

[5]See for the above remarks also Bos (2011, p. 235) with reference to Pluta's works.

[6]I owe information about this manuscript to Prof. H. Hubien (Liège).

[7]K. Halm, G. von Laubmann, W. Meyer, Catalogus codicum latinorum Bibiothecae Regiae
Monacensis. Ed. altera emendatior. Band 1.1, cdd. 1–2323 compl., p. 140.

[8]For a list of questions, see Bos (2011, pp. 257–265).

[9]The square initial letter has text written around it: Circa nobile et multum utile necnon
delectabile.

Et quaeritur primo, utrum tantum quinque sunt habitus intellectuales. Pro huius queestionis decisione est notandum primo quod secundum Philosophum, sexto Ethicorum[10], quinque ponuntur habitus intellectuales, scilicet sapientia, prudentia, intelligentia, ars et scientia. Quorum habituum sufficientia sic sumitur: omnis habitus intellectualis vel est [...]

*Expl.*: Sed istud iterum non approbat via moderna que non ponit realem distinctionem inter subiectum et propriam passionem. Et ideo dicendum est quod propriae passiones non suscipiunt intentionem et remissionem. Nec ridere est propria passio, sed esse risibile.

### 3.2. ff. 186v–237r: Quaestiones in Praedicamenta

*Inc.*: Quaeritur primo, utrum aequivocum sit univocum.
Pro intellectu quaestionis est notandum primo quod de subiecto libri scientiae praedicamentorum sunt diversi modi dicendi. Nam quidam, ut Simplicius et Boethius, dicunt quod subiectum scientiae libri praedicamentorum est decem voce genera significantes.

*Expl.*: Hoc tamen esse imperfectum non est esse substantiale, quia alias poneretur inchoatio formarum quam negant moderni philosophi, sed hoc esse imperfectum est esse quantitativum plus recipiens materiam quam formam, ut habet declarari circa primum Physicorum.

### 3.3. ff. 237v–254v: Quaestiones super De interpretatione Aristotelis.[11]

*Inc.*: 'Circa librum Periermeniarum movetur talis quaestio prima, utrum enuntiatio sit subiectum scientiae libri Periermeniarum. Pro intellectu quaestionis est notandum primo quod, quamvis subiectum multipliciter capitur, hic tamen 'subiectum' debet capi pro attributionis scientiae subiecto.

*Expl.*: Ratio est ista quia in modalibus divisis distribuunt et particularisant tempus more signorum universalium et particularium, quia isto modo sunt primae impositionis et sunt ampliativi, sicut autem non est in modalibus compositis ex quo tunc sunt termini secundarum intentionum.[12]

### 4. f. 254v: Anonymus, Quaestio utrum omne ens aut sit in anima aut extra animam.

This short question immediately follows Nicholas' commentary on the *Perihermeneias*. It is written by the same hand that wrote the marginal notes, viz. the headings in Nicholas' commentary (hand M³).

f. 255r–256r: Anonymus, Quaestio utrum Deus ponatur in praedicamentis.

f. 256v: Anonymus, De modis praedicamentalibus.

f. 257r–v: Anonymus, Auctoritates.

---

[10] Aristoteles, *Ethica Nicomachea*, VI, 3, 1139 b.
[11] This text is written in the square initial.
[12] De quo laudetur Deus gloriosus perhenniter (sic) *add.* M.

f. 258r–269v: Anonymus, De relationibus iuxta traditionem Modernorum.

*Inc.*: Circa praedicamentum relationis incidunt quaedam dubitationes. Quarum prima est ista: utrum relatio sit ens reale extra animam.
*Expl.*: Et sic est finis dubiorum de relationibus iuxta traditionem moderno-rum. Deo gratias.

f. 270r–v: Anonymus, Quaestio utrum relatio nullo modo sit intelligibilis.

f. 271r–v: Anonymus, Quaestio utrum praedicamentum logicum, naturale et metaphysicum sint eadem vel diversa.

ff. 272r–274v: Anonymus, Quaestio utrum praedicamentum qualitatis, vel qualitas, sit res diversa a substantia vel quantitatis.

f. 274v–275r: Anonymus, De principio individuationis iuxta traditionem modernorum.

ff. 275v–f.276v: Anonymus, Circa primas duas proprietates praedicamenti qualitatis dubitatur [...]

## 4   The Form of the Questions

Nicholas' commentary on the old logic is a set of questions. In by far the largest number of cases, the questions take the following form:

1. The question itself;

2. Some notes by Nicholas (ranging from 1 to 3);

3. Conclusion or conclusions (ranging from 1 to 3);

4. Arguments pro and con (usually 2 to 5).

Nicholas calls items 1–3 the 'corpus' or 'central part' of the question.[13] Three are very few exceptions to the general scheme.

## 5   The Commentary as an 'Exercise' (*'exercitium'*)

In the incipit of the questions on Porphyry,[14] the commentary is called an *'exercitium'*, or exercise. Both students for a bachelor's and those for a master's degree were obliged to follow two kinds of courses, viz. lectures, in which a professor expounded the *littera* to students of each level, and exercises, in which the student himself could play a part. In his lectures, the master shows the contents and structures of the text and harmonizes conflicting statements. In the exercises, the students of each level each of their own level, are expected to take active part themselves and participate in disputations. The *exercitia* such as are handed down in our text, are corrected questions of the disputations, not

---

[13]See, below, the appendix, p. 20, l. 1–p- 25, l. 26.
[14]Inc.: 'Exercitium veteris artis venerabilis magistri Amsterdam etcetera. Et quaeritur primo, utrum tantum quinque sunt habitus intellectuales. Pro huius quaestionis decisione est notandum primo ...' (MS: f. 147r). The square initial letter has the following text written around it: 'Circa librum Periermeniarum movetur'.

exact reports of the actual exercises themselves.[15] In our texts the disputations are clearly solved - in other university practices, this is not always the case,[16] but rather the problem is left undecided.

# 6  Principles of Nicholas' Philosophy

## 6.1  Nicolas as a 'modernus'

Nicholas calls himself a '*modernus*'. He does not wish to be considered a follower of Ockham, not even of John Buridan and Marsilius of Inghen, to whom he frequently refers, especially to Marsilius. Nicholas sometimes criticizes William of Ockham and the *antiqui*. For instance, unlike Ockham, our master accepts a *real* difference between substance and quantity.[17] Jan Pinborg noted this difference in views between the two masters in his article on Nicholas' commentary on *De anima*.[18]

As regards Porphyry and Aristotle, he investigates the sufficiency ('*sufficientia*') of their doctrines, posing the question whether the various lists to be found in the authoritative texts were sufficiently proved as regards their definition and number. These investigations concern the following problems, viz. whether sufficient proof had been given of the doctrines 1) of the five intellectual dispositions (art, prudence, science, wisdom and intellect), 2) of the five predicables, 3) of the ten categories, 4) of the three *antepraedicamenta* (equivocals, univocals, denominatives), 5) of the three *postpraedicamenta* (opposition, priority and posteriority, simultaneity, movement and disposition (*habitus*)), 6) of the different species of quality, and 7) of the four kinds of opposing propositions (contradictory, contrary, subcontrary and subaltern propositions). Nicholas clearly does not accept traditional doctrine unconditionally, but asks for proof, and therefore belongs to those who cast doubt on traditional doctrines by no longer accepting them without proof.

Nicholas refers to many masters, in most cases to Albert the Great and Thomas Aquinas. Further he refers to Boethius, Avicenna, Averroes, Gilbertus Poirretanus, Peter of Spain, John Duns Scot, Robert Grosseteste, Roger Bacon, Henry Totting of Oyta, Johannes Aurifaber, Giles of Rome, Richard Brinkley, the author of a *Tractatus de spaera* (most probably Johannes de Sacrobosco), Ralph of England (Radulphus Anglicus = Ralph Strode ?), Thomas Manlevelt, Thomas of Cleves and Johannes Dorp. He also shows acquaintance with the grammarian Priscian.[19]

## 6.2  Nicholas as a conceptualist

In the Middle Ages, both *antiqui* and *moderni* commented on Aristotle. As already mentioned, Nicholas considers himself a *modernus*.[20]  *Via moderna*

---

[15]In the latter case we find a detailed report of the disputation that was held—which no doubt is interesting from the point of view of the history of university teaching (see Kenny and Pinborg, 1982, pp. 21–23).

[16]Kenny and Pinborg (1982, p. 34).

[17]See Bos (2011, pp. 251–256).

[18]Pinborg (1964).

[19]His acquaintance with Priscian is shown by his use of 'collectivus plurium' and 'pronomen primitivae speciei' in question 12. I owe this information to Prof. C. H. Kneepkens.

[20]*e.g.* Nicolaus de Amsterdam, In *Porph.*, qu. 6, f. 159v: 'Sed licet hec positio sic intellecta sit probabilis, iste tamen modus loquendi non est viae modernae conformis.' Here the *via*

stands here, it seems, for a *tradition of learning*, which *happens* to be con-
ceptualistic. It is not just a synonym for conceptualism or nominalism as a
philosophical approach in general.[21]

As a conceptualist, Nicholas thinks that philosophical discussions take place
on the level of concepts, and thus also on that of written and spoken language
as far as languages of those kinds are guided by concepts. Spoken or written
words are imposed, or have imposition, to signify things. Under the guidance
of concepts, humans use written and spoken words to signify things.

### 6.3    Speaking in terms of reality or in terms of logic.

Nicholas distinguishes between different ways of speaking, viz. *realiter* and *logicaliter*. Buridan approached problems in the same way.[22] In his commentary
on the old logic, Nicholas comes forward principally as a logician. His way of
speaking is *logicaliter*. However, he often compares this logical way of speaking
with another, viz. speaking *realiter*.

An example of this distinction: 'Difference' (*differentia*) can be taken in
different ways, Nicholas says, viz. *realiter* and *logicaliter*. *Realiter* it is a disposition of the subject. Then it is sometimes used in the singular number, but
usually in the plural, meaning 'different things' (*differentia*). In a most proper
sense, rationality is *in a man*. Then it is the difference which makes him belong
to the species man. One can also take the term *logicaliter*; then it is a *term*,
which is said, or can be said, of a subject, in this case of a 'man'.[23] Then the
term '*differentia*' (in the singular) is one of the five predicables. Predicables
in general may differ *logicaliter*, but may be identical *realiter*, Nicholas says.[24]
The same thing can be considered differently under different aspects.

Nicholas also uses the term *essentialiter*. For instance, a substantial form
can be associated *essentialiter* with a man. He takes '*essentialiter*' sometimes
as synonym of *realiter*, but frequently in opposition to *accidentaliter*. Then,
*essentialiter* is associated with *specifice*, because the species as such is referred

---

*moderna* is the criterion for judging views.

[21]Pinborg (1964, p. 252).

[22]Johannes Buridanus, *Quaestiones super libros Metaphysicae*, ed. Parisiis 1518 (repr.
Frankfurt a. M. 1964), VII, q. iii, f. xliii b.

[23]Nicolaus de Amsterdam, Exercitiun in *Porphyrium*, qu. 13, f. 172v: Unde 'differentia
communiter dicta' realiter loquendo est dispositio separabilis a subiectis qua aliqua differunt
accidentaliter, ut album a [a: an MS] nigro; logicaliter vero est terminus connotativus alicuius
dispositionis accidentalis qui [f. 173r] natus est esse medium ad concludendum aliquod differre accidentaliter vel idem a se ipso aliter se habente uno tempore quam alio tempore. Sed
'differentia proprie dicta' est dispositio inseparabilis a subiecto qua unum differt ab altero accidentaliter, sed logicaliter [vero add. M] est terminus connotativus dispositionis accidentalis
inseparabilis qui aptus natus est esse medium ad concludendum aliquod differre accidentaliter et inseparabiliter ut 'album' respectu 'cigni', quod respectu 'hominis' dicitur accidens
separabile. Sed 'differentia propriissime dicta' realiter loquendo est quae facit aliud, hoc est:
quae facit res differre essentialiter et specifice; logicaliter est universale quod aptum natum
est esse medium ad concludendum unam rem ab alia differre essentialiter et specifice, ut ly
'rationale'.

[24]Nicolaus de Amsterdam, *Exercitiun in Porphyrium*, qu. 13, f. 174v: Respondetur conce-
dendo quod possunt praedicari in quid, sed neganda est sequela, quod 'ergo non possunt
praedicari [praedicare M] in quale', quia praedicabilia ista sunt distincta ratione, et non
realiter.

to. So, a specific term can be used *essentialiter*, both when speaking *logicaliter* and *realiter*.[25]

Anyone who speaks about reality should be aware in what way (*logicaliter* or *realiter*) he does so. One should be careful not to confuse these ways of speaking.

It is no wonder that, when speaking in terms of reality, Nicholas often cites the thirteenth-century realists Albert the Great and Thomas Aquinas. He does not seem to take sides between the two, but he quotes both masters when he needs arguments to support his own views. According to Nicholas, Albert and Thomas were authoritative as metaphysicians, because as such they spoke *realiter*.

# 7   The Limitations of Human Knowledge

In his commentary Nicholas emphasizes the limitations of human knowledge, introducing an epistemological aspect into his text. He points out that human knowledge is unable to know *e.g.* the differences between concrete, material individuals within a species. Porphyry's Tree also makes the limitations clear, Nicholas says, in the sense that each ultimate species, for instance *man* or *ass*, has its own essential specific difference, though we know few of these.[26] For instance, we do not know the essential differences between an ox and an ass, but we can know their *propria* or proper attributes, viz. *hinnibilis* ('being able to neigh') and *rudibilis* ('being able to bray'). A *proprium* indeed is not a *differentia*, but it can be better known by a human, because both neighing and braying can be known by the senses.

According to our master, one cannot know individuals as such. A similar problem arises in the case of our knowledge of non-material, corporeal substances, viz. God and the angels. To these spiritual substances one can apply only negative or privative terms. The *differentia*, he says, is known by human knowledge only in the case of material, not spiritual substances.[27]

Nicholas distinguishes between *aptitudo* and *possibilitas* with respect to a term's signification. For instance, the term '*sol*' is a general term, though it has only a single referent. It has the aptitude to stand for more, not the

---

[25]Nicolaus de Amsterdam, *Exercitiun in Porphyrium*, qu. 13, f. 174r: Tertio: sicut compositum componitur realiter ex materia et forma, sic species componitur intentionaliter ex genere et differentia tamquam ex partibus definitionis. Et sicut materia est indeterminata, sed specificabilis, sic et genus quod specificatur per differentiam.

[26]Nicolaus de Amsterdam, *Exercitiun in Porphyrium*, qu. 17, f. 184v: Et ex hoc provenit quod omnia individua eiusdem speciei substantialis sunt eiusdem perfectionis intrinsecae et essentialis. Sic etiam in toto universo non reperiuntur duae species aequalis perfectionis; sed quaelibet species in suo ordine tenet gradum sibi determinatum eo quod unaqueque species habet propriam essentialem differentiam constitutivam, quamvis paucae tales sint nobis notae. Ideoque saepe loco differentiarum ponimus proprias passiones.

[27]Nicolaus de Amsterdam, *Exercitiun in Porphyrium*, qu. 14, f. 176v: Ibi potest dici quod sic capiendo praedictos terminos positive et non privative. Nam, ut praetactum est in separatis a materia et substantiis immaterialibus, differentia accipitur ab actu sive a gradu perfectionis. Et sic capiendo praedictas differentias positive prout connotarent actum aut gradum perfectionis secundum generalitatem suorum generum, tunc essent vere differentiae. Nichilominus tamen non essent nobis differentiae, ut videtur intendere probatio conclusionis, quia nos non possumus intelligere intellectione simplici substantias separatas. Et sic patet quomodo rationabiliter posset excusari Porphyrius in praedictarum differentiarum positione.

possibility, by which he apparently means: the natural possibility as it applies
to the course of nature.

# 8 Analysis of Question 12 of Nicholas' Commentary on Porphyry[28]

## 8.1 Structure of the question

Notanda

    Notanda 1 and 2

Definition by Porphyry

Two rationes

    Notandum 3

Exposition of the definition: two notes

Four arguments with solutions.

## 8.2 Contents of question 12.

### Meaning of the term 'individuum'.

The subject of this question is the definition of the individual. The title runs:
*Quaeritur duodecimo utrum definitio individui data a Porphyrio sit bona, in qua
dicitur: 'individuum est quod de uno particulari praedicatur* [29] *(*The problem is
whether the definition of the individual given by Porphyry is correct, in which
it is said: 'Individual is that which is predicated of one particular').

Nicholas defines *individuum* as a term: 'individuum est terminus cui ex modo
suae impositionis repugnat supponere pro pluribus univoce et divisim mediante
copula non ampliativa' ('an individual is a term which is not compatible with
reference to more things in an unambiguous way and taken in division, by way
of a copula, which is not ampliative') (p. 22, l. 28). One should understand,
he says: an individual can be said of more, like in 'hoc animal est Sortes'.
We should speak not of supposition, because this implies that '*individuum*'
can be said of more things together, but of predication. The term 'Sortes' is
individual, and there does not exist a collection of 'Sorteses' in the same way
as there exists a collection of men, of which it is true to say that they are, *e.g.*,
running.

So '*individuum*' is a term in Nicholas' view (p. 20, ll. 8–9). An individual thing in the outside world can be referred to by such an individual term
in different ways. The strictest formula is the *individuum determinatum*, of
which the individual term 'Sortes' is an example. Then there is the *individuum
vagum, e.g.* 'hoc album', 'hoc veniens'. Thirdly, we have the *individuum circumlocutum, e.g.* 'sol', 'mundus', 'Deus' or: 'filius Sophronisci', when there is
only one individual that can be referred to. This distinction can also be found
in Marsilius of Inghen.[30]

---

[28]I cannot discuss in this contribution all aspects of Nicholas' conception of the individual
as they appear in the different books of Nicholas' Commentary on the old logic.

[29]In the manuscript: ff. 169r–172v.

[30]Bos (1999).

## Relation of the individuum with imagination.

The term '*imaginari*' presents another problem. In the fourteenth and fifteenth centuries imagination played an important role in logical works. Marsilius of Inghen, for instance, distinguishes '*imaginatio*' as a separate aspect of time, that is, in a large sense, together with '*possibilitas*', as opposed to the time distinctions between past, present, and future, which are aspects of time in the strict sense.[31]

Imagination plays an important role in the commentary, as in 'Sortes imaginatur'. Then ' Sortes' is not individual (p. 23, ll. 7–1).

## 8.3   Four objections with solutions.

In the section containing objections and solutions Nicholas makes clear that the individual is the primary reality. Concepts are formed by the mind with respect to these individuals.

- Nicholas denies any objectivity in the mind about concepts, both universal and singular. They are the result of the activity of the mind. It is possible, therefore, to know a universal without any existing thing belonging to it (p. 24, l. 36–p. 25, l. 2 and p. 25, l. 35–p. 26, l. 2).

- The next objection is about the *individuum vagum*. Here a demonstrative pronoun (*hoc*) plays a part. This, the opponent says, has no sensible object and is therefore not singular (p. 26, l. 27–29). Nicholas answers that, just like the sun, it can 'singularize' (*singularisare*), *i.e.* refer to an individual thing.

- An opponent opines that only the *individuum circumlocutum* is singular: for here one *suppositum* is referred to by way of general concepts (p. 27, ll. 24–25). Nicholas denies this, because, as a good empiricist conceptualist, he refuses to accept generality before knowledge of singular.

- The final objection is about the principle of individuation. An opponent denies its existence. Nicholas affirms it, in line with what he calls the *moderni*. After a discussion he concludes by saying that the principle of individuation, in the sense of completive, or totalitive, as he labels it, is the whole nature, its own *essentia*, by which the individual concept is determined (p. 29, ll. 5–6).

---

[31]See Bos (1980, p. 102, ll. 7–8).

# Appendix

|   | **Sigla** |
| --- | --- |
| M$^1$ | = manus quae scripsit textum Nicolai de Amsterdam |
| M$^2$ | = manus quae addidit notas marginales, probabiliter eadem quae manus M$^1$ |
| M$^3$ | = manus quae addidit notas marginales, differens a manu quae scripsit textum principalem |
| M$^4$ | = manus quae addidit titulos supra columnas |
| cf. | = confer |
| in mg. | = in margine |
| <...> | = supplevi |
| (?) | = fortasse |
| add. | = addidit |
| ill. | = illegibilia / illegibiles |

*About the edition*: I have used classical Latin. I have not noted medieval spellings that diverge from the classical Latin.

### Quaeritur duodecimo utrum definitio individui data a Porphyrio sit bona, in qua dicitur: 'individuum est quod de uno particulari praedicatur'[32]

Pro intellectu quaestionis est notandum primo quod 'individuum' dupliciter
5 capitur, scilicet secundum primam intentionem et secundum secundam intentionem. Individuum prout est terminus primae intentionis[33] significat rem[34] a se indivisam et a quolibet alio divisam, et sic 'individuum' idem est quod 'singulare'. Sed 'individuum' secundum secundam intentionem prout attribuitur terminis, est de principali consideratione Porphyrii.

10 Ex quo patet quod iste terminus 'individuum' est universale et non est individuum aliquod ex eo quod ei non repugnat supponere pro pluribus univoce et divisim. Quia secundum Porphyrium[35] 'individuum' in secunda intentione est triplex: scilicet vagum, determinatum, et circumlocutum, alias dictum: ex suppositione individuum.

15 Unde individuum vagum[36] seu accidentale dicitur quod ex quibusdam septem proprietatibus consistit, quarum collectio numquam[37] potest reperiri in alio, ut hoc album, hoc veniens, quod est in prospectu cognoscentis. Res autem est in prospectu cognoscentis cum circumstantiis accidentalibus. Quare individuum vagum merito dicitur 'accidentale'. Haec[38] autem septem proprietates indi-
20 viduantes habentur in hoc metro secundum Boethium: *Forma, figura, locus, stirps, nomen, patria, tempus.* Haec septem propria continet omnis homo.

---

[32]de individuo M$^4$, *supra columnam.*
[33]intentionis: impositionis M$^1$.
[34]rem: ad *add.* M$^1$.
[35]Porphyrius, *Isagoge*, ed. L. Minio-Paluello, Bruges-Paris 1966, p. 13, ll. 21–23.
[36]individuum accipitur (?) M$^3$ *in mg.*
[37]numquam: nuncquam M$^1$.
[38]haec: hee M$^1$.

Sed aliud dicitur 'individuum determinatum'[39] quod est abstractum a conditionibus individuantibus, et ad certum genus principale limitatum, ut sunt nomina propria 'Sortes', 'Plato', 'Iohannes' et consimilia, quae sunt vera individua de quibus species in quid reperitur. Nam, licet individuo vago ut 'hic 25 homo', vel consimili termino communi capto cum [f. 169v] pronomine primitivae speciei, conveniat definitio individui de qua quaestio sicut individuo determinato, tamen individuum vagum non est istud de quo species in quid praedicatur, sed hoc tantum convenit determinato individuo.

Sed praeter ista reperiuntur tertio modo individua quae dicuntur 'circumlocuta'[40] vel 'ex suppositione',[41] ut sunt termini communes actu unicum suppositum habentes, ut isti termini 'sol', 'mundus', 'Sophronisci[42] filius', si solus 5 sit ei unus filius. Sed de istis individuis non est ad propositum, cum non sint vera individua, sed magis communia.

Secundo est notandum quod Porphyrius comparat ad invicem genus, species et individua, dicens[43] quod genus est quoddam totum, individuum autem est pars, sed species est totum et pars; est quidem totum respectu individuorum, 10 sed est pars respectu generis loquendo de parte subiectiva et de toto universali. Propter quod dicit Porphyrius quod collectum in una\<m\> naturam species est, hoc est: terminus specificus est collectivus plurium, hoc est: repraesentativus multorum in unam naturam, hoc est: sub uno conceptu communi. Et subdit Porphyrius:[44] 'magis enim istud quod genus est'; idest: genus est magis 15 collectivum quam species, quia genus sub conceptu communiori sua significata repraesentat quam species; singulare vero semper divisum est, hoc est: distincte repraesentativum.

Et tunc Porphyrius consequenter comparando tria praedicta ad invicem dicit[45] quod decem sunt generalissima, specialissima in numero vero quodam[46] sunt, non tamen definito; sed individua quae sunt post specialissima, sunt in- 20 finita.

Ratio primi, videlicet quod decem sunt generalissima, est ista quia ad ista decem stat omnis resolutio entium, nam secundum dominum Albertum[47] omnia inferiora resolvuntur in superiora. Sed secundum modernos logicos auctoritas praedicta sic exponitur, quod decem sunt diversi modi praedicandi generales de substantia prima, et ideo haec generalissima Porphyrius hic non determinat, 25 sed Philosophus in Praedicamentis[48] et in quinto Metaphysicae.[49]

---

[39]individuum determinatum M³ *in mg.*

[40]circumlocuta: circumlocutiva M³ *in mg.*

[41]individuum circumlocutum M³ *in mg.*

[42]sophronisci: suffronisci M¹.

[43]Porphyrius, *Isagoge*, translatio Boethii, ed. L. Minio-Paluello, Bruges-Paris 1966, p. 8, ll. 1–3.

[44]Porphyrius, *Isagoge*, translatio Boethii, ed. L. Minio-Paluello, Bruges-Paris 1966, p. 6, l. 23.

[45]Cf. Porphyrius, *Isagoge*, translatio Boethii, ed. L. Minio-Paluello, Bruges-Paris 1966, p. 4, l. 15 – p .7, l. 16.

[46]quodam: an quoddam ? M¹.

[47]Albertus Magnus, *Liber de praedicamentis*, ed. Borgnet, *Tractatus* IV, c. iv, p. 72b.

[48]Aristoteles, *Praedicamenta* IV, 1 b 25 – 2 a 3.

[49]Aristoteles, *Metaphysica* V, vii, 1017 a 23–31.

Ratio vero secundi, scilicet quod specialissima sunt in quodam numero, est ista quia species specialissimae constituuntur per differentias essentiales quae sunt finitae considerando saltem species et differentias quantum ad esse quod habent a natura vel in natura. Et licet species specialissimae sunt contentae in quodam numero, hic tamen numerus non est definitus, hoc est: certus no-
5 bis. Cuius ratio est ista quia, quantum ad nostram cognoscibilitatem, omnes differentiae ab eodem homine cognosci non possunt, et ideo hoc modo species specialissimae sicut et differentiae videntur rationem infiniti habere, licet tamen secundum nullam considerationem sunt infinitae.

Individua autem, quae sunt post specialissima sunt infinita, scilicet in poten-
10 tia quamvis non in actu—quia stante aeternitate mundi philosophice loquendo reperitur processus in infinitum in generationibus et corruptionibus, quae sunt sibi invicem accidentaliter subordinata secundum potentiam.

Aliae non ponuntur a Porphyrio auctoritates de generalissimis et specialis-simis quae respiciunt differentias.[50] Ideoque de istis auctoritatibus dicetur de
15 differentia in quaestione.[51]

Tertio notandum est quod Porphyrius quodam modo hic incidentaliter vide-tur determinare de definitione individui, quia, ut iam praetactum est in auctori-tatibus praeallegatis et expositis, semper superiora praedicantur vera praedi-catione de individuis, ita quod genus generalissimum praedicatur de generibus
20 subalternis, de speciebus specialissimis sub eo contentis, et de individuis. Genus autem subalternum praedicatur de speciebus specialissimis sub eo contentis et de individuis, species vero specialissima solum [f. 170r] de individuis praedi-catur. Et quia in omnibus istis praedicationibus mentio fit de individuis, ne ergo Porphyrius procedat ex ignoto, determinat hic de definitione individui
25 dicens 'individuum autem est quod de uno solo particulari praedicatur'.

Pro cuius definitionis expositione est notandum[52] quod ipsa sic debet exponi: individuum est terminus cui ex modo suae impositionis repugnat supponere pro pluribus univoce et divisim mediante copula non ampliativa.

Dicitur primo[53] notanter 'supponere' et non 'praedicari', secundum quod
30 tamen ponitur in definitione, quia secundum modernos logicos ly 'praedicatur' debet exponi per[54] 'supponere', quia verum individuum tantum praedicatur de pluribus, ut dicendo 'hoc animal est Sortes', 'hoc corpus est Sortes' et sic de aliis.

Quidam tamen hanc expositionem refutantes dicunt quod verba Porphyrii debent intelligi de praedicatione directa, et secundum eos non est necesse quod
5 ly 'praedicatur' per 'supponere' exponitur. Sed motivum istorum non procedit, et praesertim propter terminos individuales accidentales. Cuius dicti ratio est ista quia praedicatione directa in terminis accidentalibus individuum praed-icatur de pluribus, ut dicendo 'hoc album est hoc[55] album', 'Sortes est hoc album', in quibus propositionibus hoc complexum 'hoc album' praedicatur de
10 pluribus praedicatione directa; ergo expositio posita est sustinenda.

---

[50]differentias: cum hoc *add.* M[1].
[51]*vide infra*, p. 29, ll. 11–13.
[52]intellectus individui M[3] *in mg.*
[53]primo M[2] *in mg.*
[54]per: pro M[1].
[55]hoc: *corr. supralin.* M[1].

Dicitur secundo[56] notanter 'divisim', quia terminus individualis coniunctim tantum supponit pro pluribus, sicut 'forma' pro materia et forma, quae sunt plura, sed pro illis supponit coniuctim et non divisim. Similiter dicitur hoc idem propter terminos individuales pluralis numeri, sic dicendo 'isti homines trahunt navem', ubi subiectum tantum supponit pro pluribus, sed coniunctim, 15 quia non valet descensus ad aliquod singulare.

Dicitur[57] etiam notanter 'mediante copula non ampliativa', quia mediante copula ampliativa quilibet terminus individualis potest supponere pro pluribus. nam ly 'Sortes' mediante copula de ly 'imaginatur' stat pro omni isto quod potest imaginari esse Sortes. Sed iam manifestum est quod plura possunt 20 imaginari esse Sortes quam homo.

Quibus sic stantibus dicendum est *conclusive*[58] quod definitio individui data a Porphyrio et intellecta ut iam est exposita, est bona. Patet quia convenit omni contento sub definito, et facit definitum differre a quolibet alio, ut patet 25 singulas particulas transcurrenti.

*Arguitur primo sic:*[59] Nullum est individuum determinatum, ergo definitio individui minus bene dicta. Assumptum patet, quia, si aliquod esset individuum determinatum, tunc ipsum generabitur per abstractionem circumstantiarum accidentalium, quia alias non esset determinatum, sed vagum et confusum, ut dictum est in corpore quaestionis;[60] sed modo sic est quod abstractis circumstantiis accidentalibus fabricatur conceptus communis; ergo utique videtur quod post abstractionem huiusmodi circumstantiarum non causabitur conceptus individualis determinatus. Tenet consequentia ex hoc quia univer- 5 sale et individuum ex quo sunt opposita, videntur habere oppositas rationes in eorum generatione.

Confirmatur[61] quia[62] individuum determinatum, si poneretur, tunc contraheret ipsam speciem aliquid addendo ultra eam, ex quo semper inferius contrahit et restringit superius; sed individuum determinatum nihil potest addere 10 ultra aut supra speciem. [f. 170v] Quod sic patet, quia aut adderet substantiam, aut accidens. Non accidens, quia sic non reputaretur verum individuum in praedicamento substantiae. Nec etiam individuum potest addere ultra speciem aliquid substantiale, quia, si sic, tunc sequeretur quod unum individuum esset perfectius altero essentialiter, quod est contra unum[63] articulum Parisiensem[64] 15 condemnatum. Et patet hoc idem inductive, quia istud substantiale superadditum aut esset materia, aut forma, aut totum compositum, sufficienti divisione, ut patet ex secundo De anima.[65] Non materia, quia individuum determinatum

---

[56]secundo M³ *in mg.*

[57]tertio M³ *in mg.*

[58]conclusio M².

[59]contra M².

[60]*vide supra*, p. 20, l. 13.

[61]con<firmatur> M² *in mg.*

[62]an individuum addat aliquid universali M³ *in mg.*

[63]p ? *add.* M¹.

[64]Articulus Parisiensis, vide: *Chartularium universitatis Parisiensis* I, ed. H. Denifle et E. Chatelain. Parisiis 1889–1897, *locum invenire no potui.* Cf. Thomas Aquinas, *Quaestio disputata de malo*, qu. ii, art. 9, ad. 16.

[65]Aristoteles, *De anima* II, i, 412 a 6–9; II, ii, 414 a 14–16 (cf. J. Hamesse, *Auctoritates Aristotelis*, p. 177 (37)).

est iam abstractum a conditionibus materiae; nec etiam forma, quia alias plures
formae essent in eodem individuo, quod non est dicendum; nec etiam composi-
20   tum, ex consimili ratione; ergo relinquitur quod nulla debeant esse individua
essentialia determinata seu abstracta.

     *Respondetur*[66] quod modus generationis[67] conceptuum universalium et con-
ceptuum singularium determinatorum[68] non est per modum sequestrationis,
hoc est: divisionis proprietatum accidentalium a substantia, et separationis
25   earundem, ut patet ex hoc quia, si sic, tunc oporteret omnem conceptum
universalem, similiter et conceptum singularem determinatum poni in potentia imaginativa, in qua ponuntur intentiones phantasticae repraesentantes rem
concretive. Consequens autem est falsum, ex quo quilibet praedictorum conceptuum ponitur subiective in intellectu possibili. Et ideo modus generationis
praedictorum conceptuum fit elicitive et abstractive, quia intellectus solum eli-
5   ciendo abstrahit universale, videlicet deducendo istud quod fuit in virtute seu
in potentia ad esse formale et actuale.

     Pro quo notandum est[69] ulterius quod, licet conceptus singulares determi-
nati sint posteriores conceptibus universalibus, secundum quod dicit Philosophus tertio De anima[70] quod singularia intelliguntur per lineam reflexam licet
non per conceptum reflexum, ex eo quod prima notitia intellectus est singu-
10   laris vaga magis confusa et iterum fit reversa ad notitiam singularem, scilicet
determinatam, et sic fit quodam modo egressus a singularibus et regressus ad
singularia, et secundum hoc bene conceditur quod unus conceptus ex alio gener-
atur, sed improprie, quia post alium, sicut ex aurora fit dies quia post auroram
hanc, secundo Metaphysicae;[71] non tamen proprie abstractio singularis deter-
15   minati conceptus fit a conceptibus universalibus, sed fit a phantasmate quod
principiat omnes[72] conceptus, sive sint singulares sive universales.

     Ex quo patet quod conceptus universales non sunt principia aut causa ex qua
productionis conceptuum singularium determinatorum. Et ratio est ista quia,
si sic, scilicet si conceptus universales tamquam causae sufficientes producerent
20   simul cum intellectu agente conceptum singularem determinatum, sequeretur
quod de re non sensata posset haberi conceptus singularis determinatus. Consequens est contra Philosophum, septimo Metaphysicae.[73] Sed sequela patet,
quia conceptus universales de quibus formarentur conceptus singulares deter-
minati possunt haberi sine re sensata, ex quo secundum Philosophum, nono
25   Metaphysicae,[74] non sensibile potest intelligi conceptu communi, quamvis per
participationem cum rebus sensibilibus.

     Ex quibus sequitur ulterius quod conceptus universalis non generatur proprie
a conceptu singulari vago, sed magis a phantasmate, quamvis etiam non semper

---

[66]dicitur M² *in mg.*
[67]seu abstracta *iter.* M¹.
[68]quomodo abstrahitur conceptus singularis M³ *in mg.*
[69]quomodo conceptus singularis dicitur reflexivus M³ *in mg.*
[70]*Fortasse* Aristoteles, *De anima* III, 1, 425 a 24–26.
[71]Aristoteles, *Metaphysica* II, ii, 994 b 3.
[72]omnes *corr. ex* homines M¹.
[73]Cf. Aristoteles, *Metaphysica* VII, xv, 1039 b 27 – 1040 a 5 (cf. J. Hamesse, *Les Auctoritates Aristotelis*, Louvain-Paris 1974, p. 130 (182)).
[74]Aristoteles, *Metaphysica* IX, vi, 1048 b 15–21.

a phantasmate istius rei quae intelligitur universaliter, [f. 171r] sed alterius rei similis in specie.

Etergo dicendum[75] est ad argumentum quod intellectus agens sua propria virtute cum phantasmate producere potest[76] in intellectu possibili conceptum unversalem abstractum, aut etiam conceptum singularem abstractum et determinatum. Et hoc est quod dicit Marsilius circa septimum Metaphysicae, quod intellectus mere est istius potentiae et naturae abstractivae quod apprehenso 5 aliquo singulari vago potest abstrahere in communi vel in speciali istam rem ab omnibus suis accidentibus.[77]

Sed tamen inter hos conceptus abstractos potest colligi differentia talis quod conceptus universalis abstractus potest haberi de re non sensata quam repraesentat, et conceptus singularis abstractus et determinatus non potest haberi de re non sensata[78] quam repraesentat. Et ratio est ista, quia conceptus determi- 10 natus praesupponit vagum[79] seu phantasma proprium.

Et ex hoc sequitur secundum Johannem Scotum[80] quod notitia singularis determinata dicitur aliquo modo intuitiva in quantum praesupponit rem praesentem singulariter vage, et ob hoc dicit Buridanus, circa septimum Metaphysicae,[81] quod, qui numquam vidisset Sortem, non posset de eo formare concep- 15 tum supponentem pro eo solum, sed conceptus universales abstracti non habent necessariam dependentiam ab aliquo singulari, sed a quolibet per concomitantiam possunt formari seu causari, ex nono Metaphysicae.[82] Et per hoc patet quid dicendum sit ad argumentum qui[83] sunt modi generationis conceptuum abstractorum.

Ad confirmationem autem argumenti dicendum est quod species contrahitur 20 per individuum, non quidem realiter, sed secundum rationem. Et ratio huius dicti est quia species est quoddam universale quod semper est ens rationis, etergo non potest contrahi per ens reale, sed potius per ens rationis.

Sed tamen tunc remanet difficultas de modo contrahendi, videlicet quomodo[84] conceptus individualis determinatus contrahat conceptum specificum.[85] 25 Ibi ergo dicendum est quod conceptus individualis determinatus et conceptus specificus possunt dupliciter considerari: uno modo in suis realitatibus inquantum sunt accidentia in anima existentia, et sic sunt aeque existentes in anima in qua unus conceptus alium non contrahit; alio modo possunt considerari rationabiliter in ordine ad eorum significata quae determinant huiusmodi conceptus. 5 Et sic concedendum est quod conceptus individualis determinatus repraesentat

---

[75]dicitur M² *in mg.*

[76]Marsilius of Inghen, *Quaestiones in Metaphysicam: locum invenire non potui.*

[77]accidentibus: seu accidentibus *add.* M¹.

[78]quomodo differunt conceptus universalis et singularis M³ in mg.

[79]vagum: fagum (*sic*) M¹.

[80]Scotum: Scoti M¹. Johannes Duns Scotus, *Lectura in Sententias* II, dist. 3, q. 2, n. 285 (= *Opera omnia* XVII, p. 321); *Ordinatio* I, dist. 1, pars 1, qu. 2, nn. 34–36 (*Opera omnia* II, pp. 23–24); *Ordinatio* II, dist. 3, pars 2, qu. 2, n. 321 (*Opera omnia* VII, p. 553).

[81]Johannes Buridanus, *Quaestiones in Metaphysicam*, VII, q. 20 (incertum).

[82]Aristoteles, *Metaphysica* IX, iii, 1047 a 36–37 (incertum).

[83]qui: quod quaedam (?) M¹.

[84]quomodo: sensus *add. necnon del.* M¹.

[85]quomdo conceptus individualis contrahat specificum, et capiuntur dupliciter M³ *in mg.*

istud quod conceptus specificus, sed modo quodam compositionali, et sic etiam
individuum dicitur aliquid addere ultra speciem.

    Sed tunc, an istud superadditum[86] sit materia, forma, compositum, aut
10  accidens, prout quaerit confirmatio tacta, dicendum est quod individua, si essent definibilia, tunc superaddunt differentiam essentialem ultra differentiam
constitutivam speciei. Si ergo differentia significat formam, tunc superaddit
individuum formam. Si vero differentia significat totum conceptum, tunc individuum determinatum addit ultra speciem totum compositum.

15    Non tamen ex hoc sequitur quod plures essent formae substantiales in eodem
individuo, quia huiusmodi compositio, superadditio et contractio non est realis
et absoluta, sed est terminalis et respectiva ex eo quod tantum ultima differentia dat esse specificum[87] actuale et formale; aliae autem differentiae respectu
ultimae dant esse potentiale. Et licet species contrahatur tantum ad individua
20  per differentias[88] accidentales quantum est ex [f. 171v] parte nostrae cognitionis, quantum tamen est ex natura rei species contrahi posset per differentias
essentiales conceptibus singularibus determinatis correspondentes. Sic etiam,
licet individua non sunt definibilia definitione quidditativa quantum est scilicet
ex parte nostrae cognitionis, nihil tamen prohibet ea posse definiri quantum
est ex natura rei.

25    *Arguitur secundo sic:*[89] Individua vaga non sunt individua, ergo definitio
individui non videtur competere individuis vagis. Consequentia nota, et assumptum patet, quia, si esset aliquid individuum vagum, hoc maxime quod
causaretur per signum demonstrativum primitivae speciei, ut 'hoc album', 'hoc
veniens', prout dictum est prius.[90] Sed quod hoc sit falsum, patet, quia actus correspondens ly 'iste' et consimili signo demonstrativo est mere communis;
ergo non potest aliquid singularisare. Consequentia tenet ex hoc quia commune
non habet naturam singularisandi. Sed assumptum patet quia quodlibet singulare est sensibile; sed actus correspondens ly 'iste' non habet aliquod obiectum
5  sensibile; ergo actus correpondens ly 'iste' non dicitur singularis.

    *Respondetur*[91] quod, licet actus demonstrativus sit bene communis, nihilomi-
nus potest singularisare. Quemadmodum reperitur in naturalibus, quod sol qui
non est in se calidus, producit tamen calorem in istis inferioribus, sic etiam
actus demonstrativus, qui in se non est singularis eo quod nullum singulare
10  obiectum ei correspondet, producit tamen singularitatem in terminis commu-
nibus. Et hoc specialiter provenit ex eo quod actus demonstrativus demonstrat
rem prout est in prospectu cognoscentis etcetera.

    *Arguitur tertio sic:*[92] Individua tertio modo dicta sunt vera individua, ergo
posita in corpore quaestionis sunt falsa. Consequentia nota, et assumptum
15  patet. Nam ista sunt vera individua quibus correspondet conceptus individualis; sed sic est de individuis tertio modo dictis; igitur sunt vera individua.
Consequentia nota, et assumptum pro prima parte similiter. Sed assumptum

---

[86]an superadditum sit materia, forma vel compositum M³ *in mg.*
[87]specificum: aliquale *add. necnon del.* M¹.
[88]differentias: essentiales *add. necnon del.* M¹.
[89]contra. Secundo hoc M² *in mg.*
[90]*vide supra*, p. 20, l. 7.
[91]dicitur M² *in mg.*
[92]contra M² *in mg.*

pro secunda parte probatur quia dictis individuis tertio modo captis correspondet aliquis conceptus; et non universalis, ergo singularis. Tenet consequentia ex sufficienti divisione. Sed assumptum, videlicet quod eis non correspondet conceptus communis, probatur quia conceptus universalis abstrahitur ab essentiali convenientia rerum particularium. Sed quia tantum unum est singularisatum seu suppositum individuorum tertio modo captorum, ergo non est inter individua circumlocuta aliqua convenientia, ex quo convenientia est quaedam relatio inter plura; etergo relinquitur quod conceptus correspondens individuo circumlocuto sit singularis. Quod fuit probandum.                                            25

*Respondetur*[93] quod non est ponenda universalitas realis in re praecedens operationem intellectus; ergo etiam non est assignanda una convenientia praecedens operationem intellectus.

Et ex isto sequitur correlarie quod convenientia essentialis plurium individuorum est intentionalis, quia causatur per operationem intellectus. Sed quia   30
ipsa operatio intellectus est operatio et actus[94] immanens, ideo non potest effectum producere secundum esse reale, sed solum secundum esse intentionale et secundum esse cognitum. Ex isto etiam habetur quod auctoritas Porphyrii qua dicitur quod participatione[95] speciei plures homines sunt unus homo, debet retroquaeri ad sensum logicalem, videlicet quod[96] plures [f. 172r] homines con-   5
cipiuntur et significantur unico conceptu specifico et absoluto. Et sic proprie sunt unus homo intentionaliter, hoc est: habent unum conceptum eis correspondentem et communem. Et per hoc dicendum est ad argumentum quod, quia convenientia una est potior operatione intellectus, ideo non est omnino verum quod a convenientia una essentiali debet contrahi universalitas, sed causatur   10
universalitas modo in praedicta solutione primi argumenti, scilicet vel abstractive a phantasmate et non a convenientia rerum particularium, vel etiam obiective, sicut virtus aestimativa sensitiva potest ex sensatis elicere insensata.

Verum est tamen quod multi metaphysicorum et philosophantium posuerunt res esse unius vel eiusdem speciei ex una convenientia specifica individuis istius speciei aliqualiter[97] praeparata. Sed istud dictum eorum stare non potest quia   15
convenientia ex quo hic relatio[98] <est>, non distinguitur a suo fundamento.

Et ideo, ut tactum est, tenendum est conclusive quod non potest dari[99] una realis convenientia multorum individuorum, et per consequens relinquitur quod modus loquendi istorum philosophantium sit falsus. Nec motivum eorum est validum, quia res non dicuntur esse eiusdem speciei realiter ex hoc quod conve-   20
niunt in una specie reali, sed dicuntur esse eiusdem speciei realiter ex hoc quod habent aequalem perfectionem ad primum ens et aequalem imperfectionem a non ente. Et ideo etiam forma non est eiusdem speciei cum composito ex quo non habent aequales perfectiones, cum secundum mentem Philosophi, septimo

---

[93]dicitur M² *in mg.*
[94]actus: e *add. necnon del.* M¹.
[95]participatione speciei plures homines sunt unus homo, et significantur vel concipiuntur per conceptum specificum M³ (*verba scripta sub columna*).
[96]pu *add. necnon del.* M¹.
[97]aliqualiter; an adaequaliter ? M¹.
[98]relatio: revelatio M¹.
[99]dari: dare M¹.

25  Metaphysicae,[100] forma est perfectior et prior toto composito prioritate perfectionis, eo quod forma est ens actuale nullam includens potentialitatem sicut
facit compositum ratione materiae.

   *Arguitur quarto sic*:[101] Nullum est individuum, ergo conclusio cum determi-
natione falsa. Consequentia nota, et assumptum probatur quia nullum est principium individuationis, ergo nullum est individuum.[102] Consequentia nota[103]
ex hoc quod principium et principiatum dicuntur correlative. Sed assumptum
5   patet quia, si esset aliquod principium individuationis, vel hoc esset materia, vel
forma. Sed nullum istorum videtur dicendum. Quod patet primo de materia,
quia ipsa est causa convenientiae, ergo non potest esse causa individuationis
seu distinctionis. Sed quod forma non sit principium individuationis, probatur
quia forma est principium speciei, ex quo differentia adveniens generi constituit
10  speciem; ergo forma non erit principium individui.

   *Respondetur*[104] quod 'aliquid esse principium individuationis' intelligitur dupliciter:[105] Uno modo quod sit principium causationis seu constitutionis individui. Ista modo plura sunt principia individui, ex quo individuum est quid
causatum quod habet sua principia intrinseca et extrinseca. Intrinseca sunt
15  materia et forma, sed extrinseca sunt efficiens et finis.

   Alio modo potest intelligi 'principium individuationis aliquid esse' secundum
modum antiquorum, qui imaginabantur quod in materia esset quaedam universalitas modo praetacto, ut, verbi gratia, in homine dicebant aliquod universale
quod dicebant contrahi per haecceitatem aut Sorteitatem aut Platoneitatem et
20  sic de singulis. Isto modo dicendum est quod etiam non est aliquod principium
individuationis ponendum, cum nulla sit universalitas in rerum natura. Et per
consequens sequitur quod proprie loquendo nullum est principium individuationis, quia tamen unum [f. 172v] individuum distinguitur ab alio.

   Ideoque ad habendam causam huiusmodi distinctionis vocant moderni pro
25  concordia diversarum opinionum quod triplex potest assignari individuationis[106] principium, scilicet originale[107] seu extrinscum, formale seu intrinsecum,
et principium completivum seu totalitativum.

   Originale[108] principium individuationis et extrinsecum est materia signata
quantitate, seu ipsa quantitas quae primo est divisibilis, et omnia divisibilia
sunt divisibilia ratione quantitatis et materiae signatae. Et ita loquuntur de
principio individuationis antiqui doctores Aegidius, Thomas, et etiam hoc vide-
5   tur sentire Porphyrius.

   Principium vero individuationis formale et intrinsecum est ipsa forma quae
intrinsece individuat rem secundum quod vult Philosophus, secundo De

---

[100]Cf. Aristoteles, *Metaphysica* VII, viii, 1033 b 17–20.
[101]contra M² *in mg.*
[102]quod nullum sit principium individuationis M² *in mg.*
[103]nota: quia *add.* M¹.
[104]dicitur M² *in mg.*
[105]aliquid esse principium individuationis intelligitur dupliciter M³ *in mg.*
[106]tripliciter principium individuationis M³ *in mg.*
[107]originale: origenale M¹.
[108]originale M³ *in mg.*

anima[109] et septimo Metaphysicae,[110] dicens quod individuum substantiae praecedit individuum accidentis.

Sed principium individuationis completivum[111] et totalitativum est propria   10
entitas uniuscuiusque rei quia unumquodque individuat se ipsum et individuatur se ipso; etergo individuum per propriam essentiam et naturam totam, cui correspondet conceptus individualis determinatus, est individuum, et non per aliquod superadditum, et ita loquuntur communiter moderni.

Et per hoc potest responderi ad motiva in contrarium adducta in argumento.   15
Et primo ad improbationem, quando arguebatur 'materia est causa convenientiae', hoc est verum aliquorum in genere; sed tamen cum hoc stat quod sit causa materialis distinctionis et numeralis. Simili modo dicendum est de forma quod proprie loquendo non est principium speciei realis, cum nulla sit species realis, sed est tantum principium individui.   20

Et sic patet quid sit dicendum ad argumentum.

# BIBLIOGRAPHY

Bos, E. (1980). *Marsilius of Inghen, Treatises of the Properties of Terms A First Critical Edition of the Suppositiones, Ampliationes, Appellatioines, Restrictiones and Alienationes.* Springer, Dordrecht/Boston/Lancaster.

Bos, E. (1999). Thuo of viborg and marsilius of inghen. In Ebbesen, S. and Friedman, R., editors, *Medieval Analysis in Language and Cognition,* Acts of the Symposium 'The Copenhagen School of Medieval Philosophy', January 10–12, 1996, Organized by the Royal Danish Academy of Sciences and Letters, and the Institute for Greek and Latin, University of Copenhagen, Copenhagen, pages 505–521.

Bos, E. P. (2011). Nicholas of Amsterdam's conceptualism in his commentary on the logica vetus. In Baumbach, M., Mojsisch, B., and Pluta, O., editors, *Bochumer Philosophisches Jahrbuch,* Bd. 14 (2009–2010–2011), pages 233–298.

Buridanus, J. (1518). *Quaestiones super libros Metaphysicae.* Parisiis. Repr. Frankfurt a. M. 1964.

Halm, K., von Laubmann, G., and Meyer, W. (1892). *Catalogus codicum latinorum Bibliothecae Regiae Monacensis.* Altera emendatior. Band 1.1, cdd. 1–2323 compl.

Kenny, A. and Pinborg, J. (1982). Medieval philosophical literature. In Kretzmann, N., Kenny, A., and Pinborg, J., editors, *The Cambridge History of Later Medieval Philosophy.* Cambridge University Press.

Pinborg, J. (1964). Die Aristoteles-Quaestionen des Magister Nicolaus von Amsterdam. *Classica et medievalia,* 25:244–62.

Pluta, O. (2007). Materialism in the philosophy of mind: Nicholas of Amsterdam's *Quaestiones De Anima.* In Bakker, P. and Thijssen, H., editors, *Mind, Cognition and Representation: The Tradition of Commentaries on Aristotle's* De Anima, pages 109–126. Ashgate Publishing, London.

Pluta, O. (2009). Johannes Buridanus und seine Schule an der Universität Rostock im 15. Jahrhundert. *Acta Mediaevalia XXII,* pages 361–378.

---

[109]Aristoteles, *De anima* II, iii, 414 b 27.
[110]Aristoteles, *Metaphysica* VII, x, 1035 b 30.
[111]completivum M³ *in mg.*

# The Metaphysics of Plato's Cosmic Paradigm

Sarah Broadie[†] [‡]

In the *Timaeus* Plato presents an inquiry into the genesis and nature of the physical world. The account is archetypally Platonic, for it represents our cosmos as framed by divine craftsmanship in accordance with an eternal, incorporeal, intelligible, paradigm or Form. It may be obvious that this picture is metaphysically problematic. Slightly less obvious, perhaps, is the fact that it is deeply ambivalent. It admits of two contrasting interpretations, and they are the subject of this paper. Aware as I am of my inability to say anything about Logic that could interest Stephen Read, my colleague and friend of more than a decade, I have fallen back on Metaphysics as a second best for celebrating his signal contribution to philosophy at and beyond the St Andrews locations where, both nominally and really, these two most ancient disciplines continue to flourish and develop.

## 1 Cosmology or Metaphysics?

Consider the ambiguous phrase 'intelligible world'. It may call up the thought that the natural universe is accessible not only (in part, at least) to sense perception, but also to some measure of scientific understanding by us. This idea is of course present in the *Timaeus*, where it rests on the assumption that nature was designed according to a rational and benevolent plan which human intellects may reasonably hope to reconstruct to some extent. Alternatively and still in the context of Platonic cosmology, the phrase may refer to an object accessible only by intellect, an object which constitutes the eternal and purely intelligible original of which this universe is a merely temporal copy. The eternal original is called a 'world' (or 'cosmos') because the world-hood of the sensible world, which is to say its physical order and complexity-in-unity, derive from corresponding features of the intelligible model. It is worth pondering which of these two 'intelligible worlds' the *Timaeus* cosmology is principally *about*. Is it first and foremost about the natural domain, being an attempt to make more sense of this subject-matter than previous cosmologies had done—an attempt, however, whose specific shape and method is underpinned by the trans-natural metaphysics of an eternal incorporeal Form of the cosmos? Or is it primarily about that transcendent Form itself, in effect dealing with the physical cosmos as the mere taking-off point for investigation of the Form? According to the first of these understandings, Platonic cosmology basically aims to find out about

[†]Philosophy, The University of St Andrews, St Andrews KY16 9AL, UK.
Email: `sjb15@st-andrews.ac.uk`
[‡]This paper is based on Ch. 3 of Broadie (2012).

the natural world by, or in part by, conjecturing the contents of the rational, benevolent, plan in accordance with which, it assumes, the natural world was constructed. According to the second understanding, Platonic cosmology is basically a portal to some kind of purely metaphysical study of the eternal and incorporeal—the latter being the primary object of interest.[1]

I distinguish these two approaches for the sake of philosophical clarification and analysis: the aim is not to provide a division for neatly classifying historical interpretations of the *Timaeus*. Still, it would be true to say that for ancient Platonists such as Plotinus, Porphyry, and Proclus, the world of nature is the launching pad for the soul's ascent to the intelligibles and beyond; and that these philosophers were more occupied with the metaphysical problem of how the intelligible manages to be reflected (at all) in the sensible and in matter, than with constructing a picture of the physical world by conjecturing the contents of its paradigm. No doubt, therefore, they read the *Timaeus* accordingly.[2] By contrast, the modern consensus is that the *Timaeus* offers first and foremost a theory of the cosmos,[3] and I think that this is correct. If we look at the text as a whole, the following features stand out. (1) The material is announced in advance as an account of the coming to be of the physical world, not an account of something else as well (27a5–6). (2) It is indeed announced as the portal to something beyond itself, but what follows it is not an ascent to the domain of pure intelligibles, but downward immersion in the particularities of human history (actually, the pseudo-history of ancient Athens and Atlantis, 27a2–b6). (3) The exuberantly detailed scientific explanations of a very wide range of empirical phenomena go far beyond whatever could be needed for the 'portal to metaphysics' approach. (4) At one place Plato indicates that although he recognises recondite principles of reality, they cannot be made clear through an account like the present one (48c2–d1):[4] which suggests that this

---

[1]Throughout I use 'cosmos' to mean, not the sum total of physical reality, but (as the word implies) an ordered system. In the *Timaeus* account, the sum total of physical reality was at one stage not yet ordered as a system.

[2]However, this is broad and impressionistic. Caution is needed because Plotinus and Porphyry do not set out to comment comprehensively on the *Timaeus*, and because Proclus, who does, understands his task in a way that certainly accepts the cosmology as such even though for him there is a great deal more to it than just that. He seems to have no uneasiness in combining these perspectives. In the preface to his *Timaeus* commentary he says: 'This whole dialogue, throughout its entire length, has physical inquiry (*phusiologia*) as its aim' (I. 1.17–19, tr. Tarrant; cf. I. 1–4.5 and 12.25–14.3). However, for Proclus even Plato's mythical Atlantis story —given as a sort of preface and also sequel to the Timaean cosmology (see 20d7–27b9, and the sequel dialogue *Critias*)—is a contribution to *phusiologia*. Following Iamblichus, Proclus understands that story as an allegory covering the whole of metaphysical and physical reality starting with the One and the Dyad and Unlimited (I. 77. 24–78. 27; cf. 130. 10 ff.). This tells us something about what counts as physical inquiry for Proclus.

[3]However, Arthur Platt (quoted by Lloyd, 1968, p. 79) wrote: 'Plato, being first and foremost a metaphysician with a sort of religious system, would not have us study anything but metaphysics and a sort of mystic religion' (Platt, 1927). For a contrast, see Bury (1929, p. 13): 'In truth, there is but little of metaphysics in the *Timaeus*; it is mainly occupied with the attempt to give a "probable" account of matters which belong to the sciences of physics and physiology'.

[4]This statement is far from casual: it occurs in the prominent and carefully staged introduction to Plato's account of the basic physical materials. Since these materials are principles of *the formed physical cosmos*, the question arises whether they are (as *e.g.*, in Empedocles and other earlier philosophers) first principles 'of *all* things' (48c2–3).

account is not intended as *entrée* to a full-blooded examination of metaphysics for its own sake, and therefore is intended to be primarily about the natural world.

But what exactly does the difference between the two approaches amount to? In grasping it one grasps the central ambiguity of the tradition called 'Platonism', an ambiguity that can be traced back to the *Timaeus* itself. For in fact the text offers contrary clues. If we go by some (the majority), the account is primarily about the physical world albeit with eternal intelligible underpinnings; if we go by others (few but striking), it seems as if it may be primarily about an eternal intelligible the study of which we have to pursue via the natural world in the first place. The ambiguity is present because Plato's distinction of eternal paradigm and object generated in accordance with it can be developed in two radically divergent ways.

According to one way, the eternal paradigm of the cosmos is an original of which the divine Craftsman makes a copy or a representation or a reproduction in a different medium. According to the other, the paradigm is a recipe which he follows. The information that the chocolate cake about to be served has been made in accordance with a certain recipe does not leave us expecting the cake to be (in a different medium) a copy, likeness, image, representation, reproduction, imitation, or semblance of a recipe. By contrast, the blurred image, stamped on a tea-towel, of half a page of Mrs Beaton *is* a reproduction of an original—in this case, of a page in a recipe book. I shall argue that thinking of the cosmic paradigm as the *recipe* for the cosmos leads to engagement with cosmology as such, whereas thinking of it as the original of the cosmos points temptingly towards treating cosmology as merely a gateway to metaphysics. And this in turn leads to what I call 'hyper-realism' about the eternal cosmic paradigm, by contrast with a more economical but still Platonic style of realism assumed by the other approach.

## 2    Ways with Paradigms

First, we may think of the famous likeness between a Platonic Form and its this-worldly correlate (or correlates) in terms of representation: this is encouraged by Plato's statements in numerous places that this-worldly objects are imitations of Forms. It is also encouraged by the imagery whereby the this-worldly object is a shadow, reflection, or dream of the Form. Now, our first-order experience of representations, whether in words or some other medium, is dominated by interest in the things the representations are of (or that we take them to be of). Thus in dreaming we are typically taken up with what the dream is about. We often look at shadows and reflections, *e.g.*, of ourselves in the mirror, just in order to obtain information about the original objects whose shadows or reflections these are. No doubt it is partly because of the intensity of our interest in the originals that it sometimes seems as if the originals themselves are actually there, standing or happening in front of us or around us, when in fact they are in no such place and may even be non-existent, and all that is physically present to us is the representing medium. We are prone to a double mistake. We may, without realising, 'project' properties of the representing medium on to the represented original, so that the original seems to us to be, for example, 'here' when only the medium is 'here'. And we may fall under the illusion that what is in fact an image borne by the representing medium is the one and only real thing: *i.e.*, that we are dealing, not with an original and its representation, but with a single non-derivative entity.

Now, it is plain that the *transparency* of the medium, the fact that it does *not*, in our basic interaction with it, draw attention to itself, facilitates these mistakes. Suppose, however, that we manage to avoid or to correct these mistakes. In that case, we are free of the illusion that the objects represented are here with us, and of the illusion that what is in fact the image of the object is all there is. We shall now be correctly 'reading' what goes on among the objects as going on in whatever space or domain *they* are in, whether far from us or in a different world from us. But the medium will still be transparent, if it is a good one.[5] Thus now that we are reading correctly we are still taking no notice of the medium as such, and we are surely giving much less attention than before to the representations in it, since we are now sure-footedly using them as signs of the things we are interested in.

The point of this discussion is to bring out the fact that if the sensible world is essentially a representation of an intelligible original, then the right attitude towards the sensible world and things within it is not to be interested in them at all for themselves, as the natural scientist most certainly is, but to do one's best to 'look through' them at what they represent.

The existence of a causal relation (or our assumption that such a relation exists) between one set of items and another leaves it open which side is or should be the primary object of attention. Thus the fact that the *Timaeus* assumes a causal relation between an intelligible object, the Craftsman's paradigm, and the sensible cosmos [6] does not in itself preclude regarding the latter as a representation or set of signs of the former, but it certainly does not dictate this direction of interest. A medical technician reading blips on a screen is interested in them only as representing the patient's heartbeat. By contrast, the Platonic cosmologist whose concern above all is to advance natural science conjectures the contents of the world-maker's eternal paradigm in order to achieve a reasonable account of major features of the physical world. This cosmologist does not 'use' the cosmos as a means or medium by which to penetrate to truths *about the paradigm*, but refers to the paradigm as an aid or method for research *about the cosmos*.

We can, however, ask whether this specifically cosmological direction of interest is in fact the direction that most determines Plato's thinking in the *Timaeus*. It is obvious that the causal relation between heartbeats and blips on the medical screen is meant to be used to monitor the heartbeats *via* the blips (and not the other way round) because it was in order to monitor heartbeats that we created the technology that embodies that causal relation. But in the case of the sensible cosmos and its intelligible paradigm, is it in fact so clear in the text which way the direction of our interest is meant to go? Was the physical

---

[5] If the medium is a bad one, *e.g.*, foggy or noisy, what is supposed to be represented may hardly appear in it; in which case we may notice just some bit of the medium and take that to be the one and only reality.

[6] By 'causal relation' I mean no more than that the Craftsman is guided by the paradigm.

world, according to the *Timaeus*, created primarily for its own sake as a thing of order and beauty, and also as a place to be lived in, coped with, wondered at, and through rational speculation scientifically explored, by mortal rational creatures such as ourselves: or is it primarily a sensible sign-system through which such creatures should try to make out the nature of the eternal, thereby embarking on an inquiry whose subject-matter is a Platonic Form or domain of Platonic Forms?

This latter way of receiving the *Timaeus* fits the idea that this world was made as a representation of the eternal paradigm—made 'in its image'. In the last section I contrasted this with the idea that the paradigm stands to the cosmos as a recipe, prescription, design, or plan stands to a product made in accordance with it. Let us now turn to thinking about the function of a recipe or design. The primary reason for following a design when making something is not in order to create a representation of the design, or to communicate the design by means of the representation, but in order to be more effective in making the product.[7] True, someone else might be able to infer the design from the product; but there is a great deal else that a product is typically intended for than to take our minds back to the recipe for it. For example, a shuttle is made as a tool for weaving. And if it is made according to a template, this is not so that it should reveal the template in a veiled fashion, but so that it will be a better shuttle than one haphazardly made. On this line of thought, the world-maker looks, or looked, to an intelligible pattern in order to raise the chances of producing the most perfect possible physical system: that his product conforms to the pattern is not an end in itself, but ensures that the product is excellent in accordance with whatever the standard is for excellence in that type of thing.

Let us now see how the text supports each of the two approaches.

> [1] We must go back to this question about [the cosmos]: which of the two paradigms (*poteron tôn paradeigmatôn*) guided its maker when he fashioned it—the one that does not change and stays the same, or the one that has come to be? [2] Well, if this cosmos is beautiful and its craftsman good, then clearly he had the eternal paradigm in view, whereas if [...] what is irreligious for anyone even to put into words!—then he <had in view> one that has come to be. So it is evident to all that <he had in view> the eternal one. For the cosmos is the most beautiful among the things that have come to be, and he is the best among causes. This, then, is how it has come to be: it has been crafted in accordance with that which is changeless and is grasped by wisdom in a rational account (28c5–29a2).

This passage, which launches the Timaean cosmology, opens with a strange question (section [1]): strange because its wording seems to presuppose that even before our cosmos was formed from pre-existing unordered matter (30a2–6; 32c5–8; 69b2–c3) there was already on hand a *generated*, and therefore

---

[7] A secondary case occurs when one operates in accordance with a recipe in order to demonstrate or test the recipe.

presumably physical and sense-perceptible, model which the our world-maker might have adopted as his guide; but such a model must itself have been an ordered system of some kind—since unordered matter can scarcely function as the model—as distinct from the material—for producing an ordered world. I shall not halt over the interpretations, grammatical and philosophical, sparked by this puzzle. In fact the important point is that the question in section [1] is rhetorical: *of course* the divine Craftsman looked to an eternal paradigm. The question is nothing but an elaborate affirmation of its own correct answer. The reason this answer has to be the right one is then given in section [2] in the light of a general premise laid down a few lines earlier (28a6–b2): it is axiomatic (a) that this cosmos is beautiful and its maker good, and (b) (this is the general premise) that a product is beautiful if and only if its maker looks to an eternal, as distinct from generated, paradigm.

From this reasoning it would seem a straightforward conclusion that the world-maker worked from an eternal paradigm just for the sake of his product, *i.e.*, just so that the physical world would be as beautiful as any such thing could be. This rather suggests that the prime benefit to human beings from studying nature (at least if they base their study on the correct, *i.e.*, Timaean, starting point[8]) is the kind of benefit that comes from studying a wonderful rational system for its own sake. By contrast, the reasoning hardly suggests that the world-maker made this cosmos in accordance with an eternal paradigm primarily so that we (as yet not made, of course) should use the cosmos as a window through which to glimpse, for its own sake, the eternal original. This much seems fairly clear from section [2] of the passage above. But let us go back to the question of section [1]: 'Which of the two paradigms ... ?' That question, notwithstanding its purely rhetorical function, has, I now argue, the potential to shunt us towards a 'portal to metaphysics' interpretation of the Timaean cosmology.

Timaeus introduced the notion of eternal paradigms with the generalisation that beautiful products are the ones whose craftsmen follow eternal paradigms rather than generated ones (28a6–b2). He then applied the disjunction 'Looking to the eternal or the generated one?' to the particular case of the maker of this world.[9] In both generalisation and application the two kinds of paradigms are presented in a symmetrical way. This symmetry in a way is natural, because the generalisation leads up to the application, and (1) the latter is effected by demanding *a choice between two answers to the same question*. As the objects presented by the respective answers, the two paradigms are logically and rhetorically symmetrical, so to speak. Each is invoked as (2) *a method for producing the same result*. Simply as methods they are on a par. One is superior, but this can only be judged by putting them logically side by side. Furthermore, (3) *the reader apprehends both in the same way*. The reader simply *thinks* of each. (The reader is not the world-maker actually choosing between generated and eternal paradigms; nor is the reader currently getting

---

[8]By contrast, *e.g.*, with ancient atomist starting points which include only atoms, the void, chance, and necessity.

[9]This use of the disjunction seems less strange when we see it as a somewhat mechanical application of a question that can be sensibly asked about the craftsmen of our experience.

ready to make a human artefact and choosing between an actually present this-worldly example and an eternal template.) Hence one might imagine, and Plato's presentation encourages it, that the paradigms *involved in the methods* are a matching pair of objects: alternative versions, eternal and generated, of what is essentially the same type of thing. Just as the artificer who works in accordance with a generated object as paradigm works by *copying* it, perhaps in a different kind of material, so it may seem that the artificer who chooses the better method works by copying his eternal paradigm in a different medium. But this is a confusion, and one that makes it seem that the *Timaeus* offers first and foremost a cosmological gateway to trans-natural metaphysics rather than a metaphysical gateway to cosmology.

To see this, let us begin by considering what it means for a human maker to 'look to an eternal paradigm rather than to one that has merely come to be'. Plato treats it as self-evident that good makers (*i.e.*, makers of good products) look in each case to an eternal paradigm. Consequently, we should interpret the principle so that it is common sense. In common-sense terms the principle is: rather than trying directly to copy or reproduce a thing that already exists in the world, whether a shuttle someone has made or an existing political consti-tution, intelligent shuttle- or constitution-makers begin by turning back within themselves to first principles,[10] working out what such a thing essentially is and what it is for. Alternatively, they should accept the instructions of some-one else who has gone back to the first principles of the matter. It is common sense that productive work is better guided by an intellectually sought for, in-tellectually worked out, answer, than by looking at an unanalysed pre-existing object of the kind.[11] The maker who merely tries to copy or reproduce may labour over superficial characteristics of the model-object as if they were essen-tial ones, and may ignorantly reproduce characteristics that were appropriate for the context in which the first object was meant to function, but not for the context of the new one. The merely reproductive maker might copy what is actually a broken shuttle[12] or an unjust constitution through ignorance of what shuttles and constitutions really are.

However, there is an important asymmetry between the paradigm that has come to be, and what, on the common-sense interpretation, we are equating with the eternal paradigm. The eternal paradigm is an answer to a 'What is ...?' question. It is a quiddity. It is eternal because the right answer is necessarily always the same, or so the Platonist assumes. So the maker who makes the right choice of guide will be guided by a quiddity (more or less perfectly grasped by him or her). Now it surely makes no sense to try to think

---

[10]This is meant in a relaxed sense, *i.e.*, as returning to first principles of the relevant subject matter. Someone designing a gun goes back to first principles of ballistics and metallurgy, but not to first principles of sub-nuclear physics.

[11]These remarks, I hope, are enough for the present purpose, but a general account of the use of existing examples should be more nuanced. Often it is impossible, and often unnecessary, to give 'an intellectually worked out' answer to a 'What is ...?' question, if this means a verbally articulated definition. People may grasp intuitively what to aim at by being shown a sample or a demonstration, so that their successful production of new instances is not 'mindless copying' but expresses mastery of a principle. But they have to trust others to provide a good sample or accurate demonstration.

[12]Cf. *Cratylus* 389b1–3.

of the right answer to a 'What is ...'? question (by 'right answer' I mean that which the question was aiming to capture) as having any role, or making any impact, apart from being the answer to its question.[13] Let us recognise as a distinct class of 'What is ...?' questions those whose answers are sought as guidance for *bringing something into being*; and correspondingly we recognise a distinct class of (let us call them) practical quiddities. The point then is that it makes no sense to think of a practical quiddity as having any positive role except to guide the maker or practitioner. (It may also have the negative role of a standard used as the basis for criticising faulty efforts to make a thing of the kind in question.) The asymmetry with the non-eternal case is this: the non-eternal (generated, usually perceptible and physical) object used as a paradigm has a life of its own outside this context. It contributes to weaving if it is a shuttle, it constrains social activity in various ways if it is a political constitution. It makes no sense to try to think of a particular shuttle's being nothing but a physical paradigm for making shuttles or for explaining to someone what a shuttle is. Even a colour-card sample can be used otherwise than as a sample: samples can be arranged into attractive patterns, and tunes could be played using different tuning-fork sounds. And certainly a shuttle, and objects of most kinds, must have a great many other things true of them before it is true that they can be paradigms of their kinds.

I have been focusing on empirical paradigms that are in fact examples—exemplary instances—of the kind of object someone is aiming to make. But in fact the Greek word *paradeigma* does not mean 'example': it has the more general meaning of 'pattern', and what we call a pattern for something may be a plan, design, or instruction for bringing it into being.[14] However, *pointing to a good example* of F is such a central and frequent way of setting up guidance for producing an F that it is easily assumed that a *paradeigma* is essentially an example. When philosophers think of people pointing at or looking to some empirical object as the *paradeigma* of something, F, they are very likely presupposing that the object is an exemplary case of F. Hence for now in considering the use of empirical objects as paradigms I shall continue to focus on objects used as examples of the kinds they are meant to explain.

So empirical paradigm-objects are themselves instances of the kinds they illustrate: instances put to a certain use. And we use empirical objects as paradigms by trying to *copy* or *reproduce* them, *i.e.*, by trying to make some sort of *likeness* of them. However, as we have seen, they contribute to the

---

[13]One might argue for this by appealing to the etymology of 'quiddity', from the interrogative pronoun '*quid?*' = 'what?'. The thought is that quiddities are only ever presented or accessed in, through, or by answers to the definition-seeking questions 'What is ...?' or 'What is it for something to be ...?'. Thus Aristotle's terms for quiddity (τὸ τί 'εστι; and τὸ τί 'ῆν 'εἰναι;—a. k. a. 'essence') are substantivized questions. The contrast is with objects that can be presented (often by physically pointing them out) not only in correct answers to wh-questions (such as 'Who did it?', 'Which river is nearest ?'), but also in many other antecedent contexts.

[14]At *Protagoras* 326c8 (although some scholars have questioned the MSS reading) there is an unselfconscious example of a *paradeigma* that is not an example: (Protagoras speaking): 'The city compels them [sc. young adults] both to learn the laws and to live according to them <as if> according to a *paradeigma*'. The law is not itself an exemplary instance of civic behaviour, but the basic answer to the question 'What is a good citizen?'

world in other ways antecedently to our using them as paradigms. But now suppose an illusion of *symmetry* to be at work, generated by that evenly constructed question: 'Which of the two paradigms?' The illusion is that *eternal* paradigms are like non-eternal ones, the difference (admittedly momentous) consisting *only* in the difference between eternal and non-eternal, and the associated difference between intelligible and sensible! Since non-eternal, empirical, paradigms are instances of the kinds they help explain, one would now picture an eternal paradigm as a sort of instance too of the kind with respect to which it gives guidance (a 'perfect particular'). This point is a notorious implication of certain formulations of Platonism, and it was made the basis of a *reductio ad absurdum* of such formulations by Plato himself in the *Parmenides* (132c12–133a4; cf. 132a1–b2). That argument is meant to show how a certain way of conceiving of Platonic Forms generates, for any multiply instantiated characteristic *F*, an infinite regress of Forms of *F*. I shall return to this briefly in Part 3. For now, however, the main point is this: thinking about a Form as an eternal and intelligible, *rather* than perishable and sensible, paradigm easily leads to two false steps. (1) One of these steps takes us into the mind-set of assuming that the way to make something in accordance with an eternal paradigm is to *copy* or *reproduce* it. For this is how we operate when making something in accordance with an empirical paradigm. (2) The other false step gets us to a place where the Form appears as an eternal object which, as it were, does a great deal more than simply function as a paradigm. For this is how it is with empirical objects taken as paradigms. But to look at the Form in this way is, in effect, to be committed to thinking of it as enjoying a rich and in a sense concrete life of its own: a life not merely additional to its playing its role of paradigm, but metaphysically prior. If it is in this fashion that we imagine Plato's world-maker's intelligible paradigm, *i.e.*, not as a quiddity—what is expressed in an intelligent answer to the question 'What is the recipe or formula for a supremely excellent comprehensive physical system?'—but as an eternal object that itself exemplifies the kind in question,[15] then we are all set to say that the paradigm, like the cosmos made in accordance with it,[16] is a living being—only a supernal one, 'the Intelligible Animal'; and it becomes attractive to think of its life as busily and multi-directionally unfolding and being enjoyed (even though strictly in eternity) in an incorporeal domain that stretches in other directions (just as a physical shuttle exists in various contexts before someone uses it as an example of shuttles)—a domain where chains of intelligibles rise tier upon tier beyond the rather humble level at which the Intelligible Animal—almost accidentally, it can begin to seem—serves as paradigm for the

---

[15] Why should any maker need both quiddity and eternal example? And if he doesn't, the dispensable one seems to be the latter, because perhaps he can grasp the quiddity without considering any eternal example (*e.g.*, by analysing sensible examples), whereas it seems that he must have already brought the quiddity into play if he fully understands what the eternal example is an example of. This kind of criticism goes back to Aristotle's *Metaphysics*.

[16] The physical cosmos of the *Timaeus* is an intelligent, living, and in fact divine being: see 30b1–31a1; 32d1–34b9; 92c4–9.

empirical world.[17] I do not think Plato in the *Timaeus* coolly intended to pitch us into all this, but there are notable passages where his language pulls in this direction.

Before turning to them, let me introduce the term 'thick' in this connection. To conceive of an intelligible paradigm as an object essentially endowed with important properties and relations over and above any function it has of guiding thought or practice is to treat it as a 'thick' intelligible. By 'thick' I mean what people sometimes informally mean by 'concrete'. 'Concrete', however, has two unwanted connotations. (1) In an Aristotelian context it means a matter-form composite. (2) In contemporary philosophy 'concrete' is used by contrast with 'abstract', but since it is frequently assumed that everything concrete is physical or supervenient on the physical, 'concrete' is often heard as having that implication; hence the word is unsuitable for application to incorporeal entities. Instead of using 'thick' one could speak of the paradigm as having 'wide ontological role'. This is analogous to Crispin Wright's notion of 'wide cosmological role'. One of Wright's markers of the realism of discourse featuring a concept C is that the corresponding property has 'wide cosmological role' ('cosmological' because instantiations of the property have consequences in the physical world independently of our responses).[18] For an intelligible to have 'wide ontological role' (from the point of view of a given intellectual enterprise) is for it to be embedded in an incorporeal realm that extends in all sorts of interesting directions beyond the limits of that enterprise.[19]

At several junctures in the *Timaeus* Plato allows himself language that implies thickness for the cosmic paradigm. For example, the seductive collocation of *apeikazesthai* (to be made like, or in the likeness of), *eikôn*, and *eikôs* at 29c1–2 presents the physical cosmos not merely as made in accordance with the divine intelligible plan, but made so as to be a *likeness or image of* it. That use of *eikôn* of course recalls the wealth of occasions, in the *Republic* and elsewhere, when Plato glories in the language of images, copies, imitations, reflections, and shadows to indicate the relation of participating empirical particulars to their Form. And it is this current that carries him along in the famous argument that this cosmos must be all-comprehensive and therefore unique (30c2–31b3). The cosmos has those attributes, we are told, because the Craftsman made it as a likeness of the perfect Intelligible Animal, and the latter is the all-comprehensive and therefore unique intelligible of its kind.

Then there is the even more famous passage that explains why this cosmos was made to be chronological, *i.e.*, why it is configured with ever-recurring regular visible rotations (37d1–38c3). The reason was so that the life of this cosmos would resemble as closely as possible the strictly eternal life (*aiôn*[20]) of

---

[17]See, *e.g.*, the astoundingly elaborate ontology of Proclus, helpfully presented in summaries and diagrams by Festugière (1966–8, v. I, 177–9); Brisson (1998, pp. 68–9); Opsomer (2000).

[18]Wright (1992, pp. 196–99).

[19]The present discussion is about paradigms as used for practical purposes, but some of the points are probably relevant to the case of defining a thing for theoretical purposes.

[20]*Aiôn* originally meant 'natural life-span', and is first commandeered here to denote the is without was and will be of eternity. Since living things provide our most obvious examples of natural life-spans, the word strongly suggests that Plato at this moment is thinking of the

the Intelligible Animal of which it is a likeness (37d6). Time (*chronos*), which circles according to number, imitates eternal life (*aiôna mimoumenou*). There are 'likeness' words at 37c8; d2; 5; 7; 38a7; 38b8.[21]

Plato's emphasis on the status of the cosmos (or some feature of it) as a *likeness* of the paradigm (or some attribute of it) conveys that this is how the inquirer should view the cosmos. We must never forget that it is a copy, not an original. However, something like this point can be expressed in terms not of copies and originals, but in terms of recipes, plans, designs, or practical quiddities, and objects made in accordance with their specifications: the inquirer must never forget that the cosmos was made in accordance with a practical quiddity. Either message drums in Platonic awareness of the derivative status of the cosmos, so it may seem that the two messages amount to the same. But Platonic awareness of the derivative status of the cosmos can become the starting point for two different types of intellectual journey. In one, the inquirer uses the assumption that our cosmos has an eternal, intelligible, reality in its background as the methodological basis for arriving at reasonable theories about our cosmos. In the second, the inquirer regards the cosmos as point of departure (or else a barrier) for finding out more about the eternal object in the background. To the extent that one makes the second kind of journey, one lays aside interest in cosmology or in the physical world as such. One will find many questions to address whose answers make no difference to cosmology.[22]

# 3   Some Questions Arising

## 3.1   Thick intelligibles and the Third Man argument

It may be thought that if Plato's Forms are conceptualized in a way that saves them from the regress ('Third Man') arguments of the *Parmenides*, then they cannot coherently be conceptualized as 'thick' in the sense explained in Part 2. The regress paradoxes seem to be generated by the idea that Forms are perfect particulars (the 'Two Worlds' view), and it is this that ushers in the notion of them as thick entities with a teeming life of their own. Hence one might think that a successful demolition of the regresses would make the 'thick' conception untenable. If that is so, and especially if Plato has shrugged off the Third Man by the time he writes the *Timaeus*,[23] it becomes questionable whether the 'thick' interpretation of Forms is relevant at all to that dialogue, even if some of his language there does suggest it. Since the 'thick' interpretation is a topic of this paper, being linked to the question whether the *Timaeus* presents a metaphysically supported cosmology or a cosmological avenue to metaphysics, something should be said here about thick intelligibles and the Third Man.

---

paradigm as itself a living being. If that is what the paradigm is, then, as I have argued, there must be a great deal more to it than its role as paradigm for this cosmos.

[21] See also the references to copies and likenesses of eternal things in the Receptacle-passage: 50c5; d1; 51a1–2 (with Cornford's conjecture at a1); 52a5; c2–3.

[22] Perhaps the same thinker can approach the *Timaeus* cosmology in both ways although not at the same time. But an ontology of incorporeals that fits one of those ways will be either too sparse or too lavish for the other.

[23] Most scholars today regard the *Timaeus* as the later dialogue.

So let us ask: does conceiving of Forms in a way that blocks off Third Man regresses preclude conceiving of them as thick entities? In my view, the answer is No.

The regresses arise from supposing that just as the resemblance of sensible Fs to each other follows from their common participation in a distinct Form $F$ that is $F$ (self-predication), so the resemblance of the Form to the sensible Fs must be due to its and their common participation in a further form $F$ that is $F$; and so on. Just as the shared $F$-ness of the sensible Fs is not self-explanatory, but derives from a distinct Form in which they participate, so the $F$-ness shared by this Form and the sensibles must likewise derive from something else, an ulterior Form $F$. The regresses threaten disaster not merely because they are endless, but because they generate a plurality of Forms $F$ as against the official tenet that sensible Fs owe their $F$-ness to a unique Form $F$. There are, however, different ways to block such a regress *ab initio*. One can point out that the reason for the Form's resemblance to the sensibles is the same as the reason why the latter resemble each other: namely, each of them was made in the likeness of the Form; hence there is no need for explanation in terms of another Form. Alternatively, one can maintain that the Form is not $F$ in the same sense or way as the many sensibles (but in a sense or a way that is related and analogous), and therefore it should not be grouped as an $F$ thing alongside them to create a new plurality demanding another Form to account for their common $F$-ness. Each of these solutions blocks off a proliferation of Forms of $F$, thus safeguarding the uniqueness of the $F$-Form as such. But neither solution rules it out that the unique $F$-Form is embedded in an ontology vastly over-stocked (as most of us would think) with *other* intelligibles. Unchecked Third Man regresses are pernicious for Platonism because they imply the absurdity of explaining the shared $F$-ness of the sensible Fs by reference to *any* intelligible object. But the over-stocked ontology of intelligibles is objectionable for a different reason, namely because it invokes *too much* intelligible machinery to explain the $F$-ness of the sensibles, and checking the Third Man regresses leaves that problem untouched. In sum, a philosopher can side-step Third Man regresses while continuing to view the $F$-Form as a thick intelligible, *i.e.*, as carrying on its back a great deal more baggage than whatever is needed for it to be the quiddity of $F$.[24]

## 4    Mathematical Entities, and Metaphysical First Principles

As we have seen, interpreting Timaean cosmology as a portal to the metaphysics of the incorporeal is bound up with a theoretical interest in the metaphysics for its own sake. This is by contrast with the attitude that refers to the intelligible paradigm not for its own sake but for the sake of understanding this cosmos. Some may find it incredible that such opposite attitudes could fail to be distinguished, so that even Plato himself in the *Timaeus* veers between them (or so it seems from his choice of expressions), and some of his followers have been

---

[24] *e.g.*, Proclus, a fancier of thick intelligibles if ever there was one, has solutions to the regress arguments in his *Commentary on Plato's* Parmenides, 889–90; 908–9; 912, in Morrow and Dillon (1987).

so impressed by the metaphysics that they hardly noticed that, according to the sweep of the evidence, this is metaphysics strictly in the service of cosmology. But a reason for failing to distinguish is perhaps not far to seek. There *is* an incorporeal domain for which a theoretical interest in the territory for its own sake is unproblematically legitimate: the domain of pure mathematics. In geometry, moreover, we standardly use sensible representations as a means to investigate intelligible structures and relationships. In the *Republic* Plato speaks of this practice as follows:

> [...] although they use the figures that are seen, and make their statements about them, their thoughts are not about *them* but about those beings which these ones resemble (*eoike*). Their statements focus on the square itself, and the diagonal itself: not on the diagonal which they draw. And so on with the other cases. *These* very figures which they mould and draw (of which shadows and reflections in water are likenesses [*eikones*]) they now use as likenesses, and seek thereby to see *those* very figures that cannot be seen except by thought (*Republic* VI, 510d5–511a1).

This exactly hits off the 'portal to metaphysics' approach to the cosmos. The approach is wrong if one purports to be doing cosmology, but right for pure mathematics done with perceptible diagrams.

Add to this the fact that some of the objects and relationships studied by the pure mathematician play a vital part in Timaean cosmology, just as some of them do in the plans of human architects and engineers. The number-theory and the geometry can be, and are, '*applied*'. Examples in the cosmology are: the continuous proportion with four terms that explains why there must be four material elements and how they co-exist in indissoluble harmony (31b4–32c4); the sequences of ratios used to mark out the intervals in the world soul (35b4–36b5); the assignment of certain regular geometrical polyhedra to be the shapes of the four kinds of elemental particles (55d6–56b6); and the selection of specific triangles for constructing those polyhedra (53c4–55c4). Here, it is incidental to the mathematical entities as such that they are paradigmatic for world-making. At the same time, their purely mathematical nature relates them essentially to other mathematical entities which play no part in world-making: thus the cosmically appropriate ones are multiply relevant intelligibles, since they have a life beyond cosmology, and (one might well think) antecedent to cosmology. Conversely, in so far as mathematical entities are cosmically appropriate, their life outside cosmology is a logically incidental fact. Even so, some Platonists through the ages may have fallen into the confusion of assuming that features of the physical cosmos as such stand to the mathematical structures supposedly applied in designing them as the sensible diagrams drawn by pure geometers stand to the geometrical objects. From this it is no great stretch to a philosophical vision of this cosmos as a sort of a perceptible diagram by which the world-maker teaches us about its intelligible Form.

The mistake is perhaps partly to be accounted a simple-minded failure to tease out the different relations inherent in an objectively somewhat complex handful of connections and differences. These are the real connections and differences between (a) taking mathematicals as objects of study in their own right, and (b) employing them first in one, then another, sort of intellectual enterprise: *i.e.*, first (b1) in the planning and construction of an artefact in accordance with mathematical specifications, and secondly (b2) in the attempt by others to make sense of the finished object by assuming that mathematical specifications went into its design and theorising as to what precisely these were. However, add to this so to speak natural potential for confusion the fact that some of the signals Plato had sent in earlier writings either ignore or blur crucial distinctions. His fundamental contrast between sensibles and intelligibles, with the associated drama of 'turning from the sensible to the intelligible' (*Republic* VI, 508c4–d10; 509d4; VII, 514a1–520d4; 520c1–8; 522e5–525c6; 532a1–d1; cf. *Theaetetus* 175b9–d7), promotes a picture in which each side of the contrast constitutes a single (even if internally divisible) 'realm' or 'domain'. This may have fostered the impression that when we 'turn to the intelligible' it is for some single general intellectual purpose. Thus the difference between turning to intelligibles as objects of theoretical study, and as guides for practical action and production, may not have been held steadily in view.

Again, while it is tempting to look at two kinds of imperfection together—the imperfection of a geometer's diagram as compared with the circle it represents, and the imperfection of many human artefacts as compared with the demands of their ideal design—doing so easily results in the notion that the ideal objects in the two cases are objects of thought in the same way. After all, the geometer's ink-drawn circle and the wheel produced by a wagon-maker are both accessed by us through sense-perception, and they may be functionally interchangeable: the wagon-wheel can be used to illustrate a point of geometry, just as a wooden circle made for classroom purposes could be taken over to serve as the rim of a wheel. Easy, perhaps, at an early stage of reflection to move from such facts to the thought that since only one ideal circle is involved there is just one way for enlightened intellects to deal with the ideal circle.

Furthermore, in the early Academy there were intellectual pressures towards a grand unifying vision. We can make this out dimly from fragments of information preserved in Aristotle and from hints in some of Plato's dialogues. Some, including perhaps Plato himself at some stage, held that all Forms of natural objects, or perhaps the cosmic paradigm in all its aspects, turn out to consist in mathematical entities. Thus to some it must have seemed that physics could be reduced to a mathematical discipline, or at least the parts of physics that deal with natural *formations* as distinct from the material realisation. There was also the hope of running everything back to more fundamental metaphysical principles, the One and the Indefinite Dyad, whether by generating numbers from these, and from numbers lines, from lines surfaces, from surfaces geometric solids, and from them physical bodies in motion, or in some other way. Such theories do not necessitate the other-worldly focus that sees the physical cosmos as a windowpane on to intelligible realities, no more a subject of inquiry in its own right than are the geometer's drawings; but one can imagine how they might have helped to strengthen that focus.[25]

---

[25] See Aristotle's complaint against the philosophers 'called Pythagoreans', *Metaphysics* I, 989b29-990a18, especially 990a5–8: 'The causes and principles which they mention are [...]

# 5   Types of Platonic Realism

I have been contrasting reference to the intelligible cosmic paradigm as a means of understanding the physical cosmos, the object of primary concern in the *Timaeus*, with reference to that paradigm as itself the object of primary concern. This second approach has these characteristics: first, it involves turning away from the cosmos and treating cosmology not as a science in its own right but as a *praeparatio* for a science of the incorporeal as such. Secondly, it involves treating the cosmic paradigm as a thick intelligible, which is to say: focusing on, as distinct from prescinding from, aspects of this intelligible object that go beyond what is needed for it to function as a practical quiddity governing construction of the physical world. The two characteristics reinforce each other, for once a Platonist turns away from studying the cosmos in its own right there is nothing for him or her to do with the undeniably Platonic cosmic paradigm except use it as a starting point for penetrating further into the territory of the intelligibles as such; and the more interesting that sort of expedition seems to be, the less motive there is for doing cosmology.

Platonists are all in some sense realists about Platonic Forms like the cosmic paradigm of the *Timaeus*. Let me call 'hyper-realists' those for whom the paradigm is a thick intelligible, an object of a science of incorporeals as such, or analogous to a mathematical structure which can be applied in making something physical, but which it makes perfectly good sense to study for its own sake. It has been the gist of this chapter that Timaean cosmology does not presuppose hyper-realism about the paradigm. The question now arises: what then *are* the metaphysical commitments of Timaean cosmology? Well, it is committed to the reality of production-guiding quiddities. Accepting these as real does not depend on imagining them as the 'front-ends' of thick intelligibles, in the way a flower is the front-end of a plant with a root-system. We need only say that production-guiding quiddities are as real as they need to be in order to function as such. Since the most important one is the quiddity of the natural cosmos, such quiddities cannot in general be ontologically founded in the thought or practice of human beings considered as parts of corporeal nature. Hence even if they are founded in the thought and practice of rational beings, given that rational beings include the divine world-maker, their foundation is firmly situated somewhere beyond corporeal nature no less than if they somehow exist independently of all rational minds but are nonetheless "there" for rational minds to access.[26] There is enough in this Platonism to keep contemporary naturalists comfortably scandalised.

---

sufficient to act as steps even up to the higher realms of reality, and are more suited to these than to theories about nature' (tr. W. D. Ross in Barnes, 1984).

[26]This assumes that the practical quiddity of the cosmos is not somehow present as an immanent imperative in the materials from which the cosmos was formed. However, Plato is adamant that these materials are lifeless and devoid of intelligence (46d4–7). In the Platonic tradition subsequent to Plato it became a major question whether the cosmic paradigm is "internal", or "external" and prior, to the Craftsman's intellect, but the matter is not raised in the *Timaeus* even though Plato had briefly confronted it in relation to the human mind at *Parmenides* 132b3–c12. This is another indication that in the *Timaeus* Plato is not really interested in the metaphysics of the cosmic paradigm except in so far as it (a) secures the excellence of the cosmos, and (b) provides a basis for human cosmological inquiry.

It may be felt that this more moderate Platonic realism renders the quiddities too 'thin': how can they make a difference (in guiding thought and action) unless they exist, and how can they exist unless they are founded on an antecedent intelligible reality? Perhaps a Platonic answer that avoids hyper-realism would go as follows: it agrees (1) that the quiddities must have a foundation beyond themselves, and (2) that thickness must indeed pertain to them; but it says that the foundation and the thickness lie in opposite directions. Thus: (1) the quiddities (we are considering practical quiddities) are founded in the Form of the Good.[27] The latter is expressed through the intelligent bringing to be of things that are good. But a good thing cannot simply be good: it must be a good $F$ or $G$.[28] Hence the Form of the Good is expressed through one or another practical or productive specific quiddity, and is their common foundation. On the other hand: (2) these quiddities reach out to thickness by the directionality of their nature (we could say by their direction of fit). Each concrete realisation of a quiddity has properties and relations that go beyond what is needed for it to be such a realisation. However, the thickness is not on the side of the eternal and purely intelligible, but on the empirical, temporal, side.

Intellect is necessary for this metaphysical process, perhaps because the Good *is* an intellect, and the quiddities are 'in' it; but there may be other ways of articulating the role of intellect. For example, it might seem better to distinguish between world-making intellect and *the* Good, because world-making intellect interprets the Good in the way appropriate to its own function, *i.e.*, in terms of the perfection and completeness of the cosmos that is to be made. There are also other intellects, in particular those of mortal rational beings, whose task is to interpret the Good in terms of arrangements that are good for humans and can only be humanly realised. These aspects of the Good would arguably not be part of the cosmic paradigm, because (on a simple understanding) if they were, human arrangements would come about as elements of the *natural* universe, and not through the practices that depend on human culture. On this way of looking at it, the world-maker and the human agent are concerned with distinct practical quiddities and separate readings of the Good.

On the other hand, we could instead say the following. Since humans are an essential part of the divinely made world, the most far-sighted human intellects, when thinking out the practical quiddities that should guide human affairs, will do their best to see the human good in relation to basic human nature and the nature and meaning of the surrounding cosmos. Thus a humanly practical quiddity ideally incorporates reference to human physiology, human psychology, and the rest of nature in so far as this bears on the good human life. The quiddity's content will therefore include more than the goal that is to be humanly realised, because the goal appears against a background understanding of nature. So the humanly practical quiddity is, as it were, two-level:

---

[27] The Form of the Good (*Republic* VI 504c9–VII 534d2 ) does not appear explicitly in the *Timaeus*, although more than one interpretative tradition claims to find it there.

[28] The values of '$F$' and '$G$' etc. are selected with the proviso that a good $F$ etc. is a good, or a good thing. This precludes examples that are merely attributively good, *e.g.*, good terror-tactics

not an instruction through and through, but an instruction embedded in a scientifically declarative setting. We can also conceptualise the cosmic paradigm in the complementary way. According to this, its content includes not only the world of nature but also outlines of ideal human qualities and institutions (where 'ideal' means in part 'ideal given the nature of the cosmos'); however, the ideals-for-humans do not dictate tasks for the world-maker. From his point of view, these parts of the paradigm are, as it were, dormant (although not hidden), since they can only be activated by humans. Thus his paradigm too is double-layered, with some parts directly addressing the practical side of the divine world-making enterprise, and others not. This picture, which places the humanly relevant quiddities within the cosmic paradigm but at one remove or as if in quotation marks, allows for a world-maker who cares how humanity manages its fate, even though the particular developments are not under his control. Putting all this together, the far-sighted human cosmologist will look out for specific ways in which human nature has been divinely constructed so as to have the best chance of making good choices, individual and social.[29]

# BIBLIOGRAPHY

Barnes, J., editor (1984). *The Complete Works of Aristotle, the Revised Oxford Translation.* Princeton University Press, Princeton.

Brisson, L. (1998). *Le Même et l'Autre dans la Structure Ontologique du Timée de Platon.* Academia Verlag, Sankt Augustin.

Broadie, S. (2012). *Nature and Divinity in Plato's* Timaeus. Cambridge University Press, Cambridge.

Bury, R. G. (1929). *Plato: Timaeus, Critias, Cleitophon, Menexenus, Epistles, with an English translation.* Loeb Classical Library. Harvard University Press, Cambridge MA.

Cornford, F. M. (1935). *Plato's Cosmology: The Timaeus of Plato.* Hackett Publishing Company, Indianapolis/Cambridge.

Festugière, A. J. (1966–8). *Commentaire sur le Timée/Proclus; Traduction et Notes.* Librairie Philosophique J. Vrin, Paris.

Lloyd, G. E. R. (1968). Plato as a natural scientist. *The Journal of Hellenic Studies,* 88:78–92.

Morrow, G. and Dillon, J., editors (1987). *Proclus' Commentary on Plato's Parmenides.* Translated with introduction and notes by J. Dillon. Princeton University Press, Princeton.

Opsomer, J. (2000). Proclus on demiurgy and procession in the *Timaeus.* In Wright, M. R., editor, *Reason and Necessity: Essays on Plato's* Timaeus, pages 113–143. Duckworth Press, London/Swansea.

Tarrant, H. (2007). *Proclus: Commentary on Plato's Timaeus. Volume 1, Book 1: Proclus on the Socratic State and Atlantis.* Translated with introduction and notes, and with a general introduction by D. Baltzly and H. Tarrant. Cambridge University Press, Cambridge.

Wright, C. (1992). *Truth and Objectivity.* Harvard University Press, Cambridge MA.

---

[29]The *Timaeus* has many examples of how the human body is designed for human flourishing, specifically rational flourishing.

# Realism, Structural Realism and Instrumentalism

PETER CLARK[†]

## 1 Introduction

The question which I wish to address in this paper is one in what might be called the theory of theories. What is theoretical knowledge in the sciences knowledge *of*?

There are two profoundly opposed answers to this question. One is the thesis of scientific realism (perhaps the most natural common sense view) which asserts that, if we believe that our scientific theories are at least approximately true and our evidence for this belief is precisely the correctness of their experimentally checkable predictions, then we must believe to that same extent in the existence of those hypothetical entities, those theoretical entities, which those theories assert are responsible for the experimental evidence. So if we encounter in the vocabulary of empirically successful theories terms like electromagnetic field, gravitational field, elementary particle, quark or boson, or indeed terms like id, superego, libido, or terms like social propensity, individual preference or historical forces, then the thesis of scientific realism asserts that we have reason to believe that there are such things just to the extent that the theories in which those terms occur are supported by the experimental data. This is a very natural claim in the theory of theories; if theories quantify over hypothetical or theoretical entities, then those theories are asserting that such things exist and we are bound to accept that such things exist to the degree that such theories are experimentally supported.

However, as is very well known, there is an opposing view.[1] Within the modern theory of theories it gets a grip from a logical result. Take any scientific theory referred to above and formalise it into first order logic. That formalisation will provide us with a set of axioms (the core assertions of the theory) and a non-logical vocabulary. The non-logical vocabulary will sustain a partition into terms which are theoretical and terms which are observational. Then the result in the theory of theories states that for every scientific theory

[†]An original version of this paper was presented at the Conference on Freedom and Determinism: Social Sciences and Natural Sciences, organized by the University of A Corua (Ferrol Campus) and the Society of Logic, Methodology and Philosophy of Science in Spain. I am very pleased to dedicate it to my long-term friend and stalwart colleague Stephen Read.

[1]The thesis of instrumentalism is very ancient. In the context of the scientific revolution in the early Seventeenth Century it seems first to have emerged as an articulated doctrine in a dispute between Kepler (defending Tycho Brahe from a realist standpoint) and the imperial mathematician Ursus who adopted a strongly instrumentalist view with respect to astronomical hypotheses. See particularly Jardine (1984)

$T$, there is a theory $T^*$ which employs only the observational vocabulary of $T$, such that if $e$ is any statement formulated purely in the observational vocabulary of $T$, then $e$ follows from $T$ if and only if $e$ follows from $T^*$.[2] So since the evidence supporting $T$ is formulated in the observational vocabulary of $T$, $T^*$ is supported by the evidence exactly to the degree that $T$ is. But $T^*$ makes no reference to theoretical entities, so what could be the justification for the claim that the evidence supports the existence of theoretical entities, when it equally supports a theory which makes no mention of them? The claim that there is no justification is the thesis of scientific instrumentalism. It is a negative argument undermining the argument for scientific realism; is there a positive argument for instrumentalism?

There is, and it is called the pessimistic induction. That argument amounts to this: while at the empirical observational level of specific confirmed predictions science is cumulative, at the theoretical or explanatory level it is highly non-cumulative. Indeed the history of science reveals a sequence of dramatic revolutions in theory and that, despite much, often very surprising predictive success by earlier theories, subsequent theories, while retaining as predictions those earlier predictive successes, have denied that the underlying structure of unobservable reality was anything like what earlier theories said it was. Up to the present then, all past theories have been proved to be false. Newtonian gravitational theory giving way to Relativity and classical electromagnetism giving way to quantum theory, being prime examples, though the list is legion. Why do we not then reasonably infer that our current scientific theories are false? That is the pessimistic induction. But that induction further invites the question as to in what sense then were those admittedly predictively successful earlier theories even approximately true, given that such revolutions have occurred in successive theoretical accounts of the deep structure of the Universe? That is the central threat to scientific realism and a key argument for the instrumentalist position-there is no knowledge in the purely theoretical domain.

To return to our original question: what is theoretical knowledge in science knowledge of? We now have two opposed answers. The realist answer is that theoretical knowledge is knowledge of the observationally inaccessible entities ultimately responsible for the observed data. The instrumentalist answer is that theoretical knowledge in the sciences is simply a convenient heuristic device for systematically codifying and predicting the relations found in observed experience. Theoretical claims are not really capable of bearing a truth-value at all. There may be a reality beyond the observable, but it is not within the scope of science, nor can it be part of what science tells us about the World. It is not part of the cognitive content of scientific theories.

Finally, by way of introduction, it should be pointed out that it is in no way an objection to the above dilemma that the distinction between observable and theoretical vocabulary is not a fixed one and evolves with the evolution of scientific knowledge. As experimental techniques develop and the progress of

---

[2]$T^*$ is taken by some instrumentalists to be the Ramsey sentence of $T$ (see below p. 60) but there are other alternatives and it is no requirement on the instrumentalist that he take the cognitive content of T to be identified with the Ramsey sentence of T.

science provides new machinery and procedures for the investigation of nature, more and more of the physical universe becomes observable as the instruments of measurement become more and more sophisticated. At the end of the Nineteenth Century, atom and molecule were clearly regarded as unobservable entities postulated to explain the thermodynamics of gases and liquids and their behaviour in reactions and in mixtures. By 1912 Jean Perrin had completed his systematic experimental investigation of their size and the various numbers like Avogadro's number which characterise them.[3] By the beginning of the Twenty First Century, experimental methods are such that the molecule and the atom are in a host of contexts (for example surface chemistry[4]) plainly observable terms, part of the observable vocabulary in theories in which they occur. Nevertheless, despite the fact that observational techniques advance, at any stage in the investigation of nature, there is a partition to be made among observational and theoretical vocabulary, and that is enough to establish at each stage the problem posed by the two opposing theses in response to the fundamental question. Granting that the theory-observation distinction evolves does not help in avoiding the issue for any empirically minded philosopher or scientist.

The debate between realism and instrumentalism has raged down the centuries with great philosophers and scientists ranged on either side. Recently, however, a new view has emerged which seems attractive in that it captures what seems correct or insightful in both views, but without abandoning the cognitive significance of theory. This view is called Structural Scientific Realism. It is a realist view because it accepts that scientific theories describe in part an unobservable reality, but it also accepts from the instrumentalist position that the cognitive content of theories is not what the realist traditionally has thought that to be. It is to this new and exciting third view that this paper is devoted.

The core of the claim is the thesis of structuralism: theoretical knowledge is not knowledge of unobservable objects and the hidden relations among them but is always knowledge of structure.

The view has at least two forms, a modest one and a very radical one. The leading advocates of the modest view, John Worrall and Elie Zahar, describe it as being the only viable solution to the problem of giving a (minimally) realistic interpretation of the natural sciences.[5] Thereby they claim it meets the challenge of Constructive empiricism (the most sophisticated modern version of instrumentalism), which is the claim that science does not aim at the truth but at empirical adequacy alone, and solves the problem posed by the pessimistic induction.[6]

---

[3]Perrin (1910, 1916).

[4]The scanning tunneling microscope now provides virtually pictures of molecules and atoms. See for example Ertl (2008). In general, techniques involving scanning tunneling microscopy allow us to see molecules and recognize them by their shape. In appropriate circumstances, molecular populations can be placed upon a surface where they form complex but highly ordered arrays of repeated patterns. When heated, they can react and form a strong stable two dimensional polymeric array in which the component molecules can still be recognized from the scanning microscope image. See particularly Treier et al. (2009a) and Treier et al. (2009b)

[5]See especially Worrall (1989, 2007); Zahar (2001)

[6]Cf. van Fraassen (1980)

The advocates of the much more radical view do not confine themselves to epistemology but regard the thesis as having important consequences for the metaphysics of science, as an interpretation of modern physics and virtually the whole of the special sciences. James Ladyman and Don Ross' recent book "*Every Thing Must Go*" champions this cause.[7] They claim they see a need for "an ontology apt for contemporary physics, and a way of dissolving some of the metaphysical conundrums it presents" and "for a conception of how theories represent the world that is compatible with the role of models and idealisations in physics."[8] These are worthy aims indeed, but their thesis is really revolutionary. They deny that "strictly speaking there are things';" they deny that "in the material world as represented by the currently accepted scientific structures, individual objects have any distinctive status." They argue that "some real patterns behave like things, traditionally conceived, while others behave like traditional instances of events and processes," but "from the metaphysical point of view, what exists are just real patterns [...] Science motivates no separate metaphysical theories about objects, events and processes."[9] Their clarion call is "There are no things, Structure is all there is."

Now one must not underestimate the seriousness of their claim. Their claim is not that there are some queer things about in modern physics, entities with startling and peculiar properties, for we can all agree on that, but rather it is that they want to do without entities of any sort whatsoever and rely merely on the existence of patterns (to use Resnik's phrase) and structures. It is a manifest fact that modern physical theory can be formalised in first order set theory with individuals as urelements, and consequently that in such formalisation there are universally and existentially quantified expressions (the quantifiers thought of as ranging over sets and the urelements). If to be asserted to be by a theory is to be the value of a bound variable occurring in that theory, then it would appear that modern physical theory is committed to all manner of entities, objects and things which serve as the range of those variables, in the standard univocal Quinean way. Ladyman and Ross *et al.* are fully aware of this, and that is why they eschew that means of exhibiting the content of theory and the Quinean view of theoretical commitment to existence. Thus they say explicitly,

> It is not part of our realism that every time a scientist quantifies over something in formulation of a theory or hypothesis she is staking out an existential commitment [...] Indeed, we will argue that, semantic appearances notwithstanding, we should not interpret science— either fundamental physics or special sciences—as metaphysically committed to the existence of self-subsistent individuals (Ladyman et al., 2007, p. 119).

This is a very strong form of structural realism, and though I am happy to accept the existence of all sorts of structures from $\omega$ through $\mathbf{C}$ (the field of

---

[7]Ladyman et al. (2007). These are the main authors, but the volume also contains contributions jointly written with Ladyman and Ross by David Spurrett and John Collier.

[8]Ladyman et al. (2007, p. 131).

[9]Ladyman et al. (2007, p. 121).

complex numbers), to physical fields, and even if it is required by metaphysics to atomless gunk (presumably conceived of as a continuous fluid), I am very unwilling to do without objects. For it seems clear that all these structures are structures of things. One can talk of structures quite properly as themselves things, as when one thinks of the structure as an equivalence class, as an abstraction over some suitable equivalence relation itself defined over classes of objects. But structures are always structures of *some things*.

## 2   A Brief Mathematical Diversion

Structuralism finds its most fully articulated form in the philosophy of mathematics.[10] Structuralism as a general view about the nature of mathematics really got started in a remark of Dedekind in his classic of 1887 *Was sind und was sollen die Zahlen?* He says there:

> If in the consideration of a singly infinite system $N$, set in order by a transformation $\phi$, we entirely neglect the special character of the elements, simply retaining their distinguishability and taking into account only the relations to one another in which they are placed by the order setting transformation $\phi$, then are these elements called *natural numbers* or *ordinal numbers* or simply numbers and the base-element 1 is called the *base number* of the number series $N$. With reference to this freeing the elements from every other content (abstraction) we are justified in calling numbers a free creation of the human mind (Dedekind, 1963, Section 73, p. 68).

This manifesto of structuralism in its basic form, that the natural numbers should be regarded as merely place holders in any $\omega$ sequence, was replied to by Russell in 1903, before he himself temporarily adopted a structuralist view in his *Analysis of Matter*.[11] I have always thought that Russell's reply then was exactly the right one, not just to the specific claim but to the general structuralist thesis. It is worth quoting in full. He argues as follows:

> Moreover it is impossible that the ordinals should be, as Dedekind suggests, nothing but the terms of such relations as constitute a progression. If they are to be anything at all they must be intrinsically something: they must differ from other entities as points from instants, or colours from sounds. What Dedekind intended to indicate was probably a definition by means of the principle of abstraction [...] But a definition so made always indicates some class of entities having (or being) a genuine nature of their own, and not logically dependent upon the manner in which they have been defined. The entities should at least be visible to the mind's

<hr>

[10]Structuralism in recent philosophy of mathematics was revived in a classic article by Paul Benacerraf in 1965 (Cf. Benacerraf, 1965) There are basically three forms of modern structuralist views: structures as patterns as advocated by Micheal Resnik (Cf. Resnik, 1988), structures as universals as argued for by Stewart Shapiro (Cf. Shapiro, 2000), and a purely modal view advocated by Geoffrey Hellman (Cf. Hellman, 1996).

[11]Russell (1927)

eye; what the principle asserts is that, under certain conditions, there are such entities, if we only knew were to look for them. But whether when we have found them, they will be ordinals or cardinals, or even something quite different, is not to be decided off hand. And in any case, Dedekind does not show us what it is that all progressions have in common, nor give any reason for supposing it to be the ordinal numbers, except that all progressions obey the same laws as ordinals do, which would prove equally that any assigned progression is what all progressions have in common (Russell, 1903, p. 249).

# 3    Ontic Structural Realism

Let us return now to the main claim of Ross and Ladyman and their radical thesis, which we call ontic structural realism. It is clear that they and their co-authors clearly want metaphysics to fulfill an explanatory purpose, in particular they see it as performing an explanatory unification at the highest theoretical level. This is and has been since the Scientific Revolution part of the work of metaphysics. So to take a straightforward example, one might genuinely regard the metaphysical theory of Perdurantism,[12] perhaps enhanced by stage theory, as a good example of an attempt to unify the large scale picture of the four-dimensional block universe of Minkowski Space-Time in Relativity with ordinary facts about objects and how they change in our experience as codified in common sense theories. The Minkowski model of Relativity theory could be treated independently of theories about ordinary objects which change and age, but it is clearly helpful if an explanatory unification can take place and explain how we can have a unified account of both. Similarly, one might recall Seventeenth and Eighteenth Century struggles with the concept of matter, which sought to find a metaphysical concept of matter which could marry the concept of substance as a carrier for the primary qualities of matter as exhibited in mechanics, for example those of mass, inertia, impenetrability, and *vis-viva*, to the other extraordinary property of matter, that is its response to the gravitational field and all that this apparently implied about action at a distance. So fulfilling a unifying explanatory purpose has always been part of the metaphysics of science—certainly not the only part, for it has also provided a general conceptual framework in which specific exact scientific theories with empirical content may be developed. Popper, I think, gives an excellent example of this study of the Darwinian revolution subsequent to the publication of the *Origin of Species* in 1859.[13]

Now Ross and Ladyman themselves lay down a constraint on metaphysical hypotheses which they label the Principle of Naturalistic Closure (PNC): this, modulo some technical stipulations, says:

> Any new metaphysical theory that is to be taken seriously at time t should be motivated by, and only by, the service it would perform, if true, in showing how two or more specific scientific hypotheses,

---

[12]See, for example, Hawley (2001)

[13]See for example his illuminating paper Popper (1985)

at least one of which is drawn from fundamental physics, jointly explain more than the sum of what is explained by the two hypotheses taken separately, [...] (Ladyman et al., 2007, p. 37).

Given this view about the role of metaphysics embodied in the PNC, they argue for a positive and a negative thesis. They assert that:

> *The single most important idea we are promoting in this book is that to take the conventional philosophical model of an individual as being equivalent to the model of an existent mistakes practical convenience for metaphysical generalisation.* We can understand what individuals are by reference to the properties of real patterns. Attempting to do the opposite as in most historical (Western) metaphysical projects produces profound confusion. (Witness the debates about identity over time, identity over change in parts, and vagueness none of which are PNC-compatibly motivated problems.) (Ladyman et al., 2007, p. 229, their emphasis).

So they use the PNC to dismiss some, if not all, of contemporary metaphysics. This seems to me grossly unfair since much of modern metaphysics, as remarked above, has been motivated by an attempt to bring a consistency proof forward for common sense views and fundamental physics (thereby surely satisfying the PNC). But I shall not dwell upon this point. Rather let us turn to their positive ontic structuralist thesis. That is the claim that all that exists is structure or patterns, all the way down. Though they never quite spell out what they mean by this view, it is clear that they are committed to a Reductionist view that objects, atoms, molecules, quarks and tables and chairs are to be thought of as "bundles" of structural universals.

Now it seems to me evident that, whatever form of structuralism is involved, the view cannot provide an answer to the pessimistic induction argument, which after all is a fundamental issue in the realist instrumentalist debate. For where before we had revolution in underlying ontology through scientific revolutions (that observation from the history of scientific theory is what gave rise to the pessimistic induction), we now have revolutions in structure. If there was a dramatic change in ontology from say the substance of heat, phlogiston, to the kinetic energy of molecules in the transition from early theories of heat and of Carnot's thermodynamics to Late Nineteenth Century thermodynamics, then how is continuity to be restored by appeal to a transition from the structure of a continuous media subject to a conservation law over cycles to a structure of discrete moving particles governed by rectilinear motion except at collision? Mathematical structure can change discontinuously just as traditional ontology can. So where is the advantage in this talk of structures?

But there is, I think, an even more serious objection, one that Russell made long ago. The objection is that the doctrine simply isn't coherent, if it is globalised so that everything is structure. Ladyman and Ross espouse the semantic view of theories; they wish to use all the techniques of model theory, domains, isomorphisms and embeddings *etc.* to formulate and analyse the structural relations postulated by empirical theories. But they understand objects in a domain merely by the relational nexus in which they take part; objects are certain "higher order" relations holding among relations on the domain. But then, which relations hold on the domain will depend upon the objects in the domain, but this in turn depends upon which relations hold on the domain. I submit that this is viciously circular, not in the sense of understanding or definability alone, but in the ontological sense.

Now there is no doubt that we can ascribe properties and relations to relations. We can say correctly that the relation 'less than or equal to' is antisymmetric, or that the successor relation is one-one, or that the relation of isomorphism is part of the relation of ordinal similarity as is the property of being order preserving. But if all science does is speak of the relations holding among or of relations, it is perfectly consistent with the world being empty.[14] We are not given a coherent account of how the World can be unless some of the relata are individuals, but then structure can't be everything that there is.

## 4    The Modest Defence of Scientific Structural Realism

Let us now turn to the much more modest and reasonable defence of Scientific Realism proposed by Worrall and Zahar. What is it that they are defending, and why does it require a defence at all? They are defending the claim of Scientific Realism which they, I think entirely rightly, characterise as a combination of a metaphysical claim and an epistemological one. The metaphysical claim asserts that there is a mind independent reality of which scientific theories attempt to give true descriptions, and the epistemological thesis asserts that not only is this reality partially accessible to human discovery, but also that "it is reasonable to believe that the successful theories of mature science the unified theories that explain the phenomena without ad hoc assumptions have indeed latched on, in some no doubt partial and approximate way, to that structured reality, that they are, if you like, approximately true."[15]

One standard realist defence against the pessimistic induction, the no-miracles argument, is manifestly invalid. This very well known argument of Putnam and Boyd says that, if we do not grant some notion of approximate truth to successive theories, then the explanatory success of science at the empirical predictive level would be a miracle.[16] It would be a matter of the remotest chance, the remotest coincidence. But the invalidity of this argument is clear, since it hinges upon what we take the prior likelihood of a false theory having a true and interesting consequence as being. It is only on the very specific assumption that the prior likelihood of that is incredibly low, that the argument has the slightest force. After all, any sequence of events can seem miraculous if one chooses a sufficiently low prior probability for outcomes of the required kind.[17]

---

[14]Van Fraassen makes a closely related point. He puts the matter forcefully as follows: "if structure is not just there as mathematical or abstract entity, then it is not true that structure is all there is." van Fraassen (2006). This really is the core of Russell's criticism: the claim that everything is structure is self-refuting since, if these structures are concrete, why are they not individuals? Clearly they are.

[15]Worrall (2007).

[16]Putnam (1975); and Boyd (1984).

[17]See particularly Howson (2000, especially, pp. 35–60).

Indeed, further it is a requirement of the practice of science that the predictive successes of earlier theories are carried over into succeeding theories as a necessary condition for the *adequacy* of those theories. The once much vaunted problem of "Kuhn loss," as it was called, turned out to be a myth.[18] The key idea in the structuralist defence of scientific realism is really contained in what is sometimes called the "correspondence principle." This is the claim that, if we look at the history of major scientific revolutions, then an adequacy condition on succeeding theories is that they yield the predecessor theory as a limiting case. The classic example of this is special relativity and Newtonian mechanics, where the Lorentz transformations of the former yield the Galilean transformations of the latter when the velocities considered are small with respect to that of light, and where the dynamical laws of the former yield as a limit the Newtonian Second Law when again the velocities are small to respect to that of light.

Now the key claim in general of Worrall's and Zahar's position is that there is a strong notion of continuity which can be extracted from the history of theory change in science. It is continuity at the mathematical structural level, not at the ontological level.[19] As Worrall puts it:

> According to the account of theory change that underpins SSR [Structural Scientific Realism], successive theories in science have not only been successively more empirically adequate, but there has always been a *reason*, when viewed from the vantage point of the later theory, *why* the earlier theory achieved the degree of empirical adequacy that it did namely that the earlier theory continues to look approximately structurally correct: its mathematical equations are retained modulo the correspondence principle (Worrall, 2007, especially, p. 143).

This seems to me to be a modest historical thesis, which one might well accept. The difficulty is however that it comes embedded with another claim, which seems to me to be completely fallacious as an account of theoretical knowledge in science. This claim is the view that a theory's full cognitive content is captured by its Ramsey Sentence, where the Ramsey sentence of a given theory $T$, results from $T$ by replacing all the theoretical predicates occurring in $T$ by second order variables and then existentially quantifying over them. So if $T$ is an empirical theory with a theoretical vocabulary

---

[18]Kuhn loss was the supposed historical phenomenon that the explanatory successes of earlier theories at the level of successful predictions would fail to be captured by the succeeding theories.

[19]Van Fraassen in an excellent recent reply to structuralism (van Fraassen, 2006, pp. 275–307) gives a nice example of how observations reveal the structure of the phenomena behind them without revealing the qualities and inner nature of that hidden reality. His example is based on one provided by Russell in his *Problems of Philosophy* (1959). Van Fraassen writes: "Listen to the radio, and hear the sounds which were produced in the studio many miles away. In between are the radio waves which have none of the qualities of sound. But we can infer that they must have structure which encodes the structure of this sound. Thus we know a great deal about those radio waves on the basis of observation: not what qualities they have or what they are like in themselves, but their structure. And it's precisely that, and only that, which science describes (as it happens of course what Maxwell's equations describe)," (van Fraassen, 2006, p. 289).

$\Theta_1, \ldots, \Theta_n$ and with observational vocabulary $O_1, \ldots, O_k$ , then expressing $T$ as $T(\Theta_1, \ldots, \Theta_n, O_1, \ldots, O_k)$ the Ramsey sentence of $T$, denoted by $R(T)$, is the claim $\exists \Pi_1, \ldots, \exists \Pi_n\ T(\Pi_1, \ldots, \Pi_n, O_1, \ldots, O_k)$. As is very well known $T$ and $R(T)$ have exactly the same observational consequences.[20] Now why is it the case that Structural realists want to identify the cognitive content of $T$ with $R(T)$? The answer is because $R(T)$ says there are certain attributes $\Pi_1, \ldots, \Pi_n$, whose relational structure is exhibited by $R(T)$, and that that structure imposes exactly the content on the observations that $T$ does (recall that $T$ and $R(T)$ are observationally equivalent). So $R(T)$ exhibits the structural constraints that $T$ imposes on the observations.

There is however a real difficulty with this view. It is the old problem pointed out by the topologist Max Newman when criticising Russell's version of structural realism (as developed in his *Analysis of Matter*, and that based upon his distinction between knowledge by acquaintance and knowledge by description).[21] This objection has been recently greatly elaborated upon by Michael Friedman and William Demopoulos.[22] I will concentrate on Demopoulos' most recent elaboration of Newman's argument, for I think his argument is very telling.[23] Essentially, the argument boils down to a model theoretic argument of the following sort. Take a model, call it **M** in which all of the purely $O$ sentences of $T$ hold; then, provided the cardinality of **M** is sufficiently great, it can be expanded to a model **M\*** in which of course the $O$ sentences are satisfied, but in which all of the existential claims of $T(R)$ are also satisfied. This follows because of the richness of the set of subsets of the domain of **M**. It is always possible, provided the domain of **M** is sufficiently large, to find subsets of the domain which will satisfy the existential claims of $T(R)$ exhibited above.[24] What this means then is that if $T$ is consistent, all that $T(R)$ expresses is a cardinality claim on the Universe, which is manifestly not what the theoretical claims of empirical science do. This result also holds if we do not, in forming the Ramsey sentence of the theory, allow for existential quantification over so-called mixed terms, that is those terms which apply both to theoretical and observational entities. So it cannot be right to identify the cognitive content of $T$ with $T(R)$, which is what the structural realist insists we should do. This clearly presents a dilemma for the structuralist realist. Either identify the cognitive content of $T$ with $T(R)$, with resulting trivialization, or do not; but then, what is to constitute the structural content of an empirical theory

---

[20] The proof is straightforward. If an observation sentence $O$ is not a consequence of $T$, then some interpretation $I$ of $T$ satisfies $T$ but fails to satisfy $O$. But then that same interpretation will satisfy $R(T)$, since $R(T)$ is merely an existential generalisation of some predicates in $T$ but will fail to satisfy $O$. So if $O$ is a consequence of $R(T)$, then it must be a consequence of $T$ by contraposition. Similarly, if $O$ is not a consequence of $R(T)$, then some interpretation of the existentially generalised predicates of $T$ satisfies $R(T)$ but fails to satisfy $O$. Precisely that interpretation of the predicates of $T$ will then provide an interpretation of $T$ itself which satisfies $T$ but fails to satisfy $O$. Hence, by contraposition, if $O$ is a consequence of $T$, $O$ consequence of $R(T)$. So as far as $O$ consequences are concerned, $T$ and $R(T)$ are equivalent.

[21] Cf. Newman (1928).

[22] See particularly Demopoulos and Friedman (1985); Demopoulos (2003a). Cf. Demopoulos (2003b, 2007).

[23] Cf. Demopoulos (2008). See also Ketland (2004); Cruse (2005b,a).

[24] For proofs see Ketland (2004). The background model theory is explained in van Dalen (1983).

$T$? So despite their claims, nothing is gained by the structuralist account of theoretical knowledge either methodologically or ontologically, and the debate between the realist and the constructive empiricist over the interpretation of theoretical knowledge is left unresolved, by this move at least.

# BIBLIOGRAPHY

Benacerraf, P. (1965). What numbers could not be. *Philosophical Review*, 74:47–73.

Boyd, R. (1984). The current status of scientific realism. In Leplin, J., editor, *Scientific Realism*, pages 41–82. University of California Press, Berkeley.

Cruse, P. (2005a). Empiricism and Ramsey's account of theories. In Lillehammer, H. and Mellor, H., editors, *Ramsey's Legacy*, pages 105–122. Oxford University Press, Oxford.

Cruse, P. (2005b). Ramsey sentences, structural realism and trivial realization. *Studies in History and Philosophy of Science*, 36:557–576.

Dedekind, R. (1963). *Was sind und was sollen die Zahlen?; The Nature of Meaning of Numbers*. Edited by Wooster Woodruff Beman. Dover Publications, New York.

Demopoulos, W. (2003a). On the rational reconstruction of our theoretical knowledge. *British Journal for the Philosophy of Science*, 54:371–403.

Demopoulos, W. (2003b). Russell's structuralism and the absolute description of the world. In Griffin, N., editor, *Cambridge Companion to Russell*, pages 392–419. Cambridge University Press, Cambridge.

Demopoulos, W. (2007). Carnap on the rational reconstruction of scientific theories. In Friedman, M. and Creath, R., editors, *Cambridge Companion to Russell*, pages 248–272. Cambridge University Press, Cambridge.

Demopoulos, W. (2008). Some remarks on the bearing of model theory on the theory of theories. *Interpolations: Essays in Honor of William Craig, special edition Synthese*, 164:359–384.

Demopoulos, W. and Friedman, M. (1985). Russell's analysis of matter: Its historical context and contemporary interest. *Philosophy of Science*, 52:621–639.

Ertl, G. (2008). The nobel prizes 2007. In Grandin, K., editor, *Reactions at Surfaces: From Atoms to Complexity*, pages 116–139. Nobel Foundation, Stockholm.

Hawley, K. (2001). *How Things Persist*. Oxford University Press, Oxford.

Hellman, G. (1996). Structuralism without structures. *Philosophia Mathematica*, 4(3):100–123.

Howson, C. (2000). *Hume's Problem: Induction and the Justification of Belief*. Oxford University Press, Oxford.

Jardine, N. (1984). *The Birth of the History and Philosophy of Science*. Cambridge University Press, Cambridge.

Ketland, J. (2004). Empirical adequacy and ramsification. *British Journal for the Philosophy of Science*, 55:287–300.

Ladyman, J., Ross, D., Spurrett, D., and Collier, J. (2007). *Every Thing Must Go: Methaphysics Naturalized*. Oxford University Press, Oxford.

Newman, M. H. A. (1928). Mr. Russell's causal theory of perception. *Mind*, 37(146):137–148.

Perrin, J. (1910). *Brownian Movement and Molecular Reality*. Translated by F. Soddy. Taylor and Francis, London.

Perrin, J. (1916). *Atoms*. Translated by D. Hammick from the eleventh edition of Perrin, J. Constable, London.

Popper, K. R. (1985). Natural selection and its scientific status. In Miller, D., editor, *Popper Selections*, pages 239–246. Princeton University Press, Princeton NJ.

Putnam, H. (1975). What is mathematical truth? In *Mathematics, Matter and Method. Philosophical Papers*, volume 1. Cambridge University Press, Cambridge.

Resnik, M. D. (1988). Mathematics from the structural point of view. *Revue Internationale de Philosophie*, 42:400–424.

Russell, B. A. W. (1903). *The Principles of Mathematics*. Allen and Unwin, London. 2nd editition 1937.

Russell, B. A. W. (1912/1959). *Problems of Philosophy*. Clarendon Press, Oxford. Reprinted in 1959.

Russell, B. A. W. (1927). *The Analysis of Matter*. Kegan Paul, London. Reprinted in Dover Books, New York, 1954.

Shapiro, S. (2000). *Philosophy of Mathematics, Structure and Ontology*. Oxford University Press, New York.

Treier, M., Fasel, R., Champness, N., Argent, S., and Richardson, N. (2009a). Molecular imaging of polyimide formation. *Physical Chemistry Chemical Physics*, 11(8):1209–1214.

Treier, M., Richardson, N., Nguyen, M.-T., Pignedoli, C., Passerone, D., and Fasel, R. (2009b). Tailoring low-dimensional organic semiconductor nanostructure. *Nano Letters*, 9:126–131.

van Dalen, D. (1983). *Logic and Structure*. Springer, Berlin.

van Fraassen, B. (1980). *The Scientific Image*. Oxford University Press, Oxford.

van Fraassen, B. (2006). Structure: Its shadow and substance. *British Journal for the Philosophy of Science*, 57:275–307.

Worrall, J. (1989). Structural realism: The best of both worlds. *Dialectica*, 43:99–124.

Worrall, J. (2007). Miracles and models: Why reports on the death of structural realism may be exaggerated. In O' Hear, A., editor, *Philosophy of Science*, volume 61, pages 125–154. Royal Institute of Philosophy, London.

Zahar, E. (2001). *Poincaré's Philosophy: From Conventionalism to Phenomenology*. Open Court, La Salle, IL.

# Can Logical Consequence Be Deflated?

MICHAEL DE[†] [‡]

## 1   Introduction

Deflationism about truth is the view that truth is not a substantive property, *e.g.* it does not make for genuine similarity. Two truth-bearers (say, sentences) may be true without being similar or without reflecting any similarity in their subject matter or the world. Such is the case with 'Roses are red' and 'Two succeeds one': there just doesn't seem to be much in common between numbers and the successor relation and roses and redness, nor between whatever natural relations might hold between these two pairs. There is, moreover, a certain equivalence (analytic or otherwise) between asserting, believing, etc. that a sentence is true and asserting, believing, etc. the sentence itself. This equivalence suggests that truth (or the truth predicate) plays a merely expressive role and lends further support to deflationism about truth; for any notion employed for mere expressive purposes seems not to mark out any substantive feature of the world.

An interesting question is whether deflationism about truth (and falsity) extends to related properties and relations on truthbearers. Lionel Shapiro (Shapiro, 2011) answers affirmatively by arguing that a certain deflationism about truth is as plausible as an analogous version of deflationism about logical consequence. I'll call this the *equi-plausibility thesis*. If correct, logical consequence does not count as a substantive relation and instances of valid arguments need not share any substantive property, such as having a special logical form or necessarily preserving truth (assuming these properties substantive). The equi-plausibility thesis is striking, for whereas deflationism about truth is highly compelling, deflationism about logical consequence seems far less plausible. There is good reason to think that logically valid arguments do share a substantive property, such as holding in virtue of the meaning of the logical constants or necessarily preserving truth in virtue of form alone. The equi-plausibility thesis, then, constitutes an important claim deserving of careful consideration.

After presenting Shapiro's arguments for the analogy between a certain brand of deflationism about truth and about logical consequence, I argue that the argument fails on two counts. First, it trivializes to any relation between

[†]Utrecht University, Department of Philosophy, Utrecht, Netherlands. Email: mikejde@gmail.com.

[‡]Many thanks to the Foundations of Logic Consequence project in the Arché Research Centre, University of St Andrews for stimulating feedback on a first draft of this paper. This research was funded by the European Research Council under the European Community's Seventh Framework Programme (FP7/2007-2013) / ERC Grant agreement nr 263227.

truthbearers (which I'll assume for concreteness and neutrality are sentences), including substantive ones; in other words, his argument can be used to establish that deflationism about truth is as plausible as deflationism about an arbitrary sentential relation. Second, the alleged analogy between the arguments for deflationism about truth and deflationism about consequence fails. Along the way I consider what implications the failure of the equi-plausibility thesis has for deflationism about falsity.

## 2   Mere Expressive Device Deflationism

The precise formulation of deflationism that is the target of Shapiro's argument he calls *mere expressive device deflationism*, which I'll abbreviate as MEDD.[1] MEDD about truth claims that the primary role of the truth predicate is merely expressive and that the rules which underwrite this expressive role give us no reason to believe that truth is a substantive property, so we should not think truth is a substantive property.

The view is inspired by remarks of Quine on the role of the truth predicate, in particular that it allows for the expression (by finite means) of generalizations over infinitely many sentences.[2] For instance, letting $\phi_1, \phi_2, \ldots$ be an enumeration of the sentences of Peano arithmetic, one may express the infinite disjunction of sentences:

- $\phi_1$ is true (in the standard model) but not provable in Peano arithmetic;

- $\phi_2$ is true (in the standard model) but not provable in Peano arithmetic;

- ...

by the sentence

- Not every sentence true (in the standard model) is provable in Peano arithmetic.

MEDD about truth holds that the expressive role the truth predicate has is underwritten by a pair of inferential rules that equate each sentence with the statement that the sentence is true:

$$\text{T-Intro} \; \frac{p}{\text{`}p\text{' is true}} \qquad\qquad \text{T-Elim} \; \frac{\text{`}p\text{' is true}}{p}$$

Not enough has been said yet to determine whether the T-rules *alone* suffice to underwrite the expressive role of the truth predicate. That role may require that the truth predicate be *transparent* in the sense that '$p$' and the statement that $p$ is true are intersubstitutable *salva veritate* in appropriate contexts, and this will depend further on the underlying logic. While taking note of this complication, Shapiro builds into the argument for MEDD about truth the

---

[1] Shapiro abbreviates it as 'MED deflationism'.

[2] There are, of course, other secondary expressive roles the truth predicate has. *e.g.* it allows one to indirectly agree with what someone has uttered, as in 'Everything Sam uttered is true', without knowing precisely what that person has uttered.

assumption that the T-rules are sufficient to underwrite its expressive role. This is not an innocent assumption since it bears on the plausibility of MEDD about truth and hence on the significance of the "equi-plausibility" thesis. For if MEDD about truth turns out an implausible form of deflationism, the equi-plausibility thesis loses its significance. The reason the assumption lacks innocence is that MEDD about truth is much more plausible when it is assumed that the T-rules alone are sufficient to underwrite the expressive role of the truth predicate. The need for any additional rules brings into doubt (T3) (see below) of the argument for MEDD about truth, so the T-rules alone ought to be enough to give the truth predicate its primary expressive role. Whether they are in fact strong enough depends further on how strongly they are interpreted (as *e.g.* analytic or strict implications), an issue which resurfaces in §4.

## 2.1   The arguments for MEDD about truth and consequence

Now that we have seen the underlying motivation for MEDD about truth, we come to Shapiro's formulation of an argument for the thesis, which I reproduce in full.

**T1.** If it were not for the need to express a certain kind of generality, we would have no need for the predicate 'is true'. Instead of predicating 'is true' of a sentence, we could employ the sentence itself.

**T2.** To explain how 'is true' allows us to express the kind of generality in question, we need only make use of the predicate's logical features, namely, the T-rules.

**T3.** There is no reason to think that the T-rules require 'is true' to express a property whose nature is amenable to substantive characterization.

**T4.** From (T1), (T2) and (T3), it follows that there is no reason to think that in order to understand how 'is true' serves the function that is its raison d'être, we must take this predicate to express a property whose nature is amenable to substantive characterization.

**T5.** Hence we have no reason to hold that 'is true' expresses a property whose nature is amenable to substantive characterization.

Premise (T3) needs to be flagged as an important but mysterious premise. For it is not clear what it would take for a pair of inferential rules to give us reason to think that a property they refer to *is* substantive. Similarly, exactly what features of the T-rules give us no reason to think that the truth predicate picks out a substantive property? Is it that they seem to allow truth to be explained away? This cannot be so, since it is important that MEDD about truth not entail the claim that truth can be explained away. If the entailment went through, as we will see, it would show that MEDD about truth and consequence are not analogous after all. For the rules which underwrite the main role of the consequence predicate certainly do not lead us to think that consequence can be explained away. It is not clear then what it is about the T-rules that justify (T3) nor whether these features are had by the C-rules (below) which underwrite the expressive role of the consequence predicate. If the C-rules lack these features, the analogy between the arguments for MEDD about truth and about consequence fails.

It is crucial for MEDD about truth that the T-rules be read in such a way that they at least preserve truth rather than, say, mere warranted assertibility (or weaker properties in the vicinity) for the following reason. It is possible that we use sentences to convey, not the truth of what they express, but rather the falsity of what they express. We might also use sentences to convey that what they express is true on a certain hypothesis. Indeed, we could use them any way we like and it is a contingent fact about us as language users that we typically use sentences to convey their truth. Now suppose a linguistic community, say the Samsons, used sentences in such a way that a sincere utterance of '$p$' conveyed that $p$ is believed by some person, Sam.[3] Then the main role of the predicate 'is believed by Sam' would (for the Samsons) be merely expressive in the sense that an utterance of ' '$p$' is believed by Sam' would convey precisely the same thing as an utterance of '$p$'. This equivalence would be underwritten by the following rules structurally identical to the T-rules:

$$\text{Sam-Intro} \ \frac{p}{\text{'$p$' is believed by Sam}} \qquad \text{Sam-Elim} \ \frac{\text{'$p$' is believed by Sam}}{p}$$

But importantly, *the Sam-rules do not preserve truth.* Rather they preserve some notion of being correct to utter: if it is correct for a Samson to utter '$p$' then it is correct for her to utter ' '$p$' is believed by Sam', and conversely. This crucial disanalogy between the T-rules and the Sam-rules prevents the Samsons from running an argument for MEDD about the property of being believed by Sam (which invokes the Sam-rules) that is parallel to the one for MEDD about truth.

By now, one may have anticipated how the argument for MEDD about logical consequence runs. It essentially replaces the T-rules in the argument for MEDD about truth by the following C-rules, making obvious changes elsewhere:

$$\text{C-Intro.} \ \frac{\text{That $p$ entails that $q$}}{\text{'$p$' has '$q$' as consequence}} \qquad \text{C-Elim.} \ \frac{\text{'$p$' has '$q$' as consequence}}{\text{That $p$ entails that $q$}}$$

These rules are assumed to underwrite the expressive role of the consequence predicate. Here is the argument for MEDD about consequence in full.

**C1.** If it were not for the need to express a certain kind of generality, we would have no need for the predicate 'is a consequence of'. In place of '$s_2$ is a logical consequence of $s_1$', we could employ sentences $s_1$ and $s_2$ themselves, joined by a suitable sentential connective.

**C2.** To explain how 'is a consequence of' allows us to express the kind of generality in question, we need only make use of the predicate's logical features, namely, the C-rules.

---

[3]The sentential variable here is to be filled with a sentence, such as 'Snow is white', rather than a name of the sentence. This explains why it occurs in quotes in the first instance.

**C3.** There is no reason to think that the C-rules require 'is a consequence of' to express a property whose nature is amenable to substantive characterization.

**C4.** From (C1), (C2) and (C3), it follows that there is no reason to think that in order to understand how 'is a consequence of' serves the function that is its raison d'être, we must take this predicate to express a property whose nature is amenable to substantive characterization.

**C5.** Hence we have no reason to hold that 'is a consequence of' expresses a property whose nature is amenable to substantive characterization.

Note that the unwritten assumption that the main role of the consequence predicate is merely expressive is much more contentious than it is for the truth predicate. Locutions of the form ' '$q$' follows from '$p$' ' are much more natural than those of the form 'That $p$ entails that $q$' which suggests that the connective- rather than predicate-involving locutions play a merely expressive role. The same is not true for truth: an utterance of $p$ is almost always more natural than an utterance of ' '$p$' is true', suggesting that the latter are only used in special circumstances, *e.g.* in making generalizations. This already marks a disanalogy between (the arguments for) MEDD about truth and consequence, but those discussed in §4 are far more worrying for the equi-plausibility thesis.

## 3   Trivializing the Equi-plausibility Thesis

Consider the following rules:

$$\text{Jan-Intro.} \quad \frac{\text{It is believed by Jan that } p}{\text{'}p\text{' is believed by Jan}}$$

$$\text{Jan-Elim.} \quad \frac{\text{'}p\text{' is believed by Jan}}{\text{It is believed by Jan that } p}$$

The Jan-rules necessarily preserve truth (unlike the Sam-rules, recall). Moreover, they have the same form as the C-rules: the predicate-involving statement is interchangeable with the connective-involving statement. Making suitable changes in the argument for MEDD about consequence, do we obtain an analogous argument for MEDD about the sentential—*and clearly substantive*—property of being believed by Jan? Not quite. One key premise of MEDD about consequence is that the primary role of the consequence predicate is expressive. The premise may be objectionable, but certainly not to the extent that its analog for MEDD about being believed by Jan is—there just is no reason to think that the primary role of 'is believed by Jan' is expressive. So there is yet no completely analogous argument for MEDD about being believed by Jan, at last not one involving the Jan-rules.

However, suppose we introduce a predicate which is *by stipulation* both extensionally identical to 'is believed by Jan' and whose primary role is expressive; call it 'is Janned'. We may, moreover, stipulate that its expressive role is underwritten by the following pair of rules:

$$\text{Janned-Intro} \quad \frac{\text{It is believed by Jan that } p}{\text{`}p\text{' is Janned}}$$

$$\text{Janned-Elim} \quad \frac{\text{`}p\text{' is Janned}}{\text{It is believed by Jan that } p}$$

There is now an argument for MEDD about *being believed by Jan* which completely parallels the one for MEDD about consequence. We have a predicate, 'is Janned' whose primary role is expressive and underwritten by a pair of truth-preserving rules that provide just as much reason as the C-rules (*i.e.* none, according to the argument) for thinking that the property they involve is substantive.

Indeed, we may rerun a parallel strategy for *any* sentential relation for which we can introduce a corresponding predicate. In other words, *the equi-plausibility thesis trivializes.* Since some sentential relations are substantive, either the analogy between MEDD about truth and other relations fails or there is already something wrong with MEDD about truth itself. Since MEDD seems a plausible deflationist position, the problem is likely to be located in the analogy.

Trivializing MEDD will require in certain cases introducing both a predicate and a corresponding sentential connective used in formulating the rules which underwrite the expressive role of the predicate. In the case of Jan's beliefs, we needed only to introduce a predicate whose primary role—it was stipulated—is expressive and, moreover, underwritten by the Janned-rules. The corresponding sentential connective, 'it is believed by Jan that' already exists in English, so we did not need to introduce it alongside 'is Janned'.

In general, let $R$ be any $n$-place *sentential* relation. Then the following three claims, which are enough to show that the equi-plausibility thesis trivializes, are all highly plausible:

1. we can introduce an $n$-place predicate '$s_1, \ldots, s_n$ stand in $R$' denoting $R$ and a corresponding $n$-place sentential connective $\mathcal{R}(s_1, \ldots, s_n)$ expressing that $s_1, \ldots, s_n$ stand in $R$;

2. the primary role of '$s_1, \ldots, s_n$ stand in $R$' is (perhaps by stipulation) expressive;

3. the expressive role of '$s_1, \ldots, s_n$ stand in $R$' is (perhaps by stipulation) underwritten by the pair of rules:

$$R\text{-Intro} \quad \frac{\mathcal{R}(s_1, \ldots, s_n)}{\text{`}s_1, \ldots, s_n \text{ stand in } R\text{'}} \qquad R\text{-Elim} \quad \frac{\text{`}s_1, \ldots, s_n \text{ stand in } R\text{'}}{\mathcal{R}(s_1, \ldots, s_n)}$$

An equi-plausibility claim concerning MEDD about truth and $R$ follows straight-forwardly.

How might an MEDD deflationist respond to this trivializing argument? First, they might demand that 'suitable sentential connective', as it occurs in premise (C1), requires that the connective already exist in natural language. There are two problems with this response. One is that it appears to block the argument for MEDD about consequence itself since likely there is no connective 'entails' in any natural language, let alone English, that exactly corresponds with any philosopher's sense of logical entailment. Two, while the response blocks MEDD from trivializing, it does not block the equi-plausibility of MEDD about *being believed by Jan* and MEDD about consequence and truth since 'is believed by Jan that' already exists in natural language. So while this response blocks the equi-plausibility thesis from trivializing, we still have the equi-plausibility of MEDD about a deflationary-looking notion like truth with MEDD about a substantive notion like *being believed by Jan* which is bad enough to undermine Shapiro's argument.

Second, one might respond to the trivializing argument by claiming that only properties expressible by predicates characterizable by inferential rules are admissible in MEDD arguments. For the fact that the expressive role of the truth (and consequence) predicate is claimed to be underwritten by such rules is essential to the argument for MEDD about truth (and consequence). The thought would be that MEDD about such properites look equally plausible because these notions, being characterizable by inferential rules, appear to be (broadly) logical and deflatable. (Indeed, most deflationists think of truth as logical.)

Consider the property *being believed by Jan*. It doesn't appear to be char-acterizable by inferential rules in the sense that there is a predicate expressing the property that is characterized by inferential rules. But indeed it is: it is characterized, among many others, by the Jan- and Janned-rules! Indeed, for any sentential relation for which we introduce (by stipulation, say) a predicate and a corresponding connective, we get rules characterizing the relation for free.

One might deny that such rules need not genuinely characterize a sentential relation. The problem now is that whatever genuine characterizability amounts to, I do not see how it can rule out *being believed by Jan* as being characterized by the Jan- or Janned-rules without also ruling out logical consequence (and perhaps truth even) from being ruled out as being characterized by the C-rules (T-rules in the case of truth). The rules are exactly analogous, equating state-ments involving a sentential operator with corresponding statements involving a sentential predicate.

Moreover, if logical consequence is not ruled out on the grounds of being an inferentialist-friendly logical notion, then it looks like the sort of deflationism involved no longer has anything to do with *mere expressive device* deflationism. Rather, the deflationist position now appears to be that consequence is deflat-able *in virtue of being* an inferentialist-friendly logical notion. So maintaining that only inferentialist-friendly notions yield plausible MEDD arguments cannot save the equi-plausibility thesis from trivializing.

The upshot is that MEDD about any sentential relation is as plausible about MEDD about consequence. For any sentential relation we can introduce a predicate and corresponding sentential connective expressing the relation such that the main role of the predicate is both expressive and underwritten by a pair of rules completely parallel to the C-rules. Since there are substantive and non-substantive sentential relations, there must be something wrong with the argument from MEDD about consequence. It simply isn't true that *all* sentential relations are equally plausibly deflatable. The problem with the argument, I shall now argue, is that the analogy fails.

## 4    The Disanalogy Between Truth and Consequence

There are two crucial points of disanology in the arguments for MEDD about truth and consequence: the first concerns the third premises (T3) and (C3) and the second the T- and C-rules. Recall that (T3) claims that the T-rules give us no reason to think that the truth predicate picks out a substantive property. What justifies this premise? One thought is that the T-rules allow the elimination of all traces of reference to truth (in suitable contexts, *e.g. not* in generalizations, self-reference and indirect agreement). Clearly the C-rules do not allow the elimination of reference to logical consequence in similarly suitable contexts since they allow only the swapping of the consequence predicate with the entailment connective, where each refers in different ways to logical consequence. Recall, however, that this point about eliminability does not mark out a relevant disanalogy according to Shapiro because, unlike certain other brands of deflationism, it is not part of MEDD about consequence or truth that consequence or truth be in any sense eliminable.[4]

Yet there *is* something less plausible about (C3) when compared with (T3). What is it about the C-rules that gives us no reason to think that the consequence predicate picks out a substantive property? It cannot be anything about the eliminability of the notion of logical consequence, since there is no such eliminability. And it cannot be the mere fact that the C-rules underwrite the expressive role of the consequence predicate, for then the Janned-rules would equally give us no reason to think that 'is Janned' picks out a substantive property. Indeed, there isn't much reason to think (C3) is true, not even if one holds MEDD about truth. On the other hand (T3) has independent plausibility from the fact *e.g.* that the T-rules permit the eliminability of reference to truth (in suitable contexts) even if that eliminability is not supposed to be part and parcel of MEDD about truth. Why else would (T3) be plausible? (Recall that if (T3) isn't plausible, neither is MEDD about truth, and thus the equi-plausibility thesis loses any import.)

The second point of disanalogy concerns the interpretation of the C-rules. It is crucial to the argument for MEDD about consequence that the C-rules be read so that in each the conclusion *logically follows from* the premise. If they are read as anything weaker than strict implications they will fail to secure transparency

---

[4]The primarily expressive function of the truth predicate implies that reference to truth, outside of certain expressive purposes, *is* eliminable. When the truth predicate isn't playing its expressive role, reference to truth will be eliminable. In an important sense, then, the eliminability of reference to truth *is* part of MEDD about truth.

in the contexts required for the expressive role of the consequence predicate to be underwritten by them (*i.e.* the C-rules). In fact, transparency may even require that they be read as strictly stronger than strict implications—indeed, as logical entailments.

There are still other reasons (besides those concerning transparency) that suggest the C-rules need to be read as logical entailments. For if they are read so that the premise *merely* strictly implies the conclusion, the failure of the rules to preserve truth in all logically possible circumstances brings (C3) into doubt. The fact that the rules do not apply generally suggests that there is a substantive feature of logical consequence that explains precisely the cases under which the C-rules fail and those under which they hold. Why else would the rules necessarily—in the merely alethic rather than logical sense— preserve truth? It is not clear any answer could be given without positing consequence to be a substantive property. It follows that the plausibility of the argument for MEDD about consequence requires that the C-rules be taken as logical entailments.

But this need to read the C-rules as logical entailments introduces a circularity into the argument for MEDD about consequence that is not present in the case of truth. The circularity is this. The C-rules are to suggest that the consequence predicate picks out no substantive property. However, this is only plausible if the rules themselves do not essentially invoke the very relation they suggest is not a substantive property. Shapiro may not think eliminability is part of MEDD, but if (contra Shapiro) it must be (because the plausibility of third premises of MEDD arguments hinges on it) then there is a sense in which reference to consequence can never be eliminated in the argument for MEDD about consequence—for the C-rules themselves must be regarded as logical entailments.

Notice that some of these considerations apply equally to MEDD about truth: the T-rules must too be regarded as logical entailments lest the T-rules fail to secure full transparency. The difference in this case, however, is that there is no threat of circularity since entailment needn't be thought of in terms of *truth* preservation. Entailment can be spelled out in terms quite independently of any talk of preservation of *truth*, even if such spelling out implies that entailment necessarily preserve truth. The fact that the T-rules must be taken as logical entailments in the argument for MEDD about truth brings out an important difference between MEDD and other forms of deflationism which do not require the T-rules (or the corresponding T-schema) to be read in such a way. Other forms of deflationism may read the T-schema as something other than logical equivalences, such as "cognitive equivalence" and strict implication (see *e.g.* Field, 1994, and Horwich, 1998, respectively), since they do not require that the expressive role of truth be underwritten by the T-rules alone.

## 5  MEDD about Falsity

Deflationists about truth are typically also deflationists about falsity. In particular, MEDD about falsity claims that the expressive role of falsity is underwritten by the following rules:

$$\text{F-Intro} \ \frac{\text{not-}p}{\text{`}p\text{' is false}} \qquad\qquad \text{F-Elim} \ \frac{\text{`}p\text{' is false}}{\text{not-}p}$$

The F- and C-rules look exactly analogous, and this gives Shapiro a defense against certain objections to the equi-plausibility thesis. Any objection against the equi-plausibility thesis that is equally an objection against the similar, and let us assume correct, thesis concerning MEDD about truth and falsity can't be a good objection, the defense goes, at least not by the deflationists own lights. Here is one such objection that Shapiro considers to which he uses this defense. The conclusion of the argument for MEDD about consequence cannot be right since the C-rules make essential use of an entailment connective whose nature is open to "substantive enquiry" (Shapiro, 2011, p. 328). Shapiro responds to this objection by noting that the same is true concerning MEDD about falsity: the argument makes essential use of a negation connective whose nature is also open to substantive enquiry. Thus, Shapiro concludes, the objection is not convincing, assuming that MEDD about truth and falsity are on equal footing.

I agree that the objection is unconvincing but not because it equally undermines the correct thesis that MEDD about truth and falsity stand and fall together. It fails because whatever "substantive enquiry" or substantive theorizing amounts to, the fact that a property is open to substantive enquiry need not entail that the property is substantive. Surely people can substantively theorize about non-substantive properties. There is, nonetheless, an important disanalogy between the arguments for MEDD about falsity and consequence such that arguments put against the latter do not necessary carry over, *mutatis mutandis*, to the former. The disanalogy is this.

Given the usual definition of falsity as truth of negation, viz. ' '$p$' is false' iff ' 'not-$p$' is true' (where 'iff' is understood as definitional equivalence), *the F-rules are merely special cases of the corresponding T-rules.* The F-rules are simply rewritings of the following rules:

$$\text{F-Intro} \ \frac{\text{not-}p}{\text{`not-}p\text{' is true}} \qquad\qquad \text{F-Elim} \ \frac{\text{`not-}p\text{' is true}}{\text{not-}p}$$

If we interpret them as universally quantifying over all their instances, the F-rules are *logically equivalent* to the T-rules.[5] It is no wonder, then, that deflationism (including MEDD) about truth and falsity stand or fall together.

The C-rules, however, are neither special cases of, nor are they logically equivalent to, the T-rules. Suppose, like falsity, we define logical consequence in terms of truth of entailment, so that '$p$' has '$q$' as consequence iff 'that $p$ entails that $q$ is true. Then the question is whether the C-rules are, on this definition, special cases of the T-rules, suggesting—just as in the case of falsity—that truth is deflatable if and only if consequence is. It is not difficult

---

[5]This assumes a certain feature of the underlying logic, viz. that every sentence is logically equivalent to a negation. If this is contentious, the stronger point about logical equivalence (versus being a special case of the T-rules) is only meant for emphasis. It is certainly not essential to the point at hand.

to see, however, that the C-rules are not special cases of the T-rules: the consequence predicate is binary whereas the truth predicate is not.

Conversely, there is equally no hope of setting things up so that the T-rules turn out to be special cases of the C-rules. For that to be the case we would need to find a sentence '$q$' involving only '$p$', the consequence predicate and the entailment connective which implies ' '$p$' is true'. But what sentence could '$q$' be? It cannot be the obvious candidate, ' 'not-$p$' has $p$ as consequence', for truth need not be logical truth. It can be true that ' '$p$' is true' (*e.g.* ' 'Snow is white' is true') without it being true that ' 'not-$p$' has $p$ as *logical consequence*', *i.e.* that $p$ is a *logical* truth. There is therefore no reason to think that the arguments for MEDD about falsity and consequence are as similar as it might at first seem. The F-rules may appear to be exactly analogous to the C-rules but appearances here are entirely misleading.

## 6  Conclusion

While I think the equi-plausibility thesis does not in the end succeed and that on many popular conceptions of consequence the relation is indeed a substantive one, there is at least one conception of consequence that could be viewed in a deflationary spirit. That conception takes logical consequence to be the smallest relation which necessarily preserves truth from premises to conclusion, where both necessity and truth are understood in deflationary terms. A Lewisian view of necessity, for instance, might qualify as deflationary since on that view necessary truths need not mark out any metaphysically natural property.[6] But I doubt such a conception of consequence qualifies as *logical—i.e.* I doubt strict implication and logical entailment exactly coincide. Consequence has a formality aspect that strict implication lacks. Shapiro has nonetheless given us reason to explore notions besides truth and falsity that may just fit the deflationary mold.

## BIBLIOGRAPHY

Field, H. (1994). Deflationist views of meaning and content. *Mind*, 103(441):249–285.

Horwich, P. (1998). *Truth*. Clarendon Press, Oxford, 2nd edition.

Shapiro, L. (2011). Deflating logical consequence. *The Philosophical Quarterly*, 61(243):320–342.

---

[6] All sentences that are necessary truths would, of course, express the same proposition, viz. the set of all worlds. In that sense the necessary truths have a property in common, but it is far from clear that this property is a substantive (*i.e.* sufficiently natural) one.

# A Medieval Solution to the Puzzle of Empty Names

Catarina Dutilh Novaes[†]

ABSTRACT. I discuss three medieval approaches to the semantics of proper names, especially with respect to empty names, against the background of modern theories of proper names, Millianism in particular. Rather than focusing on the matter of the meaningfulness of empty names (as is done in much of the recent literature on the topic), I concentrate on the issue of whether they should count as proper names at all. The first two medieval authors to be discussed are William of Ockham and John Buridan; the third author is a much less known figure of the beginning of the 15th century, Nicholas of Amsterdam. Despite his obscurity, Nicholas' solution to the puzzle of empty names is quite remarkable; indeed, it may even shed new light on the seemingly eternal struggle of Millianists against the challenge posed by empty names. Briefly put, Nicholas of Amsterdam offers a conditional definition of what is to count as a proper name, which is not automatically falsified in the case of non-existence of the name's bearer. I argue that Nicholas' solution to the puzzle of empty names may offer further insight as to what a Millianist solution to this puzzle that does justice to some of our basic intuitions (such as the meaningfulness and the 'proper-nameness' of empty names) might be like.

## 1 Personal Prelude

At some point in my very early days as a graduate student, as I was already working on medieval logic, I stumbled upon Stephen Read's work for the first time, and it blew me away. I thought to myself: this is what I want to do when I grow up! The combination of systematic and historical investigations, each side informing the other and making it deeper and better, was exactly the path that I wanted to pursue. Not long thereafter, in 2004, I met Stephen for the first time in St. Andrews, in a visit organized by Graham Priest (thanks, Graham!). Since then, and lucky for me, Stephen and I have had many opportunities to collaborate: he was the external reader for my PhD thesis and fulfilled his duty with much more diligence than strictly required (commenting extensively on the whole manuscript); we co-authored a paper on the Liar paradox and the fallacy secundum quid et simpliciter; he arranged for me to be a Scots Centennial Fellow in St. Andrews in 2008; I became an active and rather nosy external member of his Foundations of Logical Consequence project; we held weekly sessions of our Medieval Logic Reading Group, (thanks, the internet!);

[†]Faculty of Philosophy, University of Groningen, Groningen, The Netherlands.
Email: `c.dutilh.novaes@rug.nl`

two of my Masters students went on to become his PhD students. And these are just the main events in our regular cooperation over the years.

I can say without hesitation that there is not a single individual who contributed as much to my professional advancement as Stephen did; I do not even want to imagine what would have happened if it hadn't been for his support. Besides his philosophical acumen, his intellectual integrity and his vast knowledge of the history of logic (medieval logic in particular), what makes Stephen such a good mentor is the fact that he truly cares about people's well-being, even if this is not always immediately obvious behind his English reserve. But the mere fact that he's been putting up with this loud, pushy, overbearing Brazilian for all these years suggests that there is more than meets the eye there... I hope Stephen will continue to put up with me for many, many years to come, and I look forward to collaborating with him in all kinds of ways.

The paper below is an attempt to put in practice some of the lessons that I learned from Stephen: systematic, contemporary philosophical issues can be put in a different light if historical discussions are brought in, and historical analysis has much to benefit from a more systematic articulation of the issues in question. The topic, empty names, is not one which Stephen has done any work on (although he of course has a keen interest in medieval theories of the properties of terms), but I sincerely hope he will enjoy reading it.

## 2   Introduction

The semantics of proper names, and in particular the puzzle of empty names, has been a lively topic of discussion in the last decades; what is less well known, though, is that later Latin medieval authors shared the same pronounced interest in these issues. Given this similarity, a systematic comparison between medieval and modern discussions on proper and empty names is bound to have at least an intrinsic historical interest; but beyond that, it may even bring new insights to current debates, as I hope to show here.

In this paper, I discuss three medieval approaches to the semantics of proper names—especially but not exclusively with respect to empty names—against the background of modern theories of proper names, Millianism in particular. The first two medieval approaches to be discussed were developed by two of the most celebrated later medieval philosophers, namely William of Ockham and John Buridan (both active in the first half of the 14th century); the third approach was proposed by a much less known figure of the beginning of the 15th century, Nicholas of Amsterdam. Despite his obscurity, Nicholas' solution to the puzzle of empty names is quite remarkable. Briefly put, it offers a conditional definition of what is to count as a proper name, one which is not automatically falsified in the case of non-existence of the name's bearer. The analysis of the three medieval approaches here is not intended to be an exhaustive overview of medieval views on the puzzle of empty names; rather, my goal is systematic more than historical, and the examination of Ockham's and Buridan's positions is mostly intended to outline the originality and cleverness of Nicholas' solution against the background of some of his immediate predecessors. Moreover, a brief discussion of some recent views on the puzzle

of empty names will be offered in order to substantiate the claim that Nicholas'
solution could bring new insight to the current debate.

Thus, in the first section, I lay down the modern background for my analysis
of the medieval views to be discussed, in particular with respect to Millianism
and Russell's 1910 views on proper names. Unlike most recent discussions,
which focus on whether empty names—and more specifically on whether the
sentences in which they occur—are meaningful or not, I here focus on whether
empty names are proper names at all, *i.e.* on the issue of the demarcation of
the class of proper names. I then discuss the views of the three medieval authors just mentioned. In the conclusion, I argue that Nicholas of Amsterdam's
solution to the puzzle of empty names may offer new insight as to what a Millianist solution to this puzzle that does justice to some of our basic intuitions
(such as the meaningfulness and the 'proper-nameness' of empty names) might
look like.

# 3  Millianism and Russell on Proper Names, and Two Puzzles

The challenge posed to Millianists by the phenomenon of empty names is well
known: if the semantic content of a proper name is simply its bearer, names
with no bearers would thus have no semantic content. In other words, the
following theses appear to be incompatible:

1. Empty names are meaningful: they have semantic content

2. Empty names are indeed proper names

3. The semantic content of a proper name is solely its bearer

It seems thus that at least one of these three theses must be abandoned. One
can of course give up Millianism altogether, that is reject (3). But alternative
theories of proper names have problems of their own, so it is certainly worth
looking for a solution to the empty-name puzzle within Millianism itself—as
many have done before, usually on the basis of a rejection of (1).

Those who reject (1)[1] often acknowledge that it is indeed quite intuitive,
but then go on to argue that the intuitions of competent speakers are simply
mistaken on this particular matter: contrary to these intuitions, empty names
in fact do not have any semantic content.[2] Taking the rejection of (1) as a
starting point, a significant portion of these discussions then focuses on how
to account for the semantic and pragmatic properties of the sentences where
empty names occur. From the assumption that empty names are meaningless,
the straightforward conclusion would be that the sentences where they occur
are also meaningless, but again this seems to go against some of our fundamental intuitions concerning these sentences.[3] These sentences are usually referred

---

[1]Such as Braun (1993, 2005) and F. Adams and collaborators (Adams and Stecker, 1994;
Adams and Dietrich, 2004).

[2] "The objection claims that if ordinary speakers judge that a name is meaningful, then it
has a semantic content. This premise is incorrect: ordinary speakers judge that the names
'Vulcan' and 'Sherlock Holmes' are meaningful, even though they have no semantic content."
(Braun, 2005, p. 600).

[3]This is what Reimer (2001) refers to as 'the Problem of the Proposition Expressed'.

to as 'gappy sentences', as they seem to express 'gappy' propositions—the place occupied by the empty name thus actually corresponding to a gap. Hence, Millianists must explain away the intuitive meaningfulness and truth-valuedness of gappy sentences, and the related problems of attitude-ascription, belief and sincere assertive utterance[4], which they attempt to do with mixed results.[5] Effectively, in these investigations the focus is almost entirely shifted from the analysis of the semantics and pragmatics of empty names themselves to the analysis of the semantics and pragmatics of the sentences where they occur.

But if we can find a 'Millianist' account of empty names that nevertheless preserves the intuition that empty terms are indeed meaningful and that the sentences where they occur are not gappy, then it is arguably to be preferred over an account that sacrifices these intuitions.[6] Now, thesis (2) remains to be explored. Clearly, denying (2) amounts to a reassessment of the intuitive demarcation of what is to count as a proper name, as intuitively 'Sherlock Holmes' seems to be a proper name just as 'Julius Cesar' or 'Angelina Jolie'; but perhaps the idea that empty names are meaningful but are not really proper names is less counterintuitive than the idea that they are meaningless. They might for instance be disguised descriptions that simply fail to be satisfied by any (existing) individual.

Indeed, position $1/\sim2/$ 3 is a form of Millianism that has had its share of popularity. For example, in his 'Knowledge by Acquaintance and Knowledge by Description' (1910) Russell may be read as upholding this form of Millianism: the meaning of a member of his very restrictive class of actual proper names (the names of the entities with whom the agent has had personal contact) is simply its bearer. Thus, it is not so much that Russell proposes a descriptive account of proper names but rather that he *reduces* the actual class of proper names to a very small subclass of the intuitive class, and then claims that everything else is not a real proper name but rather a disguised description. The real challenge for this position, besides going against the intuitive demarcation, is that it requires a robust criterion for what is to count as a proper name, given that we cannot rely on our intuitive attribution of 'proper-nameness' to empty names, nor on purely syntactic features. The ultimate test for this position is how its criterion for 'proper-nameness' fares when confronted with a series of puzzles.

Thus, Russell defended the view that a proper name used to refer to an individual by a given agent is in fact a disguised description unless the agent has had the experience of direct acquaintance with the individual in question. On this account, the particular epistemic state of the agent determines the semantic properties of the terms used by him. This view suggests an approach to the demarcational issue that we could dub 'Russellianism': a name is a proper name *for me* if and only if I have had an up-close-and-personal encounter with the individual in question. This, of course, cannot happen in the case of names whose bearers do not exist, but it also affects names of past and future

---

[4]This is Braun's (2005) list of problems for the Millian.

[5]See Everett (2003) for a critique of the 'gappy' approach.

[6]Reimer (2001) offers an analysis of the role of intuitions in this debate (which she refers to as 'the Intuition Problem').

individuals, or simply names of individuals whom the agent contingently has not (yet) met. Of course, this means that only a fairly small subclass of the terms that we usually consider to be proper names are indeed proper names (and always relative to a given speaker), but this is not a problem in itself. The real problem is: how robust is the Russelian criterion?

Naturally, Russell's account has quite a few counterintuitive consequences. One of them is that whether a given term is or is not a proper name becomes a matter of one's subjective experiences; but presumably, it should be a linguistic (or in any case semantic) matter, related to the conventions accepted and correctly used by the speakers of a language. Now, an implication of Russell's account is that some terms are proper names for some people, but not for others. This is what I will refer to as the **Epistemological Puzzle** for the Russellian demarcation of proper names.

Similarly, according to the Russellian criterion, whether a term is or is not a proper name crucially depends on ontological facts, *i.e.* the actual existence of a certain individual. What about names of individuals that do not exist? On the Russellian view, they cannot be counted as proper names, and yet the problem is that, again, whether a term is a proper name should presumably be a linguistic, semantic matter, not an ontological one. This is what I will refer to as the **Ontological Puzzle**.

Notice that causal theories of reference have a solution to the epistemological puzzle that is particularly acute for the Russellian view, but fail to offer an adequate response to the ontological puzzle; that is, they fail to explain the presumed 'proper-nameness' of names of future and non-existent entities. What we are after is a theory which, when faced with both the epistemological and the ontological puzzle, will still predict that the name of a not immediately known entity, including the case of non-existing ones, is indeed a proper name, but without abandoning Millianism altogether. If such a theory can be found, especially if it is not based on dubious premises, it will most certainly be a valuable addition to our repertoire of philosophical theories, as it might vindicate many of the intuitions shared by competent speakers which are otherwise jeopardized by traditional versions of Millianism.

It might be thought that a straightforward criterion would simply be to require the existence of the (presumed) bearer for a name to be a proper name. This criterion would be less astringent than Russell's, as it would take into account the possibility of social transmission of the rigid designation, according to the familiar Kripkean story. But we simply do not always know ahead whether something does or does not exist; if a necessary criterion for a name to be a proper name is that its bearer should exist, what are we to do in cases where we simply are not sure whether the given individual exists? Are we or are we not to treat the given term as a proper name, and thus use it according to the usual semantic and pragmatic properties of proper names?

Consider the following situation: little Virginia is convinced that Santa Claus exists, and appropriately uses the phrase 'Santa Claus' as a proper name. When she is about eight, friends tell her that Santa does not exist. Suppose that she is not convinced by some newspaper editorial attesting to the contrary, and indeed no longer believes that Santa Claus exists. What happens then? Did she use the phrase as a proper name only until she stopped believing in Santa's existence, and then started using it as a disguised description (which failed to be satisfied)? Or did she only mistakenly think that the phrase was a proper name, and thus did not use it correctly all along? Proper names have specific semantic properties, which are presumably mastered by their users; is it plausible to think that a competent speaker could use a given phrase appropriately even if she cannot be sure whether it really is a proper name, *i.e.* if she does not know whether the (presumed) bearer exists? It seems odd to imagine that, semantically, little Virginia's uses of the phrase 'Santa Claus' changed radically the day she found out that Santa Claus does not exist.

Similarly, one recurrent example in the literature on empty terms is the case of Vulcan, a planet whose existence was hypothesized by Le Verrier in the $19^{th}$ century. Obviously, for Le Verrier and those following him in this belief, 'Vulcan' was a full-fledged proper name; for us, who now know that there is no such planet, 'Vulcan' will not count as a proper name if a necessary condition for proper-nameness is that its bearer should exist. But obviously, such a demarcation would require an omniscient metaphysical theory in order to be effective, a theory that can predict for each and every putative entity whether it does or does not exist. Indeed, the lesson to be learned from episodes in the history of science such as the debates on Vulcan and phlogiston, just to name two examples, is that existence is far from being a straightforward matter, as more familiar examples such as 'Santa Claus' and 'Sherlock Holmes' may seem to imply. In the same vein, whenever there is a debate concerning the existence of something, say the existence of God, is it plausible to think that the different sides of the debate use the same term, in this case 'God', with radically different semantic properties? This might jeopardize the very possibility of language as a means of communication. So existence simply cannot be what is at stake when a competent speaker uses a given term as a proper name, with its usual semantic and pragmatic properties.

## 4   Medieval Authors on Proper Names

As it turns out, these issues were also lively discussed by later Latin medieval authors (see Ashworth, 2004). In fact, the two puzzles just formulated are particularly nasty for $14^{th}$ century nominalism, which emphasizes precisely the role of singulars as the source of concept formation, and the crucial role of mental language for the signifying nature of conventional language (see Panaccio, 1999).

Roughly put, according to 14th century nominalism, a singular term is a term subordinated to/signifying a singular concept, and a singular concept is formed upon the encounter with an individual; it is the concept of that individual *qua* individual. Therefore, just as for Russell, it would be impossible to have a singular concept of an individual one has never met, and accordingly, as the names we use to talk about such individuals are not subordinated to a singular concept, they are not singular terms/proper names properly speaking.

Thus, for a $14^{th}$ century nominalist, the most straightforward option seems to be to declare that all names of individuals that an agent has not become acquainted with are in fact descriptions (essentially the Russellian position), and this holds of existing individuals that the agent has never met as well as of past, future and (non-existing) possible individuals; this is indeed the gist of Buridan's position. Furthermore, under a certain interpretation of mental singular terms, based on Ockham's notion of intuitive cognition, one may go as far as viewing as proper names only the occurrences of such terms *in the very presence of their bearers*. It would seem thus that, within medieval nominalism, the epistemological and the ontological puzzles cannot be avoided. So again, a fairly obvious way to safeguard modern Millianism as well as $14^{th}$ century semantic nominalism is to redefine the boundaries of the class of proper names/singular terms in a rather counterintuitive manner, in particular by excluding empty names.

But perhaps it *is* possible to avoid these two puzzles while maintaining an intuitive demarcation for what is to count as a proper name and the intuition of the meaningfulness of empty names, and yet to remain faithful to the general principles of Millianism and of $14^{th}$ century nominalism. I submit that such a gem can be found in Nicholas of Amsterdam's treatment of the problem of empty names; in effect, it seems to satisfy all these desiderata.

So now I first briefly survey Ockham's and Buridan's views on proper names, singular terms and singular concepts; I show that their views lead them straight into the epistemological and the ontological puzzles described above.[7] I then move on to Nicholas's analysis of 'Antichrist' and 'Adam', and argue that the concept of a proper name that emerges from his discussion avoids the two puzzles, while not relying on any questionable assumption from the point of view of either Millianism or late medieval nominalism.

## 4.1   Ockham

As is well known, the concept of mental language is one of the cornerstones of Ockham's thought; it plays as essential role for his logical and semantic theories, but also for his views on cognition as well as for his philosophy of mind. It bears certain similarities to the current notion of a 'language of thought' as expounded by Fodor *et al.*, but the comparison should be taken with a grain of salt. For our present purposes, the most significant property of the mental language hypothesis is that of accounting for many semantic features of written and spoken language.[8] Generally, Ockham holds that spoken and written words are meaningful only insofar as they are subordinated to mental terms (concepts); thus, words that are not mapped onto any mental term are prima facie meaningless. Now, if empty names are not mapped onto any mental term, they are at great risk of being deemed meaningless by Ockham's theory.

For the present purposes, it is important to note that Ockham recognizes two kinds of cognition, namely intuitive cognition and abstractive cognition. An intuitive cognition gives the cognizer a direct grasp of the individual, and,

---

[7]Again, the analysis of Ockham's and Buridan's positions on proper and empty names here is not intended to be exhaustive (as this would require considerably more space); rather, the goal is to provide an idea of the general background of late medieval nominalism in order to outline the originality of Nicholas' solution to the issue of empty names

[8]On this, see Panaccio (1999). For example: Ockham defines synonymy as the phenomenon of two or more words being subordinated to the same concept; equivocation is in turn defined as the phenomenon of a word being subordinated to more than one concept.

furthermore, it attests to its existence; it is the mere apprehension of an individual in its bare existence. Naturally, it can only occur in the presence of the given particular. Abstractive cognitions are all the intellective processes that follow this first, bare cognition of the individual in order to comprehend its nature. When I first see a man, my intuitive cognition only tells me that 'it' (whatever it is) is there; it is only by means of abstraction that I see him as a man, as white etc.[9]

When it comes to proper names, it is clear that we should be interested in the relation between certain terms and singular concepts, as presumably being subordinated to a singular concept should be Ockham's criterion for what is to count as a proper name. His remarks on the relation between singular terms and singular concepts are not as detailed as one might hope, yet it is clear that his concept of intuitive cognition is at the heart of the matter. A good illustration of this fact is a passage from question 7 in Ockham's *Questions on the Physics of Aristotle* (translation from Panaccio, 2004, p. 12):

> When the intellect apprehends a singular thing by intuition, it forms in itself an intuitive cognition, which is a cognition of this singular thing only, and is capable by its very nature to supposit for this singular thing. And just as a spoken word conventionally supposits for its significate, similarly this [intuitive] intellection naturally supposits for the thing it is an intellect of.

('To supposit for' is a semantic relation between words in sentences and things, roughly equivalent to 'to stand for'.) From this passage, it appears that, for Ockham, the intuitive cognition of a thing can play the role of standing for that thing in mental language in the same way that a proper name stands for its bearer in written and spoken language. The question is now whether intuitive cognitions are the *only* terms in mental language that can play the role usually attributed to proper names in written and spoken language; in other words, the question is whether intuitive cognitions are the only singular terms in mental language, or whether mental terms of a different nature also function semantically as singular terms in the mental realm.

In order to address this issue, a better grasp of intuitive cognitions and their epistemic and semantic properties is required. For this purpose, a passage by Panaccio is particularly informative:

> A logically proper name, in Russell's view, is never given but to a single referent, which the speaker must at some point have been directly acquainted with, this episode of direct acquaintance having fixed once and for all the referent for this particular designator. Ockham's intuitive cognitions are direct designators too; they do not have descriptive content, any more than Russell's logically proper names do. And they also presuppose a direct acquaintance with

---

[9]For Ockham's views on cognition, see two conflicting accounts in Stump (1999) and Karger (1999). Indeed, the concepts of intuitive cognition and abstractive cognition are still disputed matters among Ockham scholars.

of the agent with the object. The requirement of acquaintance, however, is even stronger in the case of Ockham's intuitive cognitions,
since such cognitions simply cannot occur (in the natural order) in
the absence of their objects. Once the speaker has been in direct
contact with a given referent, she can, in Russell's view, use its logically proper name, even when the thing is not there anymore; but
this is not so with the intuitive cognition. Ockham's intuitive acts
must correspond to an even more demanding category of signs [...]
(Panaccio, 2004, p. 13).

I now return to my original question: are intuitive cognitions the only mental
terms that can play the role of singular terms in mental language? There seem
to be a number of alternatives. Alternative (1): intuitive cognitions are not the
only singular mental terms. But then, one is left with the problem of explaining
how these other (presumed-to-be) singular mental terms that are not intuitive
cognitions come about. Are they abstractive cognitions? This may seem awkward at first sight, as abstractive cognitions are more intuitively associated
with *common* (not with singular) mental terms. But how else can we account
for the possible occurrence in mental language of a singular term/proper name
even when one is not in the presence of its bearer? There is no doubt that we
think of individuals, and thus form mental propositions presumably with singular terms standing for them, also when not in their presence. So these would
be singular mental terms of a different kind, still in want of an explanation.

Alternatively, these putative singular concepts that do not correspond to
intuitive cognitions are not singular mental terms properly speaking. If (alternative 2) intuitive cognitions are indeed the only singular mental terms, this
may come about in two ways: either (alternative 2') this semantic property
of mental terms is transferred over to conventional language, and conventional
terms are only singular insofar as they are subordinated to intuitive cognitions,
or (alternative 2") this semantic property of mental terms is not transferred
over to conventional language, and thus there are singular conventional terms
that are not subordinated to singular mental terms/intuitive cognitions. If alternative 2' is the case, then this class of 'mental proper names', defined as those
corresponding exclusively to intuitive cognitions, would determine the class of
'conventional proper names' by isomorphism between mental language and conventional language. However, this would have the counterintuitive consequence
that the vast majority of the terms that we usually view as proper names would
not be real proper names; in fact, it would seem that only proper names used
when the individual is *actually present* would count as proper names. This
would also imply that different uses of a given name *by the same agent* are
sometimes a proper name, and sometimes not (as noted by Panaccio, 2004,
p. 13), depending on whether they are subordinated to an intuitive cognition
or not. Clearly, this is a much more threatening form of the epistemological
puzzle, which concerned uses of the same name by different agents.

Moreover, it would still be necessary to explain the occurrences of 'pseudo-
proper names' in conventional language, that is, those terms that we usually
view as proper names but which do not correspond to an intuitive cognition at a
given occasion. Maybe they would be subordinated to some sort of abstractive

cognition (which would not be a singular term, under the current assumption) consisting of recovering a previously had intuitive cognition, perhaps associated with a cluster of descriptions.[10] But in this case, (according to the current assumption) such terms would simply not be proper names in conventional language, as they would not be subordinated to singular terms.

But again, this would only apply to proper names of individuals that the agent has once met (as for Russell), and not to proper names of individuals with whom the agent is not acquainted. For these, a different account would be needed, and it seems that Ockham does not give us sufficient elements for a reconstruction of what his views on this matter might have been. It is unclear, for example, given the utterly personal nature of a mental vocabulary, whether he could subscribe to a inter-personal causal transmission of the meaning of a proper name (in a Kripkean vein), or whether he would (like Buridan) espouse a sort of Russellian description-theory of proper names for the names of those individuals with whom the agent has never become acquainted.

Finally, alternative 2", of the non-isomorphism between mental and conventional language with respect to singular terms, is prima facie not entirely implausible; Ockham often points out features of conventional language that are not found in mental language, such as gender and case. Yet, it seems that a term being either singular or common is too important as a semantic feature for it not to be co-extensional in mental and conventional language.

My preferred option, the one that seems to yield the least counterintuitive consequences, is Alternative 1: (at least) some singular mental terms do not correspond to intuitive cognitions. One is still faced with the challenge of explaining what these singular mental terms not corresponding to intuitive cognitions ultimately *are*, but I take Ockham's conception of mental language to be sufficiently resourceful to be up to the challenge. Furthermore, alternative 1 does not guarantee that all presumably singular conventional terms are indeed subordinated to singular mental terms (be they intuitive cognitions or not), so we are still left with the question of whether names such as 'Antichrist' and 'Aristotle' would be singular terms in mental and in conventional language for Ockham. In other words, even Alternative 1, prima facie more plausible than the others, would require a significant amount of work if it is to be fully developed. I do not take up this challenge here; for my present purposes, it is sufficient to have shown that Ockham, just as the Millianist, seems to be in real trouble with empty (proper) names.[11]

---

[10]Ockham hints at such an idea with the concept of *"rememoratio"*, which he brings to the fore for example in *Reportatio* II, q. 12-13 and in Ordinatio I, d. 3, q. 9. Marilyn McCord Adams aptly renders *"rememoratio"* as "recordative cognition" (see Adams, 1989, pp. 515–519).

[11]As for the semantics of sentences containing proper names, Ockham treats them within the framework of supposition theory. Essentially, affirmative sentences having an empty name as subject are false, as the truth of an affirmative sentence requires the existence of what its terms stand for. Negative sentences having an empty name as subject, however, are true, because a negative sentence has two causes of truth: either one of the terms does not stand for anything, or they both stand for something, but for different things. So 'Sherlock Holmes does not exist' comes out as true on his account (see *Summa Logicae* I, ch. 72).

## 4.2 Buridan

Buridan's views on (empty) proper names are more fully developed than Ockham's, and are aptly discussed in Ashworth (2004). Here, I will focus on Buridan's *Questiones in Metaphysicam* VII.20 as transcribed in Ashworth (2004), where Buridan discusses the cases of 'Antichrist' and 'Aristotle'; it is regarding these very cases that Nicholas of Amsterdam's views differ from Buridan's.

Buridan's basic tenet with respect to singular terms in general, and proper names in particular, seems to be that "a singular term must be subordinated to a singular concept, and [...] the formation of a singular concept depends on the actual presence of the singular thing" (Ashworth, 2004, p. 136). But Buridan also discusses how we can have a singular concept of something that we have met in the past, even when this individual is no longer in front of us. In this sense, Buridan's singular terms are clearly not as restrictive as Ockham's intuitive cognitions. So 'the actual presence of the singular thing' should apparently not be understood as required at each and every moment that a given singular concept is evoked by the intellect. Once the agent has become acquainted with the individual in question, the corresponding singular term is stored, as it were, in the agent's mental vocabulary for future use as well.

> It is true that through memory we correctly conceive of a thing singularly, because we remember: that this has been within the sight of the one who conceives it ; and that he has known it in this way. And thus remembering Socrates, whom I have seen, I again conceive of him singularly, although I do not see him [now]. But if I had not seen him, I could only form a concept of him suppositing for that alone on account of a collection of common circumstances.[12]

Indeed, as the last sentence in the passage indicates, when it comes to names of individuals whom the agent has never met, Buridan clearly espouses the Russellian idea that these are strictly speaking not singular terms, as they do not correspond to singular concepts and thus cannot be proper names. Rather, if I have never met Aristotle, I can only differentiate him from all other men by means of descriptions (*circumlocutione*): he was a philosopher, he was the tutor of Alexander the Great etc. Buridan adds that the fact that this description effectively signifies one single man does not make it a singular term (just as much as 'God' is not a singular term), since if two men happened to satisfy it, then it would signify them both, but this cannot occur with singular terms (see *Questiones in Physicam* 1.7—Ashworth, 2004, p. 136, fn 60).

Furthermore, Buridan addresses the epistemological puzzle raised above by adding the clause that "I can treat 'Aristotle' as a singular term because I believe that the name was imposed or given its signification by a person who did have the appropriate singular concept" (Ashworth, 2004, p. 137). But the heart of the matter is that 'Aristotle' is not, properly speaking, a singular term for those who do not possess the appropriate singular concept.[13]

---

[12]Latin text transcribed in Ashworth (2004, p. 143, my translation).

[13]Buridan's position with respect to the proper names of individuals who exist or have

But as for the ontological puzzle, Buridan clearly bites the bullet: in the case of individuals who do not as of yet exist, nobody can have had a singular concept of them, and thus there could not have been a moment of baptism/first imposition relating a term to a singular concept. Therefore, the names that we use to talk about such individuals are in no way proper names. His example is the name 'Antichrist', which is, according to him, not a proper name for two reasons: it is a complex composed of 'anti' and 'Christ', and it could apply to several individuals (see *Quaestiones in Metaphysicam* VII.20, transcribed in Ashworth, 2004, p. 142).

So we return to our original question: is there a way to avoid the ontological puzzle? Can we formulate a theory according to which a term can be a proper name even though its bearer does not exist (and thus of whom no actual person has a singular concept), but which would be compatible with late-medieval nominalist and modern Millianist views on proper names? This is where Nicholas of Amsterdam comes in.

## 5    Nicholas of Amsterdam

Nicholas of Amsterdam is a rather obscure figure of the beginning of the 15th century; he was educated in Cologne (bachelor in 1408) and taught at different universities, all of them in Germany. Moreover, he wrote commentaries on nearly all of Aristotle's texts, many of which are still extant in manuscripts in libraries throughout Germany. Nicholas clearly was a *modernus*, that is, a philosopher working within the framework established by Buridan and his followers. Thus, broadly understood, he can be said to be a nominalist, even though his positions differ in some respects from those of the great nominalist masters such as Ockham (*e.g.* on whether quantity is a distinct category—cf. Bos, 2011) and Buridan (*e.g.* on proper names, as will be shown shortly).[14]

### 5.1    *Significare*

The passage I will focus on comes from his commentary on the 'old' logic[15], written somewhere between 1422 and 1437.[16] More specifically, it comes from Question 3 of Nicholas's commentary on De *interpretatione*, namely a question on the following definition of 'name' given by Aristotle:

> Whether what is said by the Philosopher, 'a name is a significative utterance by convention, with no bearing to time, and of which no

---

existed, but with whom the agent has had no direct contact, is a version of what are now known as 'hybrid' theories of proper names, mixing elements of causal as well as of description theories of proper names.

[14]See E. P. Bos's contribution in this volume for further details of Nicholas of Amsterdam's career.

[15]The 'old' logic (*logica vetus*) was the general name to refer to the logical texts which had remained available throughout the Latin Middle Ages (such as Aristotle's *Categories* and *On Interpretation*, and some of Boethius' commentaries and textbooks), as opposed to the *logica nova*, *i.e.* the logical texts which re-emerged in the 12th century (such as Aristotle's *Prior Analytics* and *Sophistical Refutations*, among others).

[16]The commentary is found in a single manuscript, in the Bayerische Staatsbibliothek in Munich. The text used here has been edited by E.P. Bos, and is forthcoming in the volume dedicated to Nicholas of Amsterdam. I quote here the Latin passages, as the text is as of yet of difficult access; the translations are my own.

part apart from the rest signifies something in a finite and proper way',[17] is well formulated.[18]

The key to my discussion will be his analysis of the notion of *significare* as a constituent part of the definition of a name as a significative (meaningful) utterance (*vox significativa*). His explanation of the notion of signification goes as follows:

> To signify is to represent something, some things, or somehow to a cognitive power by vitally and instrumentally changing it. But to signify is two-fold, namely naturally and by convention. To signify naturally is to represent identically to all men; to signify by convention is to signify according to the intention of the first imposer of meaning.[19]

Several points are noteworthy here. First, notice that Nicholas's definition of signification echoes the one offered by Peter of Ailly in *Conceptus et insolubilia*.

> To signify is to represent something, some things, or somehow, to a cognitive power by vitally changing it (Spade, 1980, p. 16).

This definition of signification is supposed to cover both kinds of signification, natural and conventional, including the signifying nature of mental terms and spoken terms. To explain the notion of vital change, Peter considers the counterfactual situation of God producing in a stone the act of knowing a man;[20] he says that, if this were to occur, still the stone would not have been vitally changed (Spade, 1980, §4). In short, the qualification 'vitally' refers to the fact that this change occurs in a living being, as opposed to a change occurring, say, in a mirror reflecting the image of a given object; that is, a term can be significative only to a living being capable of cognitively linking a term to the salient thing.

Notice though that Peter's general definition of signification does not contain the specification that the change has to be instrumental. It is only when explicitly discussing spoken terms (in §§55–88, after having discussed mental terms in §§10–54) that the clause of instrumental change is mentioned:

> An utterance which signifies by convention is [one that] when apprehended by hearing is apt, by the imposition it actually has to represent to a cognitive power, by vitally changing it instrumentally, something or some things or somehow [...] (Spade, 1980, p. 27).

---

[17] *De Int.*, 16a19-22.

[18] Philosopho qua dicitur 'Nomen est vox significativa ad placitum sine tempore cuius nulla pars separatim aliquid significat finita et recta' sit bene dicta.

[19] *Secundo* dicendum est quod significare est potentie cognitive aliquid vel aliqua vel aliqualiter representare ipsam instrumentaliter vitaliter immutando. Hoc autem significare est duplex, scilicet [f. 240r] naturaliter et ad placitum. Naturaliter significare est apud omnes homines idem representare; significare vero ad placitum est significare secundum voluntatem primi instituentis.

[20] In the natural course of things, obviously this cannot happen, only with God's special intervention.

Peter then goes on to explain the notion of 'instrumentally':

> [...] the word 'instrumentally' occurs here because the intellect itself
> causes in part an act of understanding in itself, or an actual act
> of knowing the thing, and in part effectively changes itself vitally.
> Now the act of knowing, or act of understanding, vitally changes the
> intellect formally, because it is formally the vital change itself. But
> a significative utterance vitally changes it instrumentally (Spade,
> 1980, p. 27).

The adverb 'instrumentally' is here opposed to 'formally'. The difference
seems to be that a 'formal change' would correspond to what Ockham calls
an intuitive cognition, that is, the pure perception of something, while an instrumental change does not have this immediate character. A *vox significativa*
causes an instrumental change in a cognitive power because it makes the intellect think of the object(s) that the word signifies (besides causing the formal
change of actually having heard the given *vox*); by contrast, a direct perception of the very object(s) would only cause a formal change in the cognitive
power. In other words, a *vox significativa* is an instrument (as it were) to evoke
in the intellect (or in any other vital creature) the concept of the thing(s) it
signifies. Formal changes in the cognitive power can only be significative terms
in mental language (if at all); this is why what is distinctive about terms in
spoken language is that they are always related, in their significative function,
to instrumental changes in the cognitive power.[21]

Back to Nicholas's definition of signification, it is clear that it is almost
verbatim taken from Peter's definition of what it means for an utterance to
signify. Nicholas does not say explicitly that, thus stated, the definition only
applies to significative utterances (as opposed to mental terms). But since in
the Aristotelian definition under scrutiny here we are dealing with **voces** *significative*, meaningful **utterances**, from the context we can infer that only the
mechanisms of signification in spoken language are being dealt with. Indeed,
the notion of signification thus stated, as necessarily related to the notion of
an instrumental change in the cognitive power, does not cover signification in
mental language.[22]

Furthermore, immediately after his definition, Nicholas adds that signification is two-fold, natural and conventional. His formulation of the distinction
emphasizes the source of signification of a given term; it is either the same for
all men, in the case of natural signification, or it is determined by the first

---

[21] Peter of Ailly also recognizes that " a thing can be called a sign in two senses. In the
first sense, because it leads to an act of knowing the thing of which it is a sign. In the second
sense, because it is itself the act of knowing the thing" (Spade, 1980, p. 17).

[22] Notice that, unlike Peter, Nicholas does not provide an explanation of what these clauses,
*i.e.* 'vitally' and 'instrumentally', are supposed to mean; this is an indication that Peter's
definition of signification was so influential in Nicholas' intellectual environment that there
was no need for such explanations. In effect, the very fact that Nicholas of Amsterdam's
definition of signification is almost word for word taken from Peter of Ailly also indicates
how influential this text was to become in the decades following its composition (see Meier-
Oeser, 2003, part 8). Whether this definition is indeed Ailly's own invention I cannot affirm;
he is in any case the earliest source using the phrase 'to represent something, or some things,
to a cognitive power' to define the notion of signification that I have come across so far.

user of the term in that sense, in the case of conventional signification. Again, since only *voces significative* are being dealt with, thus excluding concepts, utterances having natural signification are presumably the inarticulate sounds produced by brutes, which are indeed significative by not conventionally significative (see *De Int.* 16a28-29); or perhaps also some of the sounds uttered by humans such as laughter, moans, or even imitations of animal sounds. These are meaningful utterances, but they are not *nomina*, and this is presumably what the *ad placitum* (by convention) clause in the definition is supposed to take care of.[23]

## 5.2  The puzzle: are 'Antichrist' and 'Adam' *voces significative*?

After explaining each of the constitutive terms of the definition of *nomen* in six points (the second of which being the explanation of *vox significativa* just discussed), Nicholas moves on to examine possible objections to this definition, in the usual later medieval fashion. The first objection is the one that is of interest to us. It goes as follows: there are some terms that the logicians 'call names', but which do not seem to fit the definition of *vox significativa*, *i.e.* which seem to be counterexamples to the definition. This would show that the definition as explained, in particular with respect to the notion of *vox significativa*, is not correct, or in any case that it leaves out an important class of terms which the logicians consider to be names: empty names.

> Some [terms] are names according to the logician, but they are not significative utterances. Therefore, this specific part of the definition, 'significative utterance' is not well phrased. This consequence is valid; the antecedent is proved of terms such as 'Antichrist', 'Adam' and similar ones, which are names, since they supposit; but they are not significative utterances, which is proved [as follows]; if they were significative utterances, they would signify either in a common manner or in a singular manner; but none of these [is the case]; on the one hand, they are not common significative utterances, since their imposition is singular. But such utterances do not signify particularly [either], as is clear, because we cannot have singular concepts of the things signified by such terms, given that this sort of thing is not perceived, as according to the seventh book of [Aristotle's] *Metaphysics*.[24]

---

[23] This two-fold notion of signification should also cover the phenomenon of signification in mental language; Nicholas does not say explicitly that natural signification also concerns mental language, but this may be seen as implied in his definition of natural signification as that which is the same for all men.

[24] [. . .] aliqua sunt nomina secundum loycum que tamen non sunt voces significative, ergo ista particula diffinitionis 'vox significativa' est male dicta. Consequentia nota, et antecedens probatur de istis terminis 'Antichristus', 'Adam' et consimilibus, que sunt nomina, ut supponitur; sed quod non sunt voces significative, probatur, quia, si essent voces significative, vel igitur significarent communiter, vel singulariter; sed nullum istorum: nam primo, quod non sunt voces significative communiter, probatur, quia impositio eorum est singularis. Sed quod tales voces non significant particulariter, patet, quia de rebus significatis per huiusmodi rationes non possumus habere conceptum singularem, ex quo huiusmodi res non sunt sensite, ut habetur septimo *Metaphysice*.

The counterexamples to the definition given are 'Antichrist' and 'Adam', and the issue is said to hold of similar cases—presumably, cases of names whose bearer the agent is not acquainted with, either because it is a long-gone individual, such as Adam, or because it is a not-yet-existing individual, such as the Antichrist. Here is how the argument goes:

1. If they were *voces significative*, they would signify either commonly, or singularly;

2. But they are neither common nor singular terms;

3. They are not common terms because their imposition is to singulars;

4. But they are not singular terms because we cannot have singular concepts of the things they signify, as these things cannot be sensed by us;

5. Hence, they are not *voces significative*.

Obviously, this is a rather counterintuitive conclusion; there is definitely a sense in which such terms are meaningful (*pace* some modern versions of Millianism). As we know, Buridan's view of such names is that they are in a way common terms, insofar as they in fact correspond to descriptions (which could apply to several individuals, if there were several individuals satisfying them). By contrast, Nicholas's solution to the puzzle will be to say that they are indeed singular terms, and this will be made possible by a subtle but significant reinterpretation of the definition of *significare*.

## 5.3   The solution to the puzzle

As just said, Nicholas's response to this objection is, contrasting with Buridan, to maintain that these are indeed singular terms even though we do not have singular concepts of them. In other words, Nicholas rejects one of the basic nominalistic tenets concerning singular terms and singular concepts, namely that a term is a singular term only insofar as it is subordinated to a singular concept.

According to him, such terms are indeed singular terms, because they were originally imposed to signify a singular thing in a singular manner. This is rather straightforward in the case of names such as 'Adam' and 'Aristotle', and it does not differ much from Buridan's proviso that we can treat such terms as singular terms (even though they are not singular terms to us) because they were first imposed as singular terms by somebody who did have a singular concept of the individual in question. But matters are obviously more complicated with names of future and/or possible individuals, of whom nobody has (had) a singular concept in order to execute this first singular imposition. Nicholas does not seem to make a distinction between those two cases, namely between individuals of whom a particular agent does not have a singular concept, but other agents do or did, and individuals of whom no actual agent has ever had a singular concept. This distinction may seem to us to be very important, but Nicholas's solution is meant to take care of both cases at once.

Nicholas concedes that of such things (Antichrist, Adam) we cannot have singular concepts, but denies that they are not singular (conventional) terms.

His justification to dismiss the Buridanian slogan 'No singular terms without singular concepts' is based on a qualification of the notion of *representare* in the definition of *significare*: he says that in the definition, *representare* must be understood as an **aptitude**, not only as an act, and concludes that such terms have indeed the aptitude to modify the cognitive power (in a vital and instrumental way) about a given singular concept concerning these things. Therefore, since they satisfy the modified definition of *representare* and consequently of *significare* thus qualified, they are *voces significative*, and more specifically they are singular terms.

Here is the relevant passage:

> It is replied that such terms are mere singular terms, as the argument shows, since they are imposed to signify singular things in a singular manner. And as a refutation [of the objection], when it is said 'about these things we cannot have a singular concept', I accept this proposition, but the consequent [the corresponding terms are not singular terms] must be denied because 'to represent' in the definition of 'to signify' indicates an aptitude, not only an act. But because the aforementioned terms have the aptitude to change, in a vital and instrumental manner, the cognitive power about a singular concept concerning these things, for this reason the consequence is not valid.[25]

How are we to understand this 'aptitude' to change the cognitive power about a singular concept? It seems to me that this should, or at least could, be understood in terms of the counterfactual situation of an agent actually having the corresponding singular concept (having had direct contact with Antichrist himself), and how, in such cases, such a change in the cognitive power would indeed occur. That is, in the actual world nobody has a singular concept of Antichrist, but it is very well conceivable that, in a counterfactual situation, a given agent would have this singular concept; in that case, the spoken term 'Antichrist' would behave semantically and cognitively to this agent exactly as proper names whose bearers a given agent does have a singular concept of behave in actual situations.

The same holds of names such as 'Adam', of whom I do not have a singular concept: were I to become acquainted with Adam himself, then the name 'Adam' would produce exactly this kind of vital and instrumental change in my cognitive power, namely that of evoking nothing but the singular concept of Adam. In other words, for a term to be a singular term it is not required that a given agent actually have the singular concept in question; it is only required that, *were an agent to have* a singular concept of the individual in question, the term would behave for this agent as one would expect it to, that

---

[25] Respondetur quod tales termini sunt mere singulares, ut arguit argumentum, ex quo sunt imposti ad significandum rem singularem singulariter. Et ad improbationem, cum dicitur quod 'de rebus istis non possumus habere conceptum singularem', concesso isto neganda est sequela protanto quia 'representare' in diffinitione 'significare' dicit aptitudinem, et non actum solum, sed quia predicti termini habent aptitudinem ad vitaliter et instrumentaliter immutandum potentiam cognitivam sub conceptu singulari circa tales res, idcirco sequela illata non valet.

is, it would evoke the singular concept in question and thereby represent the individual in question qua individual to the cognitive power.

Arguably, this account respects the basic tenets of $14^{th}$ century nominalism; the only change it introduces is to dissociate the actual (subjective and contingent) cognitive experience of an agent from the semantic behavior of terms in conventional language. As for the fact that counterfactual reasoning is used, this is not a threat to the principles of $14^{th}$ century nominalism; indeed, counterfactual reasoning is often used by Ockham, Buridan and virtually all medieval philosophers to treat a wide variety of issues.[26]

# 6  Conclusion

I submit that Nicholas of Amsterdam's account solves the epistemological and the ontological puzzles while not making any dubious commitments (neither from the perspective of later-medieval nominalism nor from the perspective of modern Millianism). According to my interpretation of his position, a proper name is what has the aptitude to represent the specific individual in question, *qua* individual, to a cognitive power by evoking the corresponding singular concept in the latter, *should the cognitive power possess the appropriate singular concept*. But the fact that some agents do not possess a given singular concept does not represent a counterexample to the definition, as it does not change the semantic behavior of such terms (proper names) for the agents (even if only hypothetical ones) that do possess it. It is a conditional definition, which thus only excludes the cases where the antecedent (the agent has the appropriate singular concept) obtains while the consequent (the name in question represents the specific individual it names to the cognitive power) does not, but not the cases where the antecedent does not obtain.

An upshot of this view, which I take to be a positive one, is the dissociation of the linguistic and semantic property of being a proper name from the (contingent and subjective) epistemic experience of the agent as well as from ontological matters. And this is accomplished at a rather low theoretical cost: all that is required is the move to counterfactual agents in order to suppose the antecedent to be the case in the case of empty names.

In terms of modern discussions of the semantics of mythical and fictional proper names, my interpretation of Nicholas' solution bears some resemblance to the view that fictional characters do exist, albeit only as fictional characters (see Salmon, 1998). But ultimately, the *counterfactual* sort of existence of the 'bearers' of empty names that I propose here is quite different from the *actual* albeit abstract sort of existence that Salmon confers to Sherlock Holmes and other fictional characters. Moreover, the core of my proposal is rather the counterfactual existence of bearer *and* of the agent (the cognitive power); what makes a name a proper name is not simply that some single thing exists of which it can be predicated, but rather the cognitive mechanism that it triggers in a cognitive agent, namely that of representing exactly the unique individual in question qua individual upon hearing/using a proper name, provided that

---

[26]As for modern Millianism, counterfactual reasoning should not be a problem either: possible worlds and similar devices have made counterfactual reasoning more palatable than ever.

the appropriate singular concept be available. A similar 'test' allows one to recognize the meaningfulness and proper-nameness of an empty term: if the appropriate singular concept is available, the term will represent the particular individual *qua* individual to the cognitive power, which obviously would not happen if 'Sherlock Holmes' were meaningless just as 'babubabu' is. ?

Thus, Nicholas of Amsterdam's position also seems to accomplish the feat of allowing for the three apparently incompatible theses stated at the beginning of the paper to be simultaneously held. On his account, 1) empty names are not meaningless, 2) they are indeed proper names, and 3) their signification is first and foremost their bearers. The emphasis on the accompanying singular concept must not mislead us into thinking that the singular concept is the real content of a proper name, empty or otherwise. Singular concepts are crucial to explain the semantic and cognitive mechanism related to proper names, but they are not the content of proper names according to these medieval views. That a proper name signifies a given individual amounts to the fact that it represents this very individual to the cognitive power in question; the appropriate singular term plays only an instrumental role in this cognitive process. Hence, Nicholas' approach suggests an appealing Millianist solution to the problem of empty names, one where very few bullets must be bitten.[27]

# BIBLIOGRAPHY

Adams, F. and Dietrich, L. (2004). What's in a (n empty) name? *Pacific Philosophical Quarterly*, 85:125–148.

Adams, F. and Stecker, R. (1994). Vacuous singular terms. *Mind & Language*, 9(4):387–401.

Adams, M. M. (1989). *William Ockham*. University of Notre Dame Press, Notre Dame. 2 vols., 2nd rev. ed.

Ashworth, E. J. (2004). Singular terms and singular concepts: From Buridan to the early sixteenth century. In Ebbesen, S. and Friedman, R., editors, *John Buridan and Beyond: Topics in the Language Sciences, 1300–1700*, pages 121–151. The Royal Danish Academy of Sciences and Letters, Copenhagen.

Bos, E. P. (2011). Nicholas of Amsterdam's conceptualism in his commentary on the logica vetus. In Baumbach, M., Mojsisch, B., and Pluta, O., editors, *Bochumer Philosophisches Jahrbuch*, Bd. 14 (2009–2010–2011), pages 233–298.

Braun, D. (1993). Empty names. *Noûs*, 27:449–469.

Braun, D. (2005). Empty names, fictional names, mythical names. *Noûs*, 39:596–631.

Everett, A. (2003). Empty names and 'gappy' propositions. *Philosophical Studies*, 116(1):1–36.

Karger, E. (1999). Ockham's misunderstood theory of intuitive and abstractive cognition. In Spade, P. V., editor, *The Cambridge Companion to Ockham*, pages 204–226. Cambridge University Press, Cambridge.

Meier-Oeser, S. (2003). Medieval semiotics. In Zalta, E., editor, *The Stanford Encyclopedia of Philosophy*. The Metaphysics Research Lab, winter 2003 edition.

Panaccio, C. (1999). Semantics and mental language. In Spade, P. V., editor, *The Cambridge Companion to Ockham*, pages 53–75. Cambridge University Press, Cambridge.

Panaccio, C. (2004). *Ockham on Concepts*. Ashgate Publishing, London.

---

[27]Braun (2005, p. 600) recognizes that empty names trigger the same sort of cognitive process in an agent as 'real' proper names. The point is exactly that, on my proposal, it is this very cognitive process that serves to demarcate a proper name from other kinds of terms: proper names will always represent the particular individual qua individual to the agent, *should the agent have the appropriate singular concept*. The 'test' should always be performed on an agent having the appropriate singular concept, otherwise the outcome might be a 'false negative'.

Reimer, M. (2001). The problem of empty names. *Australasian Journal of Philosophy*, 79(4):491–506.

Russell, B. (1910). Knowledge by acquaintance and knowledge by description. *Proceedings of the Aristotelian Society*, 11:108–128.

Salmon, N. (1998). Nonexistence. *Noûs*, 32(3):277–319.

Spade, P. V., editor (1980). *Peter of Ailly: Concepts and Insolubles: An Annotated Translation (from Latin)*. Synthese Historical Library. D. Reidel Publishing Company, Dordrecht.

Stump, E. (1999). The mechanisms of cognition: Ockham on mediating species. In Spade, P. V., editor, *The Cambridge Companion to Ockham*, pages 168–203. Cambridge University Press, Cambridge.

# Manifestations of Logical Pluralism in the Context of Hierarchies, 1900s–1930s

IVOR GRATTAN-GUINNESS[†]

## 1 Pluralisms as an Array

For many centuries logical monism held sway: there was only one logic, the bivalent case governed by the law of excluded middle, where a proposition was either true or untrue. It had been developed in a variety of different ways, for example, syllogistic, algebraic and mathematical. From the late 19th century some non-bivalent logics began gradually to emerge, especially certain constructive, modal and many-valued logics. What did the advocates of a non-bivalent logic think they were doing? This article considers some early examples up to the 1930s.

Parallel with those innovations, and at times interacting with them, came the recognition among logicians, also gradual, that it is essential to partition any logic into its 'host logic' (a term preferred here to 'object logic') and an internal hierarchy of metalogics, metametalogics, ..., each one governed by its own axioms and principles. Comparable hierarchies were perceived for mathematics and indeed for theories in general. Present even if implicitly in Giuseppe Peano and some followers from the 1890s, they were emphasised in David Hilbert's programme of 'metamathematics' at that time and especially from the 1920s onwards; in Kurt Gödel's paper (Gödel, 1931) on the incompletability of first-order arithmetic, which quickly led Rudolf Carnap to introduce 'metalogic' as a technical term; and by some Poles, in particular Alfred Tarski coining 'metalanguage' in various writings of that time. From then onwards the category of metalogic has been of central concern; here the word 'metalogic' covers not only formal Hilbertian versions but also more informal theories, such as comparing different logics, or developing ways of teaching a logic or looking at its history. However, there seems still not to be much interest in developing the internal hierarchy further with metameta ... logics, although there are occasions on which a metalogic needs to be studied.

The histories of the establishment of logical pluralism and of hierarchies have been well recorded in the accounts of the topics just noted; a good succinct summary of several strands is given in Mangione and Bozzi (1993). The philosophical issues surrounding logical pluralism are well surveyed in Aberdein and Read (2009).

[†]Middlesex University Business School, The Burroughs, Hendon, London NW4 4BT, England. Email: ivor2@mdx.ac.uk

## 2   Modal Logics

Hugh MacColl's advocacy of necessary and possible propositions in modal logics, especially from the 1890s, has often been cited as a pioneer advocacy of logical pluralism, including in my contribution to the otherwise admirable survey (Astroh and Read, 1999) of his life and work. This is undoubtedly a correct assessment of his heritage to successors; however, in a recent reconsideration (Grattan-Guinness, 2011) I suggested that he himself was a monist, albeit of an unclear sort. The evidence comes primarily in his many letters to Bertrand Russell during the 1900s[1] and published exchanges with him in *Mind*. Various contemporary logicians and philosophers considered necessity and possibility without elevating their proposals to the status of a logic; Russell was aware of some of these authors, most notably Alexis Meinong (Anellis, 2009), but he always stuck to bivalent logic. For example, within it he defined a propositional function as 'necessary' if every proposition obtained by inserting all the values of the variable is true, 'sufficient' if at least one resulting, proposition is true, and 'impossible' if every proposition is untrue (Russell, 1919). Part of his clash with Russell was his persistent failure to understand that a propositional $f$ is never a proposition, but instead took it to be a proposition that is sometimes true and otherwise untrue—a strange difficulty to find in someone with a mathematical training.

However, Russell was himself guilty of obscurity. In particular, his normal clarity was absent from his logical writings on 'implication', for he indifferently covered derivation, inference and consequence (see especially his 1906). MacColl did not merely regard Russell's stance over implication as different from his own; it was *in error*, so that 'the whole subject of formal logic needs recasting' (1908, p. 454). But MacColl's alternative conception is also hard to grasp; he added the truth-values 'necessary' and 'possible', which applied to propositions in implicational form when some semantic context linked antecedent with sequent; in other words, his position intersected with we now call relevance logic. His distinction between truth and necessity was that between truth as a matter of fact and truth as a matter of principle, together with a dual distinction between untruth and impossibility. He also considered probability logics, and appears to have seen all these logics as parts of some monistic jumbo logic. As was then normal, he did not grasp hierarchies, so that he had no proper means of describing his position.

MacColl died in 1909, just when the next pioneer in modal logics was emerging. C. I. Lewis completed his doctorate at Harvard University in 1910, and soon was publishing papers on his conception of 'strict' implication. He too found unsatisfactory the treatment of implication, by then published in A. N. Whitehead's and Russell's *Principia Mathematica* (1910); but he did not cite MacColl as his source, and was not impressed with his predecessor's work when he came across it.

Lewis launched his debut paper on implication with two 'somewhat startling theorems', that 'a false proposition implies any proposition' and 'a true proposition is implied by any proposition' (1912). He contrasted his own individuation

---

[1]There are 26 letters from MacColl, kept by Russell (itself a significant fact) and housed in the Bertrand Russell Archives at McMaster University, Canada.

of 'intensional' modalities in necessity and possibility with Russell's traditional 'extensional' version but did not reject the latter. He compared his pluralism with that of non-Euclidean geometries, but in a somewhat curious way. In this paper he accepted that non-Euclidean geometries could be constructed, but that Euclidean geometry was the "correct" one for treating space; so similarly, 'The present [Russellean] calculus of propositions is untrue in the sense in which non-Euclidian geometry is untrue' (p. 530).

A much more profound and fully pluralist conception of geometries had come in mid 19th century from Bernhard Riemann, who saw *each* geometry as characterized by a metric upon its geodesics (Torretti, 1978); for instance but *not* in any special way, Euclidean geometry was based upon the geodesics furbished by Pythagoras's theorem. Lewis turned in this direction in a later paper when he asserted that the difference between bivalent and modal propositional calculi 'sufficiently resembles that of a [sic] Euclidean and a non-Euclidean geometry to make the analogy worth bearing in mind. Like two geometries, material and strict implication are equally self-consistent mathematical systems; but they apply to different worlds' (Lewis, 1914); that is, he preferred his strict version but did not reject the material competitor. He seems to have maintained this understanding of the analogy in his later writings. For example, his textbook (1918) on 'symbolic logic', which is primarily devoted to algebraic logic, ends with separate chapters on 'the system of strict implication' and on Peano-Russell bivalent 'logistic', in that order.

## 3   Many-valued Logics

Soon after Lewis's book appeared, the Polish-born American Emil Post published his doctorate (1921) on a 'general theory of elementary propositions', in which he reworked the propositional calculus without quantification that launched *Principia Mathematica* (1910). A difficulty lay in 'this incurable defect as a logic of propositions, that it used informally in its proofs the very propositions whose formal statements it tried to prove'. Apparently this 'was entirely overcome in *Principia Mathematica*', but at the cost of 'giving up the generality of outlook that characterized symbolic logic'. This was his way of construing internal hierarchies, for 'the theorems of this paper are *about* the logic of propositions but are *not included therein*' (1921): that is, he separated the host (bivalent) logic and its metalogic and focussed upon the latter.

To formulate the propositional calculus Post contributed the 'truth-table' method of determining the values of compound propositions (pp. 165–173).[2] He then generalized it to 'm-valued truth-systems' (pp. 173–176), a name that he related to 'two-valued algebra' in Lewis (1918, p. 222); these logics exhibit logical pluralism because they seem 'to have the same relation to ordinary logic that geometry in a space of an arbitrary [finite] number of dimensions has to the geometry of Euclid. Whether these "non-Aristotelian" logics will have a direct application we do not know' (1921, p. 164); he proved some basic properties but did not offer any interpretations (pp. 180–185).

---

[2]Post has some anticipators here, including Peirce, and Russell with Wittgenstein (Anellis, 2012).

Around the same time the Pole Jan Lukasiewicz began publishing on three-valued logic. He too saw it as a complement to bivalent logic, but he also mentioned some interpretations. One was modality, with 'possibly' as the third value but not explicitly 'necessary' as a fourth, and no citation of MacColl or Lewis (1971, pp. 87–89; 1920, pp. 172–176; 1930).[3] Another was future propositions, where he suggested 'indeterminate' as a suitable name both for them and their external negations. He stressed logical pluralism, 'as much as non-Euclidian systems of geometry differ from Euclidian geometry' (1922, p. 126; 1930, p. 175) and proved some 'incompatibility' theorems between this and bivalent logic(1930, pp. 161–164). He also reduced the analogy with geometries: namely, that while non-Euclidean geometries are interpretable in Euclidean geometry, bivalent logic is interpretable in many-valued logics, not vice versa (1941, pp. 293–294).

## 4    Temporal Logics?

Lukasiewicz's example of indeterminate propositions involved time. So did some of MacColl's 'variable propositions', such as 'Mrs. Brown is not at home'; but he treated it in terms of probability values, although a temporal reading seems to be at least as natural a reading. The virtual absence of temporal logics among logical pluralists is to me a mystery of this period, and indeed in the history of logic since antiquity. Although Aristotle had considered temporal propositions, as Lukasiewicz for one knew well (1971, pp. 177–178), neither he nor many successors decided that temporal logic was a logic in its own right. Yet it is easy to find propositions in which time plays a central role in the attached logic. In 'Fred drank the tea and paid the bill' the connective 'and' means 'and then' and so is not commutative over conjunction; therefore the proposition differs from 'Fred paid the bill and drank the tea'; hence both propositions belong to a non-bivalent logic.

Instead of granting temporal logic its due status, time-dependent propositions were sited in bivalent logic with time as one of the variables. In particular, W. V. O. Quine buttressed his monistic view of bivalent logic by 'treating time as a dimension coordinate with the spatial dimensions' (1970, 30); a more sophisticated treatment of time using ordered sets had been developed in (Russell, 1936). Now theories of positing dimensions surely aid the articulation of (spatio-)temporal logics rather than guarantee their reduction to part of bivalent logic. Nevertheless, the development of temporal logics seems to have waited an extraordinarily long time, until Hans Reichenbach, Arthur Prior and not many others in the 1950s (Øhrstrøm and Hasle, 2006).

## 5    Constructive Logics: The Case of Max Newman

The warfare between Hilbert and L. E. J. Brouwer in the 1920s over bivalent and intuitionist logics is too well known to require much rehearsal here. For spectators the focus fell more upon the unnecessarily polemical attacks by Brouwer than on the content of his message. Brouwer's 'Intuitionistic considerations of formalism' (1928) was arguably the last straw for Hilbert; its insults start in

---

[3]We cite various writings of Lukasiewicz from the English edition of his selected works.

the title with 'formalism' as the *name* for Hilbert's metamathematics, which Hilbert himself never used. For some reason the word has been the standard name for metamathematics ever since, and a major source of misunderstanding of the position.

The outcome of the dispute was ironic, in that logical pluralism benefited from the co-presence of both logics; but the mutual attitude of each protagonist was monistic, based upon the claim that the other was wrong (Mancosu, 1998). Conceptions of time played a prominent role in Brouwer's logic, but in such weird pseudo-psychological ways that the cause of temporal logic was not well served. The reputations of foundational studies among observers such as mathematicians must have suffered from this circus, especially the well-earned humiliation of Brouwer by Hilbert at the end of the decade (van Dalen, 1990). More profitable was the essay by Hermann Weyl (1921) on the 'new foundational crisis' in mathematics, in which he sketched out a constructivist account of some basic branches of mathematics, especially the arithmetic continuum, and also set theory and the theory of real-variable functions. He did not explicitly grant monistic status to the underlying logic, although his preference for it over bivalency comes over strongly.

This dispute influenced another contributor, who is unknown because he did not publish.[4] In 1921 two close friends at St John's College Cambridge graduated from Cambridge University. Max Neumann had entered in 1915 to take the Mathematics Tripos; but he was compelled to leave after a year, due to having a German-born father. The family changed surname to 'Newman', but Max could not return to college till 1919. He became a close friend of Lionel Penrose, who entered the college in 1919, with the most unusual intention of studying mathematical logic with Russell: he did not seem to know that Russell had been dismissed from his lectureship at Trinity College Cambridge in 1916 because of his anti-war activities. Penrose took the Moral Sciences Tripos because it had two courses in logic; but they covered traditional topics such as syllogistic and inductive logic, and some Boolean algebra, all long taught by W. E. Johnson. Penrose did study Russell's logic, but he would have had to do it on his own; and it may well be that he engaged the attention of his new friend Newman, who heard nothing about Russell's logic in the Mathematics Tripos!

Both men graduated in 1921, Newman with a distinction. The Moral Sciences Tripos contained several courses in psychology: Penrose was drawn into this subject, especially its application to logic. After graduation he decided to go to Vienna to meet its psychologists and psychoanalysts, and Newman went along with him to interact with the mathematicians. No record exists of the details of his contacts, but the activities around the Mathematics Faculty must have played a major role in the changes of his research interests in mathematics.

For example, topology became Newman's main mathematical speciality: it was not well known in Britain, but it was developing well in various other

---

[4]For more details on Newman's career as a logician and his time in Vienna see (Grattan-Guinness, 2012a). A third member of the College also went to Vienna: Rolf Gardiner (1902–1971), student of languages and later known as an ecologist, folk dancer and admirer of Nazism. His younger sister Margaret (1904–2005) also joined the boys, and remembered the visit in her autobiography (1988, pp. 62–69).

centres, including Vienna. Hans Hahn is especially notable because he was also that rare type of mathematician who took logic seriously (Sigmund, 1995). This meant not only studying the subject but also teaching it to undergraduates: while Newman was in Vienna Hahn taught a preliminary course entitled 'algebra and logic', and in ensuing years he twice ran a full course on *Principia Mathematica*. He also supervised the dissertation of Kurt Gödel on the predicate calculus, and as editor of the Austrian mathematics journal published it as (Gödel, 1930). In the following year he also published Gödel's follow-up paper (1931) on the incompletability of first-order arithmetic.

Hahn also enjoyed discourse: he had been a student at the University up to his higher doctorate in 1905, and during those years he had participated in some of the Viennese coffee-house discussion groups. After teaching elsewhere for several years he returned to Vienna as full professor of mathematics in 1921. During 1922 he led the move to appoint Moritz Schlick to the chair of natural philosophy. After taking up his post in 1923 Schlick soon formed a large discussion group with Hahn as a leading member, which became well known as the 'Vienna Circle' (Stadler, 2001). Members of the Circle did not have to subscribe to one philosophy, but Schlick and Hahn extolled positivism and empiricism, and among influences acknowledged Russell's philosophy.

Newman must have picked up much of this atmosphere during his year in Vienna. When he returned to Cambridge he specialised in topology and continued his serious interest in logic, thereby isolating himself twice over from the mathematicians. Penrose returned from Vienna with a deepened interest in psychology and started to write a doctorate on the psychology of mathematics. However around 1925 he abandoned the whole enterprise as a 'failure' and retrained as a medical doctor, which led to a distinguished career in psychiatry, genetics and statistics. While doubtless he was a ready listener to Newman's concerns about logic, he was probably not a major influence.

# 6   Newman's Pluralism

Newman showed his interest in logic soon after his return to Cambridge in 1923 when he applied for a fellowship at his old college. One submitted item was a 161−page manuscript on 'The foundations of mathematics from the standpoint of physics' (1923), in which he explored the application of mathematics to the real world of rough objects and conditions instead of the idealized entities such as smooth bodies moving through a vacuum. The topic surely shows a Viennese influence; several members of the future Vienna Circle could have raised it.

Newman's approach to his topic was logical pluralism, for he distinguished two kinds of applied mathematics *by their different logics*. Tripos-style idealisations) mass-points, vacuua, and so on) drew upon the usual bivalent classical logic, on which he cited Hilbert's recent metamathematical survey (1922) of the axioms needed in mathematical logic and set theory; but real-life applied mathematics needed the intuitionistic logic of Brouwer (1919) and Weyl (1921) cited above on the 'new foundational crisis' in mathematics. 'A rather remarkable outcome of these enquiries is that both the classical and the Brouwer-Weyl theories appear to be necessary constituents—the first to prove "consistency" and the second "existence" theorems' (Newman, 1923, fol. 8).

This long essay did not help Newman's cause for the Fellowship application. Referee Ebenezer Cunningham could not make much sense out of the manuscript and noticed that it stopped rather suddenly. Professor H. F. Baker adopted the patronising attitude of mathematicians in general to foundational studies (even though several leading colleagues advocated or attacked the various positions adopted); he regretted that 'this abstract logic has such an attraction to the writer', although the candidate was 'of world rank'. Indeed, after its bright start the essay becomes rather disappointing; logical pluralism does not feature as much as one might expect, few aspects of working with real bodies and theories are discussed, and in places it is philosophically somewhat incoherent. Newman never published it, but it must have played a major role in forming his realization of the importance of logics.

## 7    The Scope and Limitations of Logical Knowledge

These pluralist pioneers were stepping into unfamiliar territory. The modest awareness of internal hierarchies must have been a source of hesitation, for without it the pioneers would not have possessed a clear way of discussing a logic in the first place: the ' "logocentric" predicament', as Henry Sheffer nicely put it in a comment on *Principia Mathematica*, that '*In order to give an account of logic, we must presuppose and employ logic*' (1926, pp. 227–228). There was also the question of whether any logic was primarily concerned with invalid deduction and the transmission of truth-values, or the more traditional view that it treated mainly the processing of information (Sagüillo, 2009). A few remarks and quotations from some of our authors and a few critics are given here as examples; the topic deserves detailed historical study.

There was general agreement that (formal) logic was concerned with forming propositions in the propositional and predicate calculi, with valid inference, and with basic properties of truth-values; a principal task was to distinguish all of these notions from the contexts in which they are cast. For instance, in an interaction with Russell over logic(s) and algebraic topology in 1927 and 1928 (Grattan-Guinness, 2012b), Newman wrote to Russell that

> The concepts ordinarily regarded as fundamental in logic or science have won their place rather on account of their convenience than because they are truly primitive. [...] The notion I should like to take as primitive is that of things happening. In logic we are concerned with perceived happenings, which can be individualised to "one thing happening after another". This leads to the notion of "going through a row of things", & the most primitive type of proposition is that a certain process of this kind will come to an end. [...] I have hitherto pursued this idea chiefly in connection with the foundations of mathematics, but I incline to believe that it is this notion of "things happening" that is the primitive one underlying our beliefs about the external world.

This line of thought, which echoes parts of his unpublished essay, suggests that Newman had also absorbed some empiricism from Vienna, but at the cost of reducing logic to its applications; Hahn's surely preferable view was that logic

dealt exclusively with *means* of expression in language, not with the entities
or events to which it could refer (Ablondi, 2002). But at least Newman had
a stance: logicians, including textbook writers, were and are often coy about
specifying logical knowledge whichever logic is involved, and separating it from
the context it which it is being used (or, for Newman, denying that anything
needs separating). For example, 'Let p be any proposition' obviously carries a
claim of generality, but without attention paid to semantics. Does, say, 'Paris
drinks 17' count as such a proposition; or if not, why not? Does linguistics
govern logic, or should logic guide linguistics (Lenci and Sandu, 2009)? Should
logicians pay attention to sortality (Lowe, 2009) whatever logic(s) they are
using or teaching?

Logical monists defended their position by regarding pluralism as based upon
mistakes. Quine often complained that modal logics were grounded in confu-
sions between use-mention muddles of the conditional connective with implication; in individual cases the criticisms may be correct but these logics surely
have other grounds. An amusing case is the monistic textbook of Morris Cohen
and Ernest Nagel. Hierarchically they too muddled the conditional and implication (Cohen and Nagel, 1934, 47-48); monistically they complacently opined
that 'We do not believe that there is any non-Aristotelian logic in the sense in
which there is a non-Euclidian geometry [. . . ] alternative systems of logic are
different systems of notations or symbolization for the same logical facts' [p.
xv]. This description hardly captures Lewis and C. H. Langford's recent textbook (1932), which includes several of Lewis's modal logics; indeed, Cohen and
Nagel cited it only for its treatment of algebraic logic (1934, 215)! Logic, the
domain of exact reasoning, was in a confused state in the 1930s as both logical
pluralism and internal hierarchies struggled for acceptance and especially for
accurate application. The closing lines of Lewis and Langford were telling in
this respect (1932, 502):

> Those interested in the merely mathematical properties of such sys-
> tems of symbolic logic tend to prefer the more comprehensive and
> less 'strict' systems, such as [their own] S5 and Material Implica-
> tion. The interests of logical study would probably be best served
> by an exactly opposite tendency.

Today the roster of logics is large and ever increasing, albeit with many
deservedly little-studied ones sitting among some valuable innovations. My
own view of them is similar to Riemann on geometries: there are many logics,
to be characterised in the same way. I propose that its host logic is specified
by its manner of formulating well-formed propositions using connectives and
quantifiers in both propositional and functional calculi, while its metalogic has
both to contain rules of inferences and to specify its associated truth-values.
Further, a logic is always used in some context of theorising, which can come
from *any* domain of knowledge; and it always *depends* upon that context for
its reference. I emulate a distinction made by phenomenologists between the
'independent' and 'dependent parts' of a manifold, such as the weight *of* this
stone and the price *of* that loaf; weight and price cannot exist on their own,
but the stone and the loaf can (Smith, 1982). Similarly, if someone proves a

theorem in a linear algebra, say, or criticises somebody else's theory about the history of impasto techniques in art, then the logic is embedded in the well-formed (?) propositions about linear algebra or about painting, and deductions that are (in?)validly drawn from them.

One of the applications of a logic is to itself, with paradoxes as one outcome, both in the host logic and in its metalogic. While no particular "solution" of the paradox is supported or rejected, internal hierarchies profitably allows for the use not only of metalogics but also of metametalogics, .... An outline of such a characterisation of bivalent logic is given in Grattan-Guinness (2012c), together with an exploration of the varied interactions with metamathematics, axiomatisation, model theory, multisets and other theories of collections, theories of definitions, and several abstract and operator algebras.

# 8    Appendix: Despite Mathematicians, the Case of Alan Turing

Another chance for Newman to proselytize logic came in 1933 when he slipped in to some revisions of the Mathematics Tripos a new advanced course on 'Foundations of mathematics'. He taught it in the Easter terms of 1935 and 1936, covering metamathematics, the logic(ism) of Whitehead and Russell, axiomatic set theories, Gödel's theorems and Brouwer's logic (Grattan-Guinness, 2012a). Thus he did not stress logical pluralism, presumably judging it to be premature for an introductory course; however, he surely paid due attention to internal hierarchies.

Professor G.H. Hardy stopped the course in 1937: he wrote to Newman that 'though "Foundations" is now a highly respectable subject, and everybody ought to know something about it, it is, (like dancing or "groups") slightly dangerous for a bright young mathematician!'[5] Although he had been familiar with logicism from his early contacts in the 1900s with Russell and later had studied metamathematics (Grattan-Guinness, 2001), he adopted the usual attitude of mathematicians to foundational theories.

In effect as a retort, the impact of Newman's course was unexpectedly enormous, because a recent Mathematics Tripos graduate specializing in mathematical analysis sat in on the 1935 presentation. Alan Turing took from it especially metamathematics and recursion theory and rethought them in terms of his own theory of computability, forever afterwards a companion to metalogic. The rest is history (and secrecy), especially on both Turing and Newman at Bletchley Park during the war (when Newman published three technical papers on mathematical logic, one written jointly with Turing) and at the University of Manchester afterwards. But Turing's career as a logician occurred at all because Newman's happenstance of birth delayed his degree studies for three years and thereby made Penrose a contemporary student in 1919, Penrose's most unusual interest in mathematical logic led to the Vienna visit in 1922 and Newman's recognition of logic (and also topology) there with Hahn as a role

---

[5]Curiously, somebody (presumably Newman) was still allowed to put examination questions on foundations onto the Tripos papers up to his departure to Bletchley Park in 1941; further, Turing himself taught such a course in 1939 with a promised repeat in 1940 that was cancelled by his own move to Bletchley Park.

model, and changes to the Mathematics Tripos let Newman slip in his foundations course and teach it in 1935 just when Turing had graduated and was working out what to do next. What an improbable prehistory this is!

## Acknowledgments

For permission to publish from Newman's letter I thank the Archives of Saint John's College Cambridge.

## BIBLIOGRAPHY

Aberdein, A. and Read, S. (2009). The philosophy of alternative logics. In Haaparanta, L., editor, *The Development of Modern Logic*, pages 613–723. Oxford University Press, Oxford.

Ablondi, F. (2002). A note on Hahn's philosophy of logic. *History and Philosophy of Logic*, 23(1):37–43.

Anellis, I. (2009). Russell and his sources for non-classical logics. *Logica Universalis*, 3(2):153–218.

Anellis, I. (2012). Peirce's truth-functional analysis and the origin of the truth-table. *History and Philosophy of Logic*, 33:85–97.

Astroh, M. and Read, S. (1999). Hugh MacColl and the tradition of logic. *Nordic Journal of Philosophical Logic*, 2 (1998):1–234.

Brouwer, L. E. J. (1918–1919). Begründung der Mengenlehre unabhängig vom logischen Satz von ausgeschlossenen Dritten. In *Verhandlingen der Koninklijke Akademie van Wetenschappen te Amsterdam sect. 1, 12*, pages no. 5 (43 pp.), no. 12 (33 pp.). Repr. in *Collected works*, vol. 1, Amsterdam (North-Holland), 1975, 150–221.

Brouwer, L. E. J. (1928). Intuitionistische Betrachtungen über den Formalismus. *Verhandlingen der Koninklijke Akademie van Wetenschappen te Amsterdam*, 31(1):374–379. Also in *Sitzungsberichte der Königlichen Preussischen Akademie der Wissenschaften*, 48–52. Repr. in *Collected works*, vol. 1, Amsterdam (North-Holland), 1975, 409–414. English trans. in Mancosu (1998), pages 40–44.

Cohen, M. and Nagel, E. (1934). *An Introduction to Logic and Scientific Method*. Routledge, London. Abridged version 1939. Part 1 of repr. 1962; 2nd ed. (ed. J. Corcoran), Indianapolis (Hackett), 1993.

Gardiner, M. (1988). *A Scatter of Memories*. Free Association Books, London.

Gödel, K. (1930). Die Vollständigkeit der Axiome des logischen Funktionenkalküls. *Monatshefte für Mathematik und Physik*, 37:349–360. Various reprs. and transs.

Gödel, K. (1931). Über formal unentscheidbare Sätze der Principia Mathematica und verwandter Systeme. *Monatshefte für Mathematik und Physik*, 38:173–198. Many reprs. and transs.

Grattan-Guinness, I. (2001). The interest of G. H. Hardy, F.R.S., in the philosophy and the history of mathematics. *Notes and Records of the Royal Society of London*, 55:411–424.

Grattan-Guinness, I. (2011). Was Hugh MacColl a logical pluralist or a logical monist? A case study in the slow emergence of metatheorising. *Fundamenta Scientiae*, 15:189–206.

Grattan-Guinness, I. (2012a). Discovering the logician Max Newman (1897–1984). In preparation.

Grattan-Guinness, I. (2012b). Logic, topology and physics: points of contact between Bertrand Russell and Max Newman. *Russell: the Journal of Bertrand Russell Studies*, 32(1):5–29.

Grattan-Guinness, I. (2012c). A new-old characterisation of logical knowledge. *History and Philosophy of Logic*, 33:245–290.

Hilbert, D. (1922). Die logischen Grundlagen der Mathematik. *Mathematische Annalen*, 88:151–165. Repr. in *Gesammelte Abhandlungen*, vol. 3, Berlin (Springer), 1935, pages 178–191.

Lenci, A. and Sandu, G. (2009). Logic and linguistics in the twentieth century. In Haaparanta, L., editor, *The Development of Modern Logic*, pages 775–847. Oxford University Press, Oxford.

Lewis, C. I. (1912). Implication and the algebra of logic. *Mind, New Ser*, 21:522–531.

Lewis, C. I. (1914). The calculus of strict implication. *Mind, New Ser*, 23:240–247.

Lewis, C. I. (1918). *A Survey of Symbolic Logic*. University of California Press, Berkeley. Part repr. New York (Dover), 1960.

Lewis, C. I. and Langford, C. H. (1932). *Symbolic logic*. Century, New York. Repr. New York (Dover), 1959.

Lowe, E. J. (2009). *More Kinds of Being: A Further Study of Individuation, Identity, and the Logic of Sortal Terms*. Wiley-Blackwell, Chichester, 2nd edition.

Łukasiewicz, J. (1971). *Selected Works*. Trans. and ed. by L. Borkowski. North-Holland, Amsterdam.

Mancosu, P., editor (1998). *From Brouwer to Hilbert. The Debate on the Foundations of Mathematics in the 1920s*. Oxford University Press, Oxford.

Mangione, C. and Bozzi, S. (1993). *Storia della Logica da Boole ai Nostri Giorni*. Garzanti Libri, Milan.

Newman, M. H. A. (1923). *The Foundations of Mathematics from the Standpoint of Physics*. Manuscript. Saint John's College Archives, Cambridge.

Øhrstrøm, P. and Hasle, P. F. V. (2006). A. N. Prior's logic and modern temporal logic: the philosophical background. In Gabbay, D. and Woods, J., editors, *Logic and the Modalities in the Twentieth Century*, pages 399–498. Elsevier, Amsterdam.

Post, E. L. (1921). Introduction to a general theory of propositions. *American journal of mathematics*, 43:163–185. Various reprs.

Quine, W. V. O. (1970). *Philosophy of Logic*. Prentice Hall, Englewood Cliffs/New York, 1st edition.

Russell, B. A. W. (1906). The theory of implication. *American journal of mathematics*, 28:159–202.

Russell, B. A. W. (1919). *Introduction to Mathematical Philosophy*. Allen and Unwin, London.

Russell, B. A. W. (1936). On order in time. *Proceedings of the Cambridge Philosophical Society*, 32:216–228. Repr. in Logic and knowledge, London (Allen and Unwin), 1956, pages 345–363; and in *Collected papers*, vol. 10, London (Routledge), 1996, pages 122–137.

Sagüillo, J. (2009). Methodological practice and complementary concepts of logical consequence: Tarski's model-theoretic consequence and Corcoran's information-theoretic consequence. *History and Philosophy of Logic*, 30:49–68.

Sheffer, H. M. (1926). Review of *Principia Mathematica*, 2nd ed., vol. 1. *Isis*, 1(8):226–231.

Sigmund, K. (1995). A philosopher's mathematician: Hans Hahn and the Vienna Circle. *Mathematical Intelligencer*, 17(4):16–19.

Smith, B. (1982). *Parts and moments. Studies in Logic and Formal Ontology*. Philosophia, Munich.

Stadler, F. (2001). *The Vienna Circle*. Springer Publishing Company, Vienna/New York.

Torretti, R. (1978). *Philosophy of Geometry from Riemann to Poincaré*. Reidel, Dordrecht.

Turing, A. M. (1936). On computable numbers, with an application to the entscheidungs problem. *Proceedings of the London Mathematical Society*, 42(2):230–265. Various reprs. and transs.

van Dalen, D. (1990). The war of the frogs and the mice, or the crisis of *Mathematische Annalen*. The *mathematical intelligencer*, 12(4):17–31.

Weyl, H. (1921). Über die neue Grundlagenkrise der Mathematik. *Mathematische Zeitschrift*, 10:39–79. Repr. in *Gesammelte Abhandlungen*, vol. 2, Berlin (Springer), 1968, pages 143–180. English trans. in Mancosu (1998), pages 86–118.

Whitehead, A. N. and Russell, B. A. W. (1910–1913, 1925–1927). *Principia Mathematica*. 3 vols., 1st and 2nd editions. Cambridge University Press, Cambridge.

# Harmony and the Context of Deducibility

OLE THOMASSEN HJORTLAND[†]

## 1  Introduction

The philosophical discussion about logical constants has only recently moved into the substructural era. While philosophers have spent a lot of time discussing the meaning of logical constants in the context of classical versus intuitionistic logic, very little has been said about the introduction of substructural connectives. Linear logic, affine logic and other substructural logics offer a more fine-grained perspective on basic connectives such as conjunction and disjunction, a perspective which I believe will also shed light on debates in the philosophy of logic. In what follows I will look at one particularly interesting instance of this: The development of the position known as *logical inferentialism* in view of substructural connectives. I claim that sensitivity to structural properties is an interesting challenge to logical inferentialism, and that it ultimately requires revision of core notions in the inferentialist literature. Specifically, I want to argue that current definitions of proof theoretic harmony give rise to problematic nonconservativeness as a result of their insensitivity to substructurality. These nonconservativeness results are undesirable because they make it impossible to consistently add logical constants that are of independent philosophical interest.

## 2  Background

When Prior (1961) introduced the mock-connective `tonk`, he hoped to show that merely defining inference rules for a new logical constant is not sufficient to determine its meaning. In short, that *logical inferentialism* is false.[1] Simply because `tonk` is equipped with a pair of natural deduction introduction and elimination rules it does not follow that we have succesfully stipulated the semantic content of the operator. Prior's tacit assumption is that if a constant—like `tonk`—trivializes the system, then it cannot be meaningful. Its stipulation semantically misfires.

Prior's `tonk` is not a decisive objection against inferentialism, but it does present its proponents with some difficult choices. On the one hand, one can opt for an all-inclusive approach on which any set of inference rules, no matter how blatantly inconsistent, can succesfully fix the meaning of the logical constant in question. This is the attitude that Dummett (1991) styled Wittgensteinan,

---

[†]Munich Center for Mathematical Philosophy (MCMP), LMU Munich, Germany. Email: ole.hjortland@lmu.de

[1]Logical inferentialism is a thesis limited to the semantics of logical constants, in contrast to the universal inferentialism of, say, Brandom (1994).

if only losely connected to Wittgenstein. On the other hand, we can accept Prior's objection but attempt to identify criteria for successful stipulation. On the former approach tonk is perfectly meaningful, albeit still inconsistent; on the latter, tonk is the very litmus test for an adequate set of constraints on inference rules. Whatever the constraints, tonk ought to be excluded.

Belnap (1962) was an early attempt at devising a set of constraints on which ill-behaved connectives such as tonk are ruled out. Belnap suggests that what is wrong with tonk is that it is not a *conservative extension* of any (transitive) consistent system. Prawitz (1971) and Dummett (1991) followed up Belnap's criteria by offering more fine-grained analyses of the conditions under which a connective and its associated introduction and elimination rules can be conservatively added to an antecedent system.

In the subsequent literature there is a great deal of discussion of how conservativeness follows from normalization theorems (and the subformula and separability corollaries). Following Prawitz's insight that the intuitionistic connectives satisfy the *inversion principle*, a number of authors have subscribed to the view that an adequate constraint on meaningful logical constants is a *local constraint* on the associated inference rules, rather than a global constraint on the entire system. As such, conservativeness and normalisation are mere symptoms of an underlying property of the inference rules.

In the last couple of decades, highly successful work has been done on generalizing Prawitz's inversion principle. Schroeder-Heister (1984), von Plato (2001), Tennant (2002) have all discussed a generalization of natural deduction rules which facilitates a language-independent account of inversion. Schroeder-Heister (2004, 2007), Read (2000, 2010), and Francez and Dyckhoff (2012) have applied these very generalizations to give a constraint on inference rules—a constraint which after Dummett is known as *proof theoretic harmony*.[2] As a result we have a better grasp of the connections between the inversion principle, normalization, and—ultimately—consistency; there is now a better understanding of the connections between natural deduction and sequent calculus (see especially von Plato, 2001); and harmonious inference rules have been given for a range of new connectives, including modalities (*e.g.* Read, 2012). Even more importantly, Dummett and Prawitz's revisionary project of giving a justification of intuitionistic logic has run into serious problems (see Weir, 1986; Milne, 1994; Read, 2000; Rumfitt, 2000).

## 3   The Context of Deducibility

One motivation for moving from a global constraint to local constraints on inference rules is that the former is highly dependent on what Belnap calls 'the antecedent context of deducibility':

> It seems to me that the key to a solution lies in observing that even on the synthetic view, we are not defining our connectives *ab initio*, but rather in terms of an *antecedently given context of deducibility*, concerning which we have some definite notions. By that I mean

---

[2]For Dummett on harmony, see Dummett (1991, ch. 9). Schroeder-Heister prefers the term 'definitional reflection' but his constraints are nevertheless closely related.

that before arriving at the problem of characterising connectives, we have already made some assumptions about the nature of deducibility. That this is so can be seen immediately observing Prior's use of transitivity of deducibility in order to secure his ingenious result. But if we note that we already *have* some assumptions about the context of deducibility within which we are operating, it becomes apparent that by a too careless use of definitions, it is possible to create a situation in which we are forced to say things inconsistent with those assumptions (Belnap, 1962).

Cook (2005) has already explored a non-transitive consequence relation for which **tonk** is a conservative extension. Similarly, Restall (2007) has discussed the contextual sensitivity of Belnap's other criterion: *uniqueness*. In both cases the moral is the same. The global properties engendered by introducing new logical constants largely depend on prior choices about the *structural properties* of the deducibility relation, for example: Is it transitive? Does it satisfy weakening (is it monotonic)? Is it single- or multiple-conclusion? My contention is that not only are they right about this; the context of deducibility is equally important for the proper formulation of local constraints.

In fact, Dummett (1991, pp. 205–6) contains an early discussion of such structural properties. He considers the difference between a classical disjunction and a quantum logic disjunction. Dummett observes that whereas classical $\vee$-elimination allows (possibly distinct) auxiliary formulae in each subderivation (the minor premises), its quantum counterpart is restricted to subderivations where the conclusion follows from the discharged assumptions alone (*i.e.* the disjuncts). More precisely:

$$\frac{A \vee B \quad \begin{array}{c} \Gamma, [A]^u \\ \vdots \\ C \end{array} \quad \begin{array}{c} \Gamma', [B]^u \\ \vdots \\ C \end{array}}{C} \ (\vee E) \qquad \frac{A \vee B \quad \begin{array}{c} [A]^u \\ \vdots \\ C \end{array} \quad \begin{array}{c} [B]^u \\ \vdots \\ C \end{array}}{C} \ (Q \vee E)$$

The two elimination rules give rise to different classes of theorems, *e.g.* the law of distributivity is derivable in classical logic, but not in quantum logic. Nevertheless, the introduction rules are the same in each case, and The inversion principle gives the same conversion for both rules:

$$\frac{\begin{array}{c} \Pi \\ A_i \\ \hline A_1 \vee A_2 \end{array} \quad \begin{array}{c} [A_1]^u \\ \Pi_1 \\ C \end{array} \quad \begin{array}{c} [A_2]^u \\ \Pi_2 \\ C \end{array}}{C} \ (u) \quad \leadsto \quad \begin{array}{c} \Pi \\ A_i \\ \Pi_i \\ C \end{array}$$

where $i \in \{1, 2\}$. Prawitz's inversion principle and Dummett's notion of proof theoretic harmony is by and large insensitive to structural properties. This is also true for most subsequent work on harmony and related constraints. My discussion will focus on *general elimination harmony* and the work of Read (2000, 2010); Francez and Dyckhoff (2012), but the general insight applies equally well to the harmony notion advocated by Tennant (1997, 2007).

## 4   General Elimination Harmony

The idea of generalizing Prawitz's inversion principle rests on an idea developed by Martin-Löf (1984), Prawitz (1978), and Schroeder-Heister (1984). The elimination rules for each connective are put into a *general elimination* form which unifies the treatment of elimination rules.[3] The general form follows the shape of the standard disjunction elimination rule, $\vee E$ (contexts now suppressed for simplicity):

$$\frac{A \vee B \quad \overset{\displaystyle [A]^u}{\underset{\displaystyle C}{\vdots}} \quad \overset{\displaystyle [B]^u}{\underset{\displaystyle C}{\vdots}}}{C} \ (\vee E)(u)$$

Put informally, $\vee E$ says that whatever can be derived independently from each of the grounds for introducing the major premise $A \vee B$ (*i.e.* the premises $A$ and $B$ respectively) can be derived directly from the major premise itself. That is simply an instance of the inversion principle.

In fact, other connectives can also be given in a general elimination form, one for which the new rules are equivalent to the standard rules. Conjunction, for example, has the following two general elimination rules:[4]

$$\frac{A \wedge B \quad \overset{\displaystyle [A]^u}{\underset{\displaystyle C}{\vdots}}}{C} \qquad\qquad \frac{A \wedge B \quad \overset{\displaystyle [B]^u}{\underset{\displaystyle C}{\vdots}}}{C}$$

We now see the explicit duality with disjunction: There are two elimination rules because, as opposed to disjunction, conjunction has a single introduction rule with two premises. The standard conjunction elimination rules result from a simplification where $C = A$ and $C = B$ respectively. Indeed, they are equivalent since we can derive the generalized rule from the standard rules by a simple permutation:

$$\frac{A \wedge B}{\underset{\displaystyle C}{\underset{\displaystyle \vdots}{A}}} \qquad\qquad \frac{A \wedge B}{\underset{\displaystyle C}{\underset{\displaystyle \vdots}{B}}}$$

Following Read (2000) and Read (2010) we can give schemata for harmoniously inducing a set of general elimination rules from a set of introduction rules.[5] The schemata have as instances the above examples and a number of other connectives. Furthermore, it is an immediate consequence that the elimination rule of `tonk` is not harmonious with respect to the introduction rule.

---

[3]Sometimes referred to as *disjunction elimination like* rules (*del*-rules) or *parallel rules*.

[4]There is a corresponding notion of *general introduction rules* in Negri (2002) that we will not discuss here.

[5]Note that Read's schemata for general elimination harmony is somewhat revised from Read (2000) to Read (2010). I return to the difference below.

The details are as follows: Each connective $\lambda$ has a finite set $\mathcal{I}$ of $n$ introduction rules, where each such rule has a finite number $m$ of premises.[6]

$$\frac{\alpha_{1_1} \quad \cdots \quad \alpha_{1_m}}{\delta} \quad \cdots \quad \frac{\alpha_{n_1} \quad \cdots \quad \alpha_{n_m}}{\delta}$$

The introduction rule set $\mathcal{I}$ harmoniously induces a finite set $\mathcal{E}$ of $m$ elimination rules:

$$\frac{\delta \quad \overset{[\alpha_{1_1}]^u}{\underset{\gamma}{\vdots}} \quad \cdots \quad \overset{[\alpha_{n_1}]^u}{\underset{\gamma}{\vdots}}}{\gamma} \, (u) \quad \cdots \quad \frac{\delta \quad \overset{[\alpha_{1_m}]^u}{\underset{\gamma}{\vdots}} \quad \cdots \quad \overset{[\alpha_{n_m}]^u}{\underset{\gamma}{\vdots}}}{\gamma} \, (u)$$

Here $\delta$ is the major premise (and normally a formula containing a principal occurrence of the connective $\lambda$ in question). For every premise $1 \leq i \leq m$ in the introduction rules there is an $i$th elimination rule in $\mathcal{E}$ such that it has exactly one (subderivational) minor premise for each introduction rule $1 \leq j \leq n$ in $\mathcal{I}$. For each such elimination rule $1 \leq i \leq m$, the $j$th minor premise has (an arbitrary formula) $\gamma$ as conclusion, and $\alpha_{j_i}$ as assumption. When the general elimination rule is applied, each such $\alpha_{j_i}$ assumption in the minor premises is discharged. That is simply observing the idea of the inversion principle: Whatever can be derived independently from all the possible grounds of an expression, can be be derived directly from the expression itself.

It is fairly straightforward to see that both the standard rules for $\vee$ and the general elimination rules for $\wedge$ are instances of the schemata. We will therefore say that they are $GE$-harmonious. Similarly, it is evident that the inference rules for tonk are not $GE$-harmonious.

The schemata and the notion of $GE$-harmony can be extended to sets of introduction rules which themselves are hypothetical. For example the standard introduction rule for the intuitionistic conditional. Since this involves some further machinery, however, I set it aside for now (but see Read, 2000 and Read, 2010 for this and other extensions). For our purposes it is sufficient to consider simple variations of the two connectives $\wedge$ and $\vee$ that we have already looked at.

## 5 Shared Contexts and Independent Contexts

Substructural connectives have received lots of attention in a sequent calculus framework, but are less frequently studied with natural deduction rules. In sequent calculus, there is a well-known distinction between *context-sharing* (additive) and *context-independent* (multiplicative) rules.[7] Let $\wedge$ and $\otimes$ be the context-sharing and context-independent variants of conjunction:

$$\frac{\Gamma, A_i \Rightarrow C}{\Gamma, A_0 \wedge A_1 \Rightarrow C} \, (L\wedge) \qquad \frac{\Gamma \Rightarrow A \quad \Gamma \Rightarrow B}{\Gamma \Rightarrow A \wedge B} \, (R\wedge)$$

---

[6]An infinite number of introduction rules should not in principle be excluded, but note that this will potentially yield infinitary elimination rules.

[7]The distinction originally came to prominence in Girard (1987).

$$\frac{\Gamma, A, B \Rightarrow C}{\Gamma, A \otimes B \Rightarrow C} \; (L\wedge) \qquad \frac{\Gamma_1 \Rightarrow A \quad \Gamma_2 \Rightarrow B}{\Gamma_1, \Gamma_2 \Rightarrow A \otimes B} \; (R\wedge)$$

Notice how the right top-most rule has the same context $\Gamma$ in each premise sequent. It is crucial that in a substructural setting the auxiliary formulae $\Gamma$ are *multisets*, *i.e.* it matters how many copies of a single formula $A$ occurs. It is therefore significant that in the conclusion sequent there is only one copy of $\Gamma$ occurring. Contrast the right bottom-most rule where each premise sequent has possibly distinct contexts $\Gamma_1$ and $\Gamma_2$; in the sequent conclusion both (multiset) contexts are preserved. The top-most, context-sharing rule smacks of *contraction, i.e.* the structural sequent rule which allows one to collapse copies of the same formula:

$$\frac{\Gamma, A, A \Rightarrow C}{\Gamma, A \Rightarrow C}$$

In a natural deduction setting there is no explicit contradiction rule. Instead there is a corresponding policy for discharging assumptions, namely that multiple copies of the same assumption can be discharged with a single application of a hypothetical rule.[8]

Furthermore, the left-most conjunction rules also come apart. In the top-most context-sharing rule we are forced to make a choice going from bottom to top: Either preserve the right or the left conjunct, not both. If, on the other hand, we wanted to preserve both conjuncts going upwards we would have to first apply the contraction rule to the conjunction in the conclusion sequent. With the context-independent counterpart, however, we can freely bring with us a copy of each conjunct upwards.

These features of the two rule pairs can also be found in the rules for other connectives. For disjunction, the corresponding rules are simply the duals of conjunction (albeit in multiple-succedent form rather than single-succedent). In fact, we can generalize the properties to other connectives as well, but that won't matter for our discussion.

Although less discussed in the proof theoretic literature, the distinction also exists for natural deduction rules. There are several versions of linear logic in natural deduction, but here I follow Negri (2002). She shows one way to implement the distinction while staying reasonably close to the standard Prawitz style tree presentations. Here are the context-sharing rules for conjunction:

$$\frac{\begin{matrix} \Gamma^\alpha & \Gamma^\alpha \\ \vdots & \vdots \\ A & B \end{matrix}}{A \wedge B} \qquad \frac{A \wedge B \quad \begin{matrix} \Gamma, [A]^u \\ \vdots \\ C \end{matrix}}{C} \qquad \frac{A \wedge B \quad \begin{matrix} \Gamma, [B]^u \\ \vdots \\ C \end{matrix}}{C}$$

The characteristic feature of the context-sharing $\wedge I$ is the labels $\alpha$ attached to the contexts of its introduction rule. This notation is used as heuristic for the fact that after the application of the additive rule, the contexts *must be treated as a single context*. Recall the additive conjunction rules in sequent calculus:

---

[8]The correspondence has been made formal through a translation between natural deduction and sequent calculus derivations in von Plato (2001).

There is no need for the label since after the application of $\wedge R$ the contexts are merged into one copy. The label $\alpha$ indicates that whenever a formula $A$ in one copy of $\Gamma$ is discharged, an $A$ copy in the other occurrence of $\Gamma$ is also discharged. Similarly, whenever an open assumption in one copy is substituted for a derivation ending with the same formula, an identical substitution is performed on the other copy.

As a result, when an assumption in $\Gamma$ is discharged by another rule application later in the derivation, we have a form of contraction (or multiple discharge): Two copies of the formula are discharged, one in each copy of $\Gamma$.

In contrast, consider the following multiplicative rules for conjunction:

$$\cfrac{\begin{array}{cc}\Gamma_0 & \Gamma_1 \\ \vdots & \vdots \\ A & B\end{array}}{A \otimes B} \qquad \cfrac{A \otimes B \qquad \begin{array}{c}\Gamma, [A, B]^u \\ \vdots \\ C\end{array}}{C}$$

Corresponding to sequent calculus, the multiplicative conjunction $\otimes$ only has one elimination rule, and its introduction rule may be applied with (possibly) distinct assumptions $\Gamma_0$ and $\Gamma_1$.

It should be obvious that these two connectives are proof theoretically distinct. Yet, in the presence of vacuous and multiple discharge of assumptions (*e.g.* in classical logic) they become equivalent. In fact, we can then derive the context-sharing rules for $\otimes$ and the context-independent rules for $\wedge$. For example, using two copies of $A \wedge B$ we can derive the context-independent elimination rule for the additive connective $\wedge$:

$$\cfrac{A \wedge B \qquad \cfrac{A \wedge B \qquad \begin{array}{c}[A]^1, [B]^2 \\ \vdots \\ C\end{array}}{C}\,{}_{(1)}}{C}\,{}_{(2)}$$

Second, with vacuous discharge the context-sharing elimination rules are derivable for $\otimes$. Simply opt to discharge only one conjunct in each case:

$$\cfrac{A \otimes B \qquad \begin{array}{c}[A] \\ \vdots \\ C\end{array}}{C} \qquad \cfrac{A \otimes B \qquad \begin{array}{c}[B] \\ \vdots \\ C\end{array}}{C}$$

Nevertheless, it should be no surprise that the rules for $\wedge$ and $\otimes$ give rise to distinct conversions via the inversion principle:

$$\cfrac{\cfrac{\begin{array}{cc}\Gamma^\alpha & \Gamma^\alpha \\ \Pi_0 & \Pi_1 \\ A & B\end{array}}{A \wedge B} \qquad \begin{array}{c}\Sigma, [A] \\ \Pi_2 \\ C\end{array}}{C} \quad \rightsquigarrow \quad \begin{array}{c}\Gamma \\ \Pi_0 \\ \underbrace{\begin{array}{cc}\Sigma & A\end{array}} \\ \Pi_2 \\ C\end{array} \qquad\qquad \cfrac{\cfrac{\begin{array}{cc}\Gamma^\alpha & \Gamma^\alpha \\ \Pi_0 & \Pi_1 \\ A & B\end{array}}{A \wedge B} \qquad \begin{array}{c}\Sigma, [B] \\ \Pi_2 \\ C\end{array}}{C} \quad \rightsquigarrow \quad \begin{array}{c}\Gamma \\ \Pi_1 \\ \underbrace{\begin{array}{cc}\Sigma & B\end{array}} \\ \Pi_2 \\ C\end{array}$$

$$
\cfrac{
\begin{array}{cc}
\begin{array}{cc} \Gamma_0 & \Gamma_1 \\ \Pi_0 & \Pi_1 \\ A & B \\ \hline \multicolumn{2}{c}{A \wedge B} \end{array}
&
\begin{array}{c} \Gamma, [A, B] \\ \Pi_2 \\ C \end{array}
\end{array}
}{C}
\quad \leadsto \quad
\cfrac{
\underbrace{
\begin{array}{ccc}
& \Gamma_0 & \Gamma_1 \\
& \Pi_0 & \Pi_1 \\
\Gamma & A & B
\end{array}
}
\\[2pt]
\begin{array}{c} \Pi_2 \end{array}
}{C}
$$

Notice that after the uppermost reduction step for the additive conjunction it becomes explicit that there is only one copy of $\Gamma$. In contrast, the reduction step for the multiplicative conjunction keeps both contexts.

There is nothing surprising about the above: The conversions behave differently in a way reminiscent of how cut applications are pushed for the corresponding inference rules in sequent calculus. What is interesting, however, is that $GE$-harmony as articulated by Read (2000, 2010); Francez and Dyckhoff (2012) do not contain the resources to keep these connectives apart. This is a problematic omission.

In Read (2000, pp. 130–32) the theory of $GE$-harmony induces the context-independent elimination rule from the context-independent introduction rule. That appears sensible in light of the above. However, in Read (2010), and Francez and Dyckhoff (2012) the theory of $GE$-harmony is revised, and the schemata now provides the two context-sharing rules as the elimination rules induced by the context-independent introduction rule. The reason for this change is not substructural considerations, however, but problems with other connectives.

Admittedly, the asymmetry causes no problems in the presence of standard discharge policies, and this is what the authors had in mind. My only point here is that there *are* situations in which a mismatch between context-sharing and -independent does matter. In fact, there are systems in which a lack of substructural finesse will cause considerable harm. Specifically, it will engender nonconservativeness results that will make certain legitimate connectives inconsistent extensions of the systems in question. This, I argue, is sufficient motivation to take the substructural challenge to logical inferentialism seriously.

## 6  Structural Nonconservativeness

For simplicity, let us take as our starting point a system in which neither multiple nor vacuous discharge are permissible policies for assumptions. We then introduce a conjunction which is governed by asymmetric inference rules, *i.e.* a context-sharing introduction rule, and a context-independent elimination rule:

$$
\cfrac{
\begin{array}{cc}
\Gamma^\alpha & \Gamma^\alpha \\
\vdots & \vdots \\
A & B
\end{array}
}{A \sqcap B}
\qquad\qquad
\cfrac{A \sqcap B \qquad \begin{array}{c}\Gamma, [A, B]^u \\ \vdots \\ C\end{array}}{C}\ (u)
$$

Now let us assume that there is a derivation from two copies of $A$ to some conclusion $C$. Recall that there is no multiple discharge in the antecedent system, and therefore no immediate way in which the above derivation entails the existence of a derivation from one copy of $A$ to the same conclusion $C$:

$$\begin{array}{ccc} A, A & & A \\ \vdots & \rightsquigarrow & \vdots \\ \dot{C} & & \dot{C} \end{array}$$

Moreover, the following is an instance of the context-independent elimination rule for $\sqcap$:

$$\cfrac{A \sqcap A \qquad \begin{array}{c} \Gamma, [A, A]^1 \\ \vdots \\ \dot{C} \end{array}}{C} \ {\scriptstyle (1)}$$

With the context-sharing introduction rule, then, we can extend the above to the following perilous derivation:

$$\cfrac{\cfrac{\begin{array}{cc} \Gamma^\alpha & \Gamma^\alpha \\ \vdots & \vdots \\ \dot{A} & \dot{A} \end{array}}{A \sqcap A} \qquad \begin{array}{c} \Gamma, [A, A]^1 \\ \vdots \\ \dot{C} \end{array}}{C} \ {\scriptstyle (1)}$$

If we let $\Gamma$ be simply $A$, both the premises of the introduction rule are trivial, and after its application they are treated as one premise. The latter fact is merely the characteristic feature of the context-sharing introduction rule. What this means is that there is now a derivation directly from a single copy of $A$ to the conclusion $C$. Contraction is admissible.

We can drive the point home with two concrete examples.

EXAMPLE 1. Assume that prior to the introduction of the conjunction $\sqcap$ the system only contained a conditional $\rightarrow$ governed by the two standard rules:

$$\cfrac{\begin{array}{c} [A]^u \\ \vdots \\ \dot{B} \end{array}}{A \rightarrow B} \ {\scriptstyle (\rightarrow I)(u)} \qquad \cfrac{A \rightarrow B \quad A}{B} \ {\scriptstyle (\rightarrow E)}$$

As per our hypothesis that the antecedent system is contraction-free, the conditional rules do not allow multiple discharge of assumptions. But with the introduction of the conjunction, we have the return of explicit multiple discharge. We can now extend the previous derivation with an application of the conditional rules:

$$\cfrac{\cfrac{\cfrac{\cfrac{\begin{array}{cc} [A^\alpha]^2 & [A^\alpha]^2 \\ \vdots & \vdots \\ \dot{A} & \dot{A} \end{array}}{A \sqcap A} \qquad \begin{array}{c} \Gamma, [A, A]^1 \\ \vdots \\ \dot{C} \end{array}}{C} \ {\scriptstyle (1)}}{A \rightarrow C} \ {\scriptstyle (2)} \qquad A}{C}$$

The derivation is now blatantly from one copy of $A$ to $C$, with the original two assumptions of $A$ treated as one discharged assumption in the application of $\to I$ (with index 2). Since both $A$ and $C$ are arbitrary we can now make this move with any formulae in the language. This is a form of structural nonconservativeness—multiple discharge becomes admissible with the introduction of a new connective.

EXAMPLE 2. A more startling example of structural nonconservativeness results if we instead consider a less standard connective, $\bullet$, read 'bullet' (see Read, 2000, p. 141):

$$
\begin{array}{cc}
\begin{array}{c}
[\bullet]^u \\
\vdots \\
\dfrac{\bot}{\bullet} \ (\bullet I)(u)
\end{array}
&
\begin{array}{c}
[\bot]^u \\
\vdots \\
\dfrac{\bullet \quad \bullet \quad C}{C} \ (\bullet E)(u)
\end{array}
\end{array}
$$

The inference rules for $\bullet$ are $GE$-harmonious by the standards of Read (2000). Yet Read acknowledges that not only do the rules fail to normalize, they lead straight to triviality in the presence of multiple discharge and *ex falso quodlibet* for $\bot$. In short, contrary to what Dummett and Prawitz assumed, harmony does not entail consistency.

It is all the more remarkable that a connective like $\bullet$ does indeed normalize in the absence of multiple discharge of assumptions. The inference rules are perfectly consistent in contraction-free systems. All the more problematic, then, that when the conjunction $\sqcap$ is added to the system, the result is inconsistency.[9] In other words, the upshot is more than just the admissibility of contraction; the resulting system can derive anything.

It is important to note that the type of nonconservativeness result in question is a direct result of mixing context-sharing and context-independent rules. If we were to combine the context-independent introduction and elimination rules, the problematic derivation would not be possible. The context-independent introduction rule would still leave us with two separate copies of the assumption $A$, in which case no contraction has occurred. Similarly, using exclusively context-sharing rules would not lead to nonconservativeness. It is only because of the reckless combination of inference rules that the policies for discharging assumptions are indirectly altered.

The admissibility of contraction is nothing new in sequent calculus. The above sort of derivation has a more familiar sequent counterpart:

$$
\dfrac{\dfrac{A \Rightarrow A \quad A \Rightarrow A}{A \Rightarrow A \sqcap A} \ (R\sqcap) \quad \dfrac{A, A \Rightarrow C}{A \sqcap A \Rightarrow C} \ (L\sqcap)}{A \Rightarrow C} \ (Cut)
$$

Again, the $R\sqcap$ application is context-sharing (note how two copies of $A$ are collapsed into one), while the $L\sqcap$ rule application is context-independent. After an application of Cut we have transformed a sequent of the form $A, A \Rightarrow C$ into one of the form $A \Rightarrow C$. A case of contraction, if anything is. Indeed,

---

[9]See Read (2012) for details on the derivation that leads to inconsistency.

the particular inference rules for conjunction is used in **G3** systems of classical logic precisely to make contraction admissible. In contrast, the more common **G1** systems have an explicit contraction rule.[10]

## Conclusion

For all that is said so far, perhaps one might want to reply with a shrug: The examples are artificial, and have little if any impact on philosophical debates. But that contention is simply wrong, and the attitude is unfortunate. Setting aside the principle that proof theoretic harmony should apply generally to connectives of all persuasions, there are still ample reasons to take them seriously in the philosophy of logic.[11] Substructural connectives are already commonplace in the relevant logic literature, but have now permeated a number of philosophical discussions. In formal epistemology, substructural systems have been used by van Benthem (2008) and Sequoiah-Grayson (167); in debates about vagueness substructural systems have been advocated by Zardini (2008) and Cobreros et al. (2012); and in formal semantics Barker (2010) has used substructural connectives to model free choice permission. The example I am mostly interested in strikes closer to home, however.

EXAMPLE 3. Contraction-free systems have received a lot of attention in discussions of set-theoretic and semantic paradoxes. Two recent substructural approaches are Petersen (2000) and Zardini (2011), but the strategy goes back to Curry (1942) and a number of works by Ross Brady. The observation common to their work is that unrestricted comprehension (for set theory) and unrestricted truth predicates (for theories of truth) can be consistently added to contraction-free systems. These logical constants can be given a natural deduction form as follows:

$$\frac{A}{T\langle A\rangle} \ (TI) \qquad \frac{T\langle A\rangle}{A} \ (TE)$$

$$\frac{\Phi(t)}{t \in \lambda x \Phi(x)} \ (\lambda E) \qquad \frac{t \in \lambda x \Phi(x)}{\Phi(t)} \ (\lambda E)$$

It is obviously a controversial philosophical issue whether such unrestricted rules are appropriate for our theories of truth and properties respectively. But precisely because this an ongoing philosophical concern, we cannot have it short-circuited by a harmony constraint which excludes them. On the contrary, the logical inferentialist ought not impose constraints which fail to preserve the substructural nuances required for these philosophical theories.

A theory of proof theoretic harmony that is insensitive to substructural differences is in danger of permitting structural nonconservativeness, *e.g.* admissibility of contraction. The result is a theory which renders inconsistent connectives whose inference rules are philosophically motivated and perfectly well-behaved in the appropriate context of deducibility. What we are left with

---

[10]See Troelstra and Schwichtenberg (2000, p. 77) for details.

[11]Full disclosure: My position is that structural properties are indeed part of the meaning of logical connectives, and that proof theoretic semantics therefore has to reflect it (see Hjortland, 2012a). For the opposite view, see *e.g.* Paoli (2003).

is what I call the *substructuralist challenge* to logical inferentialism: A rearticulation of proof theoretic harmony in substructural terms.[12]

# BIBLIOGRAPHY

Barker, C. (2010). Free choice permission as resource-sensitive reasoning. *Semantics and Pragmatics*, 3(10):1–38.

Belnap, N. D. (1962). Tonk, plonk and plink. *Analysis*, 22(6):130–134.

Brandom, R. B. (1994). *Making it Explicit: Reasoning, Representing and Discursive Commitment*. Harvard University Press, Cambridge, MA.

Cobreros, P., Egré, P., Ripley, D., and van Rooij, R. (2012). Tolerant, classical, strict. *Journal of Philosophical Logic*, 41:347–385.

Cook, R. (2005). What's wrong with tonk(?). *Journal of Philosophical Logic*, 34:217–226.

Curry, H. B. (1942). The inconsistency of certain formal logics. *Journal of Symbolic Logic*, 7(3):115–117.

Dummett, M. A. E. (1991). *The Logical Basis of Metaphysics*. Duckworth, London.

Francez, N. and Dyckhoff, R. (2012). A note on harmony. *Journal of Philosophical Logic*, 41:613–628.

Girard, J.-Y. (1987). Linear logic. *Theoretical Computer Science*, 50:1–102.

Hjortland, O. T. (2012a). Logical pluralism, meaning-variance, and verbal disputes. *Australasian Journal of Philosophy*. To appear.

Hjortland, O. T. (2012b). Proof theoretic semantics in the substructural era. Unpublished manuscript.

Martin-Löf, P. (1984). *Intuitionistic Type Theory*. Bibliopolis, Napoli.

Milne, P. (1994). Classical harmony: Rules of inference and the meaning of the logical constants. *Synthese*, 100:49–94.

Negri, S. (2002). A normalizing system of natural deduction for intuitionistic linear logic. *Archive for Mathematical Logic*, 41(8):789–810.

Paoli, F. (2003). Quine and Slater on paraconsistency and deviance. *Journal of Philosophical Logic*, 32:531–548.

Petersen, U. (2000). Logic without contraction as based on inclusion and unrestricted abstraction. *Studia Logica*, 64(3):365–403.

Prawitz, D. (1971). Ideas and results in proof theory. In Fenstad, J. E., editor, *Proceedings of the 2nd Scandinavian Logic Symposium*, pages 235–308. North Holland, Amsterdam.

Prawitz, D. (1978). Proofs and the meanings and completeness of the logical constants. In Hintikka, J., editor, *Essays on Mathematical and Philosophical Logic*, pages 25–40. Reidel, Dordrecht.

Prior, A. N. (1961). The runabout inference ticket. *Analysis*, 21:38–39.

Read, S. (2000). Harmony and autonomy in classical logic. *Journal of Philosophical Logic*, 29:123–154.

Read, S. (2010). General-elimination harmony and the meaning of the logical constants. *Journal of Philosophical Logic*, 39(5):557–576.

Read, S. (2012). Harmony and modality. In C. Dégremont, L. K. and Rückert, H., editors, *On Dialogues, Logics and other Strange Things*. Kings College Publications. Forthcoming.

Restall, G. (2007). Proof theory and meaning: On the context of deducibility. In *Proceedings of Logic Colloquium 2007*. Cambridge University Press, Cambridge.

Rumfitt, I. (2000). "Yes" and "No". *Mind*, 109:781–820.

Schroeder-Heister, P. (1984). A natural extension of natural deduction. *Journal of Symbolic Logic*, 49(4):1284–1300.

Schroeder-Heister, P. (2004). On the Notion of Assumption in Logical Systems. In Bluhm, R. and Nimtz, C., editors, *Selected Papers Contributed to the Sections of GAP5, Fifth International Congress of the Society for Analytical Philosophy, Bielefeld, 22-26 September 2003*, pages 27–48. Mentis, Paderborn. www.gap5.de/proceedings.

Schroeder-Heister, P. (2007). Generalized definitional reflection and the inversion principle. *Logica Universalis*, 1(2):355–376.

Schroeder-Heister, P. (2012). Definitional reflection and basic logic. In Miaetti, M. E., Palmgren, E., and Rathjen, M., editors, *Advances in Constructive Topology and Logical Foundations*. To appear.

---

[12]Schroeder-Heister (2012) offers a substructural version of his definitional reflection. My own framework is outlined in Hjortland (2012b).

Sequoiah-Grayson, S. (167). A positive information logic for inferential information. *Synthese*, 2(409–431).

Tennant, N. (1997). *The Taming of the True*. Oxford University Press, Oxford.

Tennant, N. (2002). Ultimate normal forms for parallelized natural deductions. *Logic Journal of the IGPL*, 10(3):299–337.

Tennant, N. (2007). Inferentialism, logicism, harmony, and a counterpoint. In Miller, A., editor, *Essays for Crispin Wright: Logic, Language, and Mathematics, vol. 2*. OUP, Oxford.

Troelstra, A. S. and Schwichtenberg, H. (2000). *Basic Proof Theory*. Cambridge University Press, Cambridge.

van Benthem, J. (2008). Logical dynamics meets logical pluralism? *Australasian Journal of Logic*, 6:182–209.

von Plato, J. (2001). Natural deduction with general elimination rules. *Archive for Mathematical Logic*, 40(7):541–567.

Weir, A. (1986). Classical harmony. *Notre Dame Journal of Formal Logic*, 27(4):459–482.

Zardini, E. (2008). A model of tolerance. *Studia Logica*, 90(3):337–368.

Zardini, E. (2011). Truth without contra(di)ction. *The Review of Symbolic Logic*, 4:498–535.

# Affirmative and Negative in Ibn Sīnā

WILFRID HODGES[†]

## 1 Dedication

In a recent interview in The Reasoner (Aberdein, 2011), Stephen Read lets slip that he first went to Oxford as a postgraduate student to study Chomskian linguistics, not any of the things that he has since become famous for. He did study it for a while with Pieter Seuren, and he reckons 'something rubbed off'.

A few months ago Stephen asked me for some information about Ibn Sīnā's views on affirmative sentences. I sent him a translation of the relevant part of Ibn Sīnā's *ᶜIbāra* section ii.1, and he expressed some interest in learning more about Ibn Sīnā's views in this area. This paper is a first and very provisional response. It includes a translation of most of *ᶜIbāra* ii.1, and it makes a preliminary foray into the relations between logic and linguistics in Ibn Sīnā's treatment of affirmativeness. There is a different take on some of this material in Baeck (1987).

I thank Manuela Giolfo, Ruth Kempson, Amirouche Moktefi, Paul Thom and Kees Versteegh for helpful information and comments.

## 2 Aristotle on Affirmative and Negative

Aristotle in his *Categories* 10, 13a37ff, *De Interpretatione* 4f, 17a8–37; 10, 19b5–20b12 and *Prior Analytics* i.2, 25a1–13; i.46, 51b5–52b35 introduced a distinction between affirmative and negative (*kataphátikos* and *apophátikos*, or in noun form *katáphasis* and *apóphasis*). Aristotle's views are not my concern here. But already Aristotle's treatment of the notions raises some fundamental questions:

(a) What is the point of the distinction? (It is built into Aristotle's predicative syllogisms through the classification of propositions, and hence into his modal syllogisms. But the notions appear in *Categories* and *De Interpretatione* without any reference to syllogisms.)

(b) Is it just propositions that can be affirmative or negative, or can we also classify predicates as affirmative or negative? (The treatments in *Categories* and *De Interpretatione* seem to be about propositions, but the discussion in *Prior Analytics* i.46 extends the notions to predicates.)

(c) Among propositions, is it only predicative ones that can properly be called affirmative or negative, or does the classification also apply to compound sentences? (*De Interpretatione* 5 can be read either way.)

[†]Herons Brook, Sticklepath, Okehampton, Devon EX20 2PY, England.
Email: `wilfrid.hodges@btinternet.com`

(d) What is the basis for the distinction that Aristotle makes in *De Interpre-tatione* 10 between, for example, denying that a man is just and affirming that a man is not just? (The question seems to be about which sentences containing a negation are affirmative and which are negative; so an adequate answer to (a) should go some way towards answering (d) too. But to complicate matters, Aristotle comes at similar examples from another angle when he introduces negated nouns like 'not human' under the name of 'indefinite names', as in *De Interpretatione* 2.)

Here 'predicative' propositions are the standard syllogistic ones, for example the affirmative 'Every horse is an animal', 'Some horse is an animal' and the negative 'No horse is an animal', 'Not every horse is an animal'. Aristotle sometimes includes singular sentences along the lines of 'Cleon is an animal' (which is affirmative) and 'Cleon is not a horse' (which might be either affirmative or negative depending on the answer you give to (d)). A 'predicative' syllogism is one consisting of predicative sentences. Today we distinguish predicative propositions and syllogisms from modal ones, which have 'necessarily', 'possibly' or similar modalities added. Predicative syllogisms are often referred to as categorical syllogisms; it was Stephen Read who persuaded me that the same word should be used for the propositions as for the syllogisms.

One of the jobs of a commentator should be to answer questions like (a)–(d) above, rather than simply repeating what Aristotle says. But it does seem that Ibn Sīnā is the first commentator who is on record as taking these or related questions seriously. Before him, Aristotle's pupil Theophrastus already felt that (d) needed further attention. Theophrastus introduced the term 'transposed' (*ek metathéseōs*) in connection with Aristotle's examples of propositions that contain negation but are affirmative. But we don't know whether he had a general definition of *ek metathéseōs*, or even what he thought was the purpose of the notion. (See Fortenbaugh et al., 1992, pp. 148–153 for the sources.) Theophrastus' term gives the modern term 'metathetic'. The Arabic logicians rendered it as *maᶜdūl*, which literally means 'deflected'. The term seems not to have come through to the Latin West.

Here is a brief summary of some of Ibn Sīnā's contributions to (a)–(d). On (a) he provides a new distinction between affirmative and negative sentences, namely the following two principles:

**Affirmative Principle.** In every true affirmative predicative sentence the subject term is satisfied (i.e. non-empty). (*ᶜIbāra* 79.13)

**Negative Principle.** A negative predicative sentence is true when its subject term is not satisfied. (*ᶜIbāra* 81.3f)

Together these two principles — if they are true — make it essential in logic to distinguish between affirmative and negative sentences. Below we will ask whether these principles are really new with Ibn Sīnā, what he meant by them, and why he regarded them as true.

As to (b), Ibn Sīnā's views on Aristotle's discussion in *Prior Analytics* i.46 are withering. Ignoring Aristotle's own text, he quotes at length a very garbled discussion by an unknown commentator, and concludes

(1) It's fair to say that any explanation of all this is going to come from somebody other than me. At any rate there is nothing convincing about it in the commentaries. They just charge around randomly. (*Qiyās* 195.14–16)

We will note below that Ibn Sīnā normally regards 'affirmative' and 'negative' as a classification of *sentences* (spoken or written).

Ibn Sīnā devotes *ᶜIbāra* 41.15–42.15, part of his commentary on *De Interpretatione* 5, to question (c). He begins by noting that when Aristotle restricts affirmation and denial to 'simple' as opposed to 'compound' statements, he could be using 'simple statement' to mean predicative statement, or he could be using it to mean propositions as opposed to syllogisms (which are compounded from propositions). In the second case, propositional compounds have to be classifiable as affirmations or denials. Rather surprisingly, Ibn Sīnā suggests that 'Either *S* or *T*', read as an *exclusive* disjunction, should be counted as an affirmation. To us there is something negative about exclusive disjunction; but we saw in (d) that the presence of a negation doesn't automatically make a sentence a denial.

Ibn Sīnā's response to (d) is perhaps his most interesting. For comparison, consider the views of Ibn Sīnā's predecessor Al-Fārābī, a philosopher for whom Ibn Sīnā had great respect — though for Ibn Sīnā, respecting someone and agreeing with them were never the same thing. Al-Fārābī notes that Aristotle's own examples of metathetic propositions all involve a phenomenon which is found in Greek but

(2) hardly exists in the Arabic language, except as an imported irregularity:

we can attach a negative particle to a noun or adjective so that the compound behaves as a single word, which (following Aristotle) he calls an 'indefinite noun'. He remarks that the phenomenon is found also in Persian and Syriac.

(3) [...] the communities that use them do not count them as phrases; indeed, to them their shapes are the same as those of single expressions: they behave like single expressions and they inflect like single expressions. (*Shorter Treatise on ᶜIbāra*, trans. Zimmermann, 1981, p. 222)

He goes on to suggest that these indefinite nouns should be regarded as 'affirmations' (note the implied answer to (b) above) because they translate into Arabic expressions that don't contain a negative particle at all.

Al-Fārābī has a good deal to say about indefinite nouns and metathetic propositions; they are the meat of pages 105–141 of his *Commentary on ᶜIbāra* (pp. 100–137 of Zimmermann 1981, see also Thom 2008). But his explanations cited above make it a mystery what he thinks he is talking about. Since the relevant phenomenon 'hardly exists in Arabic', is he talking about doing logic in Greek (or perhaps also in Persian or Syriac)? Or is he recommending a reform of Arabic that would introduce these indefinite nouns? (Al-Fārābī's failure to detach himself from Greek can be put in a wider context; see the discussion in Zimmermann, 1981, pp. cv–cxxxix.)

Contrast this with Ibn Sīnā's approach. For Ibn Sīnā the distinction between affirmative and negative should apply across all languages, including 'possible' ones ($^c$*Ibāra* 79.2f). Since each language handles negations in its own way, the users of a language will need to use their native intuition (*šu$^c$ūr*) to determine which constructions give affirmative sentences and which give negative ($^c$*Ibāra* 79.8). We infer that for a particular language, the dividing line between affirmative and negative is an empirical fact. But then which empirical fact is it? What is the language user's intuition supposed to be detecting? Below I will argue that there is a reasonable candidate, with due deference to the dangers of anachronism. It's worth remarking that Ibn Sīnā's appeal to user's intuition, though quite natural for a modern linguist, was unusual for the Arabic linguistics of his day, which was heavily corpus-based.

## 3  Definitions

We have four words to understand: *'ijāb* 'affirmation', *salb* 'denial', *mūjib* 'affirmative' and *sālib* 'negative'. As a rough estimate of their importance, here is a tally of the number of times each of them appears per ten pages of the Arabic of $^c$*Ibāra* and *Qiyās*:

|          | *'ijāb* | *mūjib* | *salb* | *sālib* |
|----------|---------|---------|--------|---------|
| $^c$*Ibāra* | 9       | 7       | 14     | 5       |
| *Qiyās*     | 3       | 8       | 5      | 9       |

In this section I sketch how Ibn Sīnā seems to understand the relations between the four words. I beg leave to be rather dogmatic; the full reasoning would multiply the length of this paper by ten.

From Ibn Sīnā's discussion at *Maqūlāt* 255.11–14, read with some charity, it appears that the basic notions are '$x$ is affirmed of $y$ in $z$' and '$x$ is denied of $y$ in $z$', where $z$ is a sentence. Translating Ibn Sīnā's own clunky definitions into modern formats, we have:

(4)  $x$ is affirmed of $y$ in $z$ $\Leftrightarrow$ $z$ is a sentence which asserts of $y$ that it satisfies the description $x$.

In moving from 'is affirmed' to 'affirming' or 'affirmative', we suppress the first and second arguments, in effect by quantifying them out:

(5)  $z$ is affirmative $\Leftrightarrow$ $z$ is a sentence which asserts, for some $x$ and $y$, that $y$ satisfies the description $x$.

At *Maqūlāt* loc. cit. Ibn Sīnā suggests that 'denied' and 'negative' can be treated in the same way, I presume by putting 'doesn't satisfy' in place of 'satisfies'.

The two nouns 'affirmation' and 'denial' are harder to pin down, not least because Ibn Sīnā himself is not wholly consistent in his use of abstract nouns. There are some disheartening contradictions, such as

(6)  The two mutual opposites in affirmation and denial are not the affirmation and the denial [themselves]. (*Maqūlāt* 256.1f)
I mean that affirmation and denial are genuinely mutual opposites. ($^c$*Ibāra* 43.8f)

I think that in the sentence from *Maqūlāt*, Ibn Sīnā is using 'affirmation' and 'denial' as names for the *meanings* of 'affirmative' and 'negative' respectively. In the sentence from *ᶜIbāra* he is probably using 'an affirmation' to mean 'an affirmative sentence', and likewise with 'a denial'. But there may be better explanations.

It might seem more sensible to translate *salb* as 'negation' rather than 'denial', to match 'negative'. But in practice this translation could mislead. For example at *ᶜIbāra* 78.12 we have to read 'the predicate is denied' (i.e. denied of the subject). To say that the predicate is 'negated' would suggest that it has a negation at the beginning of it, which is precisely not what Ibn Sīnā wants to say here. But in some other contexts we do have to translate *salb* as 'negation', for example in 'particle of negation'.

Ibn Sīnā is clear throughout this discussion in *Maqūlāt* that affirmation and denial have to do with *sentences*, and a sentence (*qawl*) is for him a linguistic object. The fuller discussion of affirmation etc. in *ᶜIbāra* is also in terms of sentences. (He does say 'proposition' (*qaḍiyya*) at *Maqūlāt* 255.17 and twice at 256.2, and indeed many times in *ᶜIbāra*. But reading *qaḍiyya* as a linguistic object is a lot easier than reading *qawl* as a kind of meaning; for example at *ᶜIbāra* 33.5 he gives a sentence and calls it both *qawl* and *qaḍiyya*.) It should follow that in spite of their basic status in Ibn Sīnā's logic, neither 'affirmative' nor 'negative' is a notion inherited by logic from First Philosophy, the part of metaphysics that establishes basic notions and facts about existence and ideas. If 'affirmative' and 'negative' were such notions, we would expect to find them discussed in the *Ilāhiyyāt*, the volume of Ibn Sīnā's *Šifā'* dealing with metaphysics; but they are not mentioned there, as Goichon's lexicon Goichon (1938) confirms.

Nevertheless the definitions given above rest on the notion of an idea satisfying the description given by another idea, and this is undoubtedly a notion from First Philosophy. If I interpret Ibn Sīnā correctly, he intends that the difference between 'affirmative' and 'negative' lies at the level of meanings; but for any particular language, the question which sentences meet the criterion for being affirmative or negative is a matter of linguistics.

At *ᶜIbāra* 42.16f Ibn Sīnā offers separate and parallel definitions of affirmation and denial for predicative sentences. Nevertheless at *ᶜIbāra* 34.11f he has already explained that denial has to be defined in terms of affirmation and not vice versa. I think his choice for the order of definition is unfortunate. Some sentences are marked out as having negation in a certain dominant position in them; these sentences are called negative. The other sentences, the unmarked ones, don't need a special name at all.

## 4    The Distinguishing Criterion

Ibn Sīnā's discussion of the difference between denial and metathesis in *ᶜIbāra* 78.13–19.10 should be read in the light of his general views about the structure of meanings. For predicative sentences he adopted a sort of crude X-bar theory at the level of meanings. The sentence has two descriptive components: a subject (today we say Noun Phrase, NP) and a predicate (Verb Phrase, VP). Each of NP and VP consists of a head descriptive term together with various adjuncts or attachments (*lawāḥīq, ziyādāt, šurūṭ*). In a metathetic sentence there is a negation, but it is an adjunct of VP. (At *ᶜIbāra* 81.12 he briefly mentions another kind of metathesis where the negation is an adjunct of NP.) In a true denial the negation is not incorporated into NP or VP; instead it controls the relationship between the two.

This is one of a number of places where Ibn Sīnā's language of adjuncts and attachments seems to cover material that today we would handle in terms of scope. Could it be that a negative sentence is one which has a negation whose scope is the whole sentence, whereas a metathetic affirmative sentence is one where a negation occurs but has its scope confined within one of NP and VP? Thus at *ᶜIbāra* 78.15 Ibn Sīnā contrasts the two cases where

(7)    the particle of negation is included so as to deny the predicate [of the subject], or [...] it is included so as to be a part of the predicate, making the predicate the [combined] whole.

At *ᶜIbāra* 79.8f he talks of the copula (which joins NP to VP) 'taking precedence over' (*tuqaddamu*) the negation, with the effect that the sentence is affirmative. These feel to me like scope distinctions.

Can we make sense of this in terms of logical scope of negation? I think not. Put briefly, the chief criterion for an occurrence of a descriptive term $X$ to lie in the logical scope of an occurrence $P$ of a negation in a sentence $\phi(X)$ is that removing $P$ reverses the monotonicity of the occurrence, in the following sense. We say that the occurrence has upward monotonicity if $X \subseteq Y$ and $\phi(X)$ together imply $\phi(Y)$; it has downward monotonicity if $Y \subseteq X$ and $\phi(X)$ together imply $\phi(Y)$. Ideas of this kind played a major role in Scholastic thinking about syllogisms and were sometimes taken as a general justification for syllogistic reasoning (Sánchez Valencia, 1994). Logical scope in this sense is unlikely to have been what Ibn Sīnā intended, because he barely ever shows the slightest awareness of monotonicity. He makes no distinctions along the lines of distributed/undistributed. Quite generally he seems blind to the logical scopes of negations. In Hodges (2012) I give some evidence on this and suggest some reasons for this blind spot.

On the other hand there is a distinction in modern syntactic literature that seems to match Ibn Sīnā's distinction rather closely. This is the distinction introduced by Klima (1964) between sentence negation and constituent negation. In sentence negation the negating expression includes the whole sentence within its syntactic scope; in constituent negation it includes only a constituent of the sentence. It's at first sight plausible that Ibn Sīnā's negative sentences are Klima's sentence negations and Ibn Sīnā's affirmative metatheses are Klima's constituent negations.

Klima suggested some criteria for this distinction, in terms of where the particle of negation allows us to add expressions of 'negative polarity' without violating grammaticality. Later authors proposed other criteria. The criteria don't always agree, and the differences are interesting for us. Take for example the two sentences

(8)    (i) Some birds don't fly.
       (ii) Not all birds fly.

Adger offers the criterion that a negation is 'sentential' if it 'simply denies the truth of the non-negated version of the sentence' (Adger, 2003, p. 176). We note that (i) doesn't simply deny the truth of (i') below, but (ii) does simply deny the truth of (ii'):

(9)  (i') Some birds fly.
     (ii') All birds fly.

So by Adger's criterion (ii) is an instance of sentence negation but (i) is not. By contrast one of Klima's main criteria is that in cases of sentence negation one can grammatically add an affirmative tag question, but with constituent negation one can't. Thus:

(10)  (i") Some birds don't fly, do they?
      (ii") Not all birds fly, do they?

By Klima's criterion, (i) and (ii) are both instances of sentence negation. It's clear why these examples are interesting for us: both (i) and (ii) illustrate standard English translations for Aristotle's negative existentially quantified predicative statements. Should we infer from Adger that (i) is really affirmative, or is Klima's criterion enough to certify it as a denial? The reader might like to run (i) and (ii) past the further criteria proposed in Haegeman (1995).

I think I can see what is happening here. Throughout the 78 pages of Klima's seminal paper, he limits his examples almost entirely to predicative sentences (today we would say single-clause sentences), and moreover very few of his NPs carry explicit quantifiers. So he treats the NPs as referring to fixed individuals or sets, and as a result his criteria are not designed for determining whether the NPs lie within the scope of the negation. Both Haegeman's and Adger's criteria do a better job in this direction. (I think that as stated, Adger's criterion will run into trouble with Klima's negative polarity items, but that's irrelevant for us.)

However, both Haegeman and Adger generally continue the restriction to single-clause sentences. Consider another logically relevant sentence:

(11)  It's possible that no green things conduct electricity.

This is not the denial of 'It's possible that green things conduct electricity', so by Adger's criterion it is an example of constituent negation. Would Ibn Sīnā count it as negative? The evidence here is interestingly complex. Aristotle lifted the classification of predicative sentences to their modalised versions, so he would have had to regard this sentence as negative. But Ibn Sīnā normally— though not universally—tacks the modality onto the end of the sentence, as it were

(12)  No green things conduct electricity, with possibility.

By Adger's criterion I still make this a constituent negation, but the crucial difference is that in (12) the main clause is undoubtedly negative, whereas in (11) it surely has to count as affirmative.

It does seem that the distinction between sentence negation and constituent negation is problematic for compound sentences. In English the only way of making sure that a negation encloses both clauses of a compound sentence, for example a conjunction '*S* and *T*', is to preface it with 'It is not the case that [...]', which shrinks the compound sentence down to a single nominal 'that [...]'. I don't want to put words into the mouths of the syntacticians, but it seems that this could be grounds for arguing that in English any genuine compound proposition has to be reckoned affirmative. If the same applies to Arabic, then we have a confirmation of Ibn Sīnā's treatment of exclusive disjunctions as affirmations, which we mentioned in §2.

In sum: Ibn Sīnā's classification of some sentences as affirmative and others as negative makes reasonable sense if we take his 'negative sentences' to be sentences containing a negation whose syntactic (rather than logical) scope is the entire sentence. His metathetic affirmations then fall into place as sentences where a negation occurs but has a more limited syntactic scope. This notion of syntactic scope of negations is not unproblematic even for modern syntactic theory, but there is an overlap between the cases that are difficult today and those where Ibn Sīnā's views are unclear.

There remains the question why Ibn Sīnā believed the Affirmative Principle and the Negative Principle. Although the earliest statement that we have of the Affirmative Principle seems to be Ibn Sīnā's own, he signals that it had been discussed earlier, though it was denied only by some deranged individuals who 'worked themselves up into a state' about it (*ᶜIbāra* 80.3f). So evidently he thought it was the orthodox position. How could he come to think this?

Ibn Sīnā will have had in front of him the statements of Aristotle and Al-Fārābī of the Affirmative Principle *for singular sentences*:

> When Socrates doesn't exist at all, it is not true either that Socrates is ill or that he is healthy. (Aristotle *Categories* 10, 13b18f; I translate from Isḥaq's Arabic version)

(13) But if the answer 'no' is given to the question whether Socrates is wise while Socrates does not exist, we may not turn it into the metathetic affirmation 'Socrates is not-wise', but must put it negatively as 'Socrates is not wise'. (Al-Fārābī *Shorter Treatise*, trans. Zimmermann, 1981, p. 240)

So Ibn Sīnā will have been able to quote the authority of both Aristotle and Al-Fārābī for the Affirmative Principle in the case of singular sentences. Not only that, but the claim made by Aristotle and Al-Fārābī is very plausible: if Socrates is wise then surely Socrates does exist. Ibn Sīnā could reasonably suppose that for singular sentences the Affirmative Principle was an obvious truth which was widely accepted.

So the step that needs explanation is the generalisation to quantified sentences. There are passages, for example *ᶜIbāra* 80.1f, where it seems that Ibn Sīnā is trying to infer the truth of the Affirmative Principle in general from its truth in the singular case. I won't try to defend his argument, but my guess is that Ibn Sīnā felt that there is no relevant difference between singular sentences and quantified ones. He might reason that (by definition) the only difference between a particular and a universal is that a particular carries a restriction on its meaning, to the effect that it can't legitimately be used if it describes more than one thing. How could this difference affect the Affirmative Principle?

The Negative Principle should probably be inferred from the Affirmative Principle and the thesis that every affirmative sentence has a negative contradictory negation and vice versa. The contradictory negation of a sentence is true if and only if the sentence is false.

We should say something about Ibn Sīnā's remark that the subject term of an affirmative predicative sentence must be satisfied 'either in the world or in the mind (*ḏihn*)' (*<sup>c</sup>Ibāra* 79.13f). The example that he gives immediately after stating the principle (the regular icosahedron, an example he uses for the same purpose at *Qiyās* 21.7f, *Mašriqiyyūn* 12.5) shows at once why he adds the phrase 'in the mind'. We can and do reason logically about regular icosahedra, as for example in Book 13 of Euclid's *Elements*, and surely we are justified in doing this. But nobody knows for certain that there are any exact regular icosahedra anywhere in the world. There is more to be said about what he intends by 'in the mind', but it is not closely related to the distinction between affirmative and negative—and so I leave it unsaid here.

# 5   Affirmative and Negative in Syllogisms

The words 'affirmative' and 'negative' are very frequent in Ibn Sīnā's theory of predicative syllogisms. Often these words are purely for purposes of classification. Each predicative sentence is identified by its subject term, its predicate term and whether it is (1) affirmative or negative and (2) universally or existentially quantified. Ibn Sīnā, following Aristotle, classifies modal syllogisms on the basis of their underlying predicative syllogisms, so this classificatory use extends to modal syllogisms too.

There are two uses of the words 'affirmative' and 'negative' that are not purely classificatory. One is their use in the conditions of productivity, and the other is their use for justifying conversion rules.

To begin with productivity: for Ibn Sīnā a predicative syllogism is a pair of predicative sentences (the 'premises') which is 'productive' in the sense that there is a third predicative sentence which takes a term from each premise, and which follows from the pair of premises. One of the skills of a logician is to know when a pair of predicative sentences is productive. Ibn Sīnā approaches the question as follows. The first step is to determine the terms of the two premises and label each of them as subject term or predicate term. This information determines the figure of the resulting syllogism if the pair is productive. Next, the logician must check which of the premises are affirmative and which are negative. With this information the logician can rule out some premise pairs as unproductive, by using the following 'conditions of productivity':

(a) No productive premise pair consists of two negative sentences. (*Qiyās* 108.8)

(b) In second figure every productive premise pair includes a negative sentence. (*Qiyās* 111.10)

(c) In third figure every productive premise pair has affirmative minor premise. (*Qiyās* 116.15)

Then one can add the quantifiers, and some further conditions of productivity apply; some of these mention affirmative and negative.

The conditions (a)–(c) are a mixed bunch. Item (b) reflects a basic requirement on valid first-order entailments. The requirement in this case is that the predicate term which is common to the two premises should be negated in one premise and not in the other; so one need not mention affirmative and negative, though the formulation in (b) is convenient. (The underlying metatheorem is the Lyndon interpolation theorem, cf. Hodges, 1998 for more details.) By contrast item (c) is not so much a logical truth as a blemish in Aristotle's system: the premise pair

(14)  Not every $A$ is a $B$. No $A$ is a $C$.

violates (c) but does in fact entail that not every non-$B$ is a $C$. Aristotle's system ignores this sentence-form.

We turn to the use of the notions of affirmative and negative to justify the conversion rules. For Ibn Sīnā the inference relations between sentences should be read off from the meanings of the sentences. So a logician must determine the meanings of sentences before describing their inference relations. The section of $^c$*Ibāra* partially translated below is aimed in this direction: Ibn Sīnā sets out some general principles and gives precise conditions for sentences with singular subject to be true or false.

One inference relation is A-conversion:

(15)  'Every $A$ is a $B$' entails 'Some $B$ is an $A$'.

Assuming the Affirmative Principle, 'Every $A$ is a $B$' gives 'Some $A$ is a $B$', which self-evidently entails 'Some $B$ is an $A$'. Another inference relation is that

(16)  'Every $A$ is a $B$' and 'Not every $A$ is a $B$' are mutually contradictory.

The tricky case is where there are no $A$s; in this case the first sentence is false by the Affirmative Principle and the second is true by the Negative Principle. (This assumes we are correct in counting 'Not every $A$ is a $B$' as a denial.)

The two inference relations (15) and (16) are fundamental to Aristotle's system of predicative syllogisms. So it's surprising that we have no evidence for the Affirmative and Negative Principles, or any other basis for these two inference relations, before Ibn Sīnā. Perhaps if Al-Fārābī's lost longer commentary on the *Prior Analytics* is recovered it will throw some light on the matter.

We noted earlier that the distinction between affirmative and negative seems to be geared towards predicative sentences. But Ibn Sīnā didn't believe that syllogistic reasoning is in any way limited to predicative sentences. In fact he defined a larger class of syllogisms, called 'recombinant' (*iqtirānī*), which include the predicative syllogisms and depend on the same mental procedures as predicative syllogisms, but also include some propositional compounds. If the rules for recombinant syllogisms directly generalise those for predicative syllogisms, then we would expect that the Affirmative and Negative Principles generalise to the relevant propositional compounds. Does Ibn Sīnā think that they do? The evidence is conflicting.

In favour of the Affirmative Principle for some propositional compounds: at *Qiyās* 302.15–303.1 Ibn Sīnā cites the valid recombinant syllogism

(17)  In all cases, if $q$ then $r$; and in all cases, if $q$ then not $p$. Therefore it is
not always the case that whenever $r$ then $p$.

(I believe these are correct translations, but I can't guarantee that they preserve
Ibn Sīnā's intuitions about affirmative and negative.) He claims that (17) can
be proved by 'conversion' of the first premise. He must have in mind here the
proof of the analogous predicative syllogism Felapton; so the reasoning is that
the first premise entails 'Sometimes both $q$ and $r$'. If the analogy really holds,
then he is relying on an Affirmative Principle of the form

(18)  If the sentence 'In all cases, if $q$ then $r$' is true, then there is at least one
case in which $q$ is true.

At *Qiyās* 303.3–5 there is another example of the same point; it is a recombinant
analogue of Darapti.

As evidence in the other direction, Ibn Sīnā remarks at $^c$*Ibāra* 42.9 that a
negated exclusive disjunction can be paraphrased as an affirmative predicative
proposition. This is hard to reconcile with the dichotomy expressed by the
Affirmative and Negative Principles.

It does seem that Ibn Sīnā says seriously incompatible things in different
places. But there are other grounds for believing that Ibn Sīnā didn't intend
to produce a monolithic system of logic. His attitude was more along the lines
'If you mean $X$ and accept principle $Y$ then you can deduce $Z$', and he was not
too concerned to tell us what principles we should accept. The one exception
to this is the system of predicative syllogisms, which he regarded as sacrosanct
and definitive.

# 6    Translation

What follows is a translation of Ibn Sīnā's $^c$*Ibāra*, pages 76 to 82 in the Cairo
edition (Sīnā, 1970); the division into paragraphs is mine. A translation of the
entire section ($^c$*Ibāra* ii.1) is on my website at wilfridhodges.co.uk/arabic19
.pdf. I thank Amirouche Moktefi for his invaluable advice and help; blame me
for any errors of language or judgment.

/76/ Second part
Section ii.1

Two-part and three-part propositions; metathetic, simple and privative propositions    76.5
and the connection between the contradictories of these three kinds of proposition
in the singular and unquantified cases

[2.1.1] Propositions are of two kinds. Either they contain an explicit copula (in the    76.8
sense of 39.5 above)—and in some cases this copula mentions a time, but in others
it doesn't—or they don't contain an explicit copula. If the copula is explicit, the
proposition is said to be three-part, and if it is not explicit, the proposition is said to
be two-part.

[2.1.2] Two-part propositions are shorter than they ought to be, except when their    76.10
predicates are verbs. This is because it's reasonable to say that verbs contain their own
copula, since verbs have a syntactic part that signifies their subject. So the only case
where a copula is needed for signifying the connection of the predicate to the subject

is the case where the predicate is a separate and self-contained noun. When the verb contains something that signifies that there is a subject, the verb doesn't require a copula in the same way as basic nouns do. /77/ In this respect, participles behave like verbs. But verbs themselves don't express declarative propositions, because even if they signify that there is a subject, they don't contain anything to specify which subject. The need that they do satisfy is just the need for something that couples up [the predicate] with a specified subject by a copular expression that points in its direction.

77.3    [2.1.3] Arabic has this copula in the form of a noun-like particle, and it also has it in the form of a verb-like particle. In the sentence

(19)   Zayd $\left\{ \begin{matrix} huwa \\ is \end{matrix} \right\}$ alive.

the word *huwa* refers to Zayd, though the only thing that it expresses about him is
77.5    that he is indicated. But in the sentence

(20)   Zayd $\left\{ \begin{matrix} k\bar{a}na \\ was \end{matrix} \right\}$ alive.

the word *kāna* doesn't contain anything to specify Zayd. For this reason the experts in their language say that we have an ellipsis, and the verb means

(21)   $\left\{ \begin{matrix} huwa \\ he \end{matrix} \right\}$ was (alive).

Other languages handle it differently.

77.8    [2.1.4] So propositions have one of three ranks. Those of the first rank have an element that signifies and specifies the connection, those of the second rank have an element that signifies the connection but doesn't specify it, and those of the third rank don't have an element that signifies a connection at all. The propositions of the
77.10   third subdivision are the perfect two-part propositions. The propositions of the other two subdivisions are the three-part propositions, but those of the first rank are the perfect three-part propositions, and those of the second are the propositions that are three-part but not perfected three-part. In general a three-part proposition is one in which the copula is stated explicitly, as in the sentence

(22)   The human $\left\{ \begin{matrix} y\bar{u}jadu \\ is \end{matrix} \right\}$ just.

or the sentence

(23)   The human $\left\{ \begin{matrix} huwa \\ is \end{matrix} \right\}$ just.

The expressions *yūjadu* and *huwa* are not included as predicates themselves, but rather to signify that the subject 'has' the predicate. The expression *yūjadu* signifies that the subject 'has' the predicate at a time in the future. The expression *huwa*
77.15   signifies without further qualification that the subject 'has' the predicate. The copula ['is', in either form,] signifies the connection of the predicate, and the quantifier ['the'] signifies the quantity of the subject. Moreover the part that forms the copula counts as being on the predicate side of the proposition, and the quantifier /78/ counts as being on the subject side.

78.1    [2.1.5] If the proposition is three-part and the particle of negation is linked to it, then one of two cases holds: either the particle of negation is put in front of the copula, or the copula is put in front of the particle of negation. An example of the first is the sentence:

(24) Zayd $\left\{ \begin{array}{c} laysa \\ \text{is not} \end{array} \right\}$ $\left\{ \begin{array}{c} y\bar{u}jadu \\ \text{is} \end{array} \right\}$ just.

and an example of the second is the sentence

(25) Zayd himself $\left\{ \begin{array}{c} y\bar{u}jadu \\ \text{is} \end{array} \right\}$ unjust.

[2.1.6] Putting the particle of negation before the copula negates its coupling, which 78.3
makes the proposition a genuine denial. But if the copula is put before the particle
of negation, this makes the particle of negation a part of the predicate, so that the 78.5
predicate is not 'just' by itself, but the whole expression 'un-' and 'just'. Then the
expression 'is' causes the whole of 'unjust' to be predicated of 'Zayd' affirmatively as
if the proposition said

(26) Zayd fits the description 'unjust'.

So it would be legitimate to negate this proposition [in turn] by putting a second
particle of negation in front of the copula, to get the proposition

(27) Zayd $\left\{ \begin{array}{c} laysa \\ \text{is not} \end{array} \right\}$ $\left\{ \begin{array}{c} y\bar{u}jadu \\ \text{is} \end{array} \right\}$ unjust.

[2.1.7] [Aristotle] stipulates at this point [(*De Interpretatione* 10, 19b26)] that there 78.8
are two kinds of affirmative proposition and two kinds of negative proposition. The
sentence

(28) Zayd is just.

is the opposite of the sentence

(29) Zayd is not just.

and these two propositions are [known as] simple affirmative and simple negative. 78.10
The sentence

(30) Zayd is unjust.

is opposite to the sentence:

(31) Zayd is not unjust.

and these two are [known as] affirmative metathetic and negative metathetic. A proposition is described as metathetic, or transposed, when its predicate is an indeterminate noun or an indeterminate verb. If that predicate is affirmed [of the subject],
the proposition is affirmative metathetic; if the predicate is denied, the proposition
is negative metathetic.

[2.1.8] If the proposition has no copula, making it two-part, then the negation sign 78.13
is linked to its predicate. This in itself is not an indication either that the particle of
negation is included so as to deny the predicate [of the subject], or that it is included 78.15
so as to be a part of the predicate, making the predicate the [combined] whole. But
with /79/ some particles of negation, and at least in our languages particularly those
put in front of a predicate which is a verb, the thought that prevails is that the
particle of negation denies the connection. We don't know how it goes in other actual
or possible languages. Maybe some negation expressions that are attached to verbs in
these languages carry an inflection or some other kind of marker to show the intended
meaning.

[2.1.9] Likewise of those Arabic particles of negation which go in front of nouns, 79.5
some are more suggestive of denial and some of metathesis. Thus it's reasonable to
say that *laysa* fits better with denial and *ġayr* fits better with metathesis. But when
either of these is preceded by *mā*, the result is an affirmative expression. For example
if someone says

(32)   $A \left\{ \begin{array}{c} \textit{laysa bi-} \\ \text{it is not} \end{array} \right\} B.$

the mind can get the feeling that the meaning of this sentence is closer to

(33)   $A \left\{ \begin{array}{c} \textit{huwa} \\ \text{is} \end{array} \right\} \left\{ \begin{array}{c} \textit{mā} \\ \text{what} \end{array} \right\}$ is not $B.$

Then in the mind the copula *huwa*, even though it isn't stated explicitly, takes precedence over the negation, and so the mind feels the phrase as affirmative. If there is

79.10  no [explicit] indication, then the obvious reading is that the proposition is binary and has no copula.

79.11  [2.1.10] /79/ Now we must move on to settle something that really does need to be settled under this head. We say: The criterion for [the proposition to express] an affirmation is that the subject 'has' the predicate. It's impossible to reckon that an idea which is unsatisfied 'has' an[other] idea. So every subject of a [true] affirmative proposition is satisfied—either in the world or in the mind. If one says

(34)   Every icosahedron is an $X.$

79.15  what is meant by this is that every icosahedron, regardless of where it is found, is an $X$. That doesn't mean that every /80/ nonexistent icosahedron is a nonexistent $X$. If the icosahedron doesn't exist then it doesn't satisfy any description, because being nonexistent it can't satisfy any description. If it doesn't exist then how could it be the case that it satisfies something?—except for those people who work themselves up into a state of willing nonexistent things to have descriptions that are well-defined but not satisfied, so that according to them an idea can be well-defined and not satisfied. We are talking about 'well-defined' in the normal sense of this word, and what we

80.5   intend by 'satisfied' in the normal sense is no different from this. These people are entitled to use 'satisfied' to mean whatever they choose.

80.6   [2.1.11] But [the fact is that] the mind judges something to hold affirmatively of certain ideas, either on the basis that they themselves in their state of being satisfied satisfy the [relevant] predicate, or else on the basis that they satisfy the predicate in the mind, not just as mental entities, but rather on the basis that when they are satisfied, they satisfy this predicate. If they are satisfied only in the mind at the time when the mind judges this, then in this case it is impossible for us to say (for example)

(35)   $A$ is satisfied by $B$, not in the mind but in the facts themselves.

80.10  [The subject] isn't satisfied in the facts themselves, so how could an idea be satisfied by it? 'Affirmation' and 'assertion' in the usual sense are the asserting that something holds of an idea, i.e. that it is satisfied by the idea. Likewise 'denying' in the usual sense is the un-asserting that something holds of an idea, which of course amounts to the thing not being satisfied [by the idea]. It's clear from this that there is no affirmation at all unless the subject is [taken to be] as we said.

80.13  [2.1.12] In the case of ideas that aren't satisfied in any way, there is a usage in which one asserts something of them, and it looks as if the mind judges it to be the case that they are $X$'s; [but] what is meant is that if they were satisfied /81/ in the mind, then they would be $X$'s. For example one says in this sense that

(36)   The void consists of dimensions.

81.1   [2.1.13] One can truthfully deny a thing of an idea both when the idea is satisfied and when it is unsatisfied. The distinction made earlier between the simple negative proposition and the metathetic affirmative proposition is that the subject of the [true] simple negative proposition can be either satisfied or unsatisfied. It's correct to deny something of an idea that is unsatisfied. But it's not correct to assert an affirmative metathetic proposition whose subject is unsatisfied.

[2.1.14] This being agreed, some people go on to try to distinguish between the    81.5
affirmative metathetic proposition and the simple negative proposition by making the metathetic signify the absence of something that it would be natural to find in the proximate genus or the remote genus or the species, so that they say: The expression 'unjust' is true of things that lack justice but have it in their nature, or that of their genus, to be just. Thus one says about brute animals that they are irrational, and one says about the rational soul that that it is immaterial, and in both cases the meaning in question is satisfied by some things in the same genus. Also some people say that 'unjust' is parallel to 'oppressive or intermediate [between just and oppressive]', and    81.10
'non-seeing' is parallel to 'blind'. So 'non-seeing' and 'blind' amount to the same thing, so that according to them it's not correct to say of the Eternal that he is non-seeing. This is what these people say. But the correct account of the matter will    81.12
be clear from the examples we are about to give.

[2.1.15] We say: in the discourse                                              81.12

       Every body is a thing not found in a subject,
(37)   and everything that is not found in a subject is a substance,
       so every body is a substance.

what we deduced does follow. And it's a known fact that the two propositions are affirmative, and that the expression 'not' is taken as a part of the predicate, so that    81.15
it is repeated as a part of the subject. The conclusion does follow, and that's a fact. But /82/ 'not' applied to 'found in a subject' doesn't in any way indicate the absence of something that could have existed in the genus of [SUBSTANCE], since [SUBSTANCE] doesn't have a genus at all except that [EXISTING] is a kind of genus for it. If instead of that he had taken the metathetic to signify the absence of something that one would naturally expect to find somewhere in the whole of reality, that would get somewhere nearer the truth.

[2.1.16] Really the metathetic proposition is one where the particle of negation is    82.4
part of the predicate, regardless of what form the predicate takes. When we take the particle of negation, and what would be the predicate if it was taken separately and on its own, together as a single thing, and then we assert this thing of the subject    82.5
through the affirmative copula, the proposition composed in this way is affirmative. The matter and its quality are something else.

[2.1.17] Also they have read, in [Aristotle's] *Categories* and the subsequent [com-    82.8
mentaries], that the expression 'non-human' is not applied to some [kinds of] thing to the exclusion of others—[in particular] it is not applied to existing things to the exclusion of nonexistent ones; and that it can legitimately be used as a predicate. One thing that is bound to cause confusion is that the requirement that the sub-    82.10
ject of an affirmative metathetic proposition has to be satisfied is not because the expression 'unjust' itself requires this, but because the truth of the sentence requires it, regardless of whether [UNJUST] applies both to ideas that are satisfied and ideas that aren't, or applies only to ideas that are satisfied.

[2.1.18] One should know that the distinction between the sentence                  82.13

(38)   *X* is a non-*Y*.

and the sentence

(39)   *X* is not a *Y*.

is that the simple negative proposition [(39)] is broader than the metathetic affirmative proposition [(38)], in that it is true if [the subject] is and is taken to be    82.15

unsatisfied, whereas the affirmative metathetic proposition is not true in this case. It is said truthfully that

(40)    The griffin is not a thing that can see.

but it is not truthfully said that

(41)    The griffin is a thing that can't see.

This is because 'the griffin' is a name that signifies a meaning in the imagination and there is nothing satisfying it in the real world.

# BIBLIOGRAPHY

Aberdein, A. (2011). Interview with Stephen Read. *The Reasoner*, 5:205–211.

Adger, D. (2003). *Core Syntax: A Minimalist Approach*. Oxford University Press, Oxford.

Al-Fārābī (1986). *Commentary on Aristotle's De Interpretatione*. Dar el-Machreq, Beirut. Edited by Kutsch, W. and Marrow, S.

Baeck, A. (1987). Avicenna on existence. *Journal of the History of Philosophy*, 25:351–367.

Fortenbaugh, W., Huby, P., Sharples, R., and Gutas, D., editors (1992). *Theophrastus of Eresus: Sources for his Life, Writings, Thought and Influence, Part One: Life, Writings, Various Reports, Logic, Physics, Metaphysics, Theology, Mathematics*. Brill, Leiden.

Goichon, A. M. (1938). *Lexique de la Langue Philosophique d'Ibn Sina*. Desclèe de Brouwer, Paris.

Haegeman, L. (1995). *The Syntax of Negation*. Cambridge University Press, Cambridge.

Hodges, W. (1998). The laws of distribution for syllogisms. *Notre Dame Journal of Formal Logic*, 39:221–230.

Hodges, W. (2012). Notes on the history of scope. In preparation.

Klima, E. (1964). Negation in English. In Fodor, J. and Katz, J., editors, *The Structure of Language: Readings in the Philosophy of Language*, pages 246–323. Prentice-Hall, Englewood Cliffs NJ.

Sánchez Valencia, V. (1994). Monotonicity in medieval logic. In de Boer, Ale; de Hoop, H. and de Swart, H., editors, *Language and Cognition 4: Yearbook (1994)*, pages 161–174. Rijksuniversiteit Groningen, Groningen.

Sīnā, I. (1959). *Al- Maqūlāt*. Našr Wizāra al-Taqāfa wal-'Iršād al-Qūmī. Edited by Ibrahim Madkour *et al.*

Sīnā, I. (1964). *Al- Qiyās*. Našr Wizāra al-Taqāfa wal-'Iršād al-Qūmī. Edited by Ibrahim Madkour *et al.*

Sīnā, I. (1970). *Al- ᶜIbāra*. Dār al-Kātib al-ᶜArabī lil-Tabāᶜ wal-Našr, Cairo. Edited by Ibrahim Madkour *et al.*

Thom, P. (2008). Al-Fārābī on indefinite and privative names. *Arabic Sciences and Philosophy*, 18:193–209.

Zimmermann, F. (1981). *Al-Fārābī's Commentary and Short Treatise on Aristotle's De Interpretatione*. British Academy and Oxford University Press, Oxford.

# Inferring, Splicing, and the Stoic Analysis of Argument

Peter Milne[†]

In recent years, a number of authors, including the dedicatee of this volume, have advocated the employment of *general elimination rules* in the presentation of harmonious natural deduction rules for logical constants.[1] Motivated by different concerns, in Milne (2008, 2010) I have given natural deduction formulations of classical propositional and first-order logics employing what in Milne (2012b) I call *general introduction rules*; there I show how general introduction and general elimination rules are in harmony and satisfy a certain inversion principle. Here I want to show how general introduction and general elimination rules narrow, perhaps even close, the gap between Gentzen's two ways of presenting logic: natural deduction and sequent calculus. I shall also describe a surprisingly close connection with the earliest account of propositional logic that we know of, that of the Stoic logicians. We are also led to ask after the significance of Gentzen's *Hauptsatz*. Until the final section, I shall consider only propositional logic.

## 1   General Rules

The distinctive feature of general introduction rules is that they tell us when logically complex assumptions may be discharged; more bluntly, when they are not needed. The introduced connective occurs as main operator in a formula occurring *hypothetically* as a logically complex assumption discharged in the application of the rule; additionally some or all of the component propositions may occur either hypothetically (as assumptions also discharged in the application of the rule) or categorically. In general elimination rules, by contrast, the eliminated connective occurs as main operator in a formula occurring *categorically*, for we are being told what we can draw from a logically complex proposition; some or all of the component propositions may occur either hypothetically (as assumptions discharged in the application of the rule) or categorically. The conclusion of either kind of rule is "general", not determined by the proposition containing the introduced or eliminated connective. The introduction rules for conjunction and disjunction are unexciting rewrites of standard rules; not so for negation and the conditional, whose introduction rules are essentially classical.

---

[†]Division of Law & Philosophy, School of Arts & Humanities, University of Stirling, Stirling FK9 4AL, Stirling, U.K. Email: **peter.milne@stir.ac.uk**
[1]See, *e.g.*, Peter Schroeder-Heister (1984a; 1984b), Neil Tennant (1992), Stephen Read (2000; 2004; 2010), Sara Negri and Jan von Plato (2001), von Plato (2001), and Nissim Francez and Roy Dyckhoff (2012).

## conjunction

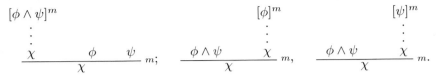

## disjunction

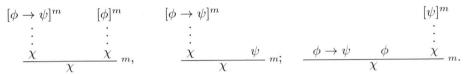

## negation

$$\cfrac{\chi \qquad \chi}{\chi}\, m; \qquad \cfrac{\neg\phi \qquad \phi}{\chi}\,.$$

with $[\neg\phi]^m$ and $[\phi]^m$ above the first, and $[\neg\phi]^m$, $[\phi]^m$ discharge points.

## conditional

These rules give us a formulation of classical propositional logic with the subformula property (cf. Milne, 2010, §2.7).

See the general form of introduction and elimination rules in figure 1.

Given the complete set of general introduction rules for a truth-functional connective (of any *arity*), we can read off a complete set of harmonious elimination rules; we can also read off the connective's truth-table. Likewise, given the complete set of general elimination rules for a connective, we can read off a complete set of harmonious introduction rules; we can again read off the connective's truth-table. And given the connective's truth-table, we can read off harmonious general introduction rules and general elimination rules. For more on why this is and ought to be the case, see Milne (2012b).

Derivable argument-forms yield derived inference rules. If $\Sigma \vdash \phi$ is derivable, we can introduce the rule

$$\cfrac{\Sigma \qquad \chi}{\chi}\, m.$$

The converse holds trivially, for, by an application of the rule, we obtain the derivation

The general form of an introduction rule is

$$
\cfrac{\cfrac{[\star(\phi_1,\phi_2,\ldots,\phi_n)]^m \qquad [\phi_{i_1}]^m \quad [\phi_{i_2}]^m \quad \cdots \quad [\phi_{i_k}]^m}{\chi \qquad \chi \qquad \cdots \qquad \chi}}{\chi \qquad \phi_{j_1} \quad \phi_{j_2} \quad \cdots \quad \phi_{j_l}}\;{}_m \quad \star\text{-introduction}
$$

where $k + l \leq n$ and $i_p \neq j_q,\, 1 \leq p \leq k,\, 1 \leq q \leq l$.

The general form of an elimination rule is

$$
\cfrac{\cfrac{[\phi_{r_1}]^m \quad [\phi_{r_2}]^m \quad \cdots \quad [\phi_{r_t}]^m}{\chi \qquad \chi \qquad \cdots \qquad \chi}}{\star(\phi_1,\phi_2,\ldots,\phi_n) \qquad \chi \qquad \phi_{s_1} \quad \phi_{s_2} \quad \cdots \quad \phi_{s_u}}\;{}_m \quad \star\text{-elimination}
$$

where $t + u \leq n$ and $r_p \neq s_q,\, 1 \leq p \leq t,\, 1 \leq q \leq u$.

Figure 1. The general form of introduction and elimination rules.

$$\frac{\Sigma \qquad [\phi]^1}{\phi} \; 1.$$

Corresponding to what is sometimes called the Rule of Assumptions—*e.g.*, in Lemmon (1965)—we have the "null rule"

$$\frac{\phi \qquad \begin{matrix} [\phi]^m \\ \vdots \\ \chi \end{matrix}}{\chi} \; m,$$

which has no proper application in natural deduction proofs laid out in tree form for there

$$\phi$$

counts as a proof with conclusion $\phi$ dependent on $\phi$ as assumption.

## 2   Splicing

We form natural deduction proof-trees by treating the conclusion of an application of one rule as the occurrence of a categorical formula in the application of another rule. Formulae standing as assumptions in the application of the first rule continue to stand as assumptions in the application of the second rule if not discharged (as hypothetically occurring side-premises) in the application of the first. A proof of the argument-form $\Sigma \vdash \psi$ is a proof tree in which only members of $\Sigma$ remain as undischarged assumptions and $\phi$ stands as the conclusion, at the root of the proof-tree.

I want to consider a different way of manipulating rules. I call it *splicing*. Splicing is carried out by cross-cancelling a hypothetical occurrence of a formula in one rule and a categorical occurrence of the same formula in another rule to obtain a new rule. Splicing is to be thought of as a new primitive operation acting directly on *rules in schematic form*. Employing splicing, we can find (general) introduction and elimination rules for logically complex formulae. For example, exclusive disjunction can be represented as $(\phi \vee \psi) \wedge \neg(\phi \wedge \psi)$. Splicing gives us in a succession of steps:

$$\frac{\begin{matrix}[(\phi \vee \psi) \wedge \neg(\phi \wedge \psi)]^m\\ \vdots \\ \chi\end{matrix} \qquad \phi \vee \psi \qquad \neg(\phi \wedge \psi)}{\chi}\,m \quad \oplus \quad \frac{\begin{matrix}[\phi \vee \psi]^m\\ \vdots \\ \chi\end{matrix} \qquad \phi}{\chi}\,m$$

$$= \quad \frac{\begin{matrix}[(\phi \vee \psi) \wedge \neg(\phi \wedge \psi)]^m\\ \vdots \\ \chi\end{matrix} \qquad \phi \qquad \neg(\phi \wedge \psi)}{\chi}\,m;$$

$$
\cfrac{[(\phi \lor \psi) \land \neg(\phi \land \psi)]^m \quad\quad\quad \cfrac{\quad\quad}{\chi} \quad\quad \cfrac{\phi \quad\quad \neg(\phi \land \psi)}{\chi}}{} \; m
\quad \oplus \quad
\cfrac{[\neg(\phi \land \psi)]^m \quad\quad [\phi \land \psi]^m}{\cfrac{\chi \quad\quad\quad\quad \chi}{\chi}} \; m
$$

$$
= \quad
\cfrac{[(\phi \lor \psi) \land \neg(\phi \land \psi)]^m \quad\quad\quad [\phi \land \psi]^m}{\cfrac{\chi \quad\quad\quad \phi \quad\quad\quad \chi}{\chi}} \; m;
$$

$$
\cfrac{[(\phi \lor \psi) \land \neg(\phi \land \psi)]^m \quad\quad [\phi \land \psi]^m}{\cfrac{\chi \quad\quad \phi \quad\quad \chi}{\chi}} \; m
\quad \oplus \quad
\cfrac{\phi \land \psi \quad\quad [\psi]^m \quad \chi}{\chi} \; m
$$

$$
= \quad
\cfrac{[(\phi \lor \psi) \land \neg(\phi \land \psi)]^m \quad\quad [\psi]^m}{\cfrac{\chi \quad\quad \phi \quad\quad \chi}{\chi}} \; m.
$$

In similar fashion, we obtain the introduction rule

$$
\cfrac{[(\phi \lor \psi) \land \neg(\phi \land \psi)]^m \quad\quad [\phi]^m}{\cfrac{\chi \quad\quad\quad\quad \chi \quad\quad \psi}{\chi}} \; m
$$

and the elimination rules

$$
\cfrac{(\phi \lor \psi) \land \neg(\phi \land \psi) \quad\quad \phi \quad\quad \psi}{\chi}
$$

and

$$
\cfrac{(\phi \lor \psi) \land \neg(\phi \land \psi) \quad\quad [\phi]^m \quad [\psi]^m}{\cfrac{\quad\quad\quad\quad\quad\quad \chi \quad\quad \chi}{\chi}} \; m.
$$

Had we spliced

$$
\cfrac{[(\phi \lor \psi) \land \neg(\phi \land \psi)]^m \quad\quad [\phi \land \psi]^m}{\cfrac{\chi \quad\quad \phi \quad\quad \chi}{\chi}} \; m
$$

with the other $\wedge$-elimination rule, *i.e.*, with

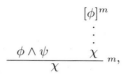

$$\frac{\phi \wedge \psi \qquad \begin{array}{c}[\phi]^m \\ \vdots \\ \chi\end{array}}{\chi}\, m,$$

we would have obtained this rule

$$\frac{\begin{array}{c}[(\phi \vee \psi) \wedge \neg(\phi \wedge \psi)]^m \\ \vdots \\ \chi\end{array} \qquad \phi \qquad \begin{array}{c}[\phi]^m \\ \vdots \\ \chi\end{array}}{\chi}\, m$$

which, being a *weakening* of the null rule, is quite acceptable but utterly uninformative regarding $(\phi \vee \psi) \wedge \neg(\phi \wedge \psi)$. (Quite generally, if we accept a rule, we can accept any weakening obtained by adding formulae whether that be in categorical occurrences or hypothetical.)

The expressive adequacy of, say, $\{\neg, \wedge, \vee\}$ (or, indeed any other expressively adequate set) in classical propositional logic translates into the capacity of splicing to be a technique for generating (sets of) general introduction and general elimination rules for arbitrary $n$-ary truth-functional connectives. By way of example, the computer programmer's favourite, 'if $\phi$ then $\psi$, else $\chi$', which we shall abbreviate as '$\looparrowright(\phi, \psi, \chi)$', is classically equivalent to $(\phi \wedge \psi) \vee (\neg\phi \wedge \chi)$. This is equivalent to the negation of $(\phi \vee \neg\chi) \wedge (\neg\phi \vee \neg\psi)$. Inspection of the results of splicing in the case of exclusive disjunction shows that splicing will yield these rules:

**introduction rules**

$$\frac{\begin{array}{c}[\looparrowright(\phi, \psi, \chi)]^m \\ \vdots \\ \upsilon\end{array} \qquad \begin{array}{c}[\phi]^m \\ \vdots \\ \upsilon\end{array} \qquad \chi}{\upsilon}\, m \quad \text{and} \quad \frac{\begin{array}{c}[\looparrowright(\phi, \psi, \chi)]^m \\ \vdots \\ \upsilon\end{array} \qquad \phi \qquad \psi}{\upsilon}\, m\,;$$

**elimination rules**

$$\frac{\looparrowright(\phi, \psi, \chi) \qquad \phi \qquad \begin{array}{c}[\psi]^m \\ \vdots \\ \upsilon\end{array}}{\upsilon}\, m \quad \text{and} \quad \frac{\looparrowright(\phi, \psi, \chi) \qquad \begin{array}{c}[\phi]^m \\ \vdots \\ \upsilon\end{array} \qquad \begin{array}{c}[\chi]^m \\ \vdots \\ \upsilon\end{array}}{\upsilon}\, m.$$

$\looparrowright(\phi, \psi, \chi)$ is also equivalent to $(\phi \to \psi) \wedge (\neg\phi \to \chi)$. Splicing, starting with this formula, gets us the very same rules.

## 2.1    Algebra ... or maybe not

With splicing and other operations that we may perform on rules, we have a certain amount of structure.

Splicing is not a function: while in any application of splicing there is only one formula cancelled, a hypothetical occurrence in one rule being crossed off against a categorical occurrence in the other, there may be more than one formula available for cancellation. So, strictly speaking, questions of associativity and commutativity do not arise. Instances of the null rule do act as *identity elements* in that, *when we can splice*, splicing with an instance of the null rule yields the original rule (and there can't be any question about which formula is up for cancellation unless the other rule involved is already an instance of the null rule or a weakening thereof). (Recall that in order to splice two rules, the same formula must occur hypothetically in one rule and categorically in the other, hence the qualification 'when we can splice'.)

Counting every rule as a weakening of itself, there is an uninteresting partial ordering given by the relation *rule X is a weakening of rule Y*.

The negation rules play a special role: splicing an introduction rule with the instance of the negation elimination rule containing the introduced formula yields an elimination rule for the introduced formula's negation. Conversely, splicing an elimination rule with the instance of the negation introduction rule containing the eliminated formula yields an introduction rule for the eliminated formula's negation.

**Duality**  Conjunction and disjunction are duals. There's an obvious duality between their respective introduction and elimination rules. We can spell it out in a simple instruction for dualising a complete set of (harmonious) general introduction and elimination rules for a connective:

> To obtain the (dual) rules for the dual connective, in each rule turn all hypothetical occurrences into categorical occurrences and all categorical occurrences into hypothetical.

Accordingly, negation is self-dual, as we would expect. The dual of $\leftrightarrow (\phi, \psi, \chi)$ is then readily seen to be $\leftrightarrow (\phi, \chi, \psi)$, a fact that can be checked rather more laboriously by writing out a truth table for $\leftrightarrow (\phi, \psi, \chi)$, turning it upside down and swapping '0's ('$T$'s) for '1's ('$F$'s) and *vice versa*.

**"The levelling of local peaks"**[2]  By inspection, we see that in the examples at hand splicing an introduction rule and an elimination rule for the same connective and cancelling the formula containing the introduced/eliminated connective produces either an instance of the null rule (in the case of negation) or a weakening of the null rule. In fact, for general introduction and elimination rules harmonious in the sense of Milne (2012b) this holds not only for the examples at hand but is always the case.

## 2.2    *bullet*

Steve Read has introduced a one-place connective which, symbolised by '•', is often nowadays called '*bullet*': *bullet* is interderivable with its negation. In his (2000), Steve gave it these (impure) introduction and elimination rules:

---

[2]The term is, of course, Dummett's.

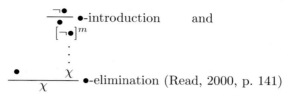

$$\frac{\neg\bullet}{\bullet} \; \bullet\text{-introduction} \qquad \text{and}$$

$$\frac{\bullet \qquad\qquad \overset{[\neg\bullet]^m}{\overset{\vdots}{\chi}}}{\chi} \; \bullet\text{-elimination (Read, 2000, p. 141)}$$

The introduction rule doesn't have a general conclusion but we can easily rectify that:

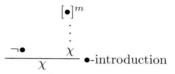

$$\frac{\neg\bullet \qquad \overset{[\bullet]^m}{\overset{\vdots}{\chi}}}{\chi} \; \bullet\text{-introduction}$$

—and now we see that, according to the recipe for dualising given above, *bullet* is self-dual.[3]

Splicing with the negation rules, we obtain these (pure) general introduction and elimination rules—

$$\frac{\overset{[\bullet]^m}{\overset{\vdots}{\chi}}}{\chi} \; m \; \bullet\text{-introduction} \qquad \text{and}$$

$$\frac{\bullet}{\chi} \; \bullet\text{-elimination (cf. Read, 2010, p. 571).}[4]$$

—which gives *bullet* the introduction rule of the *verum* constant and the elimination rule of the *falsum* constant! And upon splicing these rules for *bullet* we get neither an instance nor a weakening of an instance of the null rule, rather we get the explicitly contradictory rule

$$\overline{\chi}$$

which makes me think there's something more than a little fishy about *bullet* in the (classical) context of general introduction and elimination rules.[5]

---

[3]In the context of certain three-valued logics, such as Graham Priest's *Logic of Paradox* (Priest, 1979) or my *Logic of Conditional Assertions* (Milne, 2004), *bullet* would act as a harmless, propositional constant/0-ary connective having the intermediate truth-value. With application to the first, Steve says of *bullet* that 'it constitutes a kind of proof-conditional Liar sentence' (2000, p. 142); with application to the second, *bullet* just is the constant $N$ used, following Hailperin (1996), in defining de Finetti's binary *conditioning* connective (Milne, 2004, §§1.4-1.5, 9.1). In these contexts the negation is, of course, not governed by both *ex falso quodlibet* and the Rule of Dilemma, *i.e.*, not governed both by general introduction and by general elimination rules.

[4]Strictly, because he is being very careful regarding structural rules, Steve has two occurrences of • "above the line" in the elimination rule and would no doubt want the analogue in the introduction rule (which is mine, not his). But splicing, being based on the standard use of natural deduction rules, does not care about such niceties.

[5]For more on *bullet* in the context of general introduction and elimination rules, see Milne (2012b, §4.5).

# 3   Soundness, Completeness, and Sequent Calculus

Since rules are general in the sense that the conclusion is in effect the same (arbitrary) formula, and the indexing of discharges has no significance for splicing, we simplify our notation. Given a rule, we write '$\Sigma \Rightarrow \Delta$', where $\Sigma$ is the set of formulae occurring categorically and $\Delta$ is the set of formulae occurring hypothetically (and discharged in the application of the rule); either set may be empty. The null rule gives us all instances of $\phi \Rightarrow \phi$.[6]

We say that the rule $\Sigma \Rightarrow \Delta$ is *classically sound* if there is no assignment of truth-values to atoms under which all the formulae in $\Sigma$ are *true* and all the formulae in $\Delta$ are *false*. We confine attention to formulae built up employing $\wedge$, $\vee$, $\rightarrow$ and $\neg$.

THEOREM 1 (Soundness Theorem). *If the rule $\Sigma \Rightarrow \Delta$ is obtained by splicing from instances of the null rule and the rules for negation, conjunction, disjunction, and the conditional or is a weakening of any such rule then it is classically sound.*

**Proof.** The rules for negation, conjunction, disjunction, and the conditional are all classically sound. Weakening preserves classical soundness, as does splicing which in this setting is just Gentzen's *Schnitt*.    ∎

THEOREM 2 (Completeness Theorem). *If the rule $\Sigma \Rightarrow \Delta$ is classically sound then it is obtainable by splicing and/or weakening from instances of the null rule and the rules for negation, conjunction, disjunction, and the conditional.*

**Proof.**[Proof sketch] The idea of the proof is that we can replicate the operational rules of Gentzen's calculus *LK* for $\neg$, $\wedge$, $\vee$, and $\rightarrow$. We can also replicate the effects of Gentzen's structural rules. Proof is then by recursion on the structure of proofs of classically sound sequents in *LK*.

**negation** Suppose we have derived $\Sigma, \phi \Rightarrow \Delta$. By splicing with the negation introduction rule, we obtain $\Sigma \Rightarrow \neg\phi, \Delta$.
  Suppose, next, that we have derived $\Sigma \Rightarrow \phi, \Delta$. By splicing with the negation elimination rule, we obtain $\Sigma, \neg\phi \Rightarrow \Delta$. Thus we replicate the left and right introduction rules for negation in Gentzen's *LK*.

**conditional** Suppose we have derived $\Sigma, \phi \Rightarrow \psi, \Delta$. By splicing with one of the conditional introduction rules we obtain $\Sigma \Rightarrow \phi \rightarrow \psi, \psi, \Delta$; by splicing with the other conditional introduction rule and recalling that $\Sigma$ and $\Delta$ stand for sets, we obtain $\Sigma \Rightarrow \phi \rightarrow \psi, \Delta$.
  Suppose, next, that we have derived $\Sigma_1 \Rightarrow \phi, \Delta_1$ and $\Sigma_2, \psi \Rightarrow \Delta_2$. By splicing the first with the elimination rule for the conditional, we get $\Sigma_1, \phi \rightarrow \psi \Rightarrow \psi, \Delta_1$; by splicing this with $\Sigma_2, \psi \Rightarrow \Delta_2$ we obtain, just as we should, $\Sigma_1, \Sigma_2, \phi \rightarrow \psi \Rightarrow \Delta_1, \Delta_2$.

**conjunction and disjunction** These are treated similarly.

---

[6]Note that $\star(\phi_1, \phi_2, \ldots, \phi_n)$ and $*(\phi_1, \phi_2, \ldots, \phi_n)$ are dual only where $\Sigma \Rightarrow \star(\phi_1, \phi_2, \ldots, \phi_n), \Delta$ is an introduction rule for $\star$ if, and only if, $\Delta, *(\phi_1, \phi_2, \ldots, \phi_n) \Rightarrow \Sigma$ is an elimination rule for $*$ and likewise, *mutatis mutandis*, for $\star$-elimination and $*$-introduction rules.

Structural rules: contraction and permutation are hidden from view in the use of sets, rather than sequences; in the present context Gentzen's Weakening (Thinning, Augmentation) just is the weakening of a rule by adding side-formulae either categorically or hypothetically (left or right); splicing is Cut.

We now appeal to the known completeness of $LK$.                    ■

What starts out as, seemingly, only a notational convenience turns out to be not just a genuine sequent calculus but, in effect, Gentzen's $LK$.

Of course, the system is not exactly Gentzen's $LK$. But now, notice that the uses made of splicing/cut to show derivability of Gentzen's rules satisfy this constraint: in every application

$$\frac{\Sigma_1, \phi \Rightarrow \Delta_1 \qquad \Sigma_2 \Rightarrow \phi, \Delta_2}{\Sigma_1, \Sigma_2 \Rightarrow \Delta_1, \Delta_2}$$

of splicing/cut, $\phi$ is a subformula of at least one formula in $\Sigma_1 \cup \Sigma_2 \cup \Delta_1 \cup \Delta_2$.

This is the rule of *Analytic Cut* of Raymond Smullyan's (1968a), where a system is developed in order to show that 'The real importance of cut-free proofs is not the elimination of cuts per se, but rather that such proofs obey the subformula principle' (Smullyan, 1968a, p. 560).[7]

## 4   The Stoic Analysis of Argument

The Stoic account of propositional logic proceeds by presenting a handful of basic argument-forms and by reducing more complex arguments to these by a using a fixed number of techniques. Viewed coarsely, the approach is similar to Gentzen's sequent calculus account: there are basic argument forms taken as valid and a set of rules for generating valid argument-forms from valid argument forms. In detail there are philosophically significant differences and a difference of direction: reduction of the more complex to less rather than the other way around. Perhaps a better approximation to Stoic intentions would be achieved by inverting the proof-trees of a sequent calculus so that one works downwards from the complex forms towards the basic argument-forms,[8] although the difference of direction may not be of great moment when giving a formal account of Stoic logic.

The basic argument forms, the *indemonstrables*, are, in effect, direct elimination rules. (By 'direct' I mean that all formulae save one occur categorically.) Stoic logicians provide elimination rules for conditionals and (exclusive) disjunctions and for negations of conjunctions.

According to Benson Mates,

> The Stoics maintained that their system of propositional logic was complete in the sense that every valid argument could be reduced to a series of arguments of five basic types. Even the method of reduction was not left vague, but was exactly characterized by four

---

[7]In serendipitous conformity with Smullyan's dictum, I showed that the $\{\wedge, \vee, \rightarrow, \neg, \exists\}$-fragment of the system for classical logic in Milne (2010) has the subformula property using model-theoretic means.

[8]Cf. Corcoran (1974). See also Frede (1974, pp. 186–190).

meta-rules, of which we possess two, and possibly three. Whether or not the Stoic system was actually complete could be decided only with the help of the missing rules (Mates, 1961, p. 4).

The claim to completeness is, *if meant in the modern sense*, well wide of the mark.[9] But we can give a formulation of classical propositional logic Stoic in spirit—at least in some respects.

Splicing a rule with instances of the negation elimination rule, hypothetical occurrences of formulae are replaced by categorical occurrences of their negations. Likewise, splicing a rule with instances of the negation introduction rule, categorical occurrences of formulae are replaced by hypothetical occurrences of their negations. We obtain these rules for the conditional, conjunction and exclusive disjunction:

$$\phi \to \psi, \phi \Rightarrow \psi, \quad \phi \to \psi, \neg\psi \Rightarrow \neg\phi, \quad \neg(\phi \to \psi) \Rightarrow \phi, \quad \neg(\phi \to \psi) \Rightarrow \neg\psi;$$
$$\phi \wedge \psi \Rightarrow \phi, \quad \phi \wedge \psi \Rightarrow \psi, \quad \neg(\phi \wedge \psi), \phi \Rightarrow \neg\psi, \quad \neg(\phi \wedge \psi), \psi \Rightarrow \neg\phi;$$
$$\phi + \psi, \phi \Rightarrow \neg\psi, \quad \phi + \psi, \psi \Rightarrow \neg\phi, \quad \phi + \psi, \neg\phi \Rightarrow \psi, \quad \phi + \psi, \neg\psi \Rightarrow \phi,$$
$$\neg(\phi+\psi), \phi \Rightarrow \psi, \quad \neg(\phi+\psi), \psi \Rightarrow \phi, \quad \neg(\phi+\psi), \neg\phi \Rightarrow \neg\psi, \quad \neg(\phi+\psi), \neg\psi \Rightarrow \neg\phi.$$

Here the rules for the conditional, the negated conjunction, and the (exclusive) disjunction are exactly the Stoic indemonstrables (at least if we accept informal ancient accounts—see, *e.g.*, Mueller, 1978, pp. 10–11). The rest are present in order to spell out the truth-functional accounts of these connectives (accounts by-and-large accepted by Stoic logicians only in the cases of negation and conjunction, necessitarian readings being favoured for the conditional and exclusive disjunction).

Splicing $\neg\neg\phi, \neg\phi \Rightarrow$ and $\Rightarrow \neg\phi, \phi$, we get the double negation elimination argument-form/rule $\neg\neg\phi \Rightarrow \phi$; similarly, we may obtain $\phi \Rightarrow \neg\neg\phi$. We need some rule to get complex consequences, not just atomic formulae and their negations, double negations, triple negations, *etc.* For this we need some indirect rule, such as the Stoic's *first thema*:

$$\text{if } \Sigma, \phi \Rightarrow \psi \text{ then } \Sigma, \neg\psi \Rightarrow \neg\phi.$$

This gives us a complete set of rules for a pseudo-Stoic, natural deduction account of classical propositional logic (with exclusive disjunction as primitive), confined to argument-forms with at least one premiss. (And by splicing with the negation rules we can get back from these rules to general introduction and elimination rules.)[10]

---

[9]See Hitchcock (2005) on what might have been intended. See Mueller (1979) and Milne (1995, 2012a) for more on the completeness of Stoic logic.

[10]In the interests of historical accuracy, I should say that (*a*) the Stoics had no analogue of the null rule, considering arguments with fewer than two premisses not to be syllogisms; (*b*) they had no analogue of Weakening, declaring arguments invalid in virtue of redundancy of premisses (although exactly what that amounts to is unclear), and (*c*) they had a rule, the third *thema*, whose effect is very much like Gentzen's Cut rule. Stoic logicians seem to have recognised the equivalence in meaning of a proposition and its double negation although how this was accommodated formally is unclear—one possibility is along the lines of the account of the contrary in Read (1988, pp. 178–182) (see Mueller, 1979, p. 204). But what is important here is the style of their analysis: basic argument-forms and a set of procedures for the transformation of argument-forms. Regarding their treatment of negation we should

I have just said that the *rules* for the conditional, the negated conjunction, and the (exclusive) disjunction are *exactly* the Stoic indemonstrables but a while back I said that the indemonstrables are *argument-forms*. What we see is that there is really no difference between taking (single conclusion) general introduction and elimination rules for natural deduction and combining rules by splicing and taking argument-forms and generating new ones by Cut. We have two ways of presenting the same underlying structure, albeit that the starting points may seem quite different.

## 4.1   Tableaux

The "Stoic" argument-forms/rules all have a complex formula occurring in the antecedent/occurring categorically and a single formula in the succeedent/occurring hypothetically. Using the negation rules we can move all bar the complex formula across to the succeedent, adding or deleting negations as we go. When we do so, what we have are, in effect, the rules for Smullyan's (1968b) analytic tableaux. We can mimic the elaboration of tableaux (trees) by splicing/cutting—we have to take a little care in setting this up, for we have to mimic both what Smullyan calls [non-branching] $\alpha$ rules and what he calls $\beta$ [branching] rules.[11]

The negation rules let us turn categorical occurrences of negated formulae into hypothetical occurrences of the unnegated original and *vice versa*. Consequently, we can mimic tableaux directly with putative rules, splicing on the main formula, not side formulae. The argument-form $\Sigma \vdash \phi$ is valid if, and only if, every permitted sequence of splices on (complex) main formulae, starting from

$$[\phi]^m$$
$$\vdots$$
$$\frac{\Sigma \qquad \chi}{\chi}\ m.$$

terminates in an instance of the null rule or a weakening thereof.[12]

---

note, too, a couple of remarks of Gentzen's:

  o For *negation* ($\neg$) the situation is not quite as simple; here there are several distinct forms of inference and these cannot be divided clearly into $\neg$-introductions and $\neg$-eliminations. (Gentzen, 1936, §4.56)

  o The following must be said about the *rules of inference* for *negation*; as already mentioned at 4.56, the choice of elementary forms of inference is here *more arbitrary* than in the case of the other logical constants. (Gentzen, 1936, §5.26)

[11]It is no co-incidence that our rules/argument-forms for the pseudo-Stoic formulation of classical logic are close to the rules of the unsigned version of the tableaux system *KE* in D'Agostino and Mondadori (1994).

[12]Given the links between natural deduction with general introduction and elimination rules and Smullyan's analytic cut sequent calculus, on the one hand, and between the latter and Carlo Cellucci's (2000) analytic cut trees, on the other, the way of mimicking trees by splicing rules just suggested should be in some sense equivalent to Cellucci's tableaux system; spelling out the equivalence is work for another occasion.

## 4.2   Negation and two kinds of disjunctions

The Stoics have disjunctive syllogism as one of their five indemonstrables, albeit their disjunction is exclusive. The late Michael Dummett called disjunctive syllogism (with inclusive disjunction) 'a fundamental form of argument' (1991, p. 293). Treating it as basic goes hand in hand with a suggestion Dummett made on another occasion:

> We must first recall that a non-classical negation can be readily introduced in terms of justifiability alone. The utterance "$\phi$ or $\psi$" may now be thought of as expressing a conditional claim to be able to justify the claim "$\phi$", given a justification of "Not $\psi$", or, conversely, to justify the claim "$\psi$", given a justification of "Not $\phi$": this is, in effect, to take the logical law *modus tollendo ponens* as giving the basic meaning of disjunction.

He went on to say:

> The interpretation of "or" proposed above in effect equates "$\phi$ or $\psi$" with "If not $\phi$, then $\psi$, and, if not $\psi$, then $\phi$", understood intuitionistically, a rendering of course weaker than the ordinary intuitionistic interpretation of "$\phi$ or $\psi$" (Dummett, 1990, pp. 7–8, with a change of notation).[13]

Rather than settle for one or other disjunction, Steve has urged that there are two disjunctions in common usage, one governed by Gentzen's ∨-introduction, another governed by disjunctive syllogism—see (Read, 1988, pp. 31–34) and (Read, 1994, pp. 60, 160, 163). By distinguishing the two, the "Lewis proof"[14] that anything follows from a contradiction, which infers "$\phi$ or $\psi$" from "$\phi$" and then "$\psi$" from "$\phi$ or $\psi$" and "$\neg\phi$", is seen to trade on an ambiguity. Given the strongly classical nature of general introduction and elimination rules, it is unsurprising that this route to blocking the proof is unavailable in the present setting. It is interesting to see why not, though.

Our sequent calculus started out as a convenient means for the representation of general introduction and general elimination rules. We can read it again as a system of rules for multiple conclusion natural deduction somewhat along the lines of Boričić (1985) in that proofs are in tree form. But splicing with the negation rules allows us to turn any multiple conclusion rule into a plurality of impure, single conclusion rules—and to recover pure multiple conclusion rules from a family of impure, single conclusion rules. Thus, *in the present setting*, there is *essentially no difference* between Gentzen's ∨-elimination rule and the left and right forms of *disjunctive syllogism*,

---

[13]That "$\phi \vee \psi$" says nothing more nor less than "if not $\phi$, $\psi$, and if not $\psi$, $\phi$" is by no means a new idea. We find this statement in Mill's *System of Logic*:

> As has been well remarked by Archbishop Whately and others, the disjunctive form is resolvable into the conditional; every disjunctive proposition being equivalent to two or more conditional ones. "Either A is B or C is D," means, "if A is not B, C is D; and if C is not D, A is B" (Mill, 1843, Book 1, Ch. IV 'Of propositions', sec. 3, p. 110); 1859, p. 56.

[14]William of Soissons's proof, as Steve doubtless prefers me to say—see Martin (1986).

$$\frac{\neg\phi \qquad \phi \vee \psi}{\psi} \quad \text{and} \quad \frac{\neg\psi \qquad \phi \vee \psi}{\phi}.$$

Splicing $(\neg\phi \to \psi) \wedge (\neg\psi \to \phi)$ to obtain general introduction rules, one arrives naturally at these *three* rules—

$$
\begin{array}{c}
(\neg\phi \to \psi) \wedge (\neg\psi \to \phi) \\
\vdots
\end{array}
\qquad\qquad\qquad
\begin{array}{c}
(\neg\phi \to \psi) \wedge (\neg\psi \to \phi) \\
\vdots
\end{array}
$$

$$
\frac{\chi \qquad\qquad\qquad \phi}{\chi} \quad , \qquad
\frac{\chi \qquad\qquad\qquad\qquad \psi}{\chi} \quad \text{and}
$$
$$(\neg\phi \to \psi) \wedge (\neg\psi \to \phi)$$

$$
\begin{array}{c}
\vdots \\
\end{array}
$$

$$\frac{\chi \qquad\qquad \phi \qquad \psi}{\chi}$$

—but the third, being a weakening of each of the previous two, is redundant.

*In the present setting* one cannot coherently tell Steve's story of there being two disjunctions, for when spelt out in terms of general introduction and elimination rules, the supposedly distinct connectives have the same introduction and elimination rules. In itself, this in no way serves to impugn Steve's account of how to by-pass the Lewis proof; it merely serves to underline the classical nature of the setting provided by (my account of) general introduction and general elimination rules.

## 5   Gentzen's *Hauptsatz*

According to Dummett, it was Gerhard Gentzen 'who, by inventing both natural deduction and the sequent calculus, first taught us how logic should be formalised' (Dummett, 1991, p. 251). In view of what we have—all too briefly—seen of the Stoic approach to argument, such a claim may seem to slight the achievement of Stoic logicians. However, on an earlier occasion Dummett had been more specific in the credit he gives Gentzen. There he said,

> It can be said of Gentzen that it was he who first showed how proof theory should be done. By replacing the old axiomatic formalizations of logic by sequent calculi, and, in particular, by the cut-free systems, he not only corrected our conceptual perspective on logic, but also restored the balance of power as between proof-theoretic methods and algebraic methods (Dummett, 1973, p. 434).

In the light of this clarification, perhaps Dummett is not unfair to the Stoics. Their system was nothing like a *cut-free* sequent-calculus. But what is the significance of cut-free systems?

Gentzen sums up the *Hauptsatz* like this:

> HAUPTSATZ Every *LJ-* or *LK*-derivation can be transformed into an *LJ-* or *LK*-derivation with the same endsequent and in which the inference figure called a 'cut' does not occur.

and notes this consequence

Corollary of the Hauptsatz (subformula property) In an *LJ*- or *LK*-derivation without cuts, all occurring formulae are subformulae of the formulae that occur in the endsequent (Gentzen, 1935, §§2.5 & 2.513).

A page or so before the statement of the Hauptsatz, Gentzen had said,

> In general, we could *simplify* the calculi in various respects if we attached no importance to the *Hauptsatz*. To indicate this briefly: the inference figures [right ∧-introduction, left ∨-introduction, left ∧-introduction, right ∨-introduction, left ∀-introduction, right ∃-introduction, right ¬-introduction, left ¬-introduction, and left →-introduction] in the calculus *LK* could be replaced by basic sequents according to the following schemata:
>
> $$\phi, \psi \Rightarrow \phi \mathbin{\&} \psi \quad \phi \lor \psi \Rightarrow \phi, \psi \quad \phi \land \psi \Rightarrow \phi \quad \phi \land \psi \Rightarrow \psi$$
> $$\phi \Rightarrow \phi \lor \psi \quad \psi \Rightarrow \phi \lor \psi \quad \forall x \phi x \Rightarrow \phi a \quad \phi a \Rightarrow \exists x \phi x$$
> $$\Rightarrow \phi, \neg\phi \quad \text{(law of excluded middle)}$$
> $$\neg\phi, \phi \Rightarrow \quad \text{(law of contradiction)}$$
>
> These basic sequents and our inference figures may easily be shown to be equivalent. (Gentzen, 1935, §2.2, with modernisation of nomenclature and changes of notation).

The propositional basic argument-forms are *exactly* the rewrites of the general introduction and general elimination rules for conjunction, disjunction, and the conditional of §1 when put in the sequent format of §3. (The sketch of a proof of the completeness theorem above goes some way towards filling in the steps in proving one half of the easily shown equivalence.)

Let us remind ourselves

- that we obtained our sequent calculus by a straight-forward rewriting of the rules of a natural deduction calculus for propositional logic that has the subformula property;

- that the rules for Gentzen's cut-free sequent calculus are derived rules of our sequent calculus;

- that there is an easy back-and-fore switch we can do between our sequent calculus and the "Stoic" form in which all basic argument-forms have a single conclusion;

- that we can reread the "Stoic" formulation as a set of impure, single conclusion natural deduction elimination rules (keeping Dilemma as the sole indirect rule).

(There's one further fact that bears mention: the most natural way to transcribe general introduction and elimination rules into a sequent system yields a sequent calculus in which all operational rules are left and right *elimination* rules (see Milne, 2012b, §6)!)

What is common to all these systems is that, if Cut is used, its uses may be constrained—in deriving Gentzen's operational rules, we cut only side formulae/minor premisses in rules governing connectives—, and, quite generally, although derivations may not contain only subformulae of premisses and conclusion of the derived argument-form, what formulae may appear can be restricted, say, perhaps, to subformulae of premisses and conclusion of the derived argument-form *and their negations*. Do we then "attach no importance to the *Hauptsatz*"? Hardly—the *Hauptsatz* provides an elegant (and vivid) way to make the broader point about *constraints* on cuts/formulae. This is made clearer when we consider the first-order case.[15]

# 6   The Move to First Order

We can readily cast the standard ∃-introduction rule of natural deduction in general introduction form; the standard (Gentzen) ∃-elimination rule is already in general elimination form. When added to the natural deduction formulation of classical propositional logic from which we started out, we have a formulation of the $\{\neg, \wedge, \vee, \rightarrow, \exists\}$-fragment of classical first-order logic *with the subformula property*.[16]

When we add the (general introduction and general elimination rewrites) of the standard rules for the universal quantifier, we no longer have the subformula property. We *do* have an optimal strengthening of the subformula results obtained, as consequences of normalization theorems, by Dag Prawitz (1965, §§3.1, 3.2, 4.1, and 4.2), for the ∨- and ∃-free fragment of classical first-order logic, and by Gunnar Stålmarck (1991), for full classical first-order logic. We have:

> When $\Sigma \vdash \phi$ there is a proof in which, over and above subformulae of members of $\Sigma \cup \{\phi\}$, only $\neg\phi$ and negations of instances of universal generalizations that are themselves subformulae of members of $\Sigma \cup \{\phi\}$ occur. But $\neg\phi$ need not occur if $\phi$ itself has negation dominant, and, likewise, the negation $\neg\xi(v/c)$ of an instance of a subformula $\forall v\xi$ need not occur if $\xi$ has negation dominant. Those non-subformulae that do occur need occur only as assumptions discharged in applications of Dilemma. If a non-subformula that is the negation $\neg\xi(v/c)$ of an instance of a subformula $\forall v\xi$ does so occur, it occurs in an application of Dilemma whose immediate conclusion is $\xi(v/c)$, and, likewise, if $\neg\phi$ does occur as an assumption discharged in an application of Dilemma, it is an application whose immediate conclusion is $\phi$ (cf. Milne, 2010, § 3.5.3, Theorem 8).

---

[15]There's a parallel that would bear closer scrutiny than I have had time to give it. Inspired, on the one hand, by Smullyan's remark, quoted above, regarding the subformula principle and, on the other, by Smullyan's own demonstration of the equivalence of standard tableaux and cut-free sequent calculi (Smullyan, 1968b), a number of authors have advocated nonstandard tableaux systems which, among other things, allow for more efficient proofs—*e.g.* Boolos (1984), D'Agostino and Mondadori (1994), Cellucci (2000).

[16]As noted above, Milne (2010) contains a model-theoretic proof; Tor Sandqvist has an unpublished constructive proof.

One might, as I did in Milne (2010), grub around trying to loosen up the rules for the universal quantifier in order to restore the subformula property. But it is more in line with present concerns to note that, classically, $\forall$ is dual to $\exists$ and use this fact to obtain the standard introduction and elimination rules for $\forall$. As a first step in this direction, we notice with some alarm that the sequent rewriting in the manner of §3 of the (standard and general) elimination rule for $\exists$ gives us

$$\exists x \phi x \Rightarrow \phi a,$$

(where $x$ replaces *all* occurrences of $a$ in $\phi a$) which is far from classically sound (a fact which no doubt accounts for the absence of a basic argument-form replacing left $\exists$-introduction—and likewise right $\forall$-introduction—in Gentzen's list, quoted above).

The proof-theoretic semantics tradition has its roots in the work of Gentzen, especially his (1935), and Prawitz' (1965), which largely followed Gentzen's style of natural deduction. In an appendix, (Prawitz, 1965, Appendix C, §3) discusses "rules for existential instantiation" which take their inspiration from Quine's (1950a) and (1950b).[17] Read as a rule, the sequent above is exactly a rule of existential instantiation and, as such, must be subject to constraints. In terms of splicing, I suggest that in splicing

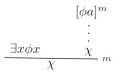

the formula cancelled *must* be $\phi a$, and in any such splicing $a$ does not occur in any other formula featuring either hypothetically or categorically in the instance of the rule with which it is spliced. (Since the conclusion is treated as "general", *for the purposes of splicing* we do not need to say anything specific about occurrences of $a$ in the conclusion.) Now, suppose we have

$$\Sigma, \phi a \Rightarrow \Delta,$$

where $a$ does not occur in any formula in $\Sigma$, nor in any formula in $\Delta$. Then we may splice with $\exists x \phi x \Rightarrow \phi a$ to obtain

$$\Sigma, \exists x \phi x \Rightarrow \Delta.$$

We have replicated Gentzen's *LK* rule for left $\exists$-introduction, with exactly Gentzen's restriction—see Gentzen (1935, §1.22).

Dualising—*i.e.*, splicing $\neg \exists x \neg \phi x$ with negation rules—to obtain an introduction rule for $\forall$, we end up with

$$\phi a \Rightarrow \forall x \phi x,$$

where $x$ replaces all occurrences of $a$ in $\phi a$ and when spliced $\phi a$ *must* be the formula cancelled; in any such splicing $a$ does not occur in any other formula featuring either hypothetically or categorically in the instance of the rule with which it is spliced.

---

[17]See Anellis (1991) and Pelletier (1999) for details of the decade-and-a-half long travail to perfect this approach.

Now, suppose we have

$$\Sigma \Rightarrow \phi a, \Delta,$$

where $a$ does not occur in any formula in $\Sigma$, nor in any formula in $\Delta$. Then we may splice with $\phi a \Rightarrow \forall x \phi x$ to obtain

$$\Sigma \Rightarrow \forall x \phi x, \Delta.$$

We have replicated Gentzen's *LK* rule for right $\forall$-introduction with exactly Gentzen's restriction—see again Gentzen (1935, §1.22).

## 6.1   $\varepsilon$-terms

$$\exists x \phi x \Rightarrow \phi a,$$

is not sound when $a$ is read as a standard name. We can make it sound by giving $a$ a special reading *in context*: $a$ stands for some one of the items satisfying $\phi x$, if there are any, else it is any item (in the domain of discourse). The interpretation of $a$ is tied to the predicate $\phi x$ and its interpretation. To mark that dependence, let us subscript $a$ accordingly.

Working from the (classical) equivalence of $\forall x \phi x$ and $\neg \exists x \neg \phi x$, we can use splicing in order to obtain an introduction rule for $\forall x \phi x$. What we end up with is

$$\phi a_{\neg \phi x} \Rightarrow \forall x \phi x.$$

By doing the minimum to retain classical soundness at first-order, we end up with the $\varepsilon$-calculus rules for the existential and universal quantifiers—see Hazen (1987).

# 7   Conclusion

Smullyan showed how proofs with analytic tableaux and cut-free derivations in Gentzen's sequent calculus *LK* match up; Prawitz showed how normalised natural deduction proofs employing Gentzen's rules are a close but not perfect match.

If we are prepared to side with Smullyan, apparently against Gentzen, on the true significance of the *Hauptsatz*, there is merit in investigating other approaches. In particular, that the formulation of classical propositional logic employing (what I have called) general introduction and elimination rules should match Smullyan's analytic cut sequent calculus is, if only from a purely technical/practical point of view, a mark in its favour. That, as I think they are, general introduction and elimination rules are philosophically well motivated— a claim I have done little to substantiate here but address at length in Milne (2012b)—is an added bonus.

In philosophy, analogies are sometimes helpful. In more formal inquiries, what is often more important is seeing that one is describing the very same phenomenon in different ways. That the first step in the direction of the confluence of ideas sketched above should have been taken by the earliest investigators of propositional logic is a remarkable coincidence.

# BIBLIOGRAPHY

Anellis, I. (1991). Forty years of "unnatural" natural deduction and quantification: A history of first-order systems of natural deduction, from Gentzen to Copi. *Modern Logic*, 2:113–152.

Anellis, I. (1992). Correction. *Modern Logic*, 3:98.

Boolos, G. (1984). Don't eliminate cut. *Journal of Philosophical Logic*, 13(4):373–378.

Boričić, B. (1985). On sequence-conclusion natural deduction systems. *Journal of Philosophical Logic*, 14:359–377.

Cellucci, C. (2000). Analytic Cut Trees. *Logic Journal of the IGPL*, 8:733–750.

Corcoran, J. (1974). Remarks on Stoic Deduction. In Corcoran, J., editor, *Ancient Logic and Its Modern Interpretations: Proceedings of the Buffalo Symposium on Modernist Interpretations of Ancient Logic, 21 and 22 April, 1972*, volume 9 of *Synthese Historical Library*, pages 169–181. Reidel, Dordrecht.

D'Agostino, M. and Mondadori, M. (1994). The taming of the cut. Classical refutations with analytic cut. *Journal of Logic and Computation*, 4(3):285–319.

Dummett, M. A. E. (1973). *Frege: Philosophy of Language*. Duckworth, London, second edition.

Dummett, M. A. E. (1990). The source of the concept of truth. In Boolos, G., editor, *Meaning and Method: Essays in Honor of Hilary Putnam*, pages 1–15. Cambridge University Press, Cambridge.

Dummett, M. A. E. (1991). *The Logical Basis of Metaphysics*. Duckworth, London.

Francez, N. and Dyckhoff, R. (2012). A note on harmony. *Journal of Philosophical Logic*, 41:613–628.

Frede, M. (1974). *Die Stoische Logik*, volume 88 of *Abhandlungen der Akademie der Wissenschaften in Göttingen. Philologisch-Historische Klasse. Dritte Folge*. Vandenhoeck & Ruprecht, Göttingen.

Gentzen, G. (1935). Untersuchungen über das logische Schließen. *Mathematische Zeitschrift*, 39:176–210, 405–31. English translation by Manfred Szabo as 'Investigations into Logical Deduction', *American Philosophical Quarterly*, 1, 1964, pages 288–306, 2, 1965, pages 204–218; also in M.E. Szabo (ed.), *The Collected Papers of Gerhard Gentzen*, North-Holland, Amsterdam, 1969, pages 68–131.

Gentzen, G. (1936). Die Widerspruchfreiheit der reinen Zahlentheorie. *Mathematische Annalen*, 112:493–565. English translation by Manfred Szabo as The Consistency of Elementary Number Theory in M.E. Szabo (ed.), *The Collected Papers of Gerhard Gentzen*, North-Holland, Amsterdam, 1969, pages 132–201.

Hailperin, T. (1996). *Sentential Probability Logic: Origins, Development, Current Status, and Technical Applications*. Lehigh University Press, Bethlehem/Pennsylvania.

Hazen, A. (1987). Natural deduction and Hilbert's ε-operator. *Journal of Philosophical Logic*, 16(4):411–421.

Hitchcock, D. (2005). The Peculiarities of Stoic Logic. In Peacock, K. A. and Irvine, A. D., editors, *Mistakes of Reason: Essays in Honour of John Woods*, Toronto Studies in Philosophy, chapter 13, pages 224–242. University of Toronto Press, Toronto.

Lemmon, E. J. (1965). *Beginning Logic*. Nelson, London.

Martin, C. (1986). William's machine. *Journal of Philosophy*, 83(10):564–572.

Mates, B. (1961). *Stoic Logic*. University of California Press, Berkeley/Los Angeles, 2nd edition.

Mill, J. S. (1843). *A System of Logic, Ratiocinative and Inductive, Being a Connected View of the Principles of Evidence, and the Methods of Scientific Investigation*, volume I. John W. Parker, London, first edition. Published in two volumes.

Mill, J. S. (1859). *A System of Logic, Ratiocinative and Inductive, Being a Connected View of the Principles of Evidence, and the Methods of Scientific Investigation*. Harper & Brothers, New York.

Milne, P. (1995). On the completeness of non-philonian stoic logic. *History and Philosophy of Logic*, 16:39–64.

Milne, P. (2004). Algebras of intervals and a logic of conditional assertions. *Journal of Philosophical Logic*, 33:497–548.

Milne, P. (2008). A Formulation of First-Order Classical Logic in Natural Deduction with the Subformula Property. In Peliš, M., editor, *The Logica Yearbook 2007*, pages 97–110. Filosofia, Institue of Philosophy, Czech Academy of Sciences, Prague.

Milne, P. (2010). Subformula and separation properties in natural deduction via small Kripke models. *Review of Symbolic Logic*, 3(2):175–227.

Milne, P. (2012a). Completeness theorems for stoic logic. *Notre Dame Journal of Formal Logic*. Forthcoming.

Milne, P. (2012b). Inversion principles and introduction rules. To appear in a Festschrift for Dag Prawitz edited by Heinrich Wansing.

Mueller, I. (1978). An Introduction to Stoic Logic. In Rist, J., editor, *The Stoics*, pages 1–26. University of California Press, Berkeley/Los Angeles.

Mueller, I. (1979). The completeness of stoic propositional logic. *Notre Dame Journal of Formal Logic*, 20(1):201–215.

Negri, S. and von Plato, J. (2001). *Structural Proof Theory*. With an appendix by Arne Ranta. Cambridge University Press, Cambridge.

Pelletier, F. J. (1999). A brief history of natural deduction. *History and Philosophy of Logic*, 20(1):1–31.

Prawitz, D. (1965). *Natural Deduction: A Proof-Theoretical Study*. Almqvist & Wiksell, Stockholm.

Priest, G. (1979). The logic of paradox. *Journal of Philosophical Logic*, 8:219–241.

Quine, W. V. O. (1950a). *Methods of Logic*. Holt, New York.

Quine, W. V. O. (1950b). On natural deduction. *Journal of Symbolic Logic*, 15:93–102.

Read, S. (1988). *Relevant Logic: A Philosophical Examination of Inference*. Basil Blackwell, Oxford.

Read, S. (1994). *Thinking About Logic*. Oxford University Press, Oxford.

Read, S. (2000). Harmony and autonomy in classical logic. *Journal of Philosophical Logic*, 29:123–154.

Read, S. (2004). Identity and harmony. *Analysis*, 64:113–119.

Read, S. (2010). General-elimination harmony and the meaning of the logical constants. *Journal of Philosophical Logic*, 39(5):557–576.

Schroeder-Heister, P. (1984a). Generalized rules for quantifiers and the completeness of the intuitionistic operators &, ∨, →, ⋏, ∀, ∃. In Richter, M., Börger, E., Oberschelp, W., Schinzel, B., and Thomas, W., editors, *Computation and Proof Theory. Proceedings of the Logic Colloquium held in Aachen, July 18-23, 1983, Part II*, volume 1104 of *Lecture Notes in Mathematics*, pages 399–426. Springer, Berlin/Heidelberg/New York/Tokyo.

Schroeder-Heister, P. (1984b). A natural extension of natural deduction. *Journal of Symbolic Logic*, 49(4):1284–1300.

Smullyan, R. (1968a). Analytic cut. *Journal of Symbolic Logic*, 33(4):560–564.

Smullyan, R. (1968b). *First-Order Logic*, volume 43 of *Ergebnisse der Mathematik und ihrer Grenzgebiete*. Springer, New York. Reprinted with new preface, New York, Dover Publications, 1995.

Stålmarck, G. (1991). Normalization theorems for full first order classical natural deduction. *Journal of Symbolic Logic*, 56(1):129–149.

Tennant, N. (1992). *Autologic*. Edinburgh University Press, Edinburgh.

von Plato, J. (2001). Natural deduction with general elimination rules. *Archive for Mathematical Logic*, 40(7):541–567.

# Read on Bradwardine on the Liar

GRAHAM PRIEST[†]

**Dedication**: It is the greatest of pleasures contribute this essay to my oldest philosophical colleague, co-author, and friend, Stephen Read, and to contribute it to this celebration of his work. Steve is an accomplished logician, shrewd philosopher, and medievalist *extraordinaire*. For the best part of 40 years now (gulp...), we have beeing cooperating—writing, reading each other's work, discussing, agreeing, disagreeing, attending conferences and organising reseach projects together. In the process, I have learned an enormous amount from him. In particular, he it was who introduced me in St Adrews to the fascinating world of medieval logic in the first year of my first philosophy position, and who has continued to show me its depths and sophistication since then. Thank you, Steve. Dedicating this essay to him is a small and inadquate token of my gratitude.

## 1 The $T$-Schema and its Bradwardinization

In a number of recent papers, Stephen Read has revived a solution to the Liar paradox proposed by the 14th Century philosopher Thomas Bradwardine, phrasing it in modern terms and defending it.[1] A generally accepted principle concerning truth is the $T$-schema:

$$T\langle A\rangle \leftrightarrow A$$

where $A$ is any non-indexical sentence, and $\langle A\rangle$ is its name. With standard techniques of self-reference, we can find a sentence, $L$, of the form $\neg T\langle L\rangle$, so that:

$$T\langle L\rangle \leftrightarrow \neg T\langle L\rangle$$

A modicum of logic then delivers the contradiction $T\langle L\rangle \wedge \neg T\langle L\rangle$. Read rejects the $T$-schema in favour of:

$$T\langle A\rangle \leftrightarrow \forall p(\langle A\rangle : p \rightarrow p)$$

[†]Departments of Philosophy, The Universities of Melbourne and St Andrews, and the Graduate Center, City University of New York. Email: gpriest@gc.cuny.edu
[1]See, *e.g.*, Read (2002, 2006, 2008b,a).

where '$\langle A \rangle : p$' is to be understood as '$\langle A \rangle$ says that $p$'. Let us call this the Bradwardinized form of the $T$-schema. The thought here is that (an unambiguous) $\langle A \rangle$ may say many things, and for it to be true, *all* of them must hold. We may assume that $\langle A \rangle$ says that $A$, $\langle A \rangle : A$. Let $C$ be the conjunction of all the other things that it says; then what the Bradwardinized form of the $T$-schema is telling us is that:

$$T \langle A \rangle \leftrightarrow (A \wedge C)$$

The left-to-right direction of the $T$-schema is clearly forthcoming; but not the right-to-left. Moreover, taking $A$ to be $L$ gives us:

$$T \langle L \rangle \leftrightarrow (\neg T \langle L \rangle \wedge C)$$

It quickly follows that $\neg T \langle L \rangle$, but then also that $\neg C$. The route back to $T \langle L \rangle$ is blocked.

Read's solution has been discussed at some length in the essays in Rahman et al. (2008) and solutions of this general kind are also discussed in Field (2007, ch. 7). In this paper, I want to table a couple of other points about the solution—both of them objections.

## 2   Denotation Paradoxes

First, if the solution is to be a robust one, it must apply to all paradoxes in the same family: same sort of paradox, same sort of solution.[2] How wide that family is, and, in particular, whether it extends to the set theoretic paradoxes,[3] may be moot. But it would be generally agreed that the family contains the paradoxes concerning satisfaction, denotation, and other semantic notions.

The naive $S$ (satisfaction) schema is:

$$\forall x (xS \langle A \rangle \leftrightarrow A_y(x))$$

where $xSy$ means that $x$ satisfies $y$,[4] $A$ is any formula of one free variable, $y$, and $A_y(x)$ is the result of substituting $x$ for all free occurrences of $y$ (subject to preventing clashes with bound variables). Substituting $\neg ySy$ for $A$ quickly leads to the Heterological paradox. The "Bradwardinized" version of the $S$-schema is, presumably:

$$\forall x (xS \langle A \rangle \leftrightarrow \forall P (\langle A \rangle : P \rightarrow Px))$$

where the second-order quantifiers range over properties, and '$\langle A \rangle : P$' means that '$A$' expresses $P$. It is easy to check that the Heterological paradox is now solved in much the same way as the Liar.[5]

---

[2]See Priest (2002, 11.5).

[3]As argued in Priest (2002, Part 3).

[4]Where this may be taken to entail that $y$ is a formula.

[5]Thus, we may suppose that $\langle A \rangle : \lambda y A$. If the other properties expressed by $\langle A \rangle$ are $\{P_i : i \in I\}$, let $C(y)$ be $\bigwedge_{i \in I} P_i y$. Then we have: $xS \langle A \rangle \leftrightarrow (\lambda y A(x) \wedge \lambda y (C(y))(x))$, so $xS \langle A \rangle \leftrightarrow (A_y(x) \wedge C(x))$. The left-to-right direction of the $S$-schema is forthcoming, but not the right-to-left. Now taking $\neg ySy$ for $A$ gives $xS \langle \neg ySy \rangle \leftrightarrow \neg xSx \wedge C(x)$. Let $t$ be $\langle \neg ySy \rangle$. Substituting this for $x$, we have $tSt \leftrightarrow \neg tSt \wedge C(t)$. $\neg tSt$ follows, but so does $\neg C(t)$, and the path back to $tSt$ is blocked.

The paradoxes of denotation are, however, a very distinctive sub-family of the semantic paradoxes;[6] distinctive enough that solutions proposed to other paradoxes of self-reference do not necessarily carry over to them.[7] So it is here. These paradoxes depend, in the first instance, on the naive $D$ (denotation) schema:

$$\forall x(\langle n \rangle \, Dx \leftrightarrow n = x)$$

where $xDy$ means that $x$ denotes $y$, and $n$ is any name. The Bradwardized form of this, by analogy with the cases for truth and satisfaction, is:

$$\forall x(\langle n \rangle \, Dx \leftrightarrow \forall y(\langle n \rangle : y \rightarrow y = x))$$

It is less than clear how to read '$\langle n \rangle : y$' here. In the cases of truth and satisfaction, the paradoxes are blocked by supposing that sentences and predicates have "excess content". By analogy, we must suppose that names have "excess content" in a similar way. '$\langle n \rangle : y$' expresses the thought that $y$ is part of the content of the name $n$, whatever we should take this to mean. I leave it to those sympathetic to the solution to make sense of this idea.[8]

Given that $\langle n \rangle : n$, it follows from the Bradwardinized $D$-schema that $\langle n \rangle \, Dx \rightarrow x = n$. But we don't have the converse. In particular we can not get $\langle n \rangle \, Dn$ from $n = n$. Now, if one consults a formal proof of the simplest of the denotational paradoxes, Berry's, then one can see that the two claims about denotation required for the proof are that for a certain descriptive term, $t$, (i) $\langle t \rangle \, Dx \rightarrow x = t$ and (ii) $\langle t \rangle \, Dt$.[9] One may therefore use the proof as a *reductio* to establish that $\neg \langle t \rangle \, Dt$.

I confess that this strikes me as something of a *reductio* of the Bradwardine line itself. A sentence with a binary relation, $aRb$ holds just if the objects denoted by '$a$' and '$b$' stand in the relation (expressed by) $R$. How could it be that the name '$t$' does not denote the object denoted by '$t$'? Maybe some funny business is going on if '$t$' has more than one denotation. But the left-to-right half of the $D$-schema entails that if a term has a denotation, it is unique.[10] Or again, maybe something strange is going on if '$t$' has no denotation. But the proof of the Berry paradox shows, using just the left-to-right half of the $D$-schema, that the condition in the description $t$ is satisfied by a unique object; so that the term does have a denotation. $t$ may be taken to be the description $\iota y A$, where $A$ is '$y$ is the least natural number that is not denoted by a name (description) of less than 100 words'. Standard considerations (employing, I

---

[6]First, they use descriptions essentially. Second, the argument for each of the contradictory conjuncts, $C$ and $\neg C$, does not go by way of establishing $C \leftrightarrow \neg C$: an independent argument is given for each horn or the contradiction.

[7]See Priest (2006b).

[8]Actually, there is a way of avoiding the issue. We can define $\langle n \rangle \, Dx$ as $xS\langle v = n \rangle$. The Bradwardinised $S$-schema then gives $\forall x(\langle n \rangle \, Dx \leftrightarrow \forall P(\langle v = n \rangle : P \rightarrow Px))$. It is then the condition $v = n$ that has "excess content". But it seems rather arbitrary to insist that $D$ *must* be a defined notion.

[9]See Priest (2006a, 1.8). The second of these can be inferred from the $D$-schema and $t = t$. This is the only place in which the right-to-left direction of the $D$-schema is employed.

[10]In truth, something already seems to have gone wrong at this stage. If the deotation of a term is unique, how can it have "excess content"?

note again, only the left-to-right part of the $D$-schema) establish that $\exists! y A$.[11]
By the very way that descriptions work:

**(*)** $\exists! y A \rightarrow \forall x (A_y(x) \rightarrow \langle \iota y A \rangle Dx)$

It follows that $\exists x \langle \iota y A \rangle Dx$. For good measure, given that:

**(**)** $\exists! y A \rightarrow A_y(\iota y A)$

we have $\langle \iota y A \rangle D \iota y A$. That is, $\langle t \rangle Dt$, and we are back with an explicit contradiction.

The only move here would seem to be to deny (*). Even though there is a unique thing satisfying $A$, '$\iota y A$' does not denote it; '$\iota y A$' has no denotation. How, then, are descriptions supposed to work? The basic principle of descriptions, that $\exists! y A \rightarrow A_y(\iota y A)$, would itself seem to lose all rationale. At the very least, Read owes us a theory of definite descriptions. Moreover, if (**) fails, this on its own, is sufficient to avoid the Berry conclusion, since the principle is appealed to in the argument for it. The Bradwardinian machinery is otiose. Indeed, if $t$ really does have no denotaton, $\exists x \, xDt$ no longer follows from $\forall x (\langle t \rangle Dx \leftrightarrow x = t)$, since we cannot instantiate the quantifier with $t$ (and even if we could, depending on one's theory of non-denotation, $t = t$ might not be true). We do not have to give up the naive $D$-Schema at all.

# 3   Propositional Quantification

Let us now turn to the second problem: the Bradwardine solution to the Liar itself. This has to be phrased using propositional quantification. Some have found such quantification problematic, and reject the notion entirely. Clearly, Read is in no position to do this; let us grant its legitimacy, at least for the sake of argument. There is certainly a grammatical awkwardness in reading propositional quantification in English. Thus, '$\exists p \, p$' is something like 'some proposition is such that it'. One feels the need to stick 'is true' on the end. But propositional quantification dispenses with the need for this. And just because of that fact, propositional quantification allows us to express what normally requires the truth predicate. Indeed, the plain vanilla $p$ says, in effect, that $p$ is true. It appears this allows us to formulate the liar paradox without an explicit truth predicate.

Thus, consider a proposition, $a$, that is identical to its own negation; that is, a proposition of the form 'not me'. By the standards of propositional quantification, this is certainly meaningful. And since every proposition is equivalent to itself, $a$ is equivalent to its own negation. So we are back with a contradicton.

The obvious reply here is to deny that '$a$' refers to anything; that is, to say that $a$ does not exist. But on what grounds can one do this? $a$ is obviously self-referential ('not me'). But there would appear to be nothing problematic about self-reference as such. Merely consider: 'this proposition is being expressed by me now', 'this proposition can be expressed by a sentence with 11

---

[11]Given that there is only a finite number of terms with the required number words, provided that each term has at most one denotation, the number of numbers denoted by them is finite. There must therefore be numbers that are not denoted, and so a least. For details, see Priest (2006a, 1.8).

words'. Neither is it a problem to construct a theory of ungrounded propositions to do justice to propositions of this kind. One such is given by Barwise
and Etchemendy (1987). In their non-well-founded theory, given any boolean
function of propositions, $F(x)$, there are solutions to the fixed-point equation
$x = F(x)$.[12]

At the very least, the solution needs to be backed up by a theory of propositions, and not one specially rigged to give the result. One, can of course, use
the paradox as a *reductio* of the claim that $a$ exists. But this is cheap: if one
builds any pre-condition into a principle employed in a paradoxical argument,
one can use the argument as a *reductio* of this. Moreover, and again, if one has
to resort to this move, it finesses the whole Bradwardinian machinery. One can
endorse the plain unvarnished $T$-schema: this simply applies to propositions,
and the liar sentence does not express a proposition.

And in the last instance, denying the existence of the paradoxical proposition does not work; as usual, strengthened paradoxes arise. By techniques of
diagonalisation, one can certainly find a term, $b$, of the form $\exists q\, q = b \wedge \neg q$.[13]
Now, suppose that $b$; that is, $\exists q(q = b \wedge \neg q)$. Then $\neg b$ by elementary quantifier
rules and the substitutivity of identicals. Conversely, suppose that $\neg b$. Then
$b = b \wedge \neg b$, and so $\exists q(q = b \wedge \neg q)$; that is, $b$.

And now, if one denies that '$b$' refers to anything, that is, one asserts that
$b$ does not exist, we are back in trouble. For suppose that $b$ does not exist,
*i.e.*, that $\neg \exists q\, q = b$. From this it follows that $\neg \exists q(q = b \wedge \neg q)$, which is
$\neg b$. Moreover, it follows that $b = b \wedge \neg b$, and by existential quantification,
$\exists q(q = b \wedge \neg q)$, that is, $b$. (Both of these steps might be taken to fail of $b$ does
not exist. But since $\neg b$ (is true), $\neg b$ must exist; so, then, must $b$.)

One might try to avoid this objection by ramification, though there is no
reason to suppose that Bradwardine had any inclination in this direction (and,
as we shall see, reasons why he should not have). Propositional quantifiers
come in a hierarchy, indexed, say, by the natural numbers. All propositions
have a rank, which is the greatest index of all bound variables in the formula
specifying it;[14] and quantifiers range only over propositions of lower rank. Thus,
our paradoxical proposition is a proposition, $b$, of the form $\exists q_n(q_n = b \wedge \neg q_n)$,
for some $n$. From $b$ we can now infer $\neg b$; so $\neg b$. When we go in the reverse
direction, we can get to $b = b \wedge \neg b$. But since $b$ is a proposition of rank $n$, we
cannot move to $\exists q_n(q_n = b \wedge \neg q_n)$, only to $\exists q_{n+1}(q_{n+1} = b \wedge \neg q_{n+1})$.

---

[12]One might wonder why this does not yield inconsistency in the form of the proposition
such that $x = \neg x$. The answer is that such objects are not guaranteed to satisfy excluded
middle, $x \vee \neg x$, in a situation (and, for that matter, they may also satisfy $x \wedge \neg x$ in a situation).
The internal logic of propositions is First Degree Entailment. This might suggest moving
from a classical to a non-classical logic to accommodate non-well-founded propositions. But
if one is to do this, one might just as well have done it with the pristine $T$-schema.

[13]This actually requires the language to contain the notion of identity between propostions.
(As in Bloom and Suszko, 1971, 1972.) But this hardly seems problematic: if we can quantify
over propositions, we can, presumably, talk about their identity. Diagonalisation is normally
applied to formulas, not terms; but it can be applied to terms just as well. See Priest (1997).

[14]Actually, even at this stage there is a problem, since there is no particular reason as to
why only one formula should specificy the proposition. But let that pass.

Ramification brings familiar problems, however.[15] For a start, ramification seems far too strong. It rules out the possibility of saying perfectly intelligible things.[16] The natural expression of the law of excluded middle with propositional quantification is: $\forall p(p \lor \neg p)$ (where that very proposition is within the scope of the quantifier). After ramification, there is no proposition that expresses this: the closest one can get is $\forall p_n(p_n \lor \neg p_n)$, for some particular $n$; this is obviously weaker. One might try to invoke the device of typical ambiguity, so that the formula is to be taken as asserted for all values of $n$. But an appeal to typical ambiguity works only when we are dealing with a universally quantified sentence. Thus, the natural way to express the dialetheic thesis, and say that some contradictory sentence is true, is $\exists p(p \land \neg p)$, and this is not equivalent to a typically ambiguous assertion of $\exists p_n(p_n \land \neg p_n)$, which asserts the existence of many more dialetheias—one of each type.[17]

And in the case of the Bradwardine solution, ramification is particularly disasterous. If we are going to have to resort to some kind of ramification, we might just as well have resorted to it in the first place, ramifying the truth predicate, à la Tarski. The net effect is the same, and is much simpler, dispensing, as it does, with propositional quantification altogether. Finally, Bradwardine's account of truth cannot even be formulated with ramified quantifiers. The nearest we can get is:

$$T \langle A \rangle \;\leftrightarrow\; \forall p_n(\langle A \rangle : p_n \to p_n)$$

for some rank, $n$, but which? It might be thought that this would be determined by $A$. Unfortunately, it cannot. According to Read's account, *saying that* is closed under entailment. But $A$ will entail propositions of arbitrarily high rank; say, for arbitrarily high $m$, $A \lor \forall p_m(p_m \lor \neg p_m)$. Thus, no $n$ is going to be adequate in a statement of the theory of truth.[18]

## 4    Conclusion

Bradwardine's solution to the liar paradox is a very clever one, both by the standards of the great period of medieval logic and by contemporary standards; and Read's revival and careful contemporary defence of it are much to be welcomed. But what we seem to learn, in the end, is that the solution, though not subject to some of the perhaps more obvious objections, is sunk by essentially the same kinds of considerations that sink all consistent solutions to the paradoxes, such as their inability to handle other paradoxes of the same kind, and extended paradoxes.

What Bradwardine would have said about these matters, we can, of course, only speculate.[19]

---

[15]See Priest (2006a, 1.5), and Priest (2002, ch. 10).

[16]Including, most notably, the theory itself. For to say, as I did, that all propositions have some rank is exactly to quantify over all propositions, which is exactly what, according to the theory, cannot, grammatically, be done. The theory is then self-refuting.

[17]There is also something rather disingenuous with typical ambiguity, even in the universal case. What is *meant* by a typically ambiguous assertion of $\forall p_n A(p_n)$, is exactly $\forall n \forall p_n A(p_n)$. The effect of ramification is to disallow ourselves the ability to say what we mean.

[18]Nor does appealing to substitutional quantification resolve any of these problems.

[19]Versions of this paper were given to the Philosophy Department, University of Con-

# BIBLIOGRAPHY

Barwise, J. and Etchemendy, J. (1987). *The Liar: an Essay on Truth and Circularity.* Oxford University Press, Oxford.

Bloom, S. and Suszko, R. (1971). Semantics for the sentential calculus with identity. *Studia Logica*, 28:77–82.

Bloom, S. and Suszko, R. (1972). Investigations into the sentential calculus with identity. *Notre Dame Journal of Formal Logic*, 13:289–308.

Field, H. (2007). *Saving Truth from the Liar.* Oxford University Press, Oxford.

Priest, G. (1997). On a paradox of Hilbert and Bernays. *Journal of Philosophical Logic*, 26:45–56.

Priest, G. (2002). *Beyond the Limits of Thought.* Oxford University Press, Oxford, second edition.

Priest, G. (2006a). *In Contradiction: A Study of the Transconsistent.* Oxford University Press, Oxford, 2nd edition.

Priest, G. (2006b). The paradoxes of denotation. In Bolander. Thomas; Hendricks, V. and Pedersen, S. A., editors, *Self-Reference*, chapter 7. CSLI, Stanford.

Rahman, S., Tulenheimo, T., and Genot, E., editors (2008). *Unity, Truth and the Liar: The Modern Relevance of Medieval Solutions to the Liar Paradox.* Springer, Heidelberg.

Read, S. (2002). The liar paradox from John Buridan to Thomas Bradwardine. *Vivarium*, 40:189–218.

Read, S. (2006). Symmetry and paradox. *History and Philosophy of Logic*, 27:307–318.

Read, S. (2008a). Further thoughts on Tarski's T-scheme and the liar. In Rahman, S., Tulenheimo, T., and Genot, E., editors, *Unity, Truth and the Liar: The Modern Relevance of Medieval Solutions to the Liar Paradox*, pages 205–228. Springer, New York.

Read, S. (2008b). The truth schema and the liar. In Rahman, S., Tulenheimo, T., and Genot, E., editors, *Unity, Truth and the Liar: The Modern Relevance of Medieval Solutions to the Liar Paradox*, pages 3–17. Springer, New York.

necticut, September 2009, the Logic Group, Melbourne University, May 2011, and at the conference *Paradoxes of Truth and Denotation*, LOGOS Group, University of Barcelona, June, 2011. My thanks go to the audiences helpful comments, and especially to Lloyd Humberstone, Tomas Kowalski, Greg Restall, Dave Ripley, and Sven Rosencrantz. Last, but by no means least, thanks go to Steve Read himself for his comments and discussions of previous versions of the paper.

# *Solvitur Ambulando.* Meaning-constitutive Principles and the Inscrutability of Inference

> It is difficult to begin at the beginning. And not try to go further back.
>
> *On Certainty*, §471[1]

The distinctive thesis of logical inferentialism is that the meaning of the logical constants is solely determined (as well as wholly exhausted) by their inferential role.[2]

In turn, their inferential role is taken to be specified by what I shall call Meaning-Constituting Clauses (MCC), the clauses, that is, that operationally specify the inferences that have to count as valid if the relevant expressions are to be assigned their intended meaning.[3]

The thesis is in the first instance a *meaning-theoretic* claim concerning the way in which the logical constants have the meaning they have. But it is also, inevitably, a thesis concerning how best to represent our logical beliefs (how best to model our beliefs regarding the connectives).[4]

Moreover, given inferentialism's strongly epistemic flavour (the meaning of the connectives is given by stating precise constraints that have to hold for movements to and from sentences containing them to be justified), it is natural to read the main inferentialist thesis as incorporating a claim about the epistemology of meaning and indeed of inference.[5]

---

[†]University of Stirling, FK9 4LA, Scotland, UK. Email: w.b.pedriali@stir.ac.uk.

[1]I'd settled on this epigraph before noticing that it also inaugurates Horwich (2010a). I depart from his quietist reading of it, however.

[2]For doubts about the parenthetic claim see Dummett (1991, p. 205). In this paper, I limit myself to a discussion of logical inferentialism. Whether, and in what way, inferentialism can be generalised to all expressions in the language is a complex issue which I shall not address here. See Brandom (2009, p. 123) for discussion.

[3]I follow (and slightly) adapt standard terminology (and ideas) to be found in *e.g.*, Peacocke (1986, pp. 3, 12; ch. 4), Peacocke (1992, p. 19), Boghossian (2008a, p. 218), Horwich (1998, ch. 6) and (2005a, p. 142), Boghossian (2000, p. 249) and (2008d, p. 259), Eklund (2007, pp. 561–62), Peacocke (2008, p. 114).

[4]See for instance the discussion in Read (2004, p. 175).

[5]As Peacocke (2008, p. 26) correctly notes, inferentialism "aims to explain content in terms of what can *rationally* lead us to make a judgement with that content" (my emphasis).

Accordingly, I think it is fair to attribute to logical inferentialists, especially to the (substantial) extent that they see themselves as giving a *proof-theoretical* (and *use*-based) semantics,[6] (at least) the following three claims regarding MCC.

Firstly, and in contrast to the standard reading of the Tarskian clauses for the connectives, MCC are said to be *non-representational.*[7] On the inferentialist story, that is, the notions of truth and reference do not have explanatory priority in the determination of the semantic properties of the target expressions. What matters, rather, is the inferential role of the expressions involved, as specified in the MCC.

Secondly, MCC are *self-justifying*, in the sense that they are said not to admit (or require) further grounds for us to be justified in holding them to be valid.[8] Note that the claim that MCC are self-justifying does double duty: it (supposedly) blocks any justificatory regress, whilst also securing the autonomy of logic—no extra-logical grounding is required to guarantee the epistemic good standing of the privileged MCC.[9]

Lastly, their meaning-constitutive character entails that there is an *Understanding-Assent Link* (UAL) from grasp of their content to the possession of a disposition to assent to them (or unconditionally to infer according to the specifications contained therein).[10] Note that UAL are not an optional component in the inferentialist account, for they play an essential role in explaining both the sense in which MCC are self-justifying and the sense in which MCC are properly said to be meaning-constituting. In short, UAL are supposed to be mapping the royal road from the meaning-constitutive character of MCC to their self-justifying status.[11]

On the inferentialist view, then, the meaning of the logical constants grounds not just our knowledge of basic logical laws but it also provides the structural basis on which our linguistic competence rests. We are competent with the connectives, we understand them properly, only if we are disposed to infer according to the MCC specifications.

In addition, MCC also furnish us with *the* explication of how we are *moved* to infer under specific constraints, and indeed of how we can do so in a fully

---

[6]See *e.g.*, the discussion in Read (1988, ch. 9), the survey article Sundholm (1989) and the classic post-Gentzen formulations in *e.g.*, Dummett (1973), Dummett (1991), Prawitz (1978), Prawitz (2006).

[7]See *e.g.*, Brandom (2000, ch. 1), Read (2010, p. 558). One can read the non-representationalist label in two ways: *i*) logical expressions do not make a representational claim about ways the world is (or must be); *ii*) logical expressions mean what they do, not in virtue of determining a particular truth-function but rather in virtue of determining specific reasoning modes. I take the latter to be the sharper (and more appropriate) reading.

[8]See *e.g.*, Read (2000, p. 124) and Read (2010, p. 558).

[9]See *e.g.*, Read (2000, pp. 123,131), Read (2010, p. 558).

[10]The UAL terminology comes from Williamson (2007, p. 74). Its ancestor is probably Peacocke (1992, p. 19).

[11]The claim that meaning is constituted by an inclination to accept certain paradigmatic instances of a particular schema is not exclusive to inferentialists. For instance, Horwich (2010b, p. 6) argues that the meaning of the truth predicate is constituted by our inclination to accept instances of the Equivalence Schema ($\langle p \rangle$ is true $\leftrightarrow p$). What is distinctive to inferentialism is precisely that the claim about inclinations is inextricably linked to the claim about justification (by contrast, Horwich does not accept the latter claim).

rational manner (that is, even in the absence of anything that could count as *evidence* in favour of the legitimacy of our most basic inferential steps).

Accordingly, MCC are said to provide a neat account of the cognitive architecture of our inferential practices by means of a bridge principle from competence *qua* semantic understanding to performance under normative constraints in actual reasoning, a principle (the appropriate UAL) that is indeed constitutive of the meaning of the logical constants.

My purpose in this note is to rehearse and try to address challenges (both familiar and unfamiliar) to the last two claims. I will however conclude that inferentialism cannot succeed in giving a proper (and exhaustive) account of the architecture of inference because the three claims above are jointly inconsistent with the meaning-theoretic aims of inferentialism.

# 1 Epistemic Conceptions of Meaning and Understanding

To the extent that it takes seriously its leading claim that the meaning of the connectives is determined by the conditions for their *justified* use, inferentialism can be seen as endorsing an epistemic conception of meaning.[12]

In addition, inferentialism is also committed to a particularly strong version of the epistemic conception of linguistic understanding (EPU) with respect to meaning.[13] On this view, to understand an expression is to know its meaning.[14] More precisely: we understand an expression only if we know its meaning.[15]

Now, there is a class of sentences for which EPU forces a stronger commitment. Analytic sentences, we are told, are such that on grasping their meaning we *eo ipso* grasp their truth value (truth in the case of analytic truths, falsity in the case of counter-analytic falsehoods).[16]

From there, it's only a short step to the meaning-constitutive proposal canvassed by the inferentialist. In the case of the MCC for the logical constants, that is, understanding plays an even greater role. It's not just that understanding their meaning goes hand in hand with assenting to their truth (or rather, their validity). The claim now is that you also acquire, *purely in virtue of that understanding*, an unconditional disposition to infer according to the specifications therein contained.[17]

---

[12]See Skorupski (1997a) for discussion of that conception.

[13]Here I adapt terminology from Pettit (2002, p. 521).

[14]The classic statement of EPU is in Dummett (1996, p. 3). See also his (1991, ch. 4) and Platts (1979, ch. II). See Longworth (2008, 2010) for further discussion.

[15]Pettit (2002, p. 521) formulates the EPU thesis too strongly (as a bi-conditional). There are reasons to resist the right-to-left direction. See *e.g.*, Peacocke (1976, p. 170), Fricker (2003, p. 332) and Williamson (2000, p. 110, fn. 4). Pettit himself attacks the left-to-right direction. See Gross (2005) and Pettit (2005) for further discussion. Prawitz (1978, p. 30) explicitly endorses EPU. Boghossian (2008c, p. 226) draws some useful EPU-related distinctions.

[16]This is of course the modern, post-Kripke conception of analyticity. See *e.g.*, Boghossian (2008a, p. 198), Boghossian (1997, p. 334), Boghossian (2008c). See Williamson (2007, ch. 4) for criticism.

[17]A reader of Williamson (2003) and Horwich (2005a) might be tempted to conclude that the principal (and perhaps the only) target of their attack is Boghossian. But as *e.g.*, the discussion in Prawitz (1978, p. 27, 30) shows, the competence/performance bridge from understanding to dispositions is a key commitment of inferentialist theories of meaning (at least of the Dummett/Prawitz variety).

This is one (perhaps *the*) sense in which MCC are self-justifying. When challenged on the good standing of a particular inferential move, reasoners need do no more than cite the appropriate MCC. If they are to mean, say, the conditional by 'if..., then...', then they have to be disposed to infer according to the relevant MCC—say, conditional proof, or *Modus Ponens* (MPP). Conversely, they infer according to MPP because they attach the canonical meaning to 'if..., then...'.[18]

So far so good. Or rather: it is clear that there are several trouble spots in and around EPU. But at least we can now see where inferentialism is coming from. On this proposal, we have a promising way of addressing the traditional difficulties in locating the source(s) of our *a priori* and analytic knowledge by locating them in linguistic understanding.[19]

The *ur*-thought here is that we have a good grasp, or so it seems, of the notion of understanding the meaning of the expressions of the language we have mastered. By grounding basic logical knowledge (BLK) in semantic competence with a privileged class of expressions (the connectives), we can conveniently bypass the familiar (and formidable) problems associated with other candidate explanations of that knowledge, namely, appeal (more or less desperate) to rational insight or the justificatory regress that awaits us as soon as we attempt to justify BLK by means of *further* inferential knowledge (*i.e.*, knowledge that itself involves inference).[20]

Before we proceed, let me note in passing that the proper way to read the inferentialist project is as one of (Carnapian) *rational reconstruction* of our inferential practices. The inferentialist, that is, is giving an account of what we get up to when we reason according to, say, MPP, such that we can be *described* as reasoners acting under rational constraints at all times, regardless of whether or not it is appropriate to credit us as accessing, again at all times, the conceptual resources deployed in the theoretical reconstruction of our reasoning moves.

The crucial point here is that the sort of conceptual sophistication posited on the inferentialist model is not one possession of which is *necessary* for competence. It *is* however a necessary condition on the availability of *reflectively*

---

[18]That Boghossian intends to secure justification for our BLK by means of understanding-based analyticity is clear from *e.g.*, Boghossian (2012, pp. 224–5).

[19]While inferentialism entails some form of EPU, the converse does not hold. Peacocke's (2008, p. 158) rationalism, for instance, is certainly committed to the view that "semantic understanding is the source of the thinker's appreciation of the logical validity of the logical axioms (and the primitive rules)". At the same time, Peacocke rejects proof-theoretic accounts of that understanding, and proposes it be grounded instead on the standard notions of truth and reference as employed in familiar truth-conditional approaches.

[20]The shape of the dilemma is efficiently rehearsed in the openings of *e.g.*, Boghossian (2008d), Hale (2002) and Wright (2002, 2004a). See also Peacocke (2008, p. 158) for an interesting suggestion. Let me note here that Boghossian's (2008a) defence of the epistemic conception of analyticity has the merit of making manifest the underlying commitments incurred by inferentialism, in particular its reliance on semantic understanding as the crucial engine of its distinctive meaning-theoretic claims. Boghossian (2008a, p. 210) pays due tribute to Coffa (1991) for elegantly tracing the emergence of the ancestors of this view back to the logical positivists. Horwich (2005a, 135, fn. 3) speaks of views of this sort (from Hilbert to Peacocke and Wright and Hale) as *semantogenetic* accounts of basic epistemic norms.

*appreciable* warrant for our reasoning modes that it be accessible to (and indeed *actually* possessed by) the reflective subject.[21]

While this move ensures that the objection to inferentialism in *e.g.*, William-son (2007, p. 97) (roughly: that the ordinary notion of semantic understanding with respect to an expression is not uniquely realised) is quickly despatched, the fact remains that the difficulties for the inferentialist arise *already* at the level of the rational reconstruction project, as we shall see in §6. So much so that it would already be an achievement if *those* difficulties could be neutralised. It would then be a task for another day to address externalist worries about the proper accounting of the employment by children and non-human animals (or even ordinary thinkers) of basic modes of reasoning that, on too strong a reading of the internalist/inferentialist model, might seem not to be plausi-bly attributed (or accessible) to subjects lacking the required meta-conceptual sophistication.

Now, the theorist formulating the appropriate MCC must resort to conceptual sophistication for (at least) one reason. The inferentialist cannot boldly go con-ventionalist and allow that any old MCC will determine a meaning for the target connective. On the contrary, she must insist that MCC aim to capture a priv-ileged class of connectives that respect certain well-specified proof-theoretical properties, a class, moreover, grounded in our best reasoning practices.[22]

This move is required so as to address the notorious challenge posed by Prior's (1961) *tonk* connective that threatens the explanatory priority claim made by inferentialists. Given that claim, it might be thought that any pair of introduction/elimination rules would determine a meaning and that any thinker who understood those rules should find them compelling. And yet the reac-tion to the *tonk* rules is one of repulsion,[23] for observing those rules would precipitate the understander into complete reasoning paralysis.

The upshot is that the inferentialist thesis needs to be appropriately re-stricted so as to screen off any connective whose meaning is (allegedly) deter-mined by rules of inference that no sane reasoner would (or *could*) employ.[24]

---

[21]See Wright (2002, p. 59), Boghossian (2008d, p. 259) and Boghossian (2008b, p. 270). There is a similar distinction mooted in Peacocke (1992, p. 29) between *attribution* and *pos-session* conditions for concepts. We can attribute concept-involving beliefs to agents lacking full possession of a given concept. Such agents would entertain concept-involving attitudes that are *deference-dependent*—their conceptual/linguistic competence necessarily involves willingness to defer to the experts in the community. As we shall see, the distinction won't help parrying the main Horwich-Williamson objection against UAL. Moreover, in my view appeals to deference are for the most part idle. We are simply replacing the inscrutability of reference (or in this case: the inscrutability of *inference*) with *the inscrutability of deference* (the hard problems arise *even when we try to account for an expert's concept-possession*). There are other distinctions in the literature that can be invoked to provide a rational recon-struction reading of inferentialism. For instance, Higginbotham's (1998a, p. 150) distinction between concept possession and conceptual competence (we can possess a concept in the absence of an adequate conception of it: see also a parallel distinction at the linguistic level in Higginbotham (1998b, p. 430)), and the cognate distinction between implicit and explicit conceptions of a concept defended in Peacocke (1998).

[22]Dummett (1991, ch. 9, 10) is essential reading here.

[23]Indeed, to (mis-)paraphrase Peacocke (1992, 6), *tonk* rules are *primitively repelling*.

[24]Note that the inferentialist must be careful to formulate the formal properties that block overgeneration (*e.g.*, conservativeness, harmony, invertibility and so on) in terms that keep proof-theoretic notions as explanatorily prior to truth-theoretic ones.

Ideally, the restrictions will be formulated by identifying *proof-theoretical* properties wholly internal to the MCC involved in a manner that would show, *via essential appeal to their* epistemic *goodness*, that the MCC satisfying those properties are *precisely* those that are grounded in our reasoning practice.[25]

If the inferentialist were to succeed in this dual task, we would then have, at last, a *purely* proof-theoretic explanation of *why* the connectives that we *do* employ in our practice are in fact *rationally* grounded.

The meaning-constituting thesis, then, would be shown to apply only to those connectives that are so basic to our thinking as to be, as it were, *architecturally* beyond challenge, as well as constitutively inalienable. And again all of this would be captured in purely proof-theoretic terms.

It would then follow that, properly speaking, meaning-constituting clauses are, rather, to be construed as *practice-constituting* clauses. Only those MCC that determine a meaning for those connectives that alone can determine a genuinely rational reasoning practice are to be accepted as truly *meaning-*constitutive.[26]

## 2   MCC, Normativity and Rationality

We have seen how, on a broadly inferentialist story, semantic (and/or conceptual) competence provides the grounding for our BLK. Semantic competence does more than that, though. For it also grounds the (standardly made) claim that logic is a normative discipline.[27] Logic, that is, is supposed to be the science of reasoning: or rather, the science of *good* reasoning.[28]

From that perspective, what the MCC for the connectives do is lay down the standards of inference that mark out correct from incorrect reasoning. To reason correctly is to follow the MCC specifications. Mistaken reasoning is reasoning contrary to those specifications.

---

[25]See *e.g.*, Read (2000, 2010) for discussion of the precise profile of those properties and Read (1988, 187) for some philosophical motivation. Boghossian (2008d, p. 262) (and elsewhere) attempts to screen off overgeneration problems via an appeal to the representational properties of the concepts involved (only concepts capable of being used for representational purposes can be genuinely meaning-constituting). That seems to me to be a mistaken strategy for an inferentialist to take. For what is left now of the non-representationalist claim?

[26]It is a vexed issue whether *e.g.*, *tonk*-rules (and inconsistent rules in general) constitute *a* meaning (Boghossian denies they do) or whether they do fix a meaning to which, however, no practice could correspond (whether they point to co-ordinates in logical space that do not exist at all, as *Tractatus* §3.032 would put it). Wright (2002, pp. 62–65) discusses the more subtle case of a Frege-derived Basic Law V-like *course-of-values* operator. Other problematic examples include the naïve truth-predicate and the naïve comprehension principles in set theory. A strategy that has gained much attention lately is going for an inconsistentist theory of meaning. See *e.g.*, Eklund (2002), Patterson (2007b,a), Azzouni (2006, 2007), Scharp (2007), Armour-Grab (2007).

[27]Indeed, perhaps *the* normative discipline *par excellence*. For a recent discussion of the claim that logic is normative see Field (2009) and Milne (2009).

[28]See *e.g.*, the textbook definitions in Shoenfield (1967, 1), Lemmon (1965, pp. 4–5), Tourlakis (2003, p. 1), Hedman (2004, p. xii) and Restall (2005, p. 1). See also e.g Shoesmith and Smiley (1978, p. x), van Benthem (1995, p. 271) and Dummett (1981b, 15). Others, *e.g.*, Harman (1999, pp. 28, 46), disagree.

MCC, then, also convey principles of normative governance for our reasoning, principles that encase norms of correct inference and they do this purely on the basis of their semantic properties.[29]

Now, it has become standard to define rationality as responsiveness to reasons.[30] But rules are reasons of a certain kind—that's why they have normative import for us.[31] And rules-as-reasons generate standards-setting *oughts* in suitably responsive beings.

In particular, the MCC for the logical constants set the most basic norms of reasoning and to be rational is to respond appropriately to their content. That is, MCC provide standing reasons to warrantedly infer according to a specific pattern. Recognition of those reasons provide a motivating reason to infer accordingly. MCC are thus also *mandate-conferring* and they are so to the extent that the validity of the specified mode of reasoning directly and immediately flows from the meaning stipulations.

On apprehending the rule (on realising what it asks of *us*), we apprehend its validity and hence we apprehend the mandate that the rule confers on *reasons-recognition*. If you recognise that there are grounds for asserting the premises, you must also recognise, given a recognition of the reasons *additionally* provided by the rule, that those very same grounds are grounds for asserting the conclusion.

I emphasised 'additionally', for here lies in wait a vicious regress, made famous by Carroll (1895).

## 3   The Carroll Regress

In a way, the regress problem (CR) highlighted by Carroll in that note is perfectly general. It affects (just about) any judgement we might make, not just judgements concerning validity. The difficulty, that is, is that any judgement—or any thought, as Frege (1906, p. 174) observed—[32] always projects from the particular to the general, from the case at hand to a wider more encompassing generality. If the question of justification is raised with respect to the legitimacy of the projection, the regress looms.

---

[29]The claim that meaning is normative is normally traced back to Kripke (1982) (but see also Wright (1980, p. 19). The challenge against that claim started with Bilgrami (1992, pp. 110–113) and continues in *e.g.*, Glüer and Pagin (1999), Wikforss (2001), Glüer (2001), Boghossian (2008b,e), Horwich (2005b, ch. 5, 6), Hattiangadi (2006, 2008), Glüer and Wikforss (2009). For a recent defence of the normativity thesis see Whiting (2007). See also the discussion between Ginsborg (2012) and Haddock (2012). I lack the space to defend the normativity thesis on behalf of the inferentialist here. Very roughly, my view is that we can resist the anti-normative attack by appealing to a distinction between semantic norms of *expectation* and norms of *fulfilment*. The former, but not the latter, impose purely semantic obligations with respect to conditions of use. Here I'm taking a cue from remarks in Husserl's *Sixth Investigation* (2001, ch. 1, §10), Heyting (1983, pp. 58–9), Wittgenstein (1930, §33) and (1953, §445). Soames (1991, pp. 215ff.) discusses an idea by James Higginbotham along similar lines. Smith (1994, pp. 85–7) speaks of expectations with respect to moral norms. For the purposes of this paper, I shall take it for granted that the sceptics' attack can be resisted.

[30]See *e.g.*, Scanlon (1998, ch. 1), Raz (1999, p. 11), Owens (2000, p. 3), Skorupski (1997b, 2010) and Parfit (2011, ch. 1).

[31]Raz (1999, p. 67).

[32]As Dummett (1981a) established, Frege's *Kernsätze* are a response to Lotze's *Logik*.

More specifically, the form the regress takes for an account of inference is the following. We start with the question of what justifies a movement in thought. Externalists (and Tarskians) will answer: the *fact* that the inference is valid. That answer is not available to the inferentialist, though. The meaning-determining rules are rules for *use*: it is their *actual* role in inference that determines meaning, and they earn their keep in virtue of their being self-justifying. The inferentialist, then, can only give an internalist answer: what justifies the movement mandated by the MCC, from the thinker's perspective, is the thinker's *awareness* that the inference is valid (*i.e.*, that it is an instance of a valid pattern of reasoning, that the MCC one has implicitly consulted is a *good* one, and not a bad companion).[33]

Accordingly, the recognition of the reasons that justify one in drawing the inference must include the recognition that the rule is valid *and* that the instance at hand is an instance of the premises. On standard views the rule, however, does not provide a reason to believe in its validity.

And now the CR can get started. For before we can move to the conclusion of an inference, we must also recognise an *additional* reason, one that incorporates the judgement concerning the rule's validity and of what follows from that recognition: namely, that *if* the two premise-reasons are recognised, and if one accepts/recognises the validity of the rule, one may *then*, and only then, infer to the conclusion via an application of that rule.[34]

To sum up, the epistemic architecture of validly drawn inference as responsiveness-to-reasons requires the recognition of three things.[35] We must recognise that the rule of inference we may cite to justify the move is valid; that the instance under consideration (the premises) is indeed an instance of the general pattern stated in the law (in the case of MPP, the minor and major premise) *and* that we have a *further* standing mandate such that *whenever* we accept the validity of the law while also recognising the instance in front of us as a genuine instance of the premise-pattern, we are then entitled to move to the conclusion.[36]

---

[33]Note that this requirement is in fact non-negotiable for the inferentialist: for the MCC to genuinely determine a meaning, they must be self-justifying, they must provide all the material required for their justification and that of their employment. Under inferentialism, there is no separating the question of what justifies a logical law from that of what justifies a move sanctioned by that law.

[34]Russell (1903, §45) spells out the regress in more or less this form and credits its origin to Bradley's *Logic* (1883). Elsewhere, §38, Russell discusses the Carroll Regress explicitly (or implicitly, as in Principia §*2.38). The Regress plays also a crucial part in Quine's (1966b, p. 104), (1966a, p. 115) attacks on conventionalism about logic.

[35]Recall that we are engaged in a process of rational reconstruction. We are asking what makes properly conducted inference a rational process. Correct reasoning may of course occur in the absence of (explicit or inexplicit) reasons-recognition properly so-called.

[36]I suppose those who find Carroll's Tortoise "a familiar subject of ridicule" (Hawthorne, 2004, 39) will resist the idea that *all* these requirements must be in place for an inference to be legitimately drawn. I submit they have failed to take the full measure of the regress. Far from being a ridiculous request, the Tortoise's demand is perfectly proper. We must recognise the rule as valid for it to count as a *reason* to infer to the conclusion. But the MPP rule is silent regarding both the *need* to accept the rule itself and the fact that the rule is itself a reason. Hence the regress.

The problem, clearly, is that the third step is both necessary and regress-inducing, since it is itself, as just noted, a *further* law of reasoning that we must *also* accept.[37] Citing that law will however trigger the regress to a further conditional, and so on. The pattern pointed out by Carroll's tortoise, then, is one that generates ever-increasing inferential complexity as a pre-condition for carrying out the simplest inferential task.[38]

Note that the problem for the inferentialist derives from the fact that the MCC-rules were meant to be self-justifying, that is, meant to provide *all the material* required for constructing a piece of practical reasoning terminating in an intention (or an expectation) to infer (whether or not fulfilled).

What the Regress shows, however, is that it is impossible finitely to state MCC that satisfy these requirements. The upshot is that there is no finite axiomatisation available for our *reflectively controlled* inferential practices. If rationality is responsiveness to reasons, it seems as if, given inferentialism, it can only be responsiveness to *infinitely many* reasons *all at once*.

# 4   Regress-Stopping Moves

What can the inferentialist say in response? Let me first note that given the inferentialist perspective, the most common response to the CR—that the Regress teaches us the distinction between axioms and rules—would be no help at all.[39] Why? Because that distinction leaves the main point of the CR unanswered.

As the Tortoise mockingly tells Achilles, everything logic tells us must be worth writing down (or in our current terminology: every reason that we must recognise for our inferences to be validly drawn must be stated as a premise).[40] Only what can be written down in a formally unexceptionable manner can *force* us to reason according to the canons of logic. But what the Regress teaches us is precisely that we cannot fully articulate all that is required for inference on pain of infinite regress. The rules spelt out in the MCC are thus motivationally

---

[37]I think the problem actually already starts from the demand that the validity of the rule be recognised. The rule itself will typically only give instructions as to what one might do, given the existence of grounds for asserting the premises. It merely spells out the consequences of those premises.

[38]The neatest rehearsals of the regress problem for the inferentialist is in Wright (2002, §12). The suggestion at fn. 17 is highly promising. We could perhaps block the regress by positing an axiom schema *of the same form as* MPP, generating infinitely many instances of ever-more complex conditionals. This would give us an axiomatisation for our inference-drawing practice but at the cost of making it, as Wright (2001, 74) has noted, an inferential *supertask*.

[39]Priest (1979, p. 291) draws the distinction in terms of the rules/beliefs contrast: the latter provide content, the former structure to the architecture of inference. This is surely right but it still leaves unanswered the question of what justifies a particular move. Priest (2002, p. 45), like Dummett (1973, p. 454), goes externalist: validity facts justify without being part of the overt premise-structure of an argument. But this confuses internal and external reasons, propositional and doxastic justification and also leaves obscure why recognition of premise-reasons should suffice to justify the move to the conclusion. To be fully rational, the reasoner must recognise the premises as *structured reasons*, instances of a valid pattern of inference. The puzzle remains, and the distinctions standardly invoked merely re-name the problem.

[40]Curiously enough, Frege anticipated the CR (in *Begriffsschrift* §13, as Sullivan (2004, p. 685) has noted) while also insisting on a requirement that actually triggers it, namely, that "what is essential to an inference must be counted as part of logic" (Frege, 1980, p. 79).

inert, they do not provide sufficient reason to infer. As soon as we *reflect* on what the rules are *really* asking of us, we realise we would need one further rule to make the examined rule effective.

So, the standard response to CR is a non-starter. Equally unpromising is the proposal sketched by Wittgenstein at *Tractatus* §5.132, one whereby we are invited to avoid the detour via generality altogether. In inference, the proposal goes, we do not appeal to general laws to sanction a particular move. The justification for a particular move from premises to conclusion is evinced from the relation holding between the particular premises and the conclusion. The relation is wholly internal to the propositions on either side of the turnstile. There is no relation external to the particular inference, joining it up to a general schema. Any appeal to rules of inference would thus be superfluous.[41]

Now, a first problem with the suggestion is that the idea is clear in outline, but opaque in application.[42] Nothing is said, beyond metaphorical appeal to visual vocabulary,[43] to make good the proposal, to give *some* indication of how facts about validity, whether local or global, could be apprehended in a way that does not involve inference (or grasp of propositional content).

More seriously for our concerns, the rational insight proposal (whether or not implemented with a Tractarian flavour) is also profoundly inimical to inferentialism, because, exactly as Wittgenstein intended, it would simply make MCC wholly redundant. Grasp of validity would no longer be given a semanto-genetic explanation. On this proposal, we do not infer as we do because of our general mastery of the meaning of the connectives but rather because we can *see*, in a *particular* case, that a set of premises does entail a given conclusion.

Nor could MCC be claimed to be self-justifying under this suggestion. Our apprehension of BLK would rather be explained via an appeal to some faculty of rational insight, perhaps construed as a logic faculty, possibly along lines similar to the Chomskian appeal to a language faculty.[44] But once again, that would make MCC redundant (the logic faculty would pick out patterns of inference *directly*).

---

[41] There are interesting (but far from exact) parallels here with the ethical particularism of *e.g.*, Dancy (2004). Perhaps the label *logical particularism* would be appropriate for a view of this kind.

[42] Wittgenstein argued that once properly regimented (*i.e.*, via a translation into a language containing the Sheffer stroke as its only connective) the premises-conclusion relation would be immediately apparent. As far as I can tell, applied to the case of MPP, the inference would look like this: $((\varphi \mid (\psi \mid \psi)) \mid \varphi) \mid ((\varphi \mid (\psi \mid \psi)) \mid \varphi) \vdash (\psi \mid \psi) \mid (\psi \mid \psi)$. Hardly the most pellucid way to represent a rationally compelling mode of inference!

[43] See Wittgenstein (1998, 100) and *Tractatus* §5.13 and §6.122. See also Russell (1903, §45). Proops (2002) has a useful discussion of this issue.

[44] Hanna (2006) develops a book-length approach to this issue, an approach he calls "logical cognitivism", that posits the existence of a logic faculty whereby we grasp, more or less directly, facts about validity. The problem of course is that the sort of normativity we require for logic ought to be *invariant with respect to contingent dispositions*. See also Hale (2002, p. 298). In discussion at the conference on the *a priori* at the Northern Institute of Philosophy in Aberdeen in June 2012, Boghossian disclosed that he has somewhat relented his long-standing opposition to the notion of rational insight.

# 5 Understanding, Again

Rational insights, or other forms of quasi-perceptual stories, then, are no friends of inferentialism. Accordingly, to escape the CR the inferentialist seems to have no other option but to go for an account whereby we do have "spontaneous normative responses" in particular cases,[45] but where those responses can be traced *in their entirety* back to *purely semantic* properties.

In other words, under pressure from the CR, the inferentialist is naturally drawn to her third claim, the one concerning UAL.[46] Given UAL, understanding the meaning of the connectives generates an *immediate* compulsion (more cautiously: a standing disposition) to infer to the conclusion of the appropriate inferential steps. The result is that the semantically-engendered disposition neatly side-steps the regress. We are justified in moving to the conclusion by the mere grasp of the meaning of the connectives. Why? Because to understand the MCC is to *know* that the rule therein encased is valid (that's EPU again). A regress-inducing detour via a general schema is no longer needed. One infers with justification *purely on the authority of the language.*

Are we then home and dry? Not quite. Here is the next problem for the inferentialist.

To escape the CR and preserve the self-justifying claim with respect to the MCC, the inferentialist has had to insist that understanding and acknowledgment of validity are co-occurrent phenomena. And now the trouble is that it seems as if we can make perfect sense of cases where full understanding of the MCC goes in hand in hand with refusal to infer in accordance with it, and indeed with the denial that the MCC is valid.

# 6 The Deviant Logician Objection

What causes trouble for the inferentialist, that is, is that perfectly competent logicians who reject the validity of a given logical law (or its corresponding rule of inference) can (perhaps) be convicted of many things but not of lack of *understanding.* Call this the Deviant Logician Objection (DLO).

The hardest (and most oft-quoted) case of all is that of McGee (1985).[47] It seems clear that no-one could seriously doubt McGee's competence with the

---

[45] As Skorupski (1997a, p. 31) usefully puts it in connection with the rule-following paradox.

[46] Could the inferentialist instead go for some version of the entitlement account as detailed in *e.g.*, Wright (2004b)? I do not think so. Entitlement could not support the self-justifying claim in the desired manner—the warrant that entitlement could provide requires buttressing by wider considerations, mostly of the pragmatic variety.

[47] It is sometimes said that McGee was challenging a thesis about the semantics of natural language (how best to model the 'if...then' connective) or that he was merely challenging the transmission of assertibility conditions under known entailment. This is not the case at all. McGee (1985, pp. 462, 463, 468, 469) is specifically targeting the claim that MPP is a valid law of inference. That's what makes the case so awkward for the inferentialist. The DLO has become familiar in the literature after Williamson (2003), but as far as I can tell it was actually first raised as a problem for inferentialism and conceptual role semantics by Horwich (1998, ch. 6) and Horwich (2005a). The exchanges between Williamson (2003, 2011) and Boghossian (2008b, 2011, 2012) brought the issue into sharper focus but also raised a lot of dust (in particular the discussion about conjunction seems like an unwanted accretion of epicycles). As Boghossian has recently conceded, again in discussion at the NIP conference in June 2012, the hardest case is indeed McGee's and that's the only one I'll be discussing here.

conditional. Nor could we invoke deference mechanisms either, or appeal to incomplete understanding—McGee *is* an expert to whom the community had better defer in matters of competence with the conditional. And yet he does not accept that MPP, wholly unrestricted, is a valid law of reasoning.[48]

More generally, the problem for inferentialism is two-fold. Firstly, we have the joint claims that use fixes the meaning of a connective and that competence is manifested by assent to the MCC. This entails that anyone who challenges aspects of use (denying, say, that the conditional satisfies the law of exportation; or denying that MPP applies to conditionals containing embedded conditionals) is talking about some *other* connective (there is no common object of the understanding shared by the participants to the dispute).

The only way for the inferentialist to account for logical disagreement would then be to insist that classical and deviant logicians are trying to elucidate one concept and one concept only (*the* conditional).[49]

This move would however force externalism on inferentialism, and the distinctive meaning-theoretic thesis of inferentialism would not survive (something other than the proof-theoretic specifications in the MCC determine *which* connective we are talking about).[50]

Secondly, it is a crucial plank of the Prawitz/Dummett view that there *are* canonical ways of specifying the meaning-determining rules. In particular, to individuate the meaning of a connective there must be precisely specified modes of reasoning that both define its semantic content, and unconditional assent to which classifies speakers as competent.

But as Putnam (1978, p. 99) noted long ago,[51] not every change of use entails a change of meaning. And this is due (largely but not exclusively) to the fact that there are no canonical specifications for understanding. It follows that variations (even radical) in patterns of use may leave (ordinary) competence attributions unimpaired.[52]

In the case of logical terms, the problem is particularly acute, for it seems an

---

[48]Hale (2002, pp. 290–1, fn. 18) suggests that the MPP-UAL should be formulated for suitably simple inferences of the kind that McGee could *not* object to. Sure. But the UAL claim concerns *validity*, truth-preservation in *all* cases. The disagreement is precisely as to whether we *should* restrict MPP. And it seems rational to *raise* that question, a question that is however strictly *unthinkable* on a fundamentalist reading of inferentialism.

[49]Read's (1988, p. 155) response to the meaning-variance argument is that we can provisionally fix the reference of a logical constant by means of beliefs about its inferential properties. Once the reference-fixing job has been done, we can then proceed to criticise any of the beliefs involved in that job. The suggestion is intriguing but ultimately it seems to me that it underestimates the force of the argument. If the inferentialist concedes that we can *alter* any of our beliefs regarding a connective without affecting the identity of that connective, then she has already renegaded on the key inferentialist claim concerning meaning-determination.

[50]I assume here that content is individuated in terms of (settled) meaning stipulations. Martí (1998, 166) makes a similar point in her discussion of Higginbotham (1998a). In Quine's (1970, p. 81) terminology, the point is that if we insist that there is an 'essence' to a concept (the conditional, in this case) which we may possess imperfectly, we are thereby abandoning the inferentialist thesis that there can be *no more* to concept individuation that settled dispositions to infer.

[51]The argument(s) in full are in Putnam (1975). See also Williamson (2007, ch. 4).

[52]I think Williamson's cases do strain credibility somewhat. But the basic point is solid. We do not cease to understand a connective as we raise doubts, whether or not sound, as to validity.

essential part of the history of logic that we *do* in fact test meaning-stipulations to ensure they deliver the desired results. And pressure towards logical revision (or deviancy), and doubts as to validity (whether prolonged or casually entertained, as one experiments with recreational logics) should not be seen as weakening *in any way* one's understanding of the target connective.

Matters, however, are even worse than that for the inferentialist. For leaving logical deviancy aside, it seems a key *requirement* of rationality that it be possible to *entertain* doubts about the validity of a logical law and it seems absurd to claim that *as we entertain those doubts* our *understanding* lapses.[53]

When we doubt, when we *wonder* whether a logical law holds, it seems imperative that we be able to assess the validity *precisely of the law under scrutiny*! When (or if) we recant, and recognise that the doubt was not rationally held, that very recognition must arise *with respect to the connective in question* and no other.[54]

But if any doubt raised about validity equates to meaning-change (as the inferentialist committed to UAL has to say), it seems impossible to even *test* a law for validity.[55]

On the inferentialist story, any time we call a law into question, *merely* into question, our understanding lapses. And it's not just that, as Quine would have it, we are talking about something else.[56] Rather, if inferentialism is right, in cases of this kind, we do not even know *what* we are talking about any more. On this account, we slip in and out of understanding as doubts about validity are raised and quelled, surely an undesirable result.[57]

The trouble for the inferentialist here is that to respond to the CR (and to hold on to the self-justifying claim) she had to eliminate *any* gap between understanding and disposition to infer (between grasp of meaning and judgement regarding validity). But by doing so, she has now to face the contrary need

---

[53]To generalise a point made in *e.g.*, Korsgaard (1996, p. 93), it is a distinctive requirement of rationality that we possess (and exercise) a capacity to *distance* ourselves from our beliefs, no matter how basic *they* may be. And yet, the inferentialist commitment to UAL robs us precisely of that capacity. In other words, *temporary* rational doubt that leaves the object of understanding unchanged *must* be possible. But this is precisely what UAL denies could *ever* happen.

[54]Incidentally, let me note that we should distinguish between the rationality of doubting a logical law and the rationality of raising the question whether that law could be doubted.

[55]Indeed, it seems impossible even to make sense of the very idea of something (some *one* thing) being *beyond* rational doubt.

[56]As is familiar, the so-called meaning-variance argument originates with Quine (1970, ch. 6).

[57]In his presentation at the NIP conference referred above, Boghossian retrenched his position, doubtlessly because of this objection. He now thinks that understanding generates an *attraction* towards the mode of inference sanctioned by the MCC. It is not clear whether he thinks of the inclination as *entailed* or as *constitutive* of the understanding, or even as causally triggered by MCC-understanding. I think the regrouping does not gain much useful ground to the inferentialist however. For one thing, the *source* of that attraction, if genuine, can just as well be traced back to *custom*, communitarian reinforcement and reward, rather than to semantic understanding properly so-called. Moreover, deviant logicians can well be quite relaxed about their contrarian inferential inclinations and contemplate with disapproving wonderment the classicist abandon with MPP. Finally, the whole point of positing inferential disposition is that they be, to adapt terminology from Eflin (2003, p. 53), *non-transitory*.

to leave *enough* of a gap to allow for the practice of rationally *raising* doubts concerning validity, a practice that characterises the history of logic.[58]

The DLO therefore stands undefeated, or so I submit.[59]

# 7   Constitutivity, Again

> "Giving grounds [...] comes to an end—but the end is not certain propositions' striking us immediately as true, *i.e.*, it is not a kind of *seeing* on our part; it is our *acting*, which lies at the bottom of the language-game."[60]

I think we should conclude that the proper response to the DLO is to abandon the UAL claim. This however would immediately raise the CR threat again while also requiring a different defence of the self-justifying claim. What could the inferentialist do at this point, then?

Our problem was that the MCC-norms that supposedly guide our reasoning must not be idle. Even when they are not reflectively access*ed*, they must still, at all times, remain reflectively access*ible* (or else it is not clear in what sense they have normative import for *us*).[61] And yet the CR and the UAL puzzles bring out an apparent limitative result in the epistemology of BLK. We need more reasons in the architecture of inference that can be explicitly expressed in a proper characterisation of inference.[62]

The difficulty seems due to the baffling character of rules. They play an essential part in an account of rationality and yet they seem to escape explicit inclusion in that account.

---

[58]Clearly, it seems more reasonable to say that grasp of a given MCC gives you mastery of *what it would be like* to infer according to its specifications. But with that move, the self-justifying claim goes out of the window. For the same reason, it would be no good to say that here one is confusing two issues (what determines the meaning of the logical constants, and which logical constants there *actually* are) that are best kept separate. What matters, one might think, is that *whatever connectives we adopt as logical* their meaning is determined by the rules for their use. The point is: the correct MCC must contain *within themselves* everything that can ensure that our choice of logic is justified.

[59]We should note a rather embarrassing point too. If inferentialism is right, we could not even make sense of the lively debate within inferentialism itself regarding the precise character of the proof-theoretic properties that MCC have to satisfy. Any change in those properties will generate a new connective. Perhaps one response here could be to endorse a *cluster* theory of the connectives (by analogy with Searle's cluster theory of proper names). Kripke might have something to say about that too, though.

[60]Wittgenstein (1969, §204).

[61]As *e.g.*, Owens (2000, p. 13) notes, responsiveness to reasons does not demand *concurrent* reflection on whatever reasons are salient at a context. Reasons must nevertheless be both accessible in principle and play a motivational role even when not brought directly to consciousness or else logic precipitates into what anthropologists would call unmarked behaviour. See Railton (2006).

[62]There is another temptation at this point, and it is to connect this issue to the discussion of the Wittgensteinian conception of nonsense in the *Tractatus* that divides American from British readings of that work (see *e.g.*, Diamond (1991, ch. 2, 3), Witherspoon (2000), Hacker (2000), Conant (2002), Hacker (2003) and Diamond (2005)). We might that is propose that some reasons can only be *shown* and not *said*, that some BLK is ineffable. The proposal pursued in the text can be seen as a variant of this idea.

While grappling with the difficulty, Sellars (1950, p. 155) had proposed that rules are not to be stated. They are, rather, to be *lived.* How could we flesh out that sketchy but intriguing remark? Here's one way.

We could think of MCC not as providing *reasons* to be accessed and responded to (and indeed *used* in inference) by reasoners.

Rather, what the rules stated in the MCC do is describe *reasoners.* In turn, reasoners *exemplify* MCC. By acting in accordance with the MCC, they *embody* those stipulations.[63]

MCC, then, do not *tell* us how to think. They show us, rather, *what it is* to think.[64] They tell what it is to be a reasoner. A reasoner is someone who moves between thoughts in that manner.[65]

MCC then are to be explained has being both *practice-constituting* and *agency-constituting.*[66]

Rational thinkers respond to reasons-in-context (the grounds for asserting the premises) and move *directly* to asserting the conclusion not because of a recognition of the validity of the MCC taken as a *separate* reason but rather because to be rational is to respond to premises-grounds by exemplifying the reasoning behaviour described in the MCC, a behaviour that is triggered by those premises in appropriately sensitive thinkers.[67]

Note that on this proposal the structural understanding that underpins our grasp of MCC is not understanding of the structure of meanings but rather of the structure of *reasoning.*[68] It is indeed an understanding of a *dynamic* structure (an *unfolding* piece of reasoning) rather than a static one (a network of standing reasons).[69]

Are we out of the woods by making this switch in the epistemic status of

---

[63]We could put it this way: we infer *in the shadow* of the concept operationally expressed by the MCC.

[64]This is the sense in which they are *sui generis* propositions.

[65]The remarks by Gentzen that sparked off inferentialism were famously hedged: the introduction rules are definitions only in a manner of speaking (*sozusagen*). On the proposal under scrutiny, Genzten's *so to speak* becomes *by so speaking.* By *saying* what they say, and by being exemplified by reasoners, the MCC define not just the meaning of the connectives but also what it is to think and reason.

[66]The account would differ from the pragmatic one given in Enoch and Schechter (2008). The constitutivity claim is meant to be immune from pragmatic encroachment.

[67]One might object that this is just a fanciful re-working of the classic response to the CR mentioned above. We replace the rule/axiom distinction with the rather woolly transformation of rules of inference into *Lebensformen* patterns (in the same sense that a knitting pattern provides a way for a knitter to be, that is!). I hope the text does enough to dispel the plausibility of the objection.

[68]We could put the point in slightly Gricean terms: by drawing an MCC-inference, we represent ourselves as knowing that the inference is legitimately drawn.

[69]Sellars (1963a, p. 169) famously said that by treating perceptual episodes as states of knowing we place those episodes in the logical space of reasons. The idea behind the proposal canvassed in the text is that by grasping MCC we are placing *ourselves* in the space of reasons. To adapt terminology from Sellars (1963b), MCC are the *entry-points* to the space of rationality, the invisible lines along which the world and the space of rationality make contact *through* our agency. To further motivate the proposal, one could also invoke Humboldt's insistence that we conceive of language not as the product of an activity (*ergon*) but as the activity itself (*energeia*). See Lafont (1999, ch. 2) for a quick introduction to Humboldt's conception of language, a conception, I should add, that I think inferentialists should enthusiastically embrace.

MCC? After all, for all that has been said so far, it is still obscure how the move from the premises to the conclusion is justified *by* the MCC (and the requirement that it be so justified seems essential to inferentialism).

Furthermore, if all MCC do is describe *reasoners* (or reasoning modes), rather than providing *reasons*, whence their motivational impact?[70] Why should we be compelled to infer in that way and no other?

And what of the DLO? If we disagree as to whether the conditional must satisfy exportation or must instead be restricted in some other way, or if we disagree about how to save logic from the semantic paradoxes, what can possibly arbitrate between opposing parties if all that one is doing is choosing *one* way to reason among others, one way to be an agent among other possible ones? What is distinctive about the *right* MCC, that is?

And finally, if we take up and exemplify a given MCC *without reasons*, properly speaking, in what sense are we acting rationally?[71]

I think these objections do carry force, but unfortunately I do not have the space to fully address all of them here. I'll just say that it seems to me that one promising route here would be to show that only some MCC are constitutive of rationality.[72] Only some ways for an agent to be are correct.

Bad companions would thus be screened off by considerations regarding what *could* constitute a rational practice.[73] Since to be an agent is inescapable,[74] and since some basic modes of reasoning (including MPP) are essential to being an agent,[75] the correct MCC will be those that are jointly genuinely constitutive of agency.[76]

---

[70]One could perhaps say that *by describing perfectly rational reasoners* MCC provide reasons to exemplify the reasoning behaviour they sanction. Perhaps.

[71]As BonJour (2005, p. 121) points out, if an agent has no insight into validity, then she has no reason (and hence no entitlement) at all to hold the conclusion to be true.

[72]One difficulty is to do so without succumbing to the crude and pragmatic idea, to quote from Williamson (2003, p. 290), that we need those rules because we could not do without logic.

[73]Obviously, this has strongly holistic overtones and radical Quinian talk of "adjustments elsewhere" might be invoked to show that perhaps even *tonk* could count as practice-constituting if some other rule of inference neutralised the *tonk*-induced slide into triviality. At that point, the best one could do is invoke considerations of theoretical elegance, and we would have completely lost the autonomy of logic.

[74]The claim is controversial. See Ferrero (2009) and Enoch (2011) for two opposing views. Note that what needs sustaining, to make the proposal have bite, is the claim that by endorsing it we are going beyond entitlement strategies such as Wright's (2004b, p. 161). It's not that we can do *no better* than taking certain things for granted (the hinge-like MCC). It is that *what it is to be a reasoner* is to take certain principles (the *right* MCC) for granted.

[75]Is a *tonk*-reasoner an agent? It is often claimed (*e.g.*, Horwich (2005a, p. 153)) that no-one could reason according to *tonk*-rules (but see Wright (2002, pp. 62–3)). And yet it seems that a *tonker* (to coin a neologism), in her brief and perilous existence, could still count as an agent. I am not really sure there is a clear answer to this question. It seems as if we can ask whether there is such a thing as moving from one thought to absolutely *any* thought whatsoever. Would *that* count as *reasoning*, or indeed as *movement*? Frege (1998, xvi) famously spoke of a "hitherto unknown form of madness" and it seems as if tonkers would get very near the precipice of intellection properly so called.

[76]Plainly, we have substituted talk of meaning-constitutivity with talk of agency-constitutivity and therefore the problems and the responses are largely analogous. For all that, I think that the move to talk of agency opens up ways to address the DLO that would at least preserve intact ordinary notions of understanding and competence.

There are however deep problems still left unresolved. As agents, we may well be said to be exemplifying MCC. But if we insist that correct MCC are *inescapable*—that there is no other way of being an agent—we seem to lose one important aspect of being rational, namely, the very idea of responsiveness to reasons that is supposed to be constitutive of rationality. If agency (and rationality) are inescapable, *what* are we responding to, as we dutifully exemplify the MCC? Or otherwise put: what *reason* do we have to embark on the project of being an agent?[77]

## 8 Conclusion: The Inscrutability of Inference

> "The end is not an ungrounded presupposition: it is
> an ungrounded way of acting."[78]

At this point, I am only tentatively confident that my proposal can satisfactorily answer all of these questions. What seems clear to me, however, is that *even if* the agency-constitutive reading of the MCC is successful, inferentialism would not survive unscathed.

In particular, I think that, as already indicated, one lesson from this discussion is that inferentialism must give up the UAL component. An account of the logical constants that makes the very idea of logical revision incoherent is surely on the wrong footing. In other words, inferentialism must make room for a conception of understanding that allows for the phenomenon of understanding-without-compulsion.

But once this is granted, inferentialism has again got to face the threat from the CR.

To escape from that, an agency-constitutive account of MCC along the lines sketched in the preceding section seems to me to be the most promising avenue (and indeed perhaps the only one available).

There are still further concessions to be made, though. For I think that inferentialism can parry the CR only at the cost of giving up the self-justifying claim.[79] Inferentialism, that is, must acknowledge that MCC cannot carry the

---

[77]This is roughly the objection against constitutive accounts of agency contained in Enoch (2011, §2). I think this is a much stronger objection than others one might moot. For instance, a fairly common one is that constitutive accounts over-intellectualise agency. But again, this objection loses track of the rational reconstruction flavour of the project we are trying to sustain. Constitutivity theorists such as Korsgaard impose the requirement that for an act to count as rational it must *incorporate* a reason. An idea worth exploring here is to deny that the choice to be an agent (the choice to endorse one rather than another MCC) is an *act* at all. But again, in what sense would the MCC themselves be rationally *grounded*? And in what sense is the taking up of agency (as a *no-alternative* undertaking) any different from the purely brutish dispositions that internalism and inferentialism were supposed to exorcise? At the same time, one might feel that these questions sound like category mistakes, and that the account itself is fundamentally mistaken. Surely, the objection goes, the regress of reasons must come to an end. Moreover, we cannot ask for a reason to be forced to accept the dictates of Reason, can we? That's surely something that doesn't belong to the space of reasons. Surely this is one point at which logic *must* give out. But isn't saying that reasons must come to an end simply to accept that logic is not autonomous in the desired way?

[78]Wittgenstein (1969, §110).

[79]One may wonder in what sense my proposal is supposed to be a *help* to the inferentialist,

justificatory burden all by themselves. Reading them as agency-constitutive principles may explain what goes on in inference (to be reasoners, we must place ourselves in the space of reasons by exemplifying the chosen MCC).

However, that reading does little, or so it seems to me, to justify inference *on a purely logical basis* (the choice of which MCC to endorse is done on the strength of agency-constitutivity considerations that do not seem to cohere with traditional conceptions of logic).[80]

Nailing down the proof-theoretical properties that distinguish well-behaved connectives from the bad companions is thus to be seen as an enterprise of more modest scope.

If successful, it will provide us with criteria for the well-behavedness of connectives—already a considerable achievement in itself. It will however be unable to provide criteria that uniquely identify the connectives determined by our best practice. Or if the criteria should succeed in doing so, they will nevertheless fail to sustain the motivational claim. Even well-behaved MCC will not (and can not) be *unconditionally* compelling for an agent.

I think the broader conclusion we should draw, at least at this stage, is therefore that inference, as a process we engage in as we reason our way in the realm of thought, remains a deeply inscrutable activity, at least inscrutable to and in the light of reason.

Sainsbury (2002, 16) concluded a discussion of the role of logic in our thinking by conceding that the cognitive processes underpinning our inferential practices are theoretically opaque to us.

I think the conclusion must be stronger. It is not just a question of the *cognitive* architecture of inference; the difficulty arises *already* at the level of the *epistemic* architecture of inference. What is unclear, that is, is how we should carve up epistemic space and our movements across it.

There are those who think that Zeno's paradoxes still await a fully exhaustive answer. It seems to me that the situation with the Carroll Regress is worse than that. We are still in denial regarding the force of the problems it poses to a full elucidation of what is involved in an act of inferring.

In that respect, if we go back to Carroll (1895) we may ask ourselves, why Achilles and the Tortoise? Why did Carroll choose this particular pair of characters in a dialogue about the motivational force of logic?

Here's a suggestion. In the original Zeno paradox, the standard lesson was supposed to be that either motion is an illusion or that our account in terms of discrete transitions between discretely ordered points was wrong.

I think we can put matters in the same way with regard to epistemic space. Either reasoning (in the sense of: rational transitions between thoughts) is an illusion or an account in terms of discrete thought-transitions between discretely ordered propositions is wrong.[81]

---

if two out of its three main claims are to be renounced. The point is that the meaning-determination claim is non-negotiable. My proposal is intended to avoid the CR (or rather: go round it). It is however powerless to salvage the other two claims. Nothing can, I think.

[80]And one might be tempted to add: so much the worse for those conceptions. For now, I remain neutral on this issue.

[81]According to Black's (1951, p. 101) conclusion with regard to Zeno's paradox of motion, even the modern mathematical "solution" given in terms of continuity is misguided. For

We could also put the matter in terms of another Zenonian paradox, that of the arrow that couldn't get started in its trajectory. Similarly, the Carroll Regress seems to show that *if inference worked the way logicians think it does* then no reasoning could ever get started (the reasons-recognition process would go on forever).[82]

Accordingly, we seem forced towards some sort of inferential nihilism: contrary to appearances (or to our wishful thinking) we do not infer rationally at all.[83]

If the difficulties I have rehearsed are as intractable as I've made them out to be, the conclusion must be even stronger: there *could not be* rational inference properly speaking. It is architecturally impossible to infer under rational constraints.

If we attempt rationally to reconstruct our reasoning practices the best we can do is gesture at an account that would allow us to self-describe ourselves as rational reasoners (indeed: to *be* rational reasoners), *were it possible to implement that account*. But it isn't, and so we ain't.[84]

As things stand, I conclude that we can do little better than follow Achilles' inglorious stone-kicking example and claim that the problem is sorted by reasoning—*Solvitur ratiocinando*.

Inference, like motion, can only be exemplified. Rules can only be lived, as Sellars had said, not made explicit components of the logical space of reasons.

That there are correct rules of reasoning is *shown* by agents placing themselves in that space. The rules, however, can neither be *fully* stated, nor used as reasons in inference.[85]

# BIBLIOGRAPHY

Armour-Grab, B. (2007). Consistent inconsistency theories. *Inquiry*, 50(6):639–654.

Azzouni, J. (2006). *Tracking Reason. Proof, Consequence, and Truth*. Oxford University Press, Oxford.

Black, there is an important distinction between the finite number of tasks Achilles actually performs and the mathematical descriptions that we (or Zeno) can give of those tasks. There are no supertasks, in actual or in epistemic space that anyone can perform. Black's proposal however would leave the rational reconstruction project in tatters, for in that project we purport to give not just a description but a *characterisation* of how ideal agents would operate in an ideal epistemic space.

[82]If Dummett (1981a, p. 297) is right and epistemic distance is indeed more puzzling than spatial distance, I think the regress should teach us that if reasoning steps are ordered the way the logician maintains they are, then not only is there no thinking, but there is no agency either. The point is that, to quote again the Tortoise, if what logic communicates must be propositional, then the most basic commands of logic are incommunicable, for they *cannot* be propositional on pain of regress.

[83]Nihilism would in effect admit *at the theoretical level* nothing more (or nothing *better*) than the "untroubled engagement in ungrounded meaning" characteristic of the ordinary perspective, as Sullivan (2002, p. 44) elegantly put it in another context.

[84]Blackburn (1995) takes the CR seriously and concludes that the Tortoise is Humean. Movements of the will (or of the mind) cannot be explicated solely by appeal to reason.

[85]This paper draws on a presentation given at the Arché AHRC-funded Foundations of Logical Consequence workshop on the Epistemology of Logic, October 29–30, 2011, St Andrews. Thanks are due to the audience on that occasion, particularly to Timothy Williamson, Stephen Read, Graham Priest, Stewart Shapiro and Torfinn Huvenes. Additional thanks are due to the expert (and wonderfully patient) editors of this volume. Work on this paper was completed during my tenure as a Leverhulme Postdoctoral Research Fellow.

Azzouni, J. (2007). The inconsistency of natural languages: How we live with it. *Inquiry*, 50(6):590–605.

Bilgrami, A. (1992). *Belief and Meaning*. Blackwell, Oxford.

Black, M. (1951). Achilles and the tortoise. *Analysis*, 11(5):91–101.

Blackburn, S. (1995). Practical tortoise raising. *Mind*, 104(416):695–711.

Boghossian, P. (1997). Analyticity. In Hale, B. and Wright, C., editors, *A Companion to the Philosophy of Language*, pages 331–368. Blackwell, Oxford.

Boghossian, P. (2000). Knowledge of logic. In Boghossian, P. and Peacocke, C., editors, *New Essays on the A Priori*, pages 229–254. Clarendon Press, Oxford.

Boghossian, P. (2008a). Analyticity reconsidered. In *Content and Justification*, pages 195–224. Clarendon Press, Oxford.

Boghossian, P. (2008b). Blind reasoning. In *Content and Justification*, pages 267–287. Clarendon Press, Oxford.

Boghossian, P. (2008c). Epistemic analyticity: A defense. In *Content and Justification*, pages 225–233. Clarendon Press, Oxford.

Boghossian, P. (2008d). How are objective epistemic reasons possible? In *Content and Justification*, pages 235–266. Clarendon Press, Oxford.

Boghossian, P. (2008e). Is meaning normative? In *Content and Justification*, pages 95–107. Clarendon Press, Oxford.

Boghossian, P. (2011). Williamson on the *A Priori* and the analytic. *Philosophy and Phenomenological Research*, 82(2):488–497.

Boghossian, P. (2012). Inferentialism and the epistemology of logic: Reflections on Casalegno and Williamson. *Dialectica*, 66(2):221–236.

BonJour, L. (2005). Last rejoinder. In Steup, M. and Sosa, E., editors, *Contemporary Debates in Epistemology*, pages 120–121. Blackwell, Oxford.

Brandom, R. B. (2000). *Articulating Reasons*. Harvard University Press, Cambridge, MA.

Brandom, R. B. (2009). *Reason in Philosophy*. The Belknap Press of Harvard University Press, Cambridge, MA.

Carroll, L. (1895). What the tortoise said to Achilles. *Mind*, 4(14):278–280.

Coffa, A. (1991). *The Semantic Tradition from Kant to Carnap*. Cambridge University Press, Cambridge.

Conant, J. (2002). The method of the *Tractatus*. In Reck, E. H., editor, *From Frege to Wittgenstein*, pages 374–462. Oxford University Press, Oxford.

Dancy, J. (2004). *Ethics Without Principle*. Clarendon Press, Oxford.

Diamond, C. (1991). *The Realistic Spirit*. Blackwell, Oxford.

Diamond, C. (2005). Logical syntax in Wittgenstein's *Tractatus*. *The Philosophical Quarterly*, 55(218):78–89.

Dummett, M. A. E. (1973). *Frege: Philosophy of Language*. Duckworth, London, second edition.

Dummett, M. A. E. (1981a). Frege's 'Kernsätze zur Logik'. In *Frege and Other Philosophers*, pages 65–78. Clarendon Press, Oxford.

Dummett, M. A. E. (1981b). *The Interpretation of Frege's Philosophy*. Duckworth, London.

Dummett, M. A. E. (1991). *The Logical Basis of Metaphysics*. Duckworth, London.

Dummett, M. A. E. (1996). What is a theory of meaning? (I). In *The Seas of Language*, pages 1–33. Clarendon Press, Oxford.

Eflin, J. (2003). Epistemic presuppositions and their consequences. In Brady, M. and Pritchard, D., editors, *Moral and Epistemic Virtues*, pages 47–66. Blackwell, Oxford.

Eklund, M. (2002). Inconsistent languages. *Philosophy and Phenomenological Research*, 64(2):251–275.

Eklund, M. (2007). Meaning-constitutivity. *Inquiry*, 50(6):559–574.

Enoch, D. (2011). Shmagency revisited. In Brady, M., editor, *New Waves in Metaethics*, pages 208–233. Palgrave Macmillan, Basingstoke.

Enoch, D. and Schechter, J. (2008). How are basic belief-forming methods justified? *Philosophy and Phenomenological Research*, 76(3):547–57.

Ferrero, L. (2009). Constitutivism and the inescapability of agency. In Shafer-Landau, R., editor, *Oxford Studies in Metaethics*, volume 4, pages 303–333. Oxford University Press, Oxford.

Field, H. (2009). What is the normative role of logic? *Proceedings of the Aristotelian Society, Supplementary*, 83:251–268.

Frege, G. (1893/1998). *Grundgesetze der Arithmetik*. Georg Olms Verlag, Jena/Hildesheim.

Frege, G. (1906). 17 key sentences on logic. In *Posthumous Writings*, pages 174–175. Blackwell, Oxford.

Frege, G. (1980). *Philosophical and Mathematical Correspondence.* Blackwell, Oxford.

Fricker, E. (2003). Understanding and knowledge of what is said. In Barber, A., editor, *Epistemology of Language*, pages 325–366. Oxford University Press, Oxford.

Ginsborg, H. (2012). The normativity of meaning. *Proceedings of the Aristotelian Society*, 86:127–146. Suplementary Volume.

Glüer, K. (2001). Dreams and nightmares: Conventions, norms, and meaning in Davidson's philosophy of language. In Kotako, P., Pagin, P., and Segal, G., editors, *Interpreting Davidson*, pages 53–74. CSLI Publications, Stanford.

Glüer, K. and Pagin, P. (1999). Rules of meaning and practical reasoning. *Synthese*, 117:207–227.

Glüer, K. and Wikforss, Å. (2009). Against content normativity. *Mind*, 118(468):31–70.

Gross, S. (2005). Linguistic understanding and belief. *Mind*, 114(453):61–66.

Hacker, P. (2000). Was he trying to whistle it? In Crary, A. and Read, R., editors, *The New Wittgenstein*, pages 353–388. Routledge, London.

Hacker, P. (2003). Wittgenstein, Carnap and the New American Wittgensteinians. *Philosophical Quarterly*, 53(210):1–23.

Haddock, A. (2012). Meaning, justification, and 'primitive normativity'. *Proceedings of the Aristotelian Society*, 86:147–174. Supplementary Volume.

Hale, B. (2002). Basic logical knowledge. In O'Hear, A., editor, *Logic, Thought and Language*, pages 279–304. Cambridge University Press, Cambridge.

Hanna, R. (2006). *Rationality and Logic.* The MIT Press, Cambridge, MA.

Harman, G. (1999). *Reasoning, Meaning and Mind.* Clarendon Press, Oxford.

Hattiangadi, A. (2006). Is meaning normative? *Mind & Language*, 21(2):220–240.

Hattiangadi, A. (2008). Some more thoughts on semantic oughts: a reply to Daniel Whiting. *Analysis*, 69(1):54–63.

Hawthorne, J. (2004). *Knowledge and Lotteries.* Clarendon Press, Oxford.

Hedman, S. (2004). *A First Course in Logic.* Oxford University Press, Oxford.

Heyting, A. (1964/1983). The intuitionist foundations of mathematics. In Benacerraf, P. and Putnam, H., editors, *Philosophy of Mathematics*, pages 52–61. Cambridge University Press, Cambridge, 2nd edition.

Higginbotham, J. (1998a). Conceptual competence. *Philosophical Issues*, 9:149–162.

Higginbotham, J. (1998b). On knowing one's own language. In Wright, C., Smith, B., and MacDonald, C., editors, *Knowing Our Own Minds*, pages 429–441. Clarendon Press, Oxford.

Horwich, P. (1998). *Meaning.* Clarendon Press, Oxford.

Horwich, P. (2005a). Meaning constitution and epistemic rationality. In *Reflections on Meaning*, pages 134–173. Clarendon Press, Oxford.

Horwich, P. (2005b). *Reflections on Meaning.* Clarendon Press, Oxford.

Horwich, P. (2010a). Ungrounded reason. In *Truth-Meaning-Reality*, pages 197–223. Clarendon Press, Oxford.

Horwich, P. (2010b). What is truth. In *Truth-Meaning-Reality*, pages 1–11. Clarendon Press, Oxford.

Husserl, E. (1900–01/2001). *Logical Investigations*, volume 1. Routledge & Kegan Paul, London/New York.

Korsgaard, C. (1996). *The Sources of Normativity.* Cambridge University Press, Cambridge.

Kripke, S. (1982). *Wittgenstein on Rules and Private Language.* Blackwell, Oxford.

Lafont, C. (1999). *The Linguistic Turn in Hermeneutic Philosophy.* The MIT Press, Cambridge, MA.

Lemmon, E. J. (1965). *Beginning Logic.* Nelson, London.

Longworth, G. (2008). Linguistic understanding and knowledge. *Noûs*, 42(1):50–79.

Longworth, G. (2010). A plea for understanding. In Sawyer, S., editor, *New Waves in Philosophy of Language*, pages 138–163. Palgrave Macmillan, Basingstoke.

Martí, G. (1998). The significance of the distinction between concept mastery and concept possession. *Philosophical Issues*, 9:163–167.

McGee, V. (1985). A counterexample to modus ponens. *Journal of Philosophy*, 82(9):462–471.

Milne, P. (2009). What is the normative role of logic? *Proceedings Aristotelian Society*, 83:269–298. Supplementary Volume.

Owens, D. (2000). *Reason without Freedom. The problem of Epistemic Normativity.* Routledge, London/New York.

Parfit, D. (2011). *On What Matters*, volume 1. Oxford University Press, Oxford.

Patterson, D. (2007a). Inconsistency theories: The significance of semantic ascent. *Inquiry*, 50(6):575–589.

Patterson, D. (2007b). Understanding the liar. In Beall, J., editor, *Revenge of the Liar*, pages 197–224. Oxford University Press, Oxford.

Peacocke, C. (1976). Truth definitions and actual languages. In *Truth and Meaning*, pages 162–188. Clarendon Press, Oxford.

Peacocke, C. (1986). *Thoughts: An Essay on Content*. Blackwell, Oxford.

Peacocke, C. (1992). *A Study of Concepts*. The MIT Press, Cambridge, MA.

Peacocke, C. (1998). Implicit conceptions, understanding and rationality. *Philosophical Issues*, 9:43–88.

Peacocke, C. (2008). *Truly Understood*. Oxford University Press, Oxford.

Pettit, D. (2002). Why knowledge is unnecessary for understanding language. *Mind*, 111(443):519–549.

Pettit, D. (2005). Belief and understanding: A rejoinder to gross. *Mind*, 114(453):67–74.

Platts, M. (1979). *Ways of Meaning*. The MIT Press, Cambridge, MA.

Prawitz, D. (1978). Proofs and the meanings and completeness of the logical constants. In Hintikka, J., editor, *Essays on Mathematical and Philosophical Logic*, pages 25–40. Reidel, Dordrecht.

Prawitz, D. (2006). Meaning approached via proofs. *Synthese*, 148:507–524.

Priest, G. (1979). The logic of paradox. *Journal of Philosophical Logic*, 8:219–241.

Priest, G. (2002). *Beyond the Limits of Thought*. Oxford University Press, Oxford, second edition.

Prior, A. N. (1961). The runabout inference ticket. *Analysis*, 21:38–39.

Proops, I. (2002). The *Tractatus* on inference and entailmen. In Reck, E. H., editor, *From Frege to Wittgenstein*, pages 283–307. Oxford University Press, Oxford.

Putnam, H. (1975). What is mathematical truth? In *Mathematics, Matter and Method. Philosophical Papers*, volume 1. Cambridge University Press, Cambridge.

Putnam, H. (1978). *Meaning and the Moral Sciences*. Routledge & Kegan Paul, Boston/London/Henley.

Quine, W. V. O. (1966a). Carnap and logical truth. In *The Ways of Paradox and Other Essays*, pages 107–132. Harvard University Press, Cambridge, MA.

Quine, W. V. O. (1966b). Truth by convention. In *The Ways of Paradox and Other Essays*, pages 77–106. Harvard University Press, Cambridge, MA. Revised and enlarged edn.

Quine, W. V. O. (1970). *Philosophy of Logic*. Prentice Hall, Englewood Cliffs/New York, 1st edition.

Railton, P. (2006). Normative guidance. In Shafer-Landau, R., editor, *Oxford Studies in Metaethics*, volume 1, pages 3–33. Clarendon Press, Oxford.

Raz, J. (1999). *Engaging Reason. On the Theory of Value and Action*. Oxford University Press, Oxford.

Read, S. (1988). *Relevant Logic: A Philosophical Examination of Inference*. Basil Blackwell, Oxford.

Read, S. (2000). Harmony and autonomy in classical logic. *Journal of Philosophical Logic*, 29:123–154.

Read, S. (2004). In defence of the dog: Response to Restall. In Rahman, S., Symon, J., Gabbay, D. M., and van Bendegem, J. P., editors, *Logic, Epistemology, and the Unity of Science*, pages 175–180. Kluwer Academic Publishers, Dordrecht.

Read, S. (2010). General-elimination harmony and the meaning of the logical constants. *Journal of Philosophical Logic*, 39(5):557–576.

Restall, G. (2005). *Logic. An Introduction*. Routledge, London.

Russell, B. A. W. (1903). *The Principles of Mathematics*. Allen and Unwin, London. 2nd editition 1937.

Sainsbury, R. (2002). What logic should we think with? In O'Hear, A., editor, *Logic, Thought and Language*, pages 1–17. Cambridge University Press, Cambridge.

Scanlon, T. (1998). *What We Owe to Each Other*. The Belknap Press of Harvard University Press, Cambridge, MA.

Scharp, K. (2007). Replacing truth. *Inquiry*, 50(6):606–621.

Sellars, W. (1950). Language, rules and behavior. In Sicha, J., editor, *Pure Pragmatics and Possible Worlds. The Early Essays of Wilfrid Sellars*, pages 129–155. Ridgeview, Atascadero, CA.

Sellars, W. (1963a). Empiricism and the philosophy of mind. In *Science, Perception and Reality*, pages 127–196. Ridgeview, Atascadero, CA.

Sellars, W. (1963b). Some reflections on language games. In *Science, Perception and Reality*, pages 321–358. Ridgeview, Atascadero, CA.

Shoenfield, J. R. (1967). *Mathematical Logic.* Association for Symbolic Logic, Natick, MA.

Shoesmith, D. and Smiley, T. (1978). *Multiple-conclusion Logic.* Cambridge University Press, Cambridge.

Skorupski, J. (1997a). Meaning, use, verification. In Hale, B. and Wright, C., editors, *A Companion to the Philosophy of Language*, pages 26–48. Blackwell, Oxford.

Skorupski, J. (1997b). Reasons and reason. In *Ethical Explorations*, pages 26–48. Oxford University Press, Oxford.

Skorupski, J. (2010). *The Domain of Reasons.* Oxford University Press, Oxford.

Smith, M. (1994). *The Moral Problem.* Blackwell, Oxford.

Soames, S. (1991). Truth, meaning, and understanding. In *Philosophical Essays*, volume 1, pages 208–224. Princeton University Press, Princeton/Oxford.

Sullivan, P. M. (2002). On trying to be resolute: A response to kremer on the *Tractatus. European Journal of Philosophy*, 10(1):43–78.

Sullivan, P. M. (2004). Frege's logic. In Gabbay, D. and Woods, J., editors, *Handbook of the History and Philosophic of Logic*, pages 671–762. Elsevier, Amsterdam.

Sundholm, G. (1989). Proof theory and meaning. In Gabbay, D. and Guenthner, F., editors, *Handbook of Philosophical Logic*, volume 5, pages 165–198. Kluwer Academic Publishers, Dordrecht, 2nd edition.

Tourlakis, G. (2003). *Lectures in Logic and Set Theory.* Cambridge University Press, Cambridge.

van Benthem, J. (1995). *Language in Action.* The MIT Press, Cambridge, MA.

Whiting, D. (2007). The normativity of meaning defended. *Analysis*, 67(2):133–140.

Wikforss, Å. M. (2001). Semantic normativity. *Philosophical Studies*, 102:203–226.

Williamson, T. (2000). *Knowledge and its Limits.* Oxford University Press, Oxford.

Williamson, T. (2003). Understanding and inference. *Proceedings of the Aristotelian Society*, 77:249–293. Supplementary Volumes.

Williamson, T. (2007). *The Philosophy of Philosophy.* Blackwell, Oxford.

Williamson, T. (2011). Reply to Boghossian. *Philosophy and Phenomenological Research*, 82(2):498–506.

Witherspoon, E. (2000). Conceptions of nonsense in Carnap and Wittgenstein. In Crary, A. and Read, R., editors, *The New Wittgenstein*, pages 315–349. Routledge, London.

Wittgenstein, L. (1914–16/1998). *Notebooks 1914–1916.* Blackwell, Oxford.

Wittgenstein, L. (1930). *Philosophical Remarks.* Blackwell, Oxford.

Wittgenstein, L. (1945/1953). *Philosophical Investigations.* Blackwell, Oxford.

Wittgenstein, L. (1949–51/1969). *On Certainty.* Blackwell, Oxford.

Wright, C. (1980). *Wittgenstein on the Foundations of Mathematics.* Harvard University Press, Cambridge, MA.

Wright, C. (2001). *Rails to Infinity.* Harvard University Press, Cambridge, MA.

Wright, C. (2002). On basic logical knowledge. Reflections on Paul Boghossian's *How are Objective Epistemic Reasons Possible?* In Bermúdez, J. L. and Millar, A., editors, *Reason and Nature. Essays in the Theory of Rationality*, pages 49–84. Clarendon Press.

Wright, C. (2004a). Intuition, entitlement and the epistemology of logical laws. *Dialectica*, 58(1):155–175.

Wright, C. (2004b). Warrant for nothing (and foundations for free?). *Supplement to the Proceedings of The Aristotelian Society*, 78(1):167–212.

# Bradwardine Hypersequents

GREG RESTALL[†] [‡]

ABSTRACT. According to Stephen Read, Thomas Bradwardine's theory of truth provides an independently motivated solution to the paradoxes of truth, such as the liar (Read, 2002, 2006). In a series of papers, I have discussed modal models for Read's reconstruction of Bradwardine's theory (Restall, 2008a,b). In this paper, provide a hypersequent calculus for this theory, and I show that the cut rule is admissible in the hypersequent calculus.

It gives me great pleasure to honour Professor Stephen Read, whose work has been a profound influence on my own. His work on relevant logic (Read, 1981, 1988), on proof theoretical harmony (Read, 2000), on the logic of identity (Read, 2004) and on Thomas Bradwardine's theory of truth (Read, 2002, 2006, 2009) have been a rich source of insight, of stimulation and of provocation. In an attempt to both honour Stephen, and hopefully to give him some pleasure, I am going to attempt to cook up something original using some of the many and varied ingredients he has provided us. In this paper, I will mix and match ideas and techniques from Stephen's papers on proof theory, on Bradwardine's theory of truth, and on identity to offer a harmonious sequent system for a theory of truth inspired by Stephen Read's recovery of the work of Thomas Bradwardine.

## 1 Background

I have written before on models for Bradwardine's theory of truth as recovered by Stephen Read (Restall, 2008a,b). The crucial syntactic innovation of the formal theory of truth is the fact that truth is a defined notion and not a primitive one. The primitive notion in the theory is that expressed by the 'connecticate' "$:$", or "says that". The connecticate is half *connective* and half pred*icate*. Like a *predicate*, it takes a singular term (here on the left), and like a *connective* it takes a the sentence (here, on the right). In words, "$t : p$" says that $t$ says that $p$. The connecticate expresses *signification*, the idea that certain objects (sentences, utterances, inscriptions, whatever) signify some

[†]Philosophy Department, The University of Melbourne, Parkville 3010, Australia. Email: restall@unimelb.edu.au

[‡]Thanks to an audience at the University of Melbourne, and also to Conrad Asmus, Rohan French, Allen Hazen, David Ripley, Shawn Standefer and Zach Weber for helpful discussion of this material. Of course, I am most grateful to Stephen Read for sustained correspondence on these issues. This research is supported by Bruce Cockburn, through his album *Slice O' Life*.

things, and fail to signify others, and we express this in our formal language using signification. If $s$ is a sentence that says that $2 + 2 = 4$ we can say

$$s : 2 + 2 = 4$$

but if that very sentence does *not* say that $2 \times 2 = 4$ we can say

$$\neg(s : 2 \times 2 = 4)$$

The parentheses are there to help with disambiguation, but they are not strictly necessary. Our convention is that ':' binds as strongly as grammatically possible, so '$t : p \supset q$' is a conditional whose antecedent is '$t : p$', while in '$t : 2 + 2 = 4$' the colon cannot bind anything smaller than '$2 + 2 = 4$' since this is the smallest available sentence commencing after the colon.

Now, when is an object true? Presumably if it says something, and if whatever it says is the case. To express this, we will make use of propositional quantification. The intuitive idea of truth was straightforward:

$$Tx =_{\mathrm{df}} (\exists p)x : p \wedge (\forall p)(x : p \supset p)$$

For $x$ to be true, there must be something that $x$ says, and of anything $x$ says, it is the case. For falsity we require the opposite. $x$ is false if and only if there is something $x$ says that is not the case.

$$Fx =_{\mathrm{df}} (\exists p)(x : p \wedge \neg p)$$

Given just this raw definition of truth and of falsity, we can already learn something about the paradoxes. If $\lambda$ is a liar sentence, then it says of itself that it is not true. This can be specified precisely. $\lambda$ is a liar if and only if we have

$$\lambda : \neg T\lambda$$

Given the *definition* of the truth predicate we can reason as follows: Suppose $T\lambda$. Then we would have $(\forall p)(\lambda : p \supset p)$, and since $\neg\lambda : \neg T\lambda$ we would have $\neg T\lambda$. So, it follows that $\neg T\lambda$, and furthermore, that $F\lambda$ (since there is something that $\lambda$ does say). So, if $\lambda$ is a liar sentence, then indeed it is not true.

Now, we do not necessarily land in self-contradictary reasoning, because it does not follow that $T\lambda$ (that $\lambda$ is also true), unlike the situation with Tarski's theory of truth. For all we can conclude in this case is that *something* that $\lambda$ says (namely $\neg T\lambda$) holds, not that *everything* that $\lambda$ says holds, which is what is required for truth. So, it follows that *something* that $\lambda$ says fails to hold.[1]

This is enough to specify liar sentences and to say a little about their properties. However, it is not enough to give an account of all of the distinctive behaviour of signification. What can we say about the signification relation?

---

[1] What is this further something that $\lambda$ says? It is hard to say something general about this. Read argues (reconstructing an argument of Bradwardine) that of anything that says of itself that it is false also says of itself that it is true (Read, 2006, p. 311). I have shown elsewhere that this conclusion does not follow from the premises we have so far accepted (Restall, 2008b). There are models of Bradwardine's theory in which some liars say of themselves that they are true, and others do not.

Here are three possible principles concerning signification. (1) if $t:p$ and $t:q$, does it follow that $t:p \wedge q$? Or (2) if $t:p$ and if $p \vdash q$ does it follow that $t:q$? Finally, (3) $t:p$ and $p \supset q$ holds, does it follow that $t:q$? In an earlier paper (Restall, 2008a), I provided a modal model theory for the signification relation, according to which the principles (1) and (2) generally hold, so signification is closed under conjunction, and under entailment, but for which (3) does not hold: we may have $t:p$ and $p \supset q$ may contingently hold without $t:q$ holding. For example, if something thing (say $t$) says that Socrates is mortal, then the mere contingent truth the material conditional 'If Socrates is mortal then the 2012 Olympics was held in London' is not enough to ensure that $t$ also says that the 2012 Olympics was held in London. Signification, on these models, is closed under *entailment* but not under the material conditional. Things say all those things *entailed* by what they say, but not necessarily those things contingently *implied* by what they say.

## 2 Modal Models

In "Modal Models for Bradwardine's Theory of Truth" I introduced modals in which '$x:p$' is read as an indexed necessity operator '$\Box_x p$.' We will do the same here, with a number of simplifying assumptions. In that paper, a model consists of a frame $\langle W, O, D, \{R_d : d \in D\} \rangle$, featuring of a class of worlds $W$, a domain $O$ of objects, and a subset $D$ of $O$ of those objects which are *declarative* (those objects which signify), and for each declarative object, a binary accessibility relation $R_d$ on $W$, together with an evaluation relation $\Vdash$ relating worlds (and assignments of values to the variables) to formulas. For our presentation in this paper, we make two simplifying assumptions: (1) that *all* objects signify, so $D = O$, and (2) we will assume that signification is modally fixed: that is, for each $w, v, v' \in W$, $vR_dw$ iff $v'R_dw$. In other words, *what* an object signifies does not vary from world to world. So, the accessibility relation $R_d$ for an object $d$ can be defined by way of a class of worlds $W_d$, where we set $wR_dv$ if and only if $v \in W_d$. (We can think of $W_d$ as the set of worlds which are as $d$ describes.)

Along with those two simplifying assumptions, we will make one *liberalising* assumption, to the effect that the domain of quantification for the second order quantifiers (of which the propositional quantifiers are a special case) is a *subclass* of the standard (full) domain. We will in particular focus on Henkin models, where the domain of quantification is closed under the usual logical operations definable in the language, in the standard manner (Shapiro, 1991).

Summing up, we have the following definition of a frame, of a model and truth in a model.

DEFINITION 1 (Simple Bradwardine Frames). A structure $\langle W, D_1, D_2, \{R_d : d \in D_1\} \rangle$ is a *simple Bradwardine frame* when it is made up of

- A non-empty set $W$ of *worlds*

- A non-empty set $D_1$ of *objects*

- A non-empty set $D_2$ consisting of sets $D_2^n$ of $n+1$-tuples from $D_1 \times \cdots \times D_1 \times W$. $D_2^n$ is the range of quantification of $n$-place predicates (which vary from world to world), so $D_2^0$, a set of sets of worlds is the range of quantification of the propositional quantifiers.

- A relation $R_d \subseteq W \times W$ for each $d \in D_1$, such that for each $w, v, v' \in W$, $wR_dv$ iff $wR_dv'$.

The language we will interpret on simple Bradwardine frames is straight-forward. We have already seen the connecticate ":". In addition to this, we will use full second order quantification with $n$-ary predicates $X^n$ (for $n = 0, 1, 2, \ldots$) rather than restrict outselves to the 0-ary case of propositional quantification, which is all that is strictly necessary for formulating the theory of truth. The reason is simple: unary predicate quantification will play a role in the final section on the logic of identity, and the proof theory works smoothly with arbitrary second order quantification, so there is no problem in including it.

Furthermore, it simplifies our presentation to use explicit $\lambda$-abstraction to create complex $n$-ary predicates. Given a formula $A$ and the variables $x_1, \ldots, x_n$ the $n$-place $\lambda$-abstract $(\lambda x_1 \cdots x_n A)$ is a complex $n$-place predicate, so given $n$ terms $t_1, \ldots, t_n$, $(\lambda x_1 \cdots x_n A)t_1 \cdots t_n$ is a formula. The truth conditions for this formula are exactly the same as that of the formula $A|_{t_1 \cdots t_n}^{x_1 \cdots x_n}$ found by simultaneously substituting the terms $t_1, \ldots, t_n$ into the instances of the variables $x_1, \ldots, x_n$ that are free in $A$.

With all of that, given a Simple Bradwardine Frame, we can interpret sentences in our formal language on the frame in the usual manner:

DEFINITION 2 (Simple Bradwardine Models). An evaluation on a simple Bradwardine frame is provided by giving an extension to every relation in the language, and a denotation for every name. The *variables* in the language will be interpreted with the aid of an assignment $\alpha$ of values to variables. The value $\alpha$ assigns to an *objectual* variable such as $x$ is an object $[\![x]\!]_\alpha$ in $D_1$. The value that $\alpha$ assigns to a predicate variable $X^n$ is a *set* $[\![X^n]\!]_\alpha$ in $D_2^n$ of $n + 1$-tuples (of $n$ domain elements from $D_1$ and one world). The projection of $[\![X^n]\!]_\alpha$ on the world $w$ is thus a set of $n$-tuples from $D_1$, the extension of the $n$-place predicate at the world $w$.

Given such an assignment of values to atomic expressions, we can assign values to complex expressions, relative to the choice of a world and the choice of an assignment of values to variables.

- $\mathfrak{M}, \alpha, w \Vdash Rt_1 \cdots t_n$ iff the $n$-tuple $\langle [\![t_1]\!]_\alpha, \ldots, [\![t_n]\!]_\alpha \rangle$ is in the projection of the extension $[\![R]\!]$ at world $w$.

- $\mathfrak{M}, \alpha, w \Vdash p$ iff $w$ is in $[\![p]\!]_\alpha$.

- $\mathfrak{M}, \alpha, w \Vdash \neg A$ iff $\mathfrak{M}, \alpha, w \nVdash A$.

- $\mathfrak{M}, \alpha, w \Vdash A \wedge B$ iff $\mathfrak{M}, \alpha, w \Vdash A$ and $\mathfrak{M}, \alpha, w \Vdash A$.

- $\mathfrak{M}, \alpha, w \Vdash (\forall x)A$ iff $\mathfrak{M}, \alpha', w \Vdash A$ for every $x$-variant $\alpha'$ of $\alpha$.

- $\mathfrak{M}, \alpha, w \Vdash (\forall X^n)A$ iff $\mathfrak{M}, \alpha', w \Vdash A$ for every $X^n$-variant $\alpha'$ of $\alpha$.

- $\mathfrak{M}, \alpha, w \Vdash (\lambda x_1 \cdots x_n A) t_1 \cdots t_n$ iff $\mathfrak{M}, \alpha, w \Vdash A|_{t_1 \cdots t_n}^{x_1 \cdots x_n}$, where $A|_{t_1 \cdots t_n}^{x_1 \cdots x_n}$ is the result of simultaneously substituting the free instances of $x_1, \ldots, x_n$ in $A$ by $t_1, \ldots, t_n$, respectively.

- $\mathfrak{M}, \alpha, w \Vdash \Box A$ iff $\mathfrak{M}, \alpha, v \Vdash A$ for every world $v$.

These clauses are completely standard. They model constant domain quantified s5 with a universal accessibility relation, and with second order quantification ranging over a possibly restricted second order domain. The innovation is in the treatment of 'says that'.

- $\mathfrak{M}, \alpha, w \Vdash t : A$ iff for each $v$ where $wR_{[\![t]\!]_\alpha}v$, we have $\mathfrak{M}, \alpha, v \Vdash A$.

In other words, '$t :$' functions as a normal modal operator, using the accessibility relation $R_{[\![t]\!]}$.

This completes our definition of simple Bradwardine models and the recursive satisfaction relation. In the rest of this paper I will provide a sound and complete sequent system for the logic of this class of models.

# 3 Hypersequents

Modal reasoning makes use of not only flat assertion and denial, but also assertion and denial under *suppositions*. In the modal case, we can suppose that things obtain in some way other than they have *actually* obtained. If a sequent

$$A \vdash B$$

tells us that it would be a mistake to assert $A$ and deny $B$, then the *hypersequent*

$$A \vdash B \mid C \vdash D$$

tells us that it would be a mistake to (in one context) assert $A$ and deny $B$ and (in another context) assert $C$ and deny $D$. So, while

$$A \vdash A$$

is an axiomatic sequent—there is a clash between asserting $A$ and denying $A$. The corresponding hypersequent

$$A \vdash \ \mid \ \vdash A$$

involves no such clash. There is no clash involved in asserting $A$ in one part of a discourse and (under a different supposition) denying $A$. After all, the whole point of modal reasoning is to consider alternate possibilities.

There would be nothing to be gained in this larger hypersequent structure unless there were some way to bridge the gap between zones of a hypersequent. This is the point of the modal operators. This is a sequent that *does* involve a clash.

$$\Box A \vdash \ \mid \ \vdash A$$

Asserting that $A$ is *necessary* and (in some alternate zone) denying $A$ does involve a clash, since the job a of a claim to necessity is to range over alternate possibilities. I develop the modal proof theory for S5 and more complex modal logics in this manner (Poggiolesi and Restall, 2012; Restall, 2007, 2012).

This sort of reasoning helps with signification too. Given some object $t$ that signifies, we can suppose that things are *as $t$ describes*. This motivates taking the following sequent to involve a clash:

$$t : A \vdash \quad | \quad \vdash_t A$$

where now, the *tagged* sequent $\vdash_t A$ represents a $t$-zone—denying $A$ in a context governed by the term $t$, which is taking things to be as $t$ describes. Asserting that $t : A$ (that $t$ says that $A$) and denying $A$ in a $t$-zone therefore involves a clash. This is the kind of structure we will employ in our reasoning: a hypersequent in which the zones may be tagged with terms.

DEFINITION 3 (Bradwardine Hypersequent). A non-empty multiset of sequents of formulas

$$\Gamma_1 \vdash_{t_1} \Delta_1 \mid \cdots \mid \Gamma_m \vdash_{t_m} \Delta_m \mid \Gamma_{m+1} \vdash \Delta_{m+1} \mid \cdots \mid \Gamma_n \vdash \Delta_n$$

in which $m$ sequents are tagged with terms, and $n - m$ sequents are untagged is said to be a *Bradwardine sequent*. In this Bradwardine sequent we must have $n + m \geq 1$ but either $n$ or $m$ can be 0.

It will very soon get quite tedious to keep singling out both those component sequents which are tagged and those which are not. So, from now, we will use the convention that when tagging a sequent $\Gamma \vdash_t \Delta$, the $t$ is either a term or is *empty*, so the sequent in this case is untagged. In the case that $t$ is empty, then the signification formula $t : A$ is the necessitation $\Box A$.

Bradwardine sequents can be interpreted in a simple Bradwardine model.

DEFINITION 4 (Hypersequents in Models). The model $\mathfrak{M}$ is a *counterexample* to the hypersequent $\Gamma_1 \vdash_{t_1} \Delta_1 \mid \cdots \mid \Gamma_n \vdash_{t_n} \Delta_n$ if and only if there are worlds $w_1, \ldots, w_n$ where for each $i$, $w1R_{[\![t_i]\!]}w_i$ (and if $t_i$ is absent, then $R_{[\![t_i]\!]}$ is the universal relation) and where each element of $\Gamma_i$ is true at $w_i$ and each element of $\Delta_i$ is false at $w_i$. In other words, for every tagged sequent $\Gamma_i \vdash_{t_i} \Delta_i$ we want a world $w_i$, accessible using the $R_{[\![t_i]\!]}$ relation, where each member of $\Gamma_i$ holds and each member of $\Delta_i$ fails. If we can do that for *each* sequent in the hypersequent, we have a counterexample.

If a hypersequent has no counterexample, then we say that the hypersequent is *valid*.

Now we will use hypersequents to give an account of the rules of derivation appropriate for our theory of signification. In these statements of the rules, instead of writing out a long hypersequent, we will often write '$\Gamma \vdash_t \Delta \mid \mathcal{H}$' to indicate a hypersequent in which $\Gamma \vdash_t \Delta$ is one component sequent. Then the hypersequent '$\Gamma, A \vdash_t \Delta \mid \mathcal{H}$,' for example, is to be found by adding the formula $A$ into the anteedent of the component squent $\Gamma \vdash_t \Delta$ of the original hypersequent.

So, we start with the structural rules *Identity* and *Cut*, and *Contraction*, which govern the logical structure of formulas as such, without singling out the behaviour of any particular logical constants.

$$\Gamma, A \vdash_t A, \Delta \mid \mathcal{H} \quad (Id)$$

$$\frac{\Gamma \vdash_t A, \Delta \mid \mathcal{H} \qquad \Gamma, A \vdash_t \Delta \mid \mathcal{H}}{\Gamma \vdash_t \Delta \mid \mathcal{H}} \ (Cut)$$

$$\frac{\Gamma, A, A \vdash_t \Delta \mid \mathcal{H}}{\Gamma, A \vdash_t \Delta \mid \mathcal{H}} \ (WL)$$

$$\frac{\Gamma \vdash_t A, A, \Delta \mid \mathcal{H}}{\Gamma \vdash_t A, \Delta \mid \mathcal{H}} \ (WR)$$

The rules for propositional logical connectives behave in the expected manner, locally to a component in a sequent. Here are the rules for conjunction and negation

$$\frac{\Gamma, A, B \vdash_t \Delta \mid \mathcal{H}}{\Gamma, A \wedge B \vdash_t \Delta \mid \mathcal{H}} \ (\wedge L)$$

$$\frac{\Gamma \vdash_t A, \Delta \mid \mathcal{H} \qquad \Gamma \vdash_t B, \Delta \mid \mathcal{H}}{\Gamma \vdash_t A \wedge B, \Delta \mid \mathcal{H}} \ (\wedge R)$$

$$\frac{\Gamma \vdash_t A, \Delta \mid \mathcal{H}}{\Gamma, \neg A \vdash_t \Delta \mid \mathcal{H}} \ (\neg L)$$

$$\frac{\Gamma, A \vdash_t \Delta \mid \mathcal{H}}{\Gamma \vdash_t \neg A, \Delta \mid \mathcal{H}} \ (\neg R)$$

Other connectives can be defined in terms of conjunction and negation, and they have rules of the structure one would expect. The first-order quantifier rules are also as expected

$$\frac{\Gamma, A\vert_s^x \vdash_t \Delta \mid \mathcal{H}}{\Gamma, (\forall x)A \vdash_t \Delta \mid \mathcal{H}} \ (\forall L)$$

$$\frac{\Gamma \vdash_t A, \Delta \mid \mathcal{H}}{\Gamma \vdash_t (\forall x)A, \Delta \mid \mathcal{H}} \ (\forall R)$$

with the usual side condition that the variable $x$ is not free in the premise hypersequent at any place other than $A$ (so, we have derived $A$ on the basis of no assumptions concerning $x$, so the derivation is purely general: we have the werewithal to derive $(\forall x)A$).

The second order quantifier rules are similar, with the only complication being the syntax, according to which $X^n$ is an $n$-ary predicate variable, and $P^n$ is an $n$-place predicate—either a primitive predicate or a $\lambda$ abstraction.

$$\frac{\Gamma, A\vert_{P^n}^{X^n} \vdash_t \Delta \mid \mathcal{H}}{\Gamma, (\forall X^n)A \vdash_t \Delta \mid \mathcal{H}} \ (\forall_2^n L)$$

$$\frac{\Gamma \vdash_t A, \Delta \mid \mathcal{H}}{\Gamma \vdash_t (\forall X^n)A, \Delta \mid \mathcal{H}} \ (\forall_2^n R)$$

Exactly the same variable condition holds on the premise of $\forall_2^n R$: the variable $X^n$ occurs nowhere free in the premise of the rule other than in the consequent formula $A$.

The second order quantifier rules make use of complex predicates, and for that we need to have rules for $\lambda$ abstraction. These are straightforward:

$$\frac{\Gamma, A\vert_{t_1 \cdots t_n}^{x_1 \cdots x_n} \vdash_t \Delta \mid \mathcal{H}}{\Gamma, (\lambda x_1 \cdots x_n A)t_1 \cdots t_n \vdash_t \Delta \mid \mathcal{H}} \ (\lambda L)$$

$$\frac{\Gamma \vdash_t A\vert_{t_1 \cdots t_n}^{x_1 \cdots x_n}, \Delta \mid \mathcal{H}}{\Gamma \vdash_t (\lambda x_1 \cdots x_n A)t_1 \cdots t_n, \Delta \mid \mathcal{H}} \ (\lambda L)$$

Finally, we need rules for signification and necessitation.

$$\frac{\Gamma \vdash_{t'} \Delta \mid A, \Gamma' \vdash_t \Delta' \mid \mathcal{H}}{\Gamma, t : A \vdash_{t'} \Delta \mid \Gamma' \vdash_t \Delta' \mid \mathcal{H}} \ (:L)$$

$$\frac{\Gamma \vdash_{t'} \Delta \mid \vdash_t A \mid \mathcal{H}}{\Gamma \vdash_{t'} t : A, \Delta \mid \mathcal{H}} \ (:R)$$

$$\frac{\Gamma \vdash_{t'} \Delta \mid A, \Gamma' \vdash_t \Delta' \mid \mathcal{H}}{\Gamma, \Box A \vdash_{t'} \Delta \mid \Gamma' \vdash_t \Delta' \mid \mathcal{H}} \ (\Box L)$$

$$\frac{\Gamma \vdash_{t'} \Delta \mid \vdash A \mid \mathcal{H}}{\Gamma \vdash_{t'} \Box A, \Delta \mid \mathcal{H}} \ (\Box R)$$

This completes the presentation of the hypersequent system. Here are some example derivations. The first shows that signification is closed under *modus ponens*. (We use the obvious defined rules for the material conditional.)

$$\dfrac{\dfrac{\dfrac{\dfrac{\vdash \mid A \vdash_t A \quad \vdash \mid B \vdash_t B}{\vdash \mid A \supset B, A \vdash_t B}\,(\supset L)}{t:A \supset B \vdash \mid A \vdash_t B}\,(:L)}{t:A \supset B, t:A \vdash \mid \vdash_t B}\,(:L)}{t:A \supset B, t:A \vdash t:B}\,(:R)$$

The next derivation demonstrates the modal flavour of signification in our proof theory and in our models:

$$\dfrac{\dfrac{\dfrac{\vdash \mid \vdash_s \mid p \vdash_t p}{t:p \vdash \mid \vdash_s \mid \vdash_t p}\,(:L)}{t:p \vdash \mid \vdash_s t:p}\,(:R)}{t:p \vdash s:t:p}\,(:R)$$

This is a consequence of the modal inertness of signification: signification facts are true in *every* circumstance, and so, are signified by *anything*. For a richer and more realistic theory, we would need not only to label zones with terms, but keep track of an accessbility relation (Poggiolesi and Restall, 2012), so finer distinctions can be made. For here, however, this is enough to show some of the distinctive features of this labelled modal system.

For our next feature of the hypersequent system, we will first prove a simple lemma.

LEMMA 5. *The rule*

$$\dfrac{\Gamma \vdash \Delta \mid \mathcal{H}}{\Gamma \vdash_t \Delta \mid \mathcal{H}}$$

*is height preserving admissible. This means that if there is a derivation of the hypersequent* $\Gamma \vdash \Delta \mid \mathcal{H}$ *then there is a derivation of* $\Gamma \vdash_t \Delta \mid \mathcal{H}$ *of the same height.*

**Proof.** Take the derivation of $\Gamma \vdash \Delta \mid \mathcal{H}$ and trace upwards from the sequent $\Gamma \vdash \Delta$ to keep track of all of the ancestor sequents, and label each with $t$. The result is still a derivation. The only rule in which a sequent *must* be unlabelled is $\square R$ and in this case it is a *premise* hypersequent and not a *conclusion* hypersequent, and this sequent is not the ancestor of any component sequent in the conclusion, so any unlabelled sequents in a conclusion may be freely labelled (and the process continue) without disrupting any rules in place. ∎

LEMMA 6. *The rule*

$$\dfrac{A \vdash B}{t:A \vdash t:B}$$

*is also admissible.*

**Proof.** Given a derivation of $A \vdash B$, transform it into a derivation of $A \vdash_t B$ as in the previous lemma. From here, we reason as follows:

$$\frac{\dfrac{A \vdash_t B}{t:A \vdash \;|\; \vdash_t \; B} \; (:L)}{t:A \vdash t:B} \; (:R)$$

and we have our result. ∎

As a final example at this stage, let us look at the resoning we have already seen, to the effect that if $\lambda : \neg T\lambda$ then $\neg T\lambda$. What is perhaps a little surprising is that the crucial reasoning for about this liar sentence uses absolutely *nothing* of the logic of signification. It uses only the definition of $T$ and the rules governing the logical connectives and quantifiers. Recall that $T\lambda$ is shorthand for $(\exists p)x:p \wedge (\forall p)(x:p \supset p)$.

$$\frac{\dfrac{\lambda:\neg T\lambda \vdash \lambda:\neg T\lambda \quad \dfrac{T\lambda \vdash T\lambda}{T\lambda, \; \neg T\lambda \vdash} \; (\neg L)}{\dfrac{\lambda:\neg T\lambda, \; T\lambda, \; \lambda:\neg T\lambda \supset \neg T\lambda \vdash}{\dfrac{\lambda:\neg T\lambda, \; T\lambda, \; (\forall p)(\lambda:p \supset p) \vdash}{\dfrac{\lambda:\neg T\lambda, \; T\lambda \vdash}{\lambda:\neg T\lambda \vdash \neg T\lambda} \; (\neg R)} \; (\wedge L)} \; (\forall L)} \; (\supset L)}$$

So, the fact an object that signifies its own untruth is, in fact, untrue, depends solely on the logical vocabulary, and the definition of truth in terms of that vocabulary. Nothing need be assumed about the logical structure of signification in this reasoning. We do not use any rules for ':'.

The results of the rest of the paper follow the general structure of those in "A Cut-Free Sequent System for Two Dimensional Modal Logic" (Restall, 2012). Since the results are standard, I will sketch them here. Full proofs of this kind can be found that paper.

We have already seen what it is for a hypersequent to have a counterexample in a model, and we have defined the *valid* hypersequents as those that hold in every model.

DEFINITION 7 (Soundness). Every derivable hypersequent holds in every simple Bradwardine model. That is, derivable hypersequents are *valid*.

**Proof.** A simple induction on the length of the derivation. Axioms are all valid, and if the premises of a rule are valid, so is the conclusion. As a result, all derivable hypersequents are valid. ∎

So, the sequent calculus does not overreach the class of Bradwardine models. So far, so good. The converse is harder to show. Significantly harder.

## 4 Completeness and the Admissibility of Cut

To show completeness, we will show for any underivable hypersequent, we can find a model in which it fails. For this, we will show more, that if we have a hypersequent which cannot be derived in the absence of cut, then we have a model which forms a counterexample. We will show this using the technique of "A Cut-Free Sequent System for Two Dimensional Modal Logic" (Restall, 2012). We will embed any underivable hypersequent into a directed family of hypersequents, satisfying certain closure conditions. First, we need the notion of *extension* for hypersequents.

DEFINITION 8 (Extension of Hypersequents). $\mathcal{H}'$ extends $\mathcal{H}$ iff there is some map $f$ from the formula instances in $\mathcal{H}$ to instances of the same formulae in $\mathcal{H}'$ which preserves all hypersequent structure. This means the following two things: *first*, for each formula occurrence $A$ in $\mathcal{H}$ its corresponding occurrence $f(A)$ in $\mathcal{H}'$ shares its *shape* (it is an instance of the same formula), its *position in a sequent* (in the left or the right of the sequent), its *sequent label*, if it started with one (so if $A$ is in a $t$-sequent in $\mathcal{H}$, so is $f(A)$ in $\mathcal{H}'$); and *second*, if $A$ an $B$ are in the same sequent in $\mathcal{H}$ so are $f(A)$ an $f(B)$ in $\mathcal{H}'$.

So, for example, the hypersequent

is extended by

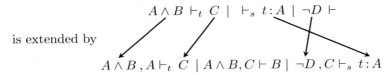

$$A \wedge B \vdash_t C \mid \vdash_s t{:}A \mid \neg D \vdash$$

$$A \wedge B, A \vdash_t C \mid A \wedge B, C \vdash B \mid \neg D, C \vdash_s t{:}A$$

by the mapping marked here. The relation of extension is reflexive and transitive (but not antisymmetric). It is a preorder but not a partial order.

DEFINITION 9 (Directed sets of Hypersequents). A set $\mathfrak{D}$ of hypersequents is DIRECTED if and only if it is (1) *closed under extension*: whenever $\mathcal{H}$ is in $\mathfrak{D}$, and $\mathcal{H}$ extends $\mathcal{H}'$ then $\mathcal{H}'$ is in $\mathfrak{D}$ too and (2) *contains upper bounds* if $\mathcal{H}$ and $\mathcal{H}'$ are in $\mathfrak{D}$ there is some hypersequent in $\mathfrak{D}$ extending both $\mathcal{H}$ and $\mathcal{H}'$.

LEMMA 10 (Models Determine Directed Sets). *The set of all hypersequents failing in some given model is directed.*

**Proof.** That the set of hypersequents failing in model is directed is straightforward. If $\mathcal{H}$ fails in a model, then so does any hypersequent $\mathcal{H}$ extends. If $\mathcal{H}$ and $\mathcal{H}'$ fail in some model, then the disjoint union of the two hypersequents extends both and also fails in that model. ■

A directed set $\mathfrak{D}$ of hypersequents will determine a frame in the following way.

DEFINITION 11 (The Frame of a Directed Set). Given a directed set $\mathfrak{D}$ of hypersequents, a component sequent in a hypersequent in $\mathfrak{D}$ determines a directed set of sequents: those to which this sequent is *extended* and each sequent that also extends to those sequents. This directed set is a *world* in the frame. A world is $R_{[\![t]\!]}$ accessible from another world if that first world is tagged by the term $t$.

DEFINITION 12 (Truth and Falsity). Given a world $w$ in a frame of a directed set $\mathfrak{D}$ we will say that a formula $A$ is true in $w$ if it appears in the left of a sequent in $w$ (once it appears in the left of a sequent in $w$, it appears in the left of all extending sequents), and it is false in $w$ if it appears in the right of a sequent in $w$.

DEFINITION 13 (Downward Closure). A directed family of hypersequents is said to be *closed downwards* if and only if the following closure conditions are satisfied.

*Negation Closure*: If $\neg A$ is true at a world, then $A$ is false at that world. If $\neg A$ is false at a world, then $A$ is true at that world. Given an underivable hypersequent $\mathcal{H}$ featuring a negation $\neg A$ as true (resp. false) at some world, it may be extended into an underivable hypersequent where $A$ is false (resp. true) at that world, because we have the following derivations, which show that if that wasn't the case, $\mathcal{H}$ would be derivable.

$$\cfrac{\cfrac{\Gamma, \neg A \vdash_t A, \Delta \mid \mathcal{H}}{\Gamma, \neg A, \neg A \vdash_t \Delta \mid \mathcal{H}}\ (\neg L)}{\Gamma, \neg A \vdash_t \Delta \mid \mathcal{H}}\ (WL) \qquad \cfrac{\cfrac{\Gamma, A \vdash_t \neg A, \Delta \mid \mathcal{H}}{\Gamma \vdash_t \neg A, \neg A, \Delta \mid \mathcal{H}}\ (\neg R)}{\Gamma \vdash_t \neg A, \Delta \mid \mathcal{H}}\ (WR)$$

*Conjunction Closure*: If $A \wedge B$ is true at a world, then $A$ and $B$ are true at that world. If $A \wedge B$ is false at a world, then either $A$ or $B$ is false at that world. Given an underivable hypersequent $\mathcal{H}$ featuring $A \wedge B$ as true (resp. false) at some world, it may be extended into an underivable hypersequent where $A$ and $B$ are true (resp. either $A$ is false or $B$ is false) at that world, because we have the following derivations, which show that if that wasn't the case, $\mathcal{H}$ would be derivable.

$$\cfrac{\cfrac{\Gamma, A, B, A \wedge B \vdash_t \Delta \mid \mathcal{H}}{\Gamma, A \wedge B, A \wedge B \vdash_t \Delta \mid \mathcal{H}}\ (\wedge L)}{\Gamma, A \wedge B \vdash_t \Delta \mid \mathcal{H}}\ (WL) \qquad \cfrac{\cfrac{\Gamma \vdash_t A, A \wedge B, \Delta \mid \mathcal{H} \quad \Gamma \vdash_t B, A \wedge B, \Delta \mid \mathcal{H}}{\Gamma \vdash_t A \wedge B, A \wedge B, \Delta \mid \mathcal{H}}\ (\wedge R)}{\Gamma \vdash_t A \wedge B, \Delta \mid \mathcal{H}}\ (WR)$$

*Necessity Closure*: If $\Box A$ is true at a world, then $A$ is true at each alternative to $A$. If $\Box A$ is false at a world, then $A$ is false at some alternative to $A$. Given an underivable hypersequent $\mathcal{H}$ featuring $\Box A$ as true at some world, and featuring some alternative to that world, $\mathcal{H}$ may be extended into an underivable hypersequent where $A$ is true at that alternative; and if $\Box A$ is false at some world, $\mathcal{H}$ may be extended into an underivable hypersequent where $A$ is false at some subjunctive alternative to that world, because of the following derivations:

$$\cfrac{\cfrac{\Gamma, \Box A \vdash_t \Delta \mid \Gamma', A \vdash_{t'} \Delta' \mid \mathcal{H}}{\Gamma, \Box A, \Box A \vdash_t \Delta \mid \Gamma' \vdash_{t'} \Delta' \mid \mathcal{H}}\ (\Box L)}{\Gamma, \Box A \vdash_t \Delta \mid \Gamma' \vdash_{t'} \Delta' \mid \mathcal{H}}\ (WL) \qquad \cfrac{\cfrac{\vdash A \mid \Gamma \vdash_t \Box A, \Delta \mid \mathcal{H}}{\Gamma \vdash_t \Box A, \Box A, \Delta \mid \mathcal{H}}\ (\Box R)}{\Gamma \vdash_t \Box A, \Delta \mid \mathcal{H}}\ (WR)$$

*Significantion Closure*: If $t:A$ is true at a world, then $A$ is true at each $t$-zone. If $\Box A$ is false at a world, then $A$ is false at some $t$-zone. Given an underivable hypersequent $\mathcal{H}$ featuring $\Box A$ as true at some world, and featuring some $t$-zone, $\mathcal{H}$ may be extended into an underivable hypersequent where $A$ is true at that $t$-zone; and if $\Box A$ is false at some world, $\mathcal{H}$ may be extended into an underivable hypersequent where $A$ is false at some $t$-zone, because of the following derivations:

$$\frac{\dfrac{\Gamma, t : A \vdash_{t'} \Delta \mid \Gamma', A \vdash_t \Delta' \mid \mathcal{H}}{\Gamma, t : A, t : A \vdash_{t'} \Delta \mid \Gamma' \vdash_t \Delta' \mid \mathcal{H}} \ (:L)}{\Gamma, t : A \vdash_{t'} \Delta \mid \Gamma' \vdash_t \Delta' \mid \mathcal{H}} \ (WL)$$

$$\frac{\dfrac{\vdash_t A \mid \Gamma \vdash_{t'} t : A, \Delta \mid \mathcal{H}}{\Gamma \vdash_{t'} t : A, t : A, \Delta \mid \mathcal{H}} \ (:R)}{\Gamma \vdash_{t'} t : A, \Delta \mid \mathcal{H}} \ (WR)$$

$\lambda$ *Closure*: If $(\lambda x_1 \cdots x_n A) t_1 \cdots t_n$ is true at a world, then so is $A|_{t_1 \cdots t_n}^{x_1 \cdots x_n}$. If $(\lambda x_1 \cdots x_n A) t_1 \cdots t_n$ is false at a world, then so is $A|_{t_1 \cdots t_n}^{x_1 \cdots x_n}$. Given an underivable hypersequent $\mathcal{H}$ featuring $(\lambda x_1 \cdots x_n A) t_1 \cdots t_n$ as true at some world, $\mathcal{H}$ may be extended into an underivable hypersequent where $A|_{t_1 \cdots t_n}^{x_1 \cdots x_n}$ is true at that world; and if $(\lambda x_1 \cdots x_n A) t_1 \cdots t_n$ as false at some world, $\mathcal{H}$ may be extended into an underivable hypersequent where $A|_{t_1 \cdots t_n}^{x_1 \cdots x_n}$ is false at that world, because of the following derivations:

$$\frac{\dfrac{\Gamma, (\lambda x_1 \cdots x_n A) t_1 \cdots t_n, A|_{t_1 \cdots t_n}^{x_1 \cdots x_n} \vdash_t \Delta \mid \mathcal{H}}{\Gamma, (\lambda x_1 \cdots x_n A) t_1 \cdots t_n, (\lambda x_1 \cdots x_n A) t_1 \cdots t_n \vdash_t \Delta \mid \mathcal{H}} \ (\lambda L)}{\Gamma, (\lambda x_1 \cdots x_n A) t_1 \cdots t_n \vdash_t \Delta \mid \mathcal{H}} \ (WL)$$

$$\frac{\dfrac{\Gamma \vdash_t (\lambda x_1 \cdots x_n A) t_1 \cdots t_n, A|_{t_1 \cdots t_n}^{x_1 \cdots x_n}, \Delta \mid \mathcal{H}}{\Gamma \vdash_t (\lambda x_1 \cdots x_n A) t_1 \cdots t_n, (\lambda x_1 \cdots x_n A) t_1 \cdots t_n, \Delta \mid \mathcal{H}} \ (\lambda R)}{\Gamma \vdash_t (\lambda x_1 \cdots x_n A) t_1 \cdots t_n, \Delta \mid \mathcal{H}} \ (WR)$$

$(\forall x)$ *Closure*: If $(\forall x)A$ is true at a world then so is $A|_s^x$ for any term $s$ in the vocabulary. If $(\forall x)A$ is false at a world then so is $A|_s^x$ for some term $s$ in the vocabulary. Given an underivable hypersequent $\mathcal{H}$ featuring $(\forall x)A$ as true at some world, $\mathcal{H}$ may be extended into an underivable hypersequent where $A|_s^x$ is true at that world; and if $(\forall x)A$ as false at some world, $\mathcal{H}$ may be extended into an underivable hypersequent where $A|_s^x$ is false at that world, for a term $s$ new to the hypersequent, because of the following derivations:

$$\frac{\dfrac{\Gamma, (\forall x)A, A|_s^x \vdash_t \Delta \mid \mathcal{H}}{\Gamma, (\forall x)A, (\forall x)A \vdash_t \Delta \mid \mathcal{H}} \ (\forall L)}{\Gamma, (\forall x)A \vdash_t \Delta \mid \mathcal{H}} \ (WL)$$

$$\frac{\dfrac{\Gamma \vdash_t (\forall x)A, A|_y^x \Delta \mid \mathcal{H}}{\Gamma \vdash_t (\forall x)A, (\forall x)A, \Delta \mid \mathcal{H}} \ (\forall R)}{\Gamma \vdash_t (\forall x)A, \Delta \mid \mathcal{H}} \ (WR)$$

where in the second derivation we choose a variable $y$ fresh to the hypersequent, so the result is indeed an instance of the rule $\forall R$. $(\forall X^n)$ *Closure*: If $(\forall X^n)A$ is true at a world then so is $A|_{P^n}^{X^n}$ for any $n$-place predicate $P^n$ in the vocabulary. If $(\forall X^n)A$ is false at a world then so is $A|_{P^n}^{X^n}$ for some $n$-place predicate $P^n$ in the vocabulary. Given an underivable hypersequent $\mathcal{H}$ featuring $(\forall X^n)A$ as true at some world, $\mathcal{H}$ may be extended into an underivable hypersequent where $A|_{P^n}^{X^n}$ is true at that world; and if $(\forall X^n)A$ as false at some world, $\mathcal{H}$ may be extended into an underivable hypersequent where $A|_{P^n}^{X^n}$ is false at that world, for predicate $P^n$ new to the hypersequent, because of the following derivations:

$$\frac{\dfrac{\Gamma, (\forall X^n)A, A|_{P^n}^{X^n} \vdash_t \Delta \mid \mathcal{H}}{\Gamma, (\forall X^n)A, (\forall X^n)A \vdash_t \Delta \mid \mathcal{H}} \ (\forall_2^n L)}{\Gamma, (\forall X^n)A \vdash_t \Delta \mid \mathcal{H}} \ (WL)$$

$$\frac{\dfrac{\Gamma \vdash_t (\forall X^n)A, A|_{Y^n}^{X^n} \Delta \mid \mathcal{H}}{\Gamma \vdash_t (\forall X^n)A, (\forall X^n)A, \Delta \mid \mathcal{H}} \ (\forall_2^n R)}{\Gamma \vdash_t (\forall X^n)A, \Delta \mid \mathcal{H}} \ (WR)$$

where in the second derivation we choose a variable $Y^n$ fresh to the hypersequent, so the result is indeed an instance of the rule $\forall_2^n R$.

So, if we start with an underivable sequent (even a sequent that cannot be derived without the use of $Cut$), we may close under these conditions to get a downard closed, directed family $\mathfrak{D}$ of hypersequents.

LEMMA 14 (Downward Closed Directed Families). *For any hypersequent $\mathcal{H}$ that cannot be derived without cut, there is a directed family $\mathfrak{D}$ of hypersequents also underivable without cut, satisfying the downward closure conditions.*

Now we have the raw materials to prove completeness.

THEOREM 15 (Completeness). *Any hypersequent which has no Cut-free derivation has a counterexample in some model.*

**Proof.**[Sketch] Take an underivable hypersequent. By the previous lemma, there is a downward closed directed family $\mathfrak{D}$ containing our starting hypersequent. Consider the frame of $\mathfrak{D}$. The worlds are the worlds of the family. The first order domain is the class of terms (including variables), the $n$-place second-order domain is the class of $n + 1$-tuples of $n$ terms and one world $\langle t_1, \ldots, t_n, w \rangle$ such that there is some predicate (complex or simple) $S$ where $S|_{t_1,\ldots,t_n}^{x_1,\ldots,x_n}$ is true at $w$. Then take the extension of the atomic predicate $P$ at world $w$ to be the set of $n$-tuples $\langle t_1, \ldots, t_n \rangle$ where $Pt_1, \ldots, t_n$ is true at $w$. This is the model. This model will, in general, make *more* statements true or false at worlds than the downward closed directed family $\mathfrak{D}$, because $\mathfrak{D}$ need not be complete at each world, while a model is. This means that more predicates may be definable in the *model* than in are given in $\mathfrak{D}$. However, a simple ordinal inductive construction due to Prawitz (1967) fills out the second order domain at stage $\alpha + 1$, adding extensions of predicates which are definable in the model defined at stage $\alpha$. The construction here is completely standard, and at the limit stage, no new predicates are added to the domain and the limit is a Henkin model. ∎

COROLLARY 16 (Cut is Admissible). *If a hypersequent is derivable with* Cut, *it is derivable without* Cut *too.*

**Proof.** We prove the contrapositive. If $\mathcal{H}$ is not derivable without *Cut*, then by the completeness theorem, it has a counterexample in some model. By the soundness theorem, it follows that this sequent is not derivable using *Cut*. So, contraposing, if $\mathcal{H}$ is derivable with *Cut*, it is also derivable without. ∎

It follows that this proof system is remarkably well behaved. The rules are in a kind of harmony, in that we do not need the rule of Cut to deliver the transitivity of the consequence relation. The rules by themselves do this well enough as it is. The left rules and the right rules are in balance.

# 5   The Logic of Identity

We'll end with a short discussion of another of Stephen Read's interests: the logic of identity (Read, 2004). I haven't included an identity predicate in the language as it stands, but this is no great loss. Given the power of second order quantification, it is possible to *define* the identity relation on the first-order domain in the usual manner.

$$t = t' \ =_{df} \ (\forall X^1)(X^1 t \equiv X^1 t')$$

Given this definition, anything *true of* $t$ is *true of* $t'$, and vice versa. This allows a substitution of $t$ by $t'$ in any sentence. Given a sentence $A|_t^x$ in which $t$ occurs somewhere, we can see that $A$ is equivalent to $(\lambda x\, A)t$, where $(\lambda x\, A)$ is a complex one-place predicate. So, $(\lambda x\, A)t \equiv (\lambda x\, A)t'$ is an instance of the universally quantified sentence $(\forall X^1)(X^1 t \equiv X^1 t')$. So, $A|_t^x \equiv A|_{t'}^x$ follows from $t = t'$, for arbitrary sentences $A$, and so, arbitrary substitution of one by another is possible.

However, in our proof theory, we want not only to substitute one term for another in a *sentence*, but also in an arbitrary *hypersequent*. In other words, we there is reason to hope that the following sequent to should derivable:

$$a = b \vdash_t \ | \ Ra \vdash_{t'} Rb$$

as it is a consequence of $Ra \vdash_{t'} Ra$, where we substitute $b$ for the second $a$ in that sequence, at the cost of adding $a = b$ in *some* zone. In general, one can define identity using the following kind of rule:

$$\frac{\mathcal{H}|_a^x}{a = b \vdash_t \ | \ \mathcal{H}|_b^x} \ (=L_1) \qquad \frac{\mathcal{H}|_b^x}{a = b \vdash_t \ | \ \mathcal{H}|_a^x} \ (=L_2)$$

which allows for the substitution of $a$ for $b$ (and vice versa) in an arbitrary hypersequent. (This rule is a generalisation of Barwise's sequent rule for identity (Barwise, 1969).[2]) It turns out that if the language is expressive enough—as it is here—we can encode an arbitrary hypersequent as an individual *sentence*, so the second order conception of identity will be strong enough for us to justify these hypersequent substitution rules as derived rules in the calculus. As an example, to give us a derivation of $\vdash_t a = b \ | \ Ra \vdash_{t'} Rb$, notice that we can reason as follows:

$$\frac{\dfrac{\dfrac{\vdash_t \ | \ Ra \vdash_{t'} Ra \ | \ Ra \vdash_{t'} Rb}{\vdash_t \ | \ \vdash_{t'} Ra \supset Ra \ | \ Ra \vdash_{t'} Rb} \ (\supset L)}{\vdash_t t':(Ra \supset Ra) \ | \ Ra \vdash_{t'} Rb} \ (:R) \quad \dfrac{\dfrac{\vdash_t \ | \ Rb, Ra \vdash_{t'} Rb \quad \vdash_t \ | \ Ra \vdash_{t'} Ra, Rb}{\vdash_t \ | \ Ra \supset Rb, Ra \vdash'_t Rb} \ (\supset L)}{t':(Ra \supset Rb) \vdash_t \ | \ Ra \vdash_{t'} Rb} \ (:L)}{\dfrac{\dfrac{t':(Ra \supset Ra) \supset t':(Ra \supset Rb) \vdash_t \ | \ Ra \vdash_{t'} Rb}{t':(Ra \supset Ra) \equiv t':(Ra \supset Rb) \vdash_t \ | \ Ra \vdash_{t'} Rb} \ (\wedge L)}{a = b \vdash_t \ | \ Ra \vdash_{t'} Rb} \ (=df)} \ (\supset L)$$

From $a = b$ in the $t$ zone, we can allow a substitution of an $a$ by a $b$ in the $t'$ zone, by encoding this transition under "$t'$ : ." If $a = b$ then $t':(Ra \supset Ra)$ sufices for $t':(Ra \supset Rb)$, and (as the right branch in this derivation shows)

---

[2]Thanks to Jeremy Seligman for pointing me to this formulation of the rules or identity (Seligman, 2001).

$t' : (Ra \supset Rb)$ is enough to ensure that we can transition from $Ra$ to $Rb$ in the $t'$ zone.

**LEMMA 17.** *In general, for any hypersequent $\mathcal{H}$ there is a formula $H$ such that there are two cut-free derivations, the first (Pack) from the premise hypersequent $\mathcal{H}$ to the conclusion $\vdash_t H$, and the second (Unpack), from axioms, to the conclusion $H \vdash_t | \mathcal{H}$.*

**Proof.** For the hypersequent $\Gamma_1 \vdash_{t_1} \Delta_1 | \cdots | \Gamma_n \vdash_{t_n} \Delta_n$ the relevant formula is

$$\bigvee_{i=1}^{n} t_i : (\bigwedge \Gamma_i \supset \bigvee \Delta_i)$$

(where if '$t_i$' is absent then '$\square$' takes the place of '$t_i$:', and as usual vacuous conjunctions and disjunctions are replaced by tautologies and conjunctions respectively). A simple induction on the construction of the formula is enough to construct the derivations *Pack* and *Unpack*. Here is a fully general case where $n = 2$, and each $\Gamma_i$ and $\Delta_i$ are small: we choose the hypersequent $A, B \vdash_{t_1} C | D \vdash_{t_2} E, F$. Here is the '*Pack*' derivation, encoding this hypersequent as a single formula.

$$\cfrac{\cfrac{\cfrac{\cfrac{\cfrac{\cfrac{\cfrac{A, B \vdash_{t_1} C | D \vdash_{t_2} E, F}{A \wedge B \vdash_{t_1} C | D \vdash_{t_2} E, F} \, (\wedge L)}{A \wedge B \vdash_{t_1} C | D \vdash_{t_2} E \vee F} \, (\vee R)}{\vdash_{t_1} A \wedge B \supset C | D \vdash_{t_2} E \vee F} \, (\supset R)}{\vdash_{t_1} A \wedge B \supset C | \vdash_{t_2} D \supset E \vee F} \, (\supset R)}{\vdash_t t_1 : (A \wedge B \supset C) | \vdash_{t_2} D \supset E \vee F} \, (:L)}{\vdash_t t_1 : (A \wedge B \supset C), t_2 : (D \supset E \vee F)} \, (:L)}{\vdash_t t_1 : (A \wedge B \supset C) \vee t_2 : (D \supset E \vee F)} \, (\vee R)$$

And here is the *Unpack* derivation:

$$\cfrac{\cfrac{\cfrac{C \vdash_{t_1} C \quad \cfrac{A \vdash_{t_1} A \quad B \vdash_{t_1} B}{A, B \vdash_{t_1} A \wedge B} \, (\wedge R)}{A \wedge B \supset C, A, B \vdash_{t_1} C} \, (\supset L)}{t_1 : (A \wedge B \supset C) \vdash_t | A, B \vdash_{t_1} C} \, (:L) \quad \cfrac{\cfrac{D \vdash_{t_2} D \quad \cfrac{E \vdash_{t_2} E \quad F \vdash_{t_2} F}{E \vee F \vdash_{t_2} E, F} \, (\vee L)}{D, D \supset E \vee F \vdash_{t_2} E, F} \, (\supset L)}{t_2 : (D \supset E \vee F) \vdash_t | D \vdash_{t_2} E, F} \, (:L)}{t_1 : (A \wedge B \supset C) \vee t_2 : (D \supset E \vee F) \vdash_t | A, B \vdash_{t_1} C | D \vdash_{t_2} E, F} \, (\vee L)$$

∎

The fact that we can *pack* and *unpack* a hypersequent $\mathcal{H}$ into a single formula $H$ means that we can get the full effect of substitution into a hypersequent by means of the second order identity rule.

$$\mathcal{H}|_a^x$$
$$\vdots$$
$$Pack \qquad Unpack$$
$$\vdots$$

$$\dfrac{\vdash_t Ha \qquad Hb \vdash_t \ | \ \mathcal{H}|_b^x}{Ha \supset Hb \vdash_t \ | \ \mathcal{H}|_b^x} \ (\supset L)$$

$$\dfrac{}{Ha \equiv Hb \vdash_t \ | \ \mathcal{H}|_b^x} \ (\wedge L)$$

$$\dfrac{}{a = b \vdash_t \ | \ \mathcal{H}|_b^x} \ (=df)$$

since the formula $Ha$ packing the hypersequent $\mathcal{H}|_a^x$ is just a substitution variant of the formula $Hb$ packing $\mathcal{H}|_b^x$. The result means that any substitution of one hypersequent by another can be encoded by a substitution at the level of individual formulas. It follows that the expressive power of the vocabulary of hypersequents does not outstrip that of the object language vocabulary.

## BIBLIOGRAPHY

Barwise, J. (1969). Logic and admissible sets. *The Journal of Symbolic Logic.*

Poggiolesi, F. and Restall, G. (2012). Interpreting and applying proof theories for modal logic. In Restall, G. and Russell, G., editors, *New Waves in Philosophy of Logic*, pages 39–62. Palgrave Macmillan.

Prawitz, D. (1967). Completeness and hauptsatz for second order logic. *Theoria*, 33(3):246–258.

Read, S. (1981). What is wrong with disjunctive syllogism? *Analysis*, 41:66–70.

Read, S. (1988). *Relevant Logic: A Philosophical Examination of Inference.* Basil Blackwell, Oxford.

Read, S. (2000). Harmony and autonomy in classical logic. *Journal of Philosophical Logic*, 29:123–154.

Read, S. (2002). The liar paradox from John Buridan to Thomas Bradwardine. *Vivarium*, 40:189–218.

Read, S. (2004). Identity and harmony. *Analysis*, 64:113–119.

Read, S. (2006). Symmetry and paradox. *History and Philosophy of Logic*, 27:307–318.

Read, S. (2009). Plural signification and the liar paradox. *Philosophical Studies*, 145(3):363–375.

Restall, G. (2007). Proofnets for S5: sequents and circuits for modal logic. In Dimitracopoulos, C., Newelski, L., and Normann, D., editors, *Logic Colloquium 2005*, number 28 in Lecture Notes in Logic. Cambridge University Press, Cambridge.

Restall, G. (2008a). Modal models for Bradwardine's theory of truth. *Review of Symbolic Logic*, 1(2):225–240.

Restall, G. (2008b). Models for liars in Bradwardine's theory of truth. In Rahman, S., Tulenheimo, T., and Genot, E., editors, *Unity, Truth and the Liar: The Modern Relevance of Medieval Solutions to the Liar Paradox*, pages 135–147. Springer, New York.

Restall, G. (2012). A cut-free sequent system for two-dimensional modal logic, and why it matters. *Annals of Pure and Applied Logic*, 163(11):1611–1623.

Seligman, J. (2001). Internalization: The case of hybrid logics. *Journal of Logic and Computation*, 11(5):671–689.

Shapiro, S. (1991). *Foundations without Foundationalism: A case for Second-order Logic.* Oxford University Press, Oxford.

# Paradoxes and Structural Rules

PETER SCHROEDER-HEISTER[†] [‡]

ABSTRACT. The derivation of many paradoxes can be blocked, if the application of structural rules is locally restricted in certain ways. This is shown independently for identity, contraction, and cut. Imposing such local restrictions is seen as an alternative to the global rejection of structural rules (notably contraction), which is no reasonable option given that structural rules are needed in mathematical reasoning.

Since the work of Fitch (1936) it is well known that the rule of contraction is crucial for the derivation of certain paradoxes. On the other hand, contraction is needed to formalize mathematical (and other) reasoning, so that giving up contraction altogether is not a viable way of avoiding them (see Read, 1994, pp. 162f, quoted from the 1995 paperback edition). This suggests to look for a restriction on contraction which is sufficient to block paradoxes without affecting 'normal' (non-paradoxical) reasoning. In this note we indicate what such a restriction might look like. As not only *contraction*, but also *identity* and *cut* are needed in paradoxical derivations, we extend our investigation to them. For each of these three structural rules, we propose provisos which formally prevent the derivation of paradoxes, without unduly restraining them as key principles of reasoning.

As our structural framework we use an intuitionistic sequent calculus whose sequents have the form $\Gamma \vdash C$ or the form $\Gamma \vdash$ , where the antecedent $\Gamma$ is a multiset of formulas and the succedent is either a formula $C$ or empty. We use notations such as $\Gamma, A \vdash C$ or $A_1, \ldots, A_n \vdash C$ in the usual way. The empty succedent is supposed to represent falsity, and the empty antecedent is supposed to represent truth. The empty sequent $\vdash$ thus represents a contradiction. In our simplified framework we only need negation $\neg$ as a logical constant. In order to represent the paradoxes, we suppose that there is a constant $R$ such that from $\neg R$ we can infer $R$ and from $R$ we can infer $\neg R$. As we are dealing only with the structural aspect of the logic of paradoxes, we are not interested in which way $R$ is construed and how these paradoxical inference rules are obtained. In naive set theory $R$ might be construed as the proposition $\{x : x \notin x\} \in \{x : x \notin x\}$, and the paradoxical rules are obtained from certain set theoretical principles. In a theory of definitional reflection $R$ might be just a constant

[†]Wilhelm-Schickard-Institut für Informatik, Universität Tübingen, Sand 13, 72076 Tübingen, Germany. Email: psh@uni-tuebingen.de.
[‡]This work goes back to investigations on definitional reasoning, which was carried out together with Lars Hallnäs. The preparation of this paper was supported by the French-German ANR-DFG project "Hypothetical Reasoning — Its Proof-Theoretic Analysis" (HYPOTHESES) (DFG Schr 275/16-2).

given by the definitional clause $R \Leftarrow \neg R$, and the paradoxical rules are obtained as rules of definitional closure and definitional reflection with respect to this definition (Hallnäs, 1991; Hallnäs and Schroeder-Heister, 1990/91; Schroeder-Heister, 1993; Schroeder-Heister, 2012a). In a theory of arbitrary propositional operators $R$ might be a nullary logical constant for which these paradoxical rules are the introduction and elimination rules (Tennant, 1982; Read, 2010).

Thus our system contains the following rules:

**Structural rules**

Identity: $\dfrac{}{A \vdash A}$ (Id)           Contraction: $\dfrac{\Gamma, A, A \vdash C}{\Gamma, A \vdash C}$ (Contr)

Cut: $\dfrac{\Gamma \vdash A \quad A, \Delta \vdash C}{\Gamma, \Delta \vdash C}$ (Cut)      Weakening: $\dfrac{\Gamma \vdash C}{\Gamma, A \vdash C} \quad \dfrac{\Gamma \vdash}{\Gamma \vdash A}$

**Negation rules**

$$\frac{\Gamma \vdash A}{\Gamma, \neg A \vdash} \ (\neg \vdash) \qquad \frac{\Gamma, A \vdash}{\Gamma \vdash \neg A} \ (\vdash \neg)$$

**Paradoxical rules**

$$\frac{\Gamma, \neg R \vdash C}{\Gamma, R \vdash C} \ (R \vdash) \qquad \frac{\Gamma \vdash \neg R}{\Gamma \vdash R} \ (\vdash R)$$

Then the derivation of contradiction looks as follows:

$$\cfrac{\cfrac{\cfrac{\cfrac{\cfrac{\cfrac{\overline{R \vdash R} \ (\text{Id})}{R, \neg R \vdash} \ (\neg \vdash)}{R, R \vdash} \ (R \vdash)}{R \vdash} \ (\text{Contr})}{\vdash \neg R} \ (\vdash \neg)}{\vdash R} \ (\vdash R) \qquad \cfrac{\cfrac{\cfrac{\overline{R \vdash R} \ (\text{Id})}{R, \neg R \vdash} \ (\neg \vdash)}{R, R \vdash} \ (R \vdash)}{R \vdash} \ (\text{Contr})}{\vdash} \ (\text{Cut})} \tag{1}$$

This derivation uses all rules of our system with the exception of weakening. If a proper paradox is expected to allow the generation of any sequent whatsoever, we could add applications of weakening at the end of this derivation to obtain $\Gamma \vdash C$ for any $\Gamma$ and $C$. However, as these applications would not affect the actual derivation of the empty sequent, we do not deal with weakening here. The legitimacy of weakening is a central matter in investigations of paraconsistency, which is a different way of dealing with the paradoxes, since it does not challenge the derivability of contradictions.

## 1   Identity

Obviously, dropping the rule of identity would block the derivation of the paradox. In fact, it would prevent us from starting any derivation whatsoever, as identity is the only axiom available. This is why identity is also called the rule of "initial sequents". However, there is a reasonable restriction on identity which can block the paradox without affecting 'standard' derivations.

**Proviso:** Identity $A \vdash A$ may only be used if no right- and left-introduction rules for $A$ are available.

The rationale behind this restriction is the following. Identity permits the introduction of a formula $A$ in an *unspecific* way: No matter what $A$ looks like, we can start with $A$ as an assertion, which depends on itself as an assumption. However, there might be *specific* ways to introduce $A$, which depend on the meaning of $A$. The proviso then says that we must use these specific ways, if they are available. For example, if $A$ has the form $\neg B$, then, rather than starting with $\neg B \vdash \neg B$ as an identity axiom, we request that $\neg B$ be introduced according to its specific meaning, *i.e.*, according to the specific introduction rules for $\neg$, yielding

$$\frac{\dfrac{B \vdash B}{B, \neg B \vdash} (\neg\vdash)}{\neg B \vdash \neg B} (\vdash\neg)$$

In the standard sequent calculus, this restriction corresponds to the common proviso that identity sequents must be atomic, so that nonatomic sequents of the form $A \vdash A$ can only be derived using the specific rules governing the constants occurring in $A$. From a more philosophical point of view, we might consider the distinction between atomic and non-atomic sentences to be the distinction between sentences for which no specific meaning rules are given in the system, and those for which specific meaning rules are available. The proviso then says that identity only applies to the unspecific case, whereas the specific case is always handled by the meaning rules. As in our context specific rules are available for $R$, $R$ is not considered atomic in this sense, so identity cannot be used for $R$. The sequent $R \vdash R$ should rather be reduced to $\neg R \vdash \neg R$ via the derivation

$$\frac{\dfrac{\neg R \vdash \neg R}{R \vdash \neg R} (R\vdash)}{R \vdash R} (\vdash R)$$

However, since $\neg R$ is not atomic either, this derivation must be reduced to

$$\frac{\dfrac{\dfrac{\dfrac{R \vdash R}{R, \neg R \vdash} (\neg\vdash)}{\neg R \vdash \neg R} (\vdash\neg)}{R \vdash \neg R} (R\vdash)}{R \vdash R} (\vdash R)$$

leading us to what we started with and showing that we cannot initiate the paradoxical derivation.

**Conclusion:** There is a plausible restriction of identity which blocks the paradoxes without affecting non-paradoxical reasoning. In the presence of restricted identity, the rules of contraction and cut can be used without any restriction.[1]

---

[1] This way of restricting identity was originally developed in the context of logic program-

## 2    Contraction

Disallowing contraction would prevent the derivation of the paradox. However, in view of the frequent use of contraction in mathematical and other reasoning, this cannot be considered a viable strategy. By adopting our distinction between specific and unspecific ways of using a sentence, we can argue for a restriction on contraction which blocks the paradox without precluding sensible uses of contraction.

If we look at the premiss $R, R\vdash$ of the application of contraction in (1), we observe that the two occurrences of $R$ result from the application of different rules. The left occurrence of $R$ in $R, R\vdash$ comes from the identity axiom $R\vdash R$. It may therefore be called an *unspecific occurrence* of $R$, since identity applies unspecifically to any formula independent of its shape. The right occurrence of $R$ in $R, R\vdash$ is the result of an introduction rule for $R$. Since this introduction rule is specific for $R$, this occurrence may be called a *specific* occurrence of $R$. By boxing the unspecific occurrences of $R$ and encircling the specific occurrences of $R$, this situation may be depicted as follows:

$$
\cfrac{
  \cfrac{
    \cfrac{
      \cfrac{
        \cfrac{\boxed{R}\vdash R}{\boxed{R},\neg R\vdash}\,(\neg\vdash)
      }{\boxed{R},\circledR\vdash}\,(R\vdash)
    }{R\vdash}\,(\mathrm{Contr})
  }{\vdash\neg R}\,(\vdash\neg)
}{\vdash R}\,(\vdash R)
\qquad
\cfrac{
  \cfrac{
    \cfrac{
      \cfrac{\boxed{R}\vdash R}{\boxed{R},\neg R\vdash}\,(\neg\vdash)
    }{\boxed{R},\circledR\vdash}\,(R\vdash)
  }{R\vdash}\,(\mathrm{Contr})
}{}
$$

$$\mathrm{(Id)}\quad\mathrm{(Id)}\quad\mathrm{(Cut)}\qquad\vdash$$

The contraction step identifies the boxed $R$ with the encircled $R$. If we argue that it makes a difference of whether we use $R$ unspecifically (in an identity sequent) or specifically (according to its meaning, as the result of a left-introduction rule), we are led to the following restriction of contraction.

**Proviso:** Contraction may only be used if the two occurrences of the sentence $A$ which are contracted into a single one, are either both specific or both unspecific. We must never contract a specific with an unspecific occurrence of $A$.

The significance of this proposal rests of course on the claim that the 'standard' uses of contraction (in mathematics and elsewhere) do *not* use the form of contraction prohibited by the proviso. This needs still to be verified — here we

---

ming with definitional reflection by Kreuger (1994). This is why we call it "Kreuger's rule" or "Kreuger's axiom". In logic programming with definitional reflection we extend logics by inference rules governing atoms which, as the common logical rules, split into right-introduction and left-introduction rules. This means that these atoms are atomic with respect to logic, but not atomic in the sense of being irreducible, because meaning-giving rules are associated with them. Therefore it is not unnatural to require that the unspecific initial sequents $A\vdash A$ be allowed only in the case in which $A$ is not further reducible to any other sentence. Formally, it can be shown that by restricting initial sequents in the way indicated, the resulting system allows the elimination of cuts and is therefore consistent. For the simplified system considered above this is easy to show, but this result holds for the general system with definitional rules for atoms as well. See Schroeder-Heister (1994).

take it for granted. Secondly, the notion of unspecific vs. specific occurrences must be made precise in such a way that paradoxes are indeed excluded by observing the proviso.

When working out this idea in detail, it turns out that the distinction between specific and unspecific occurrences of assumptions is not clear enough as it stands. An unspecific assumption can easily be turned into a specific one by using intermediate derivation steps. For example, if the critical part

$$\cfrac{\cfrac{\cfrac{\boxed{R} \vdash R}{\boxed{R}, \neg R \vdash} \; (\text{Id})}{\boxed{R}, \circledR \vdash} \; (\neg \vdash)}{R \vdash} \; (R \vdash)$$

of (1) is replaced with

$$\cfrac{\cfrac{\cfrac{\cfrac{\cfrac{\cfrac{\cfrac{R \vdash R}{R, \neg R \vdash} \; (\text{Id})}{\neg R \vdash \neg R} \; (\neg \vdash)}{\neg R \vdash R} \; (\vdash \neg)}{\circledR \vdash R} \; (\vdash R)}{\circledR, \neg R \vdash} \; (R \vdash)}{\circledR, \circledR \vdash} \; (\neg \vdash)}{R \vdash} \; (R \vdash)$$

i.e., if a derivation of $R \vdash R$ is added on top, then the boxed occurrences of $R$ become encircled, as they result from an introduction of $R$ according to the rule $(R \vdash)$. This means that both occurrences of $R$, which are contracted, are specific occurrences of $R$ and thus appear to satisfy the proviso.

To deal with such cases, we propose to introduce an indexing discipline. With every formula occurrence in a derivation, a natural number is associated as a *meaning index*, which is increased if a meaning rule (left- or right-introduction rule) is applied. Contraction is then prohibited, if the meaning indices of the sentences involved differ. In the above example, the right $R$ undergoing contraction receives a higher meaning index under this discipline than the left one, as it results from a single application of $(\vdash R)$ plus a single application of $(R \vdash)$, whereas the left $R$ results from a single application of $(R \vdash)$ alone. The result is a kind of type theory with respect to meaning, according to which the application of a meaning rules increases the type. Attaching these indices for $R$ as superscripts yields

$$\frac{\overline{R \vdash R}\ \text{(Id)}}{\cfrac{R, \neg R \vdash}{\cfrac{\neg R \vdash \neg R}{\cfrac{\neg R \vdash R^1}{\cfrac{R^1 \vdash R^1}{\cfrac{R^1, \neg R^1 \vdash}{\cfrac{R^1, R^2 \vdash}{R \vdash}\ \text{(Contr)}}\ (R \vdash)}\ (\neg \vdash)}\ (R \vdash)}\ (\vdash R)}\ (\vdash \neg)}\ (\neg \vdash)}$$

demonstrating that contraction equalizes occurrences of $R$ with unequal index.

**Conclusion:** There is a plausible restriction of contraction which blocks the paradoxes without affecting non-paradoxical reasoning. In the presence of restricted contraction, the rules of identity and cut can be used without any restriction.[2]

## 3   Cut

Derivation (1) uses cut in its last step. Without cut the empty sequent is not derivable. It is a characteristic feature of paradoxes that derivations generating them do not permit the elimination of cut. This corresponds to the fact that in natural deduction, derivations of paradoxes are not normalisable, as Prawitz (1965, Appendix B) has first observed. Therefore disallowing cut blocks the derivation of the paradox. If we insist on using cut-free systems, we can discard with the paradoxes.

However, insisting on cut-free systems (or, equivalently, on systems in which cut is admissible) asks for too much. In advanced mathematical theories, in fact: already in arithmetic, we do need cut to carry out significant proofs.[3] It is therefore worthwhile to look for a restriction of cut, which prevents paradoxes but still allows for standard mathematical reasoning.

In order to formulate such a restriction, we propose to use a type system in the style of the Curry-Howard correspondence, but adapted to the sequent calculus. A sequent $A_1, \ldots, A_n \vdash A$ now takes the form $x_1 : A_1, \ldots, x_n : A_n \vdash t : A$ for variables $x_1, \ldots, x_n$ and a term $t$. Terms are generated using certain constructors and selectors which depend on the constants available, in our case case just negation and $R$. Furthermore, certain reduction principles for terms are available which tell which terms are considered equal. Terms which cannot be further reduced are considered normal. Intuitively, normal terms codify 'real' proofs, whereas non-normal terms denote the proofs codified by their normal forms (if they exist and are unique). When using term annotations, we cannot deal with empty succedents, so we use the falsity constant $\bot$ instead.

---

[2]The idea of restricting contraction in this way was proposed in Schroeder-Heister (2004).

[3]This frequently happens, for example, when, in order to prove a statement $A$, we prove by induction a stronger statement $A'$ because $A'$ is needed as the induction hypothesis. Specialising $A'$ to $A$ means to apply a cut which is not eliminable.

In our context it is of particular importance to see that cut becomes a substitution rule:

$$\frac{\Gamma \vdash t : A \qquad \Delta, x : A \vdash s : B}{\Gamma, \Delta \vdash s[x/t] : B}$$

When performing this substitution, it may happen that the newly created term $s[x/t]$ is not normal and not normalisable, even though the terms $s$ and $t$ are in normal form. This is exactly what is taking place in the paradoxical derivation. In the term-annotated system the last step of (1) takes the form

$$\frac{\vdash t : R \qquad x : R \vdash s : \bot}{\vdash s[x/t] : \bot}$$

where the term $s[x/t]$ generated for absurdity is not normalisable, while $s$ and $t$ are normal. (For more details see the appendix.) This leads to the following restriction on the form of cut:

**Proviso:** Cut may only be used if it does not create, by means of substitution, a non-normalisable term.

The idea behind this proviso is that we should only generate terms which represent "real" proofs. Denoting by $t \downarrow$ the fact that $t$ is normalisable, we would then formulate the restricted cut rule as

$$\frac{\Gamma \vdash t : A \qquad \Delta, x : A \vdash s : B}{\Gamma, \Delta \vdash s[x/t] : B} \quad s[x/t] \downarrow$$

This way of proceeding presupposes, of course, that we use a type system and no longer just operate with the sentences (= types) alone. Furthermore, which is more involved, we must specify how to establish $t \downarrow$ for a term $t$, as this is not a syntactic property of the given proof figure or of the formal system used. So the restricted form of cut should more appropriately be formulated as

$$\frac{\Gamma \vdash t : A \qquad \Delta, x : A \vdash s : B \qquad s[x/t] \downarrow}{\Gamma, \Delta \vdash s[x/t] : B}$$

with $s[x/t] \downarrow$ as a premiss of its own. In the end this leads to a sort of free type theory where one has to add rules by means of which we can prove that a term denotes.

**Conclusion:** There is a plausible restriction of cut which blocks the paradoxes without affecting non-paradoxical reasoning. In the presence of restricted cut, the rules of identity and contraction can be used without any restriction.[4]

# 4  Summary

For each of the structural rules of identity, contraction and cut, we considered certain restricted forms which suffice for 'ordinary' mathematical reasoning,

---

[4]This restriction of cut was proposed in Schroeder-Heister (2012b). There the fact that the sequent calculus makes the use of substitution explicit in the form of the cut rule, is seen as a conceptual advantage of this format of deductive reasoning as compared to natural deduction.

but which are insufficient for the derivation of paradoxes. Even though we did not decisively argue in favour of a particular one of these restrictions, this shows that investigating constraints on the application of structural rules is a promising research programme.

## Appendix

In the term-annotated system, where we use the absurdity constant $\perp$ to represent the empty succedent, it is more convenient to consider $\neg A$ to be an abbreviation for $A \to \perp$. The term-annotated rules for implication and $R$ are as follows.

$$\frac{\Gamma, x:A \vdash t:B}{\Gamma \vdash \lambda x.t:A \to B} \qquad \frac{\Gamma \vdash t:A}{\Gamma, x:A \to B \vdash App(x,t):B}$$

together with the reduction principle

$$App(\lambda x.t, s) \rhd t[x/s] \tag{2}$$

which is the same as $\beta$-contraction, and

$$\frac{\Gamma \vdash t:R \to \perp}{\Gamma \vdash rt:R} \qquad \frac{\Gamma, x:R \to \perp \vdash t:C}{\Gamma, y:R \vdash t[x/r'y]:C}$$

together with the reduction principle

$$r'rt \rhd t \ . \tag{3}$$

With term-annotations the derivation (1) takes the form

$$\frac{\dfrac{\dfrac{\dfrac{\dfrac{\dfrac{x:R \vdash x:R}{x:R, y:R \to \perp \vdash App(y,x):\perp}}{x:R, z:R \vdash App(r'z,x):\perp}}{x:R \vdash App(r'x,x):\perp}}{\vdash \lambda x.App(r'x,x):R \to \perp}}{\vdash r\lambda x.App(r'x,x):R} \qquad \dfrac{\dfrac{\dfrac{x:R \vdash x:R}{x:R, y:R \to \perp \vdash App(y,x):\perp}}{x:R, z:R \vdash App(r'z,x):\perp}}{x:R \vdash App(r'x,x):\perp}}{\vdash App(r'r\lambda x.App(r'x,x), r\lambda x.App(r'x,x)):\perp} \tag{4}$$

It can easily be checked that the term generated for absurdity in the end sequent of (4) reduces to itself, $i.e.$ the reduction sequence based on reductions (2) and (3) (there is only a single such sequence) loops. For further discussion see Schroeder-Heister (2012b).

## BIBLIOGRAPHY

Fitch, F. B. (1936). A system of formal logic without an analogue to the Curry W Operator. *Journal of Symbolic Logic*, 1(3):92–100.

Hallnäs, L. (1991). Partial inductive definitions. *Theoretical Computer Science*, 87:115–142.

Hallnäs, L. and Schroeder-Heister, P. (1990/91). A proof-theoretic approach to logic programming: I. Clauses as rules. II. Programs as definitions. *Journal of Logic and Computation*, 1:261–283, 635–660.

Kreuger, P. (1994). Axioms in Definitional Calculi. In Dyckhoff, R., editor, *Extensions of Logic Programming. 4th International Workshop, ELP'93 (St. Andrews, U.K., March/April 1993). Proceedings (Lecture Notes in Computer Science, Vol. 798)*, pages 196–205. Springer, Berlin.

Prawitz, D. (1965). *Natural Deduction: A Proof-Theoretical Study*. Almqvist & Wiksell, Stockholm.

Read, S. (1994). *Thinking About Logic*. Oxford University Press, Oxford.

Read, S. (2010). General-elimination harmony and the meaning of the logical constants. *Journal of Philosophical Logic*, 39(5):557–576.

Schroeder-Heister, P. (1993). Rules of definitional reflection. In *Proceedings of the 8th Annual IEEE Symposium on Logic in Computer Science (Montreal 1993)*, pages 222–232. IEEE Press, Los Alamitos.

Schroeder-Heister, P. (1994). Cut Elimination for Logics with Definitional Reflection and Restricted Initial Sequents. Unpublished manuscript. (See the author's homepage).

Schroeder-Heister, P. (2004). On the Notion of Assumption in Logical Systems. In Bluhm, R. and Nimtz, C., editors, *Selected Papers Contributed to the Sections of GAP5, Fifth International Congress of the Society for Analytical Philosophy, Bielefeld, 22-26 September 2003*, pages 27–48. Mentis, Paderborn. www.gap5.de/proceedings.

Schroeder-Heister, P. (2012a). Proof-theoretic semantics. In Zalta, E., editor, *Stanford Encyclopedia of Philosophy*. http://plato.stanford.edu.

Schroeder-Heister, P. (2012b). Proof-theoretic semantics, self-contradiction, and the format of deductive reasoning. *Topoi*, 31(1):77–85.

Tennant, N. (1982). Proof and paradox. *Dialectica*, 36:265–296.

# Revising Logic in Light of Paradox

## 1 What is Truth? What is Logic?

Let us begin with a passage from Alfred Tarski's popular (Tarski, 1944, p. 348) "The semantic conception of truth and the foundations of semantics," where he lays out ingredients that together produce the Liar paradox:

> (I) We have implicitly assumed that the language in which the anti-nomy is constructed contains, in addition to its expressions, also the names of these expressions, as well as semantic terms such as the term "*true*" referring to sentences of this language; we have also assumed that all sentences which determine the adequate usage of this term can be asserted in the language. A language with these properties will be called "*semantically closed*."

> (II) We have assumed that in this language the ordinary laws of logic hold.

> (III) We have assumed that we can formulate and assert in our language an empirical premise such as the [Liar sentence] which has occurred in our argument.

By "the sentences which determine the adequate usage of" the word 'true', Tarski means the instances of the T-scheme,[1] and by the "ordinary laws of logic", he means classical logic. He points out that the empirical element in condition (III) is not essential, "for it is possible to reconstruct the antinomy of the liar without its help." What is needed, or at least what is used, is self-reference, and it is and was well-known that any language that can express a modicum of arithmetic has the resources for self-reference. Tarski concludes: "[T]he assumptions (I) and (II) prove essential. Since every language which satisfies both of these assumptions is inconsistent, we must reject at least one of them" (Tarski, 1944, p. 349)

The same options hold today. Any theorist who wants to employ something recognizable as a truth-predicate in a systematic and consistent, or at least

---

[†]The Ohio State University, Arché research Centre. Email: shapiro.4@osu.edu

[1]Of course, Tarski may be wrong in his claim that the instances of the T-scheme partly "determine the adequate usage of" a truth-predicate. If he is wrong about that, then perhaps a language can indeed be "semantically closed", according to the official definition, even if its logic is classical. Thanks to a referee for pointing this out. What counts as the proper usage of a truth-predicate is very much at issue here, and we will return to that several times below.

non-trivial, way must either restrict the T-scheme and the corresponding T-rules, somehow, or else propose a non-classical (and non-intuitionistic) logic. Tarski, of course, opts for the former:

> It would be superfluous to stress here the consequences of rejecting the assumption (II), that is, of changing our logic (supposing this were possible) even in its more elementary and fundamental parts. We thus consider only the possibility of rejecting the assumption (I). Accordingly, we decide *not to use any language which is semantically closed* in the sense given (Tarski, 1944, p. 349)

That was then; this is now. There is a wealth of philosophical and logical work that, in effect, takes the option that Tarski rejects out of hand, namely that of keeping the full, unrestricted T-scheme, or something like it, such as the corresponding inference rules or an unrestricted principle of substitution. Contradiction, or triviality, is avoided by invoking a non-classical logic.

Since at least Priest (1979), Graham Priest has urged that we accept the inconsistency—the truth and untruth of the Liar—and avoid triviality by adopting a paraconsistent logic (see Priest, 2006). J.C. Beall (2009) makes a similar proposal, invoking a different, weak logic. Although Alan Weir (1998, 2005), insists that there are no true contradictions, he develops a system that has the full T-scheme, as well as every instance of the naive comprehension scheme for set theory, as theorems. Consistency is maintained by restricting the logic. For Weir, neither excluded middle nor ex falso quodlibet is valid, in full generality. They hold only for "determinate" sentences $\Phi$, those for which we have $\neg(\Phi \leftrightarrow \neg\Phi)$. According to Weir, it is correct to reason from the determinacy of $\Phi$ to, say $(\Phi \vee \neg\Phi)$. More recently, Hartry Field (2008) provides an account that accepts the full intersubstitutivity of a sentence $\Phi$ with its truth-attribution $T <\Phi>$. For Field, the principle of excluded middle is not a logical truth. Adding excluded middle to his formal language results in classical logic, rendering it inconsistent, and trivial. The details are rich, subtle, and fascinating.

Of course, there are other, similar, systems in the literature, but these four will do for our purposes. The other major theoretical route is to follow Tarski and keep classical logic (or some straightforward extension thereof, say to three truth-values), and to restrict the T-scheme. It is a sort of optimization project.[2] Everyone starts with the obvious truth that classical logic is incompatible with the instances of the T-scheme, the corresponding rules, or intersubstitutivity. So we have to give up or at least restrict at least one of these. The idea is to do so in a way that leaves us with as rich and powerful theory as possible (short of triviality, of course), a theory that will do the legitimate work that truth does, or at least as much of this work as is possible. To adapt a phrase of Penelope Maddy (1997), we are to operate one step back from disaster.

The purpose of this paper is to explore various theses that might be claimed by those who propose an alternate, non-classical logic, in response to the semantic paradoxes (or, for that matter, for any other reason). What, exactly, are they proposing, or should they be proposing, concerning their favored logic?

---

[2]Thanks to Kevin Scharp for suggesting this way of putting things.

What should be claimed about the proposed logic, vis-à-vis ordinary classical logic (or intuitionistic logic, relevant logic, or whatever)? We ask parallel
questions concerning the other, more traditional group of theorists, those who
propose to leave the logic alone (so to speak) and restrict the T-scheme. What
can be claimed by such theorists on behalf of their account of truth, vis-à-vis
the ordinary intuitive or pre-theoretic concept of truth?

Many of the authors who address the nature of truth and/or the paradoxes
do not directly address these methodological issues, and those that do often do
not say the same things. Here we will explore possibilities.

## 2   Description: Is it (Conceptual) Analysis?

To pick a neutral term, the theorists who work in this genre—Gupta and Belnap
(1993); Kripke (1975), et al.—deliver various *theories* of truth. Each author
compares his or her theory to other accounts of truth, arguing that his or hers
is superior on whatever grounds one should use in choosing theories—whatever
those may be.

Perhaps we should think of the word "theory" here in the sense of a theory
of, say, thermodynamics. The idea is that each author is presenting us a *description* of the ordinary, pre-theoretic notion of truth, maybe something like
the results of a traditional conceptual analysis, or a semantic theory. Concerning truth alone, the theories presented by Priest, Beall, Weir, and Field are
rather simple. Each takes truth to be characterized by the platitudes, mainly
the T-scheme, a corresponding T-rule, or a principle of intersubstitutivity. It
is arguable that these platitudes do hold of the ordinary notion of truth. After
all, they are platitudes, and their status as such is usually conceded—or would
be were it not for the ensuing inconsistency (if you can get your head around
that counterfactual).

Of course, if one adopts a theory of truth like this, then, as Tarski noted,
the action concerns the logic. Suppose that the aforementioned platitudes do
hold of the ordinary notion of truth. Then, if the underlying logic of natural
language is classical (or intuitionistic), anyone who deploys the ordinary notion
of truth according to these constitutive principles is saddled with inconsistency
and perhaps even triviality. Some philosophers are content to let things rest
here, perhaps proposing ways in which the inconsistent notion is or can be
or should be deployed in a useful manner (*e.g.* Chihara, 1979, 1984; Eklund,
2002), but our four authors are not. They each present a logic on which no
triviality, and, they argue, no revenge follows from the platitudes concerning
truth. So our methodological focus then turns to the proposed logic. What is
or can be or should be claimed on behalf of this logic?

We can invoke the word theory here, too, thinking of a logic as a *theory* of
validity and logical consequence. Is this also to be understood in the sense of
a theory of thermodynamics? That is, could each author claim that his theory
gets it right, *describing* the One True notion of consequence or validity? If so,
then what is it that the logic is supposed to be getting right?

Unlike thermodynamics, the target of logic—the notion of validity—is itself normative. Logicians are not out to describe how speakers, even careful
speakers, actually reason, but how they ought to reason, or how they ought to

regulate their system of beliefs. Nevertheless, from our first perspective, logic is still a descriptive enterprise, not revisionist. On this perspective, the logician is out to describe what follows from what; their targets are the norms implicit in rational beings, as such, in our community of reasoners (see Burgess, 1992). So from this perspective, each author would be claiming that classical logic, along with intuitionistic logic and the usual relevant logics, all provide incorrect descriptions of validity and logical consequence, and that his account, at long last, provides the correct description.

At least one of our authors does make a descriptive claim about logic. Priest (*e.g.*, 2006) argues both that his dialetheic account accurately describes the notion of truth and that his para-consistent logic, called "LP", is an accurate description of the One True notion of logical consequence—or at least that the One True Logic is paraconsistent, in case LP should turn out to be not quite right.

Field does not join him in this regard. He never claims that his notion of consequence is, and always has been, the one we implicitly deploy, unbeknownst to many generations of logicians (see Field, 2009b,a). Although Field presents a number of principles that, he argues, are valid, and he presents a number of principles that, he argues, are invalid, Field does not present a deductive system. That is, Field's readers are not given a description of the canons of correct inference, nor are they given a detailed, rigorously defined proposal for how one should reason from premises to conclusion. We are not told exactly which arguments are valid and which are not. So, for Field, there simply is no sharply defined candidate to compare to classical logic, intuitionistic logic, LP, etc. At least not yet.

Field does present an elaborate model theory, based on set theory, from which he defines a highly non-effective notion of "preserving value 1." Of course, I am not about to complain about a consequence relation just because it is not effective (Shapiro, 1991), but Field himself says that his model-theoretic notion is not an accurate *description* of the consequence relation that underlies his account of truth. Since the background set theory is two-valued, it cannot accommodate the inherent (and inevitable) indeterminacies. Field's model-theoretic notions are presented as mathematical models—approximations—of the underlying notion of logical consequence. Of course, this much is fair enough. Modeling is quite useful. But, again, we are never told what, exactly, the extension of the underlying notion of consequence is. What, exactly, is his model-theoretic notion a model of? Validity is left as a primitive of the formal presentation.[3]

I submit that it is very difficult to sustain a descriptive claim on behalf of a logic brought to resolve the semantic paradoxes, Priest notwithstanding. The issues here are subtle and deep, and I will limit myself to a sketch. Suppose, for the sake of argument, and for the present, that there is a single pretheoretic or intuitive notion of logical consequence, a notion that is more-or-less sharp.

---

[3]A Fieldian could argue likewise that classical logic is not a good description of logical consequence, and that, at present, we do not have a decent such description. In other words, a Fieldian could argue that we simply do not have a good theory of logical consequence, in the present descriptive sense of "theory." Field himself does not take this line.

This intuitive notion would be whatever underlies chains of deductive reasoning in mathematics, science, and elsewhere, and what underlies ordinary criticisms and rejections of purportedly valid inferential moves, the norms we use to regulate our beliefs. This intuitive notion is perhaps what Field calls an all-purpose logic, one that applies *everywhere*. The intuitive notion is the target of the competing descriptive claims made by Priest, classical logicians, and perhaps others. The intuitive notion of consequence would also be the target of a descriptive claim by Field, Weir, et al., were they to make such a claim.

It is widely held that validity flows—somehow—from the meaning of the logical terminology, words and phrases like "or", "it is not the case that", and "for all", at least when they are used in a certain way, in deductive reasoning. Meaning, in turn, is the sort of thing that is grasped, at least tacitly, by competent speakers of a language—or ordinary competent deductive reasoners in the case at hand. Plausibly, meaning is the sort of thing that speakers grasp, implicitly, when they understand a language.

Among logicians, inferentialists claim that the meaning of (at least) logical terminology is given by inferential role, often characterized in terms of introduction and/or elimination rules. Surely, from that perspective, ordinary speakers—those who understand the language—grasp the relevant rules, at least tacitly. Michael Dummett (1973) argues that a competent speaker of a language must be able to "manifest" understanding of its logical terminology. Model-theorists think of meaning as given by truth-conditions. So someone competent with the language should grasp these truth-conditions, at least implicitly. And, on such views, the relation of validity is tied to those truth-conditions.

To be sure, these need not be the only accounts, or models, of meaning available. But whatever the logical terminology of a language might mean, it is surely plausible to insist that ordinary speakers, or at least those competent in deductive reasoning, have implicit knowledge of logical consequence, in the sense that they can reliably detect valid and invalid reasoning, at least most of the time.

A descriptive theory of logic thus has some more or less empirical consequences. If competent speakers, or at least professional mathematicians and scientists, are somehow implicitly onto the One True notion of logical consequence, then, it might be argued, there should be a characterization of this notion that can be tested against the considered verdicts of competent reasoners concerning at least many arguments. In this respect, at least, logic is not much different from other linguistic enterprises. The "data" would be felt entailments, and judgements of felicity, by those recognized as competent reasoners, just as it is in much of linguistics.

To be sure, this "data" is theory-laden, and no one pronouncement is sacrosanct. But this is the case in just about all of the sciences, linguistic or otherwise. Here, as anywhere else, there are no crucial experiments. For example, a linguist does not expect ordinary speakers to be aware of whether infelicitous sentences are unacceptable because they are ungrammatical, don't make sense, fail of anaphora resolution, etc. Similarly, a theorist should not expect ordinary speakers, even careful reasoners, to be able to distinguish logical consequence from analytic consequence, enthymematic inference, conventional implicature, presupposition resolution, etc. My point here is only that a descriptive claim on behalf of a given logic—a thesis that it describes the One True notion of logical consequence—is at least partly empirical, no less so than, say, theories of syntax and semantics within linguistics.

It seems to me that, in the case of our truth-theorists who propose alternate logics, the empirical theses are most implausible. The logics they propose are quite subtle. As noted above, the trick is to avoid contradiction, or at least triviality, while leaving the entire logical-semantic enterprise as powerful as possible. A theorist who makes a descriptive claim about logic would have to maintain that ordinary speakers, or at least ordinary folk who engage in chains of deductive reasoning—professional mathematicians at least—are somehow implicitly competent in the subtle restrictions proposed in order to avoid paradox. They would have to claim that, when push comes to shove, ordinary reasoners will reject exactly the classically valid inferences the favored logic declares to be invalid.

For example, if someone were to make a descriptive claim on behalf of, say, Field's logic, then she would be claiming that ordinary reasoners are somehow aware, at some level, that they should not invoke an instance of excluded middle if there is some reason to think that the embedded sentence is indeterminate.

Against this, it seems to me that ordinary competent reasoners, and even highly celebrated expert deductive reasoners, are ignorant of the subtle restrictions needed to avoid triviality. For the overwhelming most part, the threat of paradox due to semantic paradoxes is simply not on the deductive reasoner's radar, and the underlying logic they invoke is not equipped to deal with it.

The foregoing quasi-empirical themes are in fact pursued from the camp of relevance logicians, some of whom do pay attention to verdicts or intuitions concerning validity and invalidity. And there is overlap between relevance logics and some of those proposed to make the world safe for truth (especially Beall, 2009). But the common relevance logics—those developed by focusing on felt entailments and felt non-entailments—do not work for paradox. As far as I know, we cannot get to a logic that is safe from paradox just by paying attention to patterns of inference and judgements of validity and invalidity among competent reasoners.

Of course, this is not to say that a paradox-immune logic (if there is such a thing) cannot become natural, once we get used to it. That is, language users might evolve to the point where our basic, unreflective judgements concerning valid and invalid moves conform to the logic in question. But we simply are not used to such a logic now, and do not regulate our beliefs by its lights. So I propose that we move beyond thinking of the Priest-Beall-Weir-Field proposals as simple, descriptive claims.

We can ask our questions about the other class of truth-theories, those that leave the logic alone, and avoid paradox by restricting the truth-scheme. Tarski's own theory is the prime example.[4] A *descriptive* claim, on behalf of

---

[4]One might include, say, Kripke (1975), in this group. That would depend on whether the underlying three-valued logic is an alternative to classical logic, or an extension of it to allow for the indeterminacies. We won't engage with that question here.

such a system, would be a thesis that the ordinary notion of truth—the one deployed by ordinary, competent users of the language, is in fact restricted to sentences (or propositions) that do not themselves invoke truth. Or perhaps the claim is that the ordinary notion of truth is somehow implicitly indexed for level—there is an unarticulated constituent or a covert variable for a language or a level in the truth-hierarchy.

A descriptive theory like this would also have empirical consequences. If it is indeed part of the meaning of the English word "true", when it is used to apply to sentences and propositions in this way, that it is restricted, or that it has an unpronounced index for level, then, in some way, ordinary, competent speakers are at least tacitly aware of this, and the theory should have some consequences concerning what speakers find felicitous, what inferences they find acceptable, and the like. This is not different from any other semantic thesis that postulates an unarticulated constituent or a covert variable. And, as above, I submit that the empirical fallout of a truth theory like this is most implausible. The paradoxes, and the subtle restrictions needed to avoid them, are simply not on the radar of the ordinary, competent user of a truth predicate.

My negative conclusion concerning a descriptive claim, on behalf of either the logic or the truthpredicate, might be resisted by denying that there is the sort of empirical fallout of the various theories that I am postulating. One such line may go as follows: First, it is assumed (or argued or conceded for the sake of argument) that ordinary speakers do tend to reason in accordance with classical logic, at least in the relevant contexts of chains of deduction. Second, ordinary speakers do seem to rely on the correctness of the T-scheme. These, however, are (mere) matters of psychology, concerning what speakers tend to do. The argument continues that it cannot be that the *semantic* values of the logical particles and of the word "true" in English are given by classical logic and the T-scheme, for that would render the entire language trivial (given that the language is rich enough to formulate a Liar sentence). The quest is then to figure out what the actual semantic values of the logical particles and the truth predicate are.[5] Any differences between the use of the terms (even by careful users) and their actual semantic values, is chalked up to errors systematically made by speakers.

This line of argument presupposes that the crucial words here—the logical particles and the truth predicate—have single semantic values that dictate their proper use in all relevant contexts. The argument also assumes a deep coherence in language use, that there is one and only one correct way to use our terms (vagueness, ambiguity, and polysemy aside, perhaps). This one and only one correct usage is given by the actual semantic values of the words. I'll come to challenge this below (§4). For now, it suffices to note that, on the assumptions in question, it is not clear what the rules of our game are. If there is to be *no* empirical fallout of our semantic theories, then how should we, as neutral observers, choose between rival theories of truth? Presumably, the theories all agree on the unproblematic cases— those where a Tarskian account works. What is it that makes one of the theories the correct description of the actual semantic values of the logical particles and/or the truth predicate,

---

[5]Thanks to a referee for suggesting this line of argument.

and the other theories incorrect? How would we tell? Pending answers to these weighty questions, I propose to postpone any further consideration of this option.

Another response to my conclusions above is to eschew interest in the semantics of natural language terms altogether. The action, it might be said, does not concern the English words and phrases "true", "or", and "it is not the case that", but the *property* or *concept* of Truth, and the *relation* of Disjunction and of Negation. After all, we don't want our conclusions to be restricted to a single language, say English. This last is fair enough, I suppose. But now, I suggest, the relevant matter concerns just which concept or property is in fact picked out by the English word "true", at least in the uses we have in mind here. There is Tarskian truth, Kripkean truth, naïve truth, and others. Which one is best associated, in the relevant way, with the English word. The same goes for the logical particles.

There is classical negation, intuitionistic negation, various relevant negations, etc. Which goes with the logical particles of sufficiently regimented English, say the language used by professional mathematicians? Surely, those are empirical matters, at least in part. Or they are no less empirical than the perspective sketched above.

So I propose to move on, and consider a different orientation for our truth theories.

## 3    Prescription: Is it a Proposed Revision?

As is well-known, typical intuitionists concede that mathematicians generally accept the law of excluded middle, double negation elimination, etc., in the sense that those principles are implicit (if not explicit) in their deductive practice. That is, intuitionists do not dispute the descriptive matter broached in the last section, nor are they particularly interested in that matter. Instead, they argue that we *ought to* demur from the disputed principles. They claim that our current inferential practice is broken, and needs to be fixed.

An analogous theme here would start with a concession that the logic proposed by one of our authors—Field, Weir, Priest, Beall—is not implicit in our normative deductive practice to date. Presumably, that practice is adequately described by classical logic, or perhaps a relevant logic, but that is not so important. Our theorist would insist that, because of the semantic paradoxes, we ought to stop using that logic, in the sense that we should stop reasoning according to its norms, and start using the norms from his or her proposed logic instead.

The theme raised and examined in the previous section is that we need a new *theory* of logic, because our current theories are descriptively inaccurate. The present theme is that what we need is a new *logic*: better ways to reason, deductively; better ways to evaluate deductive reasoning; and better ways to regulate and organize our beliefs for consistency. Indeed, we need a new conception of what should *count* as consistent. It would be a call to arms for revolution.

Recall what Tarski (1944) wrote: "It would be superfluous to stress here the consequences of rejecting the assumption (II), that is, of changing our logic (supposing this were possible) even in its more elementary and fundamental parts." Consider the parenthetical remark "supposing this were possible." What is Tarski asking us to suppose is possible or, more likely, what is he suggesting is *not* possible? Changing our *theory* of logic? It is surely possible to change that. We can change a theory of anything, if a better, more accurate one comes along. Perhaps Tarski is just making a comment about how well entrenched classical logic is, or was, as a *theory* of logic. Perhaps. But that might just be a dogmatic attitude. Alternatively, Tarski may have been wondering about whether it is possible to change the *logic itself*, in the foregoing sense. He was surely aware of the main revisionist program in the early twentieth century, intuitionistic mathematics. So he would have heard of such a thing. However, Tarski may have been deeply skeptical of a revisionist enterprise, suggesting that it is much better to modify what we want to say about truth.

Weir (1998, 793) explicitly sounds a revisionist theme. He advocates restricting a generalized Cut rule, in effect giving up the transitivity of consequence. He writes:

> Certainly, to add restrictions on transitivity is a radical move, and one which would have to be made in a controlled fashion ... [S]uch restrictions [could not] be plausibly thought of as implicit in our actual practice of inference; rather they could only be revisions of that practice, revisions motivated by a desire to make better sense of it overall in the light of the difficulties we seem to land ourselves in whichever way we turn when reasoning about sets and semantics (and perhaps also in some other areas, such as the Sorites paradox).

If any of our theorists go down the revisionist route, they could soften the blow by pointing out that, after the revolution, we can maintain some semblance of our prior practice. In Field's case, that would be by adding instances of excluded middle, as non-logical premises, when we are not in danger of paradox, say when we are doing classical mathematics. In Weir's case, it would be to add principles of determinacy, in the form $\neg(\Phi \leftrightarrow \neg\Phi)$, when things are safe; and in Priest's, it would be to invoke the notion of quasi-validity, which corresponds to classical validity, when it is rational to presuppose that there is no threat of paradox. Beall has a similar line, suggesting that we need to resort to the weaker logic only when dealing with semantic notions like truth.

Even so, revisionist proposals carry costs. Presumably, such a proposal would involve a suggestion, or demand, that we revise our logic texts and classes accordingly. For example, if Field's logic is the one we all ought to adopt, then those of us charged with teaching logic should be teaching that logic; and similarly for the other proposals, if one of those is to prevail instead. The curriculum might start with classical (or relevant) logic, as a sort of first (or second) approximation, just as we learn about point masses and ideal planes in physics, before complicating the framework to make it more accurate. More advanced students should be taught the logic being proposed—if that logic is to replace classical logic in the way envisioned. And referees for professional journals in, say, linguistics, should be trained in the new logic, so that they can assess arguments accordingly, especially when unrestricted notions of truth and truth-conditions are involved.

Of course, Priest, Beall, Weir, and Field do not propose this curricular reform, even implicitly, unless Priest's (2008) lovely text in non-classical logic counts as a gentle move in that direction. Our question here, however, is whether revisionism can be, or should be, the outcome of one of the studies under consideration. Before making the revisions, however they are understood, and however far they go, we should see what the options are. Are there other, less costly, ways to confront the possibility of paradox and revenge? And, of course, we'd have to evaluate the various revisionist proposals against each other, to see which one to adopt. If there is but one logic in place now, presumably we'd want just one logic in place after the revolution. Which one?

Before going after logic, there are other, less drastic, revolutionary options to consider. One might maintain the old logic—be it classical, relevant, or whatever—and revise what we take to hold of truth. The idea would be to have the revolutionary spirit directed at the notion of truth, rather than the logic. An advocate of this approach might concede that the notion of truth— our notion of truth—is in fact characterized by, say, the intersubstitutivity principle, and propose that this notion be replaced with another one (perhaps to be expressed with a word with the same spelling, namely "truth").

One fairly natural, and hardly original, thought along these lines is to propose restricting the T-scheme, or the principle of intersubstitutivity. For example, someone impressed with Tarski's accomplishment might say that instead of deploying the current notion of truth, we introduce an openended series of truth-predicates, $truth_L$, where L is a place-holder for a description of a language, or a fragment of language, which does not contain this instance of the truth predicate. Our revisionist would suggest that we stop using our old, unrestricted truth predicate, and use these new, Tarskian, predicates instead. On this proposal, we would not have to restructure our logic curriculum, but, of course, there are other costs, many of which flow from arguments made by Kripke (1975) and others against the Tarskian account. A chasid who adopts the Tarskian revision cannot say something like "everything the Rebbe says is true." Instead, he'd have to survey (or guess at) the Rebbe's past and future pronouncements, to see which truth predicates they invoke (assuming the Rebbe also adopts the revisionist proposal), so that the chasid can insert something in the placeholder $L$ to cover all of the pronouncements. We'd have the amusing Nixon-Dean-style battles. Suppose, for example, that the Rebbe tries to say something about his hasid's present and future pronouncements—telling us not to trust them because many are not true. Moreover, someone who adopts this revisionist proposal would have to foreswear use of any predicate like, "for some language $x$, $true_x$." The parameter for language cannot be bound, at least not in this way, for that would bring back the paradox we are trying to avoid.

In fact, just about all of the proposals in the literature concerning truth can be interpreted in the revisionist spirit, no matter how they are intended by their proponents. We might consider replacing the unrestricted, freewheeling truth predicate with a context-sensitive one, or with one governed by a rule of revision, etc. Kevin Scharp (*e.g.*, 2007b; 2007a) explicitly proposes that the current, defective, notion of truth be replaced by two predicates, maintaining classical logic in the background. Each of the two replacement predicates satisfies one direction of the T-scheme universally, and satisfies the other direction for "safe" sentences. All of these revisionist programs can be compared with those that demand a revision in logic, in the foregoing sense. Each would require a cost-benefit analysis, with a hope that we—the community of truth-theorists—can find consensus.

Another option that must be considered is to not revise anything. As Chihara (1979, 1984) puts it, perhaps the cures are worse than the disease. Maybe the thing to do is to leave both the logic and the truth predicate alone, and to just be careful, relying on instinct on a case by case basis, to avoid disaster. Don't invoke the T-scheme, or intersubstitutivity, rigorously and blindly, when you sense some danger of paradox. After all, we've gotten along fairly well so far in our history, with our logic and our truth predicate, despite the supposed conflicts between them. This "proposal", or, better, non-proposal, also has its costs and benefits. It would have to be evaluated along with the others (see §5 below).

Consider, briefly, Field's account, considered as a proposal for revision of logic. On the benefit side of the ledger, of course, we would have a way to deploy the truth predicate, using the full, unrestricted substitutivity principle, in a way that is free from paradox and revenge. Or so Field argues, and I won't challenge that.

We also have to assess the costs. The downside would come from the changes to our inferential practices. As noted in the previous section, we are not given the precise extension of Field's new logic, and so it is hard to see what, exactly, we would be letting ourselves in for. In particular, we are not given a deductive system, nor are we given a model theory that will reliably test arguments for invalidity. So, to follow Field's proposal, construed along revolutionary lines, how are we supposed to train ourselves and students, concerning logic?

Both classical and intuitionistic logic have proven effective for long chains of reasoning. A mathematician can publish an article that goes on for, say, a hundred pages, with reasonable confidence that the community will come to consensus at least relatively quickly concerning whether it is correct—whether the conclusion does follow from the premises. Or at least they will if the result attracts enough interest. I do not see how there can be any assurance that deductive reasoning can be so smooth if Field's logic became the norm. It would be hard enough to evaluate each step in a long argument using his model theory, even noting that this model theory only gives us an approximation of validity.

A Fieldian revisionist might reply that in cases where we do need to execute long chains of reasoning all lie in standard mathematics, which has no threat of paradox (at least not now, thanks to Zermelo, Hilbert, et al.). In those cases, we can just add instances of excluded middle, as non-logical premises, and, in effect, make the reasoning classical. We only have to invoke the new logic, as such, when excluded middle cannot be assumed, and in those contexts, it is rare to encounter long chains of deductive reasoning. But we would still need some guidance of how to evaluate those chains of reasoning, even if they are not very long.[6]

One might note that even traditional mathematics has not always been so safe. Perhaps when paradox is lurking, there is reason to be wary of long chains of deductive reasoning anyway. Maybe we still don't have the logic quite right.

In any case, a Fieldian revisionist proposal asks us to give up a logical system—an inferential practice—that is tried and, for the overwhelmingly most part, true. It is highly articulated and useful for extended reasoning. We are to replace this with one that is left unclear, and without a definitive deductive system and model theory. I take those costs to be serious, but perhaps the Fieldian will concede this and argue that the benefits are worth it.

The logics invoked in the other proposals, those of Priest, Beall, and Weir (2005), are far more articulated than the one proposed by Field. We *are* given the extension of the notion of logical consequence, at least for formalized languages. So, in those cases, we do have a good idea of what we are in for, if a revolution motivated by one of those proposals should succeed. It still remains to be seen how useful those logics are for long sustained chains of reasoning. None of them has a straightforward, context-free natural deductive system, which can be executed efficiently, and it is proving very difficult to develop intuitions concerning which moves are correct and which are not (and, in the case of Priest, which moves are correct and incorrect), even by afficionados of the systems.[7] My point here is that the revolutionary proposals are quite costly. The benefits had better be worth it.

The situation is actually a bit worse than this. Field (2006, 2008) shows that, in just about any language that has an unrestricted truth-predicate with certain intuitive features, one cannot coherently maintain that valid arguments are truth-preserving (due to the Curry paradox). In particular, one cannot maintain that validity is truth-preserving and that modus ponens (or the usual arrow-elimination rule) is valid. The details are subtle, and vary with the various logics.[8] I won't rehearse them here.

These results suggest the revolutionary proposals call for a revision in our very conceptual scheme, and not "just" in how we ought to reason and regulate our beliefs for consistency. One might argue that it is *constitutive* of validity—as it is understood presently—that valid arguments are truth-preserving. Indeed,

---

[6]I might add that it is not at all obvious how to adapt Field's approach, and his logic, to intuitionistic analysis or synthetic differential geometry, mathematical theories where the underlying logic is intuitionistic. There we simply do not have the option of making the logic familiar by adding instances of excluded middle, since doing so would render the theory inconsistent. It is unclear how to execute a Field-like program in an intuitionistic setting.

[7]One indication of this is that most of the meta-theory, for the systems in question, is done in systems that invoke classical logic, usually classical set theory. That may be justified, if the theorist holds that the meta-theory is safe from paradox. But why should that be? The notion of truth is bound up with at least some of the meta-theoretic notions, at least prima facie. Perhaps the idea is that in some cases, at least, the reliance on classical meta-theory is something like a ladder to be kicked away after the revolution. If so, it would be good to see how efficiently we can operate without the ladder.

[8]Field's argument does not apply to some sub-structural logics (that don't have weakening or contraction) and some where the consequence relation is not transitive.

many logic texts seem to take something like the truth-preservation of valid arguments as true by definition. They begin with a thesis that if an argument is valid, then it is impossible for its premises to be true and its conclusion false. The method of constructing counterarguments seems to presuppose this. On most of the proposals for a logic change, we cannot maintain this slogan.

To be sure, it is open to our revisionist to argue that truth-preservation is (merely) a widely-held belief about validity, but is not constitutive of the notion. And after the revolution, this widely held belief will be given up. Of course, anyone with Quinean leanings will reject the very distinction between a widely-held belief and a constitutive principle. The slogan is that any principle can be given up, if we make the right adjustments elsewhere. Still, following Quine himself, it at least seems that in denying that valid arguments are truth-preserving, our revisionist is changing the subject. Perhaps our revisionist would argue that the subject has to change since, once the revolution comes, we can no longer maintain that valid arguments are truth-preserving.

In any case, the proposed revolutions in logic require us to rethink what the very target of logical study is. What is it that our logics are out to capture? What is it for an argument to *be* valid? It is not enough for our revisionist to provide us with a description of the extension of validity—either via a deductive system, a model-theoretic semantics, or an axiomatization. He or she should also tell us something about what validity *is*. What is it that the deductive system or model theory is describing, and what does that have to do with how we ought to infer deductively or how we ought to regulate our beliefs? What is the *telos* that underlies the normative notion of logical consequence, if it is not the preservation of truth?

## 4   Living and Working on the Ship of Neurath: Is it Explication, or Sharpening, or something like that?

The clash between the descriptive and prescriptive perspectives on logic, sketched in the two previous sections, is a false dilemma. As noted, the target of a descriptive claim, if one were to make it, is itself a normative enterprise. We are out to describe the notion of logical consequence that underlies or informs *correct* deductive argumentation in our present language, conceptual scheme, or whatever. Logical consequence is the relation by which we regulate our beliefs—and the relation by which we criticize and correct deductive reasoning. Perhaps there is no sharp distinction—and no distinction in kind—between changing a descriptive theory of a normative practice and changing the practice itself. This is especially plausible in cases like logic, since we sometimes use the prevailing theory of the practice to check inferences, and thus guide the very practice it is supposed to be describing (or at least we logicians sometimes like to think so).

For a rough analogy, consider the enterprise of composing a dictionary, and just think about word-spelling. Spelling is normative, in the sense that the focus is on *correct* spelling. No dictionary is out to record every way that anyone ever spells any word. Nevertheless, in some sense, practice is paramount. The way that most people, or most of the right kind of people, actually spell words, most of the time, determines how they should be spelled. At first, the lexicographer's job is straightforwardly descriptive. She is out to codify, systemize, and present the norms implicit in a linguistic community concerning the spelling of its words. At some point, however, the community might start using an established dictionary to check spelling, and thus to guide the very practice the lexicographer is out to describe. Eventually, the dictionary can become something close to a final court of appeal in such matters (putting aside the matter of incompatible, rival dictionaries). At that point, or sometime thereafter, the dictionary becomes *constitutive* of correct spelling: the perspective shifts from that of Socrates to that of Euthyphro. A given spelling is counted as correct *because* the dictionary records it that way. Again, all this is only a rough approximation, but it will do.

Another example is grammar, although that seems to be bound up with semantics and even with pragmatics. Surely it is correct to say that use determines syntax. Grammarians seem to presuppose something like this, since they rely on judgements of ordinary speakers, so-called "informants", to test their theories. To paraphrase Wittgenstein, however, what do we count as the use? Presumably, only correct use, by competent speakers. Who counts as competent? The (defeasible) data would be the utterance or publication of sentences that are not challenged for being infelicitous. Or perhaps the grammarian will begin with unreflective judgements, by competent speakers, concerning what are felicitous sentences in various contexts. Notice, however, that a well-constructed theory, once it is generally accepted, can be used to adjudicate matters of correct grammar, say by copy-editors for journals and publishing houses, not to mention school teachers.

To be sure, I am running over many delicate issues, including an important distinction between how speakers actually deploy their languages, how they think the language should be deployed, and how they were taught it should be deployed. School teachers and copy-editors have been known to accept, insist on, and even enforce, bad theories of what the grammar is. My point here is a mild one, that a good theory of grammar can sometimes, and in some way, guide the very practice it was designed to describe.

Presumably, something similar, but surely more complex, holds for semantics as well. And with semantics, it seems, we are not far from logical consequence and validity. Arguably, certain logical systems have taken on a certain guiding role in the community of careful deductive reasoners. If a dispute arises concerning a given inference, and if it is agreed that all steps in the reasoning are explicit, then one of the formal systems for classical logic can be consulted to adjudicate the matter. Classical, formal logic is *constitutive* of (classical) mathematical deductive practice, and, presumably, intuitionistic formal logic is constitutive of intuitionistic mathematical practice.[9]

There are a number of philosophical perspectives on language that dovetail with the idea that there is no distinction in kind between changing a descriptive theory of a normative practice and changing the practice itself. Some involve

---

[9]Of course, I am not claiming that mathematicians, or anyone else for that matter, defers to logical theories, or to logicians, on the matter of classical *versus* intuitionistic logic, relevant logic, etc. The present point only concerns adjudicating matters of validity within a given logical framework, say classical mathematical practice. Thanks to Alan Weir for pointing this out.

an outright rejection of what Mark Wilson (2006) calls the "classical picture", the thesis that the concepts we employ are precisely delimited in all possible situations. The opposing claim, or one opposing claim, is that there is genuine indeterminacy concerning the proper usage, to date, of many concepts or, perhaps better, what is essential to words and what they stand for. It is a truism that the use—the correct use—of each such concept, or, each such word, varies from age to age, and even person to person, and perhaps, utterance to utterance. To focus on one of the cases at hand, one might claim that there simply is no such thing at *the* ordinary notion of truth, or of *the* standard, normative rules for using the word "true."

To put it crudely, the underlying theme here is that ordinary language, and ordinary notions, and ordinary reasoning, are fraught with vagueness, loose rules, and defeasible rules of thumb, just about everywhere. It is not that anything goes. Surely that way lies madness—we do manage to use language to communicate, after all, and communication would not be possible if there were not some structure to how words are to be used. The thesis is that the rules and principles of correct usage are not completely sharp and determinate—and not fixed once and for all. As theorists about language, about concepts, and even about logic, we confront a messy and moving target. And if something like the observation at the start of this section is correct, the very act of theorizing about the target can itself move the target, once the theory in question is generally accepted.

The perspective here is of-a-piece with the Quinean attack on the analytic-synthetic distinction. The idea is that there is no sharp distinction, and no distinction in kind, between widely held beliefs and sentences somehow constitutive of the meaning of various terms. The present perspective is perhaps most consonant with Friedrich Waismann's (1945) notion of open-texture. Waismann only considers empirical terms, in ordinary language, but the idea can be—and should be—extended well beyond that.

Let $P$ be a predicate from natural language. According to Waismann, $P$ exhibits open-texture if there are possible objects $p$ such that nothing in the established use of $P$, or the non-linguistic facts, determines that $P$ holds of $p$ or that $P$ fails to hold of $p$. In effect, the sentence $Pp$ is left open by the use of the language, to date.

Here is one of the thought experiments Waismann invokes to characterize this notion:

Suppose I have to verify a statement such as 'There is a cat next door'; suppose I go over to the next room, open the door, look into it and actually see a cat. Is this enough to prove my statement?...What ...should I say when that creature later on grew to a gigantic size? Or if it showed some queer behavior usually not to be found with cats, say, if, under certain conditions it could be revived from death whereas normal cats could not? Shall I, in such a case, say that a new species has come into being? Or that it was a cat with extraordinary properties? ...The fact that in may cases there is no such thing as a conclusive verification is connected to the fact that most of our empirical concepts are not delimited in all possible directions (Waismann, 1945, pp. 121–122).

Language users introduce empirical terms to apply to certain objects or kinds of objects, and of course the terms are supposed to fail to apply to certain objects or kinds of objects. But no matter how a term gets introduced and acquires an established use, and a meaning, we can never be sure that every possible situation is covered, one way or the other. The last observation in the above passage is the key: our empirical concepts are not delimited in all possible directions. They were invoked to deal with a certain range of situations, and it is not always obvious how to apply the terms outside of that range. Sometimes, when unexpected cases arise, we, the community of language users, have to improvise.

The phrase "open texture" does not appear in Waismann's treatment of the analytic-synthetic distinction in a lengthy article published serially in *Analysis* (Waismann, 1949, 1950, 1951b,a, 1952, 1953), but the notion—or a closely related one—clearly plays a central role there. No one denies that a natural language like English is an evolving phenomenon. As new situations are encountered, and as new scientific theories develop, the extensions of predicates change. Sometimes the predicates become sharper, which is what someone who accepts open-texture would predict. As new cases are encountered, the predicate in question is extended to cover them, one way or the other. Waismann agues that when things like this happen, there is often no need to decide—and no point in deciding—whether the application of a given predicate to a novel case represents a change in its meaning or a discovery concerning the application of a term's old meaning. The contrary thesis, that there is something like the one and only correct way to go on consistent with the meaning of the term—what Wilson (2006) calls the classical picture—misrepresents the nature of language:

> Simply . . . to refer to "the" ordinary use [of a term] is naive . . . [The] whole picture is in a state of flux. One must indeed be blind not to see that there is something unsettled about language; that it is a living and growing thing, adapting itself to new sorts of situations, groping for new sorts of expression, forever changing (Waismann, 1951b, pp. 122–123).

Toward the end of the series, he writes: "What lies at the root of this is something of great significance, the fact, namely, that language is never complete for the expression of all ideas, on the contrary, that it has an essential *openness*" (Waismann, 1953, pp. 81–82).

Waismann's official definition of open-texture limits it to the application of empirical predicates (or their negations) to hitherto unconsidered, and even undreamt of, cases. In the *Analysis* series he points out that the dynamic nature of language goes well beyond this. Sometimes there are outright *changes* in the application of various words and expressions. Major advances in science often demand revisions in the accepted use of common terms: For the revolutionary scientist, "breaking away from the norm is sometimes the *only* way of making oneself understood" (Waismann, 1953, p. 84).

Waismann (1952) illustrates the point in some detail with the evolution of the word "simultaneous." The main innovative theses of the theory of relativity actually required the violation of the previous meaning of that word, what one may call its constitutive principles. How are we to understand this linguistic fallout of the theory of relativity? Are we to say that a brand new word, with a new meaning, is coined, or should we say that the old word has found some new and interesting applications, with its previous meaning intact? Did Einstein discover a hidden and previously unnoticed context-sensitivity in the established meaning of the established word "simultaneous" (or its German equivalent), even though he was not a linguist by training, and showed no special interest in that subject? Or did Einstein coin a new theoretical term, to replace an old term whose use had scientifically false presuppositions? It just so happens that the new word has the same spelling as the old word.

According to Waismann, there is often no need, and no reason, to decide what counts as a change in meaning and what counts as the extension of an old meaning to new cases—going on as before, as Wittgenstein might put it. Waismann said, in an earlier installment in the series: "there are no *precise rules* governing the use of words like 'time', 'pain', etc., and that consequently to speak of the 'meaning' of a word, and to ask whether it has, or has not changed in meaning, is to operate with too blurred an expression" (Waismann, 1951a, p. 53). The "too blurred expression" here is something like "has the same meaning as." We are encountering a borderline case of that relation.

Again, the key phrase here is "precise rules." It is not that anything goes, nor that there are no cases where it is appropriate to say that a given term is applied correctly, or incorrectly, to a new case. The fact that "has the same meaning as" has borderline cases does not entail that it has no clear cases.

As noted, Waismann only applies his notion of open-texture to empirical terms. In Shapiro (2006), I argue that the mathematical notion of a computable function (of natural numbers) is, or at least was, subject to open-texture, and that the notion of a recursive (or Turing computable) function serves to sharpen it. To ask whether the notion of a recursive (or Turing computable) function corresponds exactly to the notion of a computable function—the one implicit in earlier mathematical treatments—is to operate with the same "too blurred" notion as in Waismann's cases.

I suggest that the same goes for logic or, indeed, to the extensions and meaning of logical terms. There simply is no such thing as *the* logical norms implicit in ordinary deductive reasoning—especially if this reasoning is to include more than just the pure mathematics, in the more straightforwardly formalized branches, of the last few decades. Field (2009a) himself suggests something along these lines.

The same goes for the extension and meaning of the word "true." It is not a case of open-texture, as that is defined above. It is not that we stumbled onto situations that our previous usage of words like "true" left open, one way or the other, or that the term is somehow vague or otherwise indeterminate (although a truth-teller might count as such a case). In a sense, it is the opposite of open-texture. We stumbled onto situations where our previous usage, the rules implicit in our terms, and/or some widely shared beliefs, pull us in *opposite* directions at the same time, towards contradiction and, it seems, toward triviality if classical (or intuitionistic) logic is the standard.

From this vantage point, we can think of the Field/Priest/Beall/Weir systems as proposals for sharpening both the ordinary notion of truth and the norms of reasoning, in a way that avoids paradox and revenge. To invoke the usual metaphor, they are suggestions for tidying up the ship of Neurath. Following Waismann, we don't have to ponder whether the resulting notions— truth and the logical terms—are the same as or different from their predecessors. To do so may be to operate with too blurred an expression, namely "has the same meaning as."

A closely related, but different, meta-theme is to think of each author as proposing a Carnap-Quine-style *explication* of the notions of truth and correct inference. Each of them delivers a more sharply delimited notion of truth, along with a new logic. These notions of truth and these logics share many features with the partly inchoate ordinary notions they explicate. If this is the idea, then the main claim of each project is that the introduced items can do much of the legitimate work done by the previous notions, in a more rigorous manner.

Although many of the other accounts of truth and the semantic paradoxes do not involve a change in logic, they, too, can be considered in light of the present perspective(s), as proposed sharpenings or explications of previously messy, open-textured concepts. Tarski's seminal (1933) begins with a section entitled "The concept of true sentence in everyday or colloquial language", which highlights the paradoxes and a host of other problems dealing with concepts expressed in ordinary language. The section concludes:

> If these observations are correct, then *the very possibility of a consistent use of the expression 'true sentence' which is in harmony with the laws of logic and the spirit of everyday language seems to be very questionable, and consequently the same doubt attaches to the possibility of constructing a correct definition of this expression* (Tarski, 1933, §1, emphasis in original).

This much is consonant with the themes from Waismann broached above. At the start of the next section, Tarski writes: "For reasons given in the previous section, I now abandon the attempt to solve our problem for the language of everyday life and restrict myself entirely to formal languages." And, of course, we know what Tarski delivered, a precisely defined notion, for formalized languages that do not contain their own truth predicate. This precisely defined notion has much in common with the "colloquial" notion of truth, but it is not subject to paradox.

It is not much of a stretch to read Tarski as proposing an explication of the ordinary notion of truth, where the result can be put to work in the study of formal theories. That is, Tarski proposes to sharpen the notion so that it can be used for certain theoretical purposes.

One can construe Kripke (1975) in a similar spirit. To belabor the obvious, Kripke shows us how to introduce a rigorous, consistent truth predicate for a theory whose language contains that same truth predicate. This, of course, invokes a three-valued logic, and there are still some expressive limitations. We might read Kripke (1975) as a proposal for a more subtle explication or sharpening of the notion of truth, one that can be put to work in a wider range of cases—in particular to formal languages that contain their own truth predicate.

To be sure, explication and sharpening are not the same thing and, in each case, there are a variety of claims one might make on behalf of a candidate. A theorist might just be exploring alternatives, in a sort of hypothetical spirit. The purpose is to see what would be involved in getting the concepts in order. As useful as such an enterprise might be, we can set that perspective aside here, since there are no suggestions for practice. Nor is there a need to settle on a winner. Anything can be explored.

If our theories of truth and/or logic are understood as proposals for sharpening open-textured and/or inconsistent concepts, then there *is* a strong reason for us to settle on a winner, or perhaps to choose to reject all such theories (of which more in the next section). From this perspective, each author is demanding that we hereby start to reason and regulate our beliefs in certain way. To say the least, it would be helpful if we all spoke the same language, and reasoned according to the same norms. We are supposed to be communicating with each other. To do so, it would be inconvenient to sharpen our language in different, incompatible ways.

From this perspective, the situation is essentially the one discussed in the previous section.[10] In proposing that the concepts be sharpened in a given direction, the theorist is advocating a revolution in our conceptual scheme, either in logic or in how we use the word "true" (or both). We are told to stop using the loose, open-textured, or inconsistent notion, and use the sharpened one instead. Or we are told to stop using our old, loose logical norms and use the new ones instead. So the same features and disadvantages discussed in the previous section ensue. We'd have to change the curriculum, and the like.

Recall that an explication of a certain concept or word is supposed to be as much like the original as possible, at least in a wide range of cases, but be more useful than the original for certain purposes. So an explication need not carry the cost of a full-fledged revolution in our intellectual life. It would depend, of course, on what the purposes of the proposed explication are. If the purposes are more limited, then perhaps the costs can be borne. So what are these purposes? Why do we want a consistent, or at least non-trivial truth predicate.

Notice also that if we are thinking instead in terms of explication, then there may not be a need to choose between the different theories—it is possible to do without a single winner. It depends on what is being claimed in behalf of the given candidates. At least in principle, different explications of the same concept or word may prove useful for different purposes. Of course, to rest content with this potentially eclectic attitude, we'd need to know what

---

[10]Thanks to a referee for pointing this out.

the different purposes are, and why they are better served with the different explications.

In the closing section of this paper, we turn to this matter. It broaches the basic question of what truth is for, a topic that is discussed in the extensive literature on the nature of truth, especially by deflationists and their opponents. What do we do with truth, and could some of the things we do with truth be done better, in some ways, with an explication?

## 5   A Question from Alfred E. Neuman: Why Bother?

We do not need extensive reminders of the value of Tarski's account—however it is to be understood. The bulk of this value is preserved in all of the proposals considered here. Contexts which are capable of a Tarskian treatment are those where the truth predicate does not apply to sentences or propositions that themselves contain that very truth predicate. The key Tarskian situations are from mathematics. Truth—Tarskian truth—is invoked to give a truth-conditional, model-theoretic semantics for various theories, to compare theories for strength, and to prove soundness theorems, to the effect that the theorems of a given theory are true.

In Field's framework, in Tarskian contexts, excluded middle can be assumed, thus making the logic classical (putting intuitionistic theories aside, see note 6 above). In such contexts, Weir's principles of determinacy can also be assumed. And we can use quasi-validity in Priest or Beall's systems. In other words, all of the accounts here agree in what we may call Tarskian situations—as they had better.

But what is the *added* value of the newer proposals, especially those that change the logic? What do we gain with the added complexity, via the proposed revisions or sharpenings to logic?

Unfortunately, many of the Tarskian benefits noted just above do not extend to the more general situations, where the truth predicate applies to sentences that contain this predicate, and thus where paradox is looming. For example, relative consistency proofs generally go by induction: one proves that the axioms of a given theory are true and then proves, by induction, that truth is preserved by logical consequence. As noted in §3 above, Field (2006, 2008) shows, in compelling detail, that when it comes to languages that contain their own truth-predicates, it is inconsistent to hold that truth is preserved under logical consequence, modus ponens in particular. Moreover, his argument is substantially independent of the details of any particular account.[11]

So, to ask a blunt question, why bother? What is the reason to tinker with logic in this way, in order to get our truth predicate in order? What do we gain, beyond the benefits of using a Tarskian truth predicate in situations where it is appropriate to do so? This raises the much discussed question of what a truth predicate is for. What do we do with it?

In the philosophical literature, there are two large bodies of work on truth, with precious little overlap between them. There are accounts of the nature

---

[11] As noted, Field's argument does not apply to some sub-structural logics (that don't have weakening or contraction) and some where the consequence relation is not transitive. I won't get into the costs of adopting a logic like this.

of truth—deflation, correspondence, coherence, functionality, etc., etc.—and there is work on the paradoxes. Sometimes deflationism is characterized as the view that truth has no nature, or that there is no substantial property of truth. Weighty metaphysical matters, to be sure. If one is not a deflationist, in this sense, then a logical account of truth—ala Tarski, Kripke, Field, Priest, whatever—might be construed as providing constraints on a theory of the metaphysical nature of truth. It would help delimit the target for the metaphysician: find the nature of a property that behaves like *this*. From the opposite perspective, insights about the metaphysical nature of truth might suggest the proper restrictions on the T-scheme or the principle of intersubstitutivity, or the logic. Build your logic to accommodate *this*. One can always hope for synergy between metaphysics and logic, although in the present case, history is not particularly kind to this hope. Of course, a deflationist, one who does not think that truth has a metaphysical nature, would not look for this synergy.

Heavy metaphysics aside, Field (1994) provides one of the most sensible formulations of deflationism, in the sense that one can see what, exactly, is involved and what it would take to sustain or undermine the view. He begins by declaring opposition to widely-held "inflationist" programs that "truth conditions play an extremely central role in semantics and the theory of mind" and that "a theory of meaning and content is at least in large part a theory of truth conditions" (Field, 1994, p. 249). The main idea behind his opposing disquotational view is that "what plays a central role in meaning and content [does] not include truth conditions (or relations to propositions, where propositions are conceived as encapsulating truth conditions)" (Field, 1994, p. 253).

It is easy to see why someone who is an *in*flationist, in Field's sense, would at least strongly desire a rigorous theory of truth (or a replacement notion, or notions). That is, we can see what the purposes of the proposed explication would be. Truth (or a replacement) is to be developed in a rigorous manner to play a substantial role semantics and/or the theory of mind.

But this does not clinch the matter. Our inflationist—someone trying to develop a theory of truth-conditions for semantics or philosophy of mind—may be modest. She may be content to try to give the semantics—truth-conditions—for one chunk of language at a time. In that case, a Tarskian explication will probably suffice, and the logic can be left alone. The chunk of language in which the semantics is given need not include the chunk of language being theorized about. So the theorist can define a Tarskian truth-predicate for the target chunk within a separate meta-language, and formulate the semantics there. Much of the semantic work in contemporary linguistics can be construed in these terms.

Of course, this divide-and-conquer plan won't work if the target language-chunk itself contains an unrestricted truth-predicate, one that can apply to sentences both inside and outside the chunk. The semantics for this predicate, if there is to be one, is presumably not Tarskian.[12]

In any case, a full-blown, non-Tarskian theory of truth (or some replacement notion(s)) seems to be required—not just desired—if our inflationist has

---

[12]Thanks to Kevin Scharp here.

aspirations to formulate semantics in the very language being theorized about. That is, we cannot rely on a Tarskian truth predicate if one hopes to provide tight and complete truth-conditional principles for a natural language in which one does this providing. Clearly, a language like that would have to contain its own truth predicate. If the full T-scheme or unrestricted substitutivity holds for this truth-predicate, then the logic cannot be classical (or intuitionistic).

If this is the goal, then the proposed explication of truth indeed be acceptable, because the use of the new logic is limited. The weaker logic is a tool in the envisioned grand semantic enterprise. For almost all other purposes, we go on as before, either with the original, open-textured or inconsistent truth predicate of ordinary language or with a Tarskian truth predicate, if we have to be careful and rigorous. For almost all purposes, the logic can be left alone.

This is all for the Field-style inflationist. What of a Field-style *deflationist*, such as Field himself, someone who does *not* think we need a theory of truth, or truth-conditions, for semantics or a theory of mind? Why does *this* sort of deflationist need a rigorous, consistent, or at least non-trivial, account of truth? Why should he bother with trying to get his truth predicate and his logic in line with each other, encouraging the rest of us to do the same, in the same way? In present terms, what work is the explication supposed to do, work that the ordinary notion and the Tarskian explication cannot do?

Presumably, the action lies with truth as a device for generalization. We want to be able to say things like "everything the Rebbe says is true" and "all of the theorems of Peano arithmetic are true." The deflationist argues that this is just about *all* we need a truth predicate for. Moreover, the deflationist adds, to accomplish this generalization, all we have to go on are the platitudes—the T-scheme and intersubstitutivity—since truth has no nature.

Fair enough, perhaps. Or, in any case, I am not going to challenge this here. But, for such a deflationist, why do we need a sharp explication, one that is paradox-free? Some deflationists say that the there is no more to understanding truth than grasping the instances of the T-scheme or the intersubstitutivity principle—or that's all there would be if not for the paradoxes. From this perspective, our present truth-theorists—Field, Priest, Weir, Beall—show how to negotiate the proviso concerning paradox (in different ways). Or perhaps better, they show that the proviso *can* be negotiated. If the deflationist is willing to tinker with logic, producing one that is arguably much more complex, weak, and, arguably, less useful, then he can say that there is no more to understanding truth than grasping the instances of the T-scheme, and mean it. Complicating, and weakening, the logic makes the truth-predicate simple, about as simple as can be imagined.

Maybe the point of the enterprise is *only* to show that it is somehow possible to negotiate the proviso concerning logic. In that case, we need not settle on a winner. It does not harm the goals of deflationism if the proviso can be negotiated in several different ways, invoking several different logics. Is there anything else on the deflationist agenda? What else do we need in a theory of truth?

In particular, for our Field-style deflationist, are there any suggestions for how we should change our practice? Are we to *use* one or more of the explications? For what purpose, if not for a grand semantics or a theory of mind? Is the deflationist making a revolutionary proposal, like that broached in §3 above? Why? What is the reason for the call to arms for this revolution?

From the perspective on language sketched in the previous section, one can wonder whether the proposed revisions to our deductive practice are worthwhile. With the rejection of the classical picture of concepts, and the ensuing notion of open-texture, one might hold that *no* concept, or at least no word, has a nature, or at least none in the sense dreamt of by metaphysicians. There is no such thing as a set of non-trivial necessary and sufficient conditions that will decide every case, one way or the other. For Waismann, this applies to words like "cat" and "gold"; perhaps it applies to "true" as well. Why is it important to sharpen the notion, in the straightforward way, at such a cost to logic?

We already know how to invoke a truth-predicate over a wide range of cases, and we know how to reason deductively over a wide range of cases, including those of science and mathematics, at least so far. And we have a powerful and eminently useful formal logic to codify deductive reasoning. And we have a powerful and useful theory of Tarskian truth which serves many important theoretical purposes.

Because of the semantic paradoxes, we also know that the overall system is subject to at least temporary breakdown now and then, at least in principle. We know that we may come across situations where we have to make ad hoc maneuvers, or shrug our shoulders, depending on what is as stake.

If such cases start coming up with alarming frequency, in situations where it matters, then we can consider the massive revisions to logic to keep truth simple, and we can consider the ways to restrict the truth-predicate to keep the logic simple. And then we can decide which batch of sharpenings to adopt, in order to get past whatever crisis has emerged. But is there a theoretical crisis now? Is something broke, that our theory of truth can fix?

The situation is roughly analogous to the development of the calculus, where, for centuries, mathematicians were, for the most part, content to continue with the use of infinitesimals. They went on like that, relying on intuitive judgments, until they ran into trouble, getting conflicting results with cases that mattered. They got to a point, in the normal pursuit of their mathematical goals, where they didn't know how to go on, perhaps because their intuitions on how to deploy infinitesimals were no longer reliable. When that happened, Cauchy, Weierstrass, et al. righted the ship. Before the trouble ensued, however, there was little internal pressure to revise their framework, trenchant criticisms from the likes of Bishop Berkeley notwithstanding.

With truth, however, there arguably is no such crisis. Pending an argument to the contrary, I submit that we are better off adopting the underlying theme of Chihara (1979), that the proposed cures are worse than the disease. At least for the Field-style deflationist, at least for the present.

ACKNOWLEDGMENTS: Thanks to the participants on a workshop on paradox and revision, held at the Foundations of Logical Consequence project of the Arché Research Centre, University of St. Andrews, in March of 2011; and a similar event at the Munich Center for Mathematical Philosophy, July 2012.

Thanks especially to Kevin Scharp for discussing these matters with me and for giving valuable feedback. And to two anonymous referees of a previous version of this paper.

# BIBLIOGRAPHY

Beall, J. (2009). *Spandrels of Truh*. Oxford University Press, Oxford.

Burgess, J. (1992). Proofs about proofs: A defense of classical logic. In Detlefsen, M., editor, *Proof, logic and formalization*, pages 8–23. Routledge Publishing Company.

Chihara, C. (1979). The semantic paradoxes: a diagnostic investigation. *Philosophical Review*, 88(4):590–618.

Chihara, C. (1984). The semantic paradoxes: some second thoughts. *Philosophical Studies*, 45:223–229.

Dummett, M. A. E. (1973). The philosophical basis of intuitionistic logic. In *Truth and Other Enigmas*. Duckworth, London.

Eklund, M. (2002). Inconsistent languages. *Philosophy and Phenomenological Research*, 64:251–275.

Field, H. (1994). Disquotational truth and factually defective discourse. *Philosophical Review*, 103:405–452.

Field, H. (2006). Truth and the unprovability of consistency. *Mind*, 115:567–606.

Field, H. (2008). *Saving Truth from Paradox*. Oxford University Press, Oxford.

Field, H. (2009a). Pluralism in logic. *Review of Symbolic Logic*, 2:342–359.

Field, H. (2009b). What is the normative role of logic? *Proceedings of the Aristotelian Society, Supplementary*, 83:251–268.

Gupta, A. and Belnap, N. (1993). *The Revision Theory of Truth*. The MIT Press, Cambridge, MA.

Kripke, S. (1975). Outline of a theory of truth. *Journal of Philosophy*, 72:690–716.

Maddy, P. (1997). *Naturalism in Mathematics*. Oxford University Press, Oxford.

Priest, G. (1979). The logic of paradox. *Journal of Philosophical Logic*, 8:219–241.

Priest, G. (2006). *In Contradiction: A Study of the Transconsistent*. Oxford University Press, Oxford, 2nd edition.

Priest, G. (2008). *An Introduction to Non-classical Logic: From If to Is*. Cambridge University Press, Cambridge, 2nd edition.

Scharp, K. (2007a). Alethic vengeance. In Beall, J., editor, *The Liar's Revenge*. Oxford University Press, Oxford.

Scharp, K. (2007b). Replacing truth. *Inquiry*, 50(6):606–621.

Shapiro, S. (1991). *Foundations without Foundationalism: A case for Second-order Logic*. Oxford University Press, Oxford.

Shapiro, S. (2006). Computability, proof, and open-texture. In Olszewski, A., WoleN-ski, J., and Janusz, R., editors, *Church's Thesis after 70 Years*, pages 420–455. Oxford University Press, Oxford.

Tarski, A. (1933). Der warheitsbegriff in dem formalisierten sprachen. *Studia philosophica*, 1:261–405. translated as *The concept of truth in formalized languages*, in A. Tarski, *Logic, semantics and metamathematics*, Oxford, Clarendon Press; second edition, edited by John Corcoran, Indianapolis, Hackett Publishing Company, 1983, pages 152–278.

Tarski, A. (1944). The semantic conception of truth and the foundations of semantics. *Philosophy and Phenomenological Research*, 4:341–376. Repr. as The concept of truth in formalized languages, in A. Tarski, *Logic, semantics and metamathematics*, Oxford, Clarendon Press; second edition, edited by John Corcoran, Indianapolis, Hackett Publishing Company, 1983, pages 152–278.

Waismann, F. (1945). Verifiability. *Proceedings of the Aristotelian Society, Supplementary*, 19:119–150. Repr. in *Logic and language*, edited by Antony Flew, Oxford, Basil Blackwell, 1968, pages 117–144.

Waismann, F. (1949). Analytic-synthetic I. *Analysis*, 10:25–40.

Waismann, F. (1950). Analytic-synthetic II. *Analysis*, 11:25–38.

Waismann, F. (1951a). Analytic-synthetic III. *Analysis*, 11:49–61.

Waismann, F. (1951b). Analytic-synthetic IV. *Analysis*, 11:115–124.

Waismann, F. (1952). Analytic-synthetic V. *Analysis*, 13:1–14.

Waismann, F. (1953). Analytic-synthetic VI. *Analysis*, 13:73–89.

Weir, A. (1998). Naïve set theory is innocent. *Mind*, 107:763–798.

Weir, A. (2005). Naïve truth and sophisticated logic. In Armour-Garb and Beall, J., editors, *Deflationism and paradox*, pages 218–249. Oxford University Press, Oxford.

Wilson, M. (2006). *Wandering Significance*. Oxford University Press, Oxford.

# Necessity- and Possibility-syllogisms in Avicenna and Ṭūsī

PAUL THOM[†]

Avicenna holds a special interest for historians of modal logic because of his inventions in modal syllogistic, and the critical attention later Arabic logicians devoted to them. One of those later logicians, Naṣīr ad-Dīn aṭ-Ṭūsī (d.1274), wrote a commentary on Avicenna's *Pointers and Reminders*, a commentary which Tony Street describes in a recent paper as 'probably the finest medieval interpretation of Avicenna's logic that we have' (Street, 2012). Among the numerous insights into Avicenna's logic Street finds in Ṭūsī's commentary is the view that Avicenna's propositions of necessity or possibility involve quantification over terms, and that these terms stand for natures. I want here to show how this view can be given a formal representation. I limit myself to propositions of necessity and possibility, leaving discussion of 'absolute' propositions for another time. Let us begin with Avicenna. There are 8 combinations of necessity (L) or possibility (M) propositions in the first syllogistic figure: LLL, LLM, LML, LMM, MLL, MLM, MML, MMM. Avicenna is committed to the validity of 6 of these: LLL, LLM, LML, LMM, MLM, MMM (Thom, 2003). By virtue of standard laws of modal subordination, the validity of all 6 combinations follows from that of the LML and MMM first figure moods. These are the characteristic moods of Avicenna's syllogistic, and they could not have been accepted by Aristotle because they are equivalent to moods that Aristotle has to reject. Barbara MMM and LML are equivalent to Baroco MLL and LML, which Aristotle must reject as a consequence of rejecting Baroco QLL and LQL (where Q stands for two-way possibility) (Aristotle, 2009).

In defence of Barbara MMM and Barbara LML, Avicenna writes

> But if the judgment on $B$ is by possibility (*bil-imkān*), then there is a possibility of a possibility (*imkānu imkān*). And the mind nearly knows that it is a possibility (*wahwa qaribun min an yaʿlama ḏ-dihnu annahu imkān*), for what is possibly possible (*mā yumkinu an yumkina*) is by nature near (*qaribun ʿinda ṭ-ṭabʿ*) the judgment that it is possible (*mumkin*) (Avicenna, 1984, p. 391).

> And if *every $B$ is necessarily $A$*, then the truth is that the conclusion is necessary. In the proof of that, let us set down a consideration

[†]The University of Sydney, Sydney, Australia. Email: `paul.thom@sydney.edu.au`

nearly [self-evident] (*waǧhan qarīban*), namely: If $J$ becomes $B$, it comes to be judged as having $A$ predicated of it necessarily (Avicenna, 1984, pp. 393–394).

Ṭūsī glosses the first of these passages, using a form of words that differs from Avicenna's 'possibly possible':

Take for example $J$, which is possibly that which is possibly $A$.[1]

He puts forward two principles concerning what is possible.

Everything which is not possible is impossible to be possible (*kullu mā laysa bi-mumkinin yamtaniʻu an yakūna mumkinan*).

Everything which is not impossible to be possible is possible (*kullu mā lā yamtaniʻu an yakūna mumkinan fa-hwa mumkinun*).[2]

Commenting on Avicenna's defence of Barbara LML, Ṭūsī puts forward two principles concerning what is necessary.

Everything that is not necessary by the essence is impossible to be necessary.

Everything which is not impossible to be necessary is necessarily necessary.[3]

The first principle of each pair he takes to be primary, the second following from it by contraposition.[4]

In an earlier paper I read Avicenna's defence of Barbara MMM and LML as appealing to the modal iteration principles that what is possibly possible is possible, and what is possibly necessary is necessary; and I showed that, given these principles, Barbara MMM and Barbara LML are valid (Thom, 2008a, pp. 365–367). But Street points out that Ṭūsī is not here iterating modal operators. Rather, he understands Ṭūsī's first principle regarding the possible to be saying that 'whatever is possibly what is possibly $B$ is possibly $B$' (Street, 2012, p. 45). Street has a similar understanding of Ṭūsī's first principle regarding the necessary. He asks us to consider the reasoning

$J$ is said of things which, by their nature, are not essentially $B$, whereas $A$ is said of things which are by contrast essentially $B$. So $J$ and $A$ are said of things which are essentially different.

---

[1]Ṭūsī, Solving the Problems of Pointers and Reminders 8.2; translation in Street (2012, p. 252, my italics). Ṭūsī goes on to invoke the procedure of supposing the possible actual, as a way of demonstrating the validity of Barbara MMM. I do not consider that demonstration here, as it depends on the logic of 'absolute' propositions.

[2]Ṭūsī, Solving the Problems 8.3; translation in Street (2012, p. 252).

[3]Ṭūsī, Solving the Problems 10.5; translation in Street (2012, p. 255).

[4]Ṭūsī, Solving the Problems 8.3, 10.5.

He argues

> I think Avicenna at least as read by Ṭūsī is claiming that we have
> intuitions about Natures ( ṭabā'i' ) and the essential differences that
> separate them. So we should know (it should be primary in the
> mind or a necessity) by the reasoning given above that whatever
> is not necessarily $B$ is not possibly what is necessarily $B$. If we
> accept contraposition, then a few moments further reflection should
> convince us that we also know that whatever is possibly what is
> necessarily $B$ is necessarily $B$ (Street, 2012, p. 244).

I think it is clear that when Street refers to whatever is 'possibly what is
necessarily $B$', he means that the validity of Barbara LML rests, not on an
iteration of modalities but on quantification over terms. He holds a similar
view about the validity of Barbara MMM. He finds confirmation of this view in
Ṭūsī's reference to J being 'possibly *that which* is possibly $B$'. And he takes
the terms over which these quantifications occur to stand for natures.

So, if we want to give a formal representation of Avicenna's modal syllogistic
as construed by Ṭūsī and Street, we need to represent Avicenna's modal syllogistic as a logic of terms, where these terms can stand for natures. The formal
representation that I will outline takes its inspiration from Marko Malink's
reconstruction of Aristotle's modal syllogistic (Malink, 2006).

In order to settle on a set of primitive notions for this formal representation,
let us recall how Avicenna explains what it means to say that $A$ necessarily
belongs to every $B$:

> The meaning of this is that $A$ does not separate from it at all as
> long as it exists (mā dāma mawǧūda ḏ-ḏāt ), and not that [A] does
> not separate from it only as long as it is $B$ (Avicenna, Pointers
> 393–394; translation in Street, 2012, p. 254).

So, the truth of an affirmative necessity-proposition predicating $A$ of $B$ requires that $A$ is inseparable from $B$. But Avicenna clearly thinks that $A$ can
be inseparable from $B$ in two ways. In one way, $A$ is inseparable 'as long as it
exists'; in another way it is inseparable from $B$ 'only as long as it is $B$'. Anal-
ogously, a statement to the effect that $A$ necessarily belongs to no $B$ requires
that $A$ and $B$ be incompatible. And incompatibility, like inseparability, can
occur in two ways. In one way what is $A$ and what is $B$ remain incompatible
so long as they exist; in another way, only so long as they are described as $A$
and as $B$. Evidently then, our term-logic must be able to express statements
of inseparability and incompatibility between terms.

One way of representing statements of inseparability and incompatibility is
through an analysis in a quantified modal logic: thus the statement that $A$
is inseparable from $B$ would be analysed as having the form *Necessarily for
all x, if x is B then x is A*, and a statement of incompatibility as having
the form *Necessarily for all x, if x is B then x is not A*. In my earlier paper
I read statements of inseparability and incompatibility in this way (Thom,
2008b, pp. 365–367). And in keeping with that approach, I offered an analysis

of Avicenna's necessity- and possibility-propositions in quantified modal logic, where these propositions had both internal and external modalities (so that the universal affirmative necessity-proposition has the form *Necessarily for all x, if x is B then necessarily x is A*).

However, statements of inseparability or incompatibility between two terms don't have to be understood as having the form of universal quantifications over individuals, embedded within a necessity-operator. They can be understood, more simply, as statements to the effect that a relation of inseparability or incompatibility holds directly between a pair of terms. I take it that one element in Street's proposal is that we can represent Avicenna's syllogistic of necessity- and possibility-propositions in a logic where statements of inseparability and incompatibility are analysed in this way.

A logic of terms suitable for formalising such propositions can be constructed along the following lines. The terms that are subjects and predicates of categorical propositions will be understood as expressing *conceptions*, the latter being represented by lower-case Greek letters. $\alpha$ will be taken as the conception expressed by the term '$A$', $\beta$ as the conception expressed by the term '$B$', and $\gamma$ as the conception expressed by the term '$J$'. I will use standard notations for quantification, with $\kappa$, $\lambda$, $\mu$, $\nu$ as variables ranging over conceptions. I assume primitive relations of inseparability ($\Leftarrow$) and incompatibility ($\Downarrow$) between conceptions. The relations of separability and compatibility will be notated as ($\nLeftarrow$) and ($\nDownarrow$). Thus $\kappa \Leftarrow \lambda$ means that $\kappa$ is inseparable from $\lambda$, and $\kappa \nDownarrow \lambda$ means that $\kappa$ is compatible with $\lambda$.

Thus far, we have not addressed Avicenna's distinction between the two kinds of inseparability, or Street's idea of a nature. I think both can be handled in the following way. Implicit in Avicenna's account of the truth-conditions of necessity-propositions is a distinction between the stated subject and the underlying subject. In saying that every $B$ is of necessity $A$, we are saying something about the subject underlying the stated subject $B$. But we may be saying one of two different things. We may be saying that $A$ (or what $A$ expresses) is inseparable from the subject underlying $B$, so long as that subject exists, whether or not it continues to be $B$. Or we may be saying that $A$ (or what $A$ expresses) is inseparable from the subject underlying $B$, only so long as that subject continues to be $B$. The stated subject may be separable from the underlying subject. Consider the statement *Everyone who is writing is of necessity moving*. Movement is inseparable from a person as underlying subject so long as the person is writing, but it is separable from the person doing the writing because the person can continue to exist while not writing. Alternatively, the stated subject may be inseparable from the underlying subject. Consider the statement *Every person is of necessity a body*. Being a person is inseparable from a person so long as the person exists. Terms of this latter type are familiar from Aristotelian physics and metaphysics: they are, or express, essences (*i.e.*, Aristotelian genera, species or differentiae). Avicenna's truth-conditions for necessity-propositions implicitly distinguish such terms as a sub-class within the wider class of terms.

I will write the statement that a conception $\kappa$ is an essence: $E\kappa$. I take the notion of an essence as primitive.

Let us now consider whether plausible truth-conditions for necessity- and possibility-propositions can be stated using only the notions of inseparability, incompatibility and essence. Plausibility requires the satisfaction of at least three constraints. First, the truth-conditions must fit Avicenna's examples of true modal propositions. Second, they must preserve the relations of modal subordination between necessity- and possibility-propositions, so that a necessity-proposition of a given quality and quantity must entail the corresponding possibility-proposition of the same quality and quantity. And third, they must preserve the standard relations of equipollence linking affirmative necessities with negative possibilities, and affirmative possibilities with negative necessities. Avicenna accepts both of the latter constraints (Avicenna, 1984, p. 95).

Naǧm ad-Dīn al-Kātibī (d.1277) took universal affirmative unmodalised predications, when read 'according to the essence', to mean that everything that is an implicant of the subject is an implicant of the predicate (Street, 2012, p. 236). In a term logic based on inseparability, incompatibility and essences, this would amount to saying that the conception expressed by the predicate is inseparable from every conception from which the conception expressed by the subject is inseparable.[5] In the case of universal affirmative predications of substantial necessity, the meaning would be that the predicate-conception is inseparable from every *essence* from which the subject-conception is inseparable. But such an analysis does not fit Avicenna's examples of true predications of substantial necessity. Avicenna denies the proposition *Everything moving is necessarily changing* is a true necessity-proposition in the substantial sense he is concerned with (Avicenna, 1984, p. 266; Street, 2002, p. 133). And yet, *changing* is inseparable from every essence from which *moving* is inseparable.

As an alternative, we might take the universal affirmative necessity-proposition *Every B is by necessity A* to mean that $\alpha$ is inseparable from every essence with which $\beta$ is compatible. But again, this analysis does not fit Avicenna's examples of true modal propositions. He takes the proposition *Man is necessarily a rational body to be true* (Avicenna, 1984, p. 265; Street, 2002, p. 133). But it is not true that *rational body* is inseparable from every essence with which *man* is compatible, because a higher-level essence such as *animal* is compatible with *man* but *rational body* is not inseparable from *animal* since there are non-rational animals.

So, let us suppose that when we say that every $B$ is necessarily, or possibly, $A$, we are talking, not about every essence, but about every *nature* with which $B$ is compatible. In order to avoid the above problem about higher-level essences, we need to define a notion of nature narrower than the notion of an essence. This can be done as follows. $\kappa$ is a nature if and only if it is an essence that is inseparable from every essence which is inseparable from it.

D1. $N\kappa$ iff $E\kappa \wedge \forall\lambda[E\lambda \supset (\lambda \Leftarrow \kappa \supset \kappa \Leftarrow \lambda)]$

A nature is a most specific essence. I suggest that this is the notion that Street is employing when he says that Avicenna, as read by Ṭūsī, is claiming that in doing modal logic we rely on insights about natures.

---

[5]For difficulties with this kind of analysis, see Thom (2010).

Using D1, we can give necessity-propositions truth-conditions of the general form *A is inseparable from/incompatible with every/some nature compatible with B.*

Universal affirmative necessity: $\forall\kappa[N\kappa \supset (\beta \not\Downarrow \kappa \supset \alpha \Leftarrow \kappa)]$. It is then true, as Avicenna says, that every man is by necessity a rational body. Every nature compatible with *man* is such that *rational body* is inseparable from it.

Universal negative necessity: $\forall\kappa[N\kappa \supset (\beta \not\Downarrow \kappa \supset \alpha \Downarrow \kappa)]$. The universal negative necessity-proposition is clearly convertible, just as Avicenna says (Avicenna, 1984, p. 334; Street, 2002, p. 158). If every nature compatible with $\beta$ is incompatible with $\alpha$ then every nature compatible with $\alpha$ is incompatible with $\beta$.

Particular affirmative necessity: $\exists\kappa[N\kappa \wedge \beta \not\Downarrow \kappa \wedge \alpha \Leftarrow \kappa]$. The particular affirmative necessity-proposition is not convertible, nor does the universal affirmative necessity-proposition entail the corresponding particular with terms reversed. This is Avicenna's view, and he shows it by reference to the propositions *By necessity every laugher is a man and By necessity some man is a laugher* (Avicenna, 1984, p. 336). He takes the first to be true and the second false. These results fit our truth-conditions for the universal and particular affirmative necessity-propositions. *Man* is inseparable from every nature with which *laugher* is compatible (because the only such nature is *man* itself), but no nature compatible with *man* is such that *laugher* is inseparable from it.

The universal affirmative necessity-proposition needs to entail the particular affirmative necessity-proposition. It does not do so, given the above truth-conditions. But this problem can be resolved by adopting the following assumption.

A1. $\forall\kappa\exists\lambda[N\lambda \wedge \lambda \not\Downarrow \kappa]$

This states that for every conception there is a nature that is compatible with it. I am not aware of any text in which Avicenna asserts this, but it seems a reasonable assumption for anyone to make who believes that there are natures, provided they are prepared to exclude internally inconsistent conceptions from consideration. Such conceptions would have to be excluded because they are incompatible with every nature. For an Aristotelian, any internally consistent conception is compatible with some nature, because any such conception either is a species, differentia or genus, or is paronymous (like *writer*), or is a compound (like *writing animal*); and in each of these cases it is compatible with some nature.

Particular negative necessity: $\exists\kappa[N\kappa \wedge \beta \not\Downarrow \kappa \wedge \alpha \Downarrow \kappa]$. Avicenna considers the propositions *By necessity, not every animal is a man* (which he takes to be true) and *By necessity not every man is an animal* (which he takes to be false, Avicenna, 1984, p. 337; Street, 2002, p. 144). The first of these comes out as true on our truth-condition because there is a nature, *e.g.*, *horse* which is compatible with *animal* but is incompatible with *man*; but the second does not, since no nature compatible with man is incompatible with *animal*. The particular negative necessity is implied by the corresponding universal, given A1.

Because possibility-propositions need to be contradictory to necessity-propositions of opposite quality and quantity, they will have the following truth-conditions.

Universal affirmative possibility: $\forall\kappa\left[N\kappa \supset (\beta \not\Downarrow \kappa \supset \alpha \not\Downarrow \kappa)\right]$

Universal negative possibility: $\forall\kappa\left[N\kappa \supset (\beta \not\Downarrow \kappa \supset \alpha \not\Leftarrow \kappa)\right]$

Particular affirmative possibility: $\exists\kappa\left[N\kappa \wedge (\beta \not\Downarrow \kappa \wedge \alpha \not\Downarrow \kappa)\right]$

Particular negative possibility: $\exists\kappa\left[N\kappa \wedge (\beta \not\Downarrow \kappa \wedge \alpha \not\Leftarrow \kappa)\right]$

he modal subordination of possibility-propositions to the corresponding necessities of the same quality and quantity holds, given the following assumption

A2. $\kappa \Leftarrow \lambda \supset \kappa \not\Downarrow \lambda$

This assumption holds, given the restriction to internally consistent terms.

Given our truth-condition for universal affirmative possibilities, Barbara MMM is clearly valid. If every nature compatible with the conception expressed by the minor term is compatible with the conception expressed by the middle, and every nature compatible with the conception expressed by the middle is compatible with the conception expressed by the major, then every nature compatible with the conception expressed by the minor is compatible with the conception expressed by the major.

Ṭūsī principle for Barbara MMM can be expressed thus: All of anything, all of which is possibly something that is possibly $A$, is possibly $A$. Formally:

$$\exists\beta\Big\{\forall\kappa\left[N\kappa \supset (\gamma \not\Downarrow \kappa \supset \beta \not\Downarrow \kappa)\right] \wedge \forall\kappa\left[N\kappa \supset (\beta \not\Downarrow \kappa \supset \alpha \not\Downarrow \kappa)\right]\Big\}$$
$$\supset \forall\kappa\left[N\kappa \supset (\gamma \not\Downarrow \kappa \supset \alpha \not\Downarrow \kappa)\right]$$

His equivalent principle for Bocardo LML can be obtained from this by contraposing antecedent and consequent.

Barbara LML is also valid, given our truth-conditions for universal affirmative necessities and possibilities. If every nature compatible with the minor-conception is compatible with the middle, and every nature compatible with the middle is such that the major-conception is inseparable from it, then every nature compatible with the minor-conception is such that the major-conception is inseparable from it.

Ṭūsī's principle for this mood can be expressed thus: All of anything, all of which is possibly something that is necessarily A, is necessarily A. Formally:

$$\exists\beta\Big\{\forall\kappa\left[N\kappa \supset (\gamma \not\Downarrow \kappa \supset \kappa \not\Downarrow \beta)\right] \wedge \forall\kappa\left[N\kappa \supset (\beta \not\Downarrow \kappa \supset \kappa \Leftarrow \alpha)\right]\Big\}$$
$$\supset \forall\kappa\left[N\kappa \supset (\gamma \not\Downarrow \kappa \supset \kappa \Leftarrow \alpha)\right]$$

His equivalent principle for Baroco MMM can be obtained from this by contraposition.

Celarent MMM is valid. If every nature compatible with the minor-conception is compatible with the middle, and the major-conception is separable from every nature compatible with the middle, then the major-conception is separable from every nature compatible with the minor. Similarly for Darii MMM and Ferio MMM.

In securing the validity of Barbara MMM and Barbara LML relative to the above truth-conditions, we have relied on a bare minimum of assumptions about inseparability and incompatibility, namely A2. In particular, we made no use of logical features of these relations such as the reflexivity or transitivity of inseparability, the symmetry of incompatibility, or the principle that to be incompatible with what is inseparable from a conception is to be incompatible with it:

A3. $\kappa \Leftarrow \kappa$

A4. $(\kappa \Leftarrow \lambda \wedge \lambda \Leftarrow \mu) \supset \kappa \Leftarrow \mu$

A5. $\kappa \Downarrow \lambda \supset \lambda \Downarrow \kappa$

A6. $(\kappa \Downarrow \lambda \wedge \lambda \Leftarrow \mu) \supset \kappa \Downarrow \mu$

Furthermore, we have not relied on any special assumptions about essences and natures other than A1 and D1. We have used a semantics of terms that is based on primitive relations of inseparability and compatibility between conceptions, and a primitive notion of essence. In this semantics, natures are defined as most specific essences (D1), and we have assumed that every conception is compatible with some nature (A1). If the language contains any terms at all then, by virtue of A1, there exists at least one nature. This gives a precise sense to Street's statement that Avicenna's modal logic (as understood by Ṭūsī) is based on insights about natures and the essential differences that separate them.

The required insights are thus extremely modest in their extent. We have not assumed, as Aristotelians often do, that essences can only be related by inseparability or incompatibility:

A7. $(E\kappa \wedge E\lambda) \supset (\kappa \Leftarrow \lambda \vee \lambda \Leftarrow \kappa \vee \kappa \Downarrow \lambda)$

Nor have we assumed any of the quasi-mereological properties that Aristotelians might take to characterise the structure of essences or natures. Those properties include

**Supplementation** $(E\kappa \wedge E\lambda \wedge \kappa \Leftarrow \lambda \wedge \lambda \not\Leftarrow \kappa) \supset \exists\mu[E\mu \wedge \kappa \Leftarrow \mu \wedge \mu \Downarrow \lambda]$

If one essence falls under a second which doesn't fall under it, then there is a third essence that falls under the second and is incompatible with the first. Thus, *man* falls under *animal*, and there is a third essence, *e.g.*, *horse*, that falls under *animal* and is incompatible with *man*.

They also include

**Atomicity** $E\kappa \supset \exists\lambda[N\lambda \wedge \kappa \Leftarrow \lambda]$

Natures are the 'atoms' among essences (Aristotle's word for them being *atoma*; Aristotle, Categories 2, 2b6), so that any essence is inseparable from a nature.[6]

The semantics proposed here for Avicenna's logic of necessity- and possibility-propositions does not require the acceptance of any of these Aristotelian ideas about the structuring of essences and natures; but it is compatible with any or all of them. It is also compatible with non-Aristotelian ideas about that structuring—for example, with a Parmenidean metaphysics in which there exists only one nature, a nature which is compatible with all conceptions.

This paper has had limited aims. Further research along these lines might try to see how far the ideas presented here can be adapted to cover Avicenna's 'absolute' propositions and the associated procedure of 'supposing the possible actual'. It might also investigate the extent to which these ideas can be applied to Avicenna's logical writings other than *Pointers* and *Reminders*, and to the theories of other logicians.[7]

# BIBLIOGRAPHY

Aristotle (1963). *Categories and De Interpretatione.* Translated with notes by J.L. Ackrill. Clarendon Press, Oxford.

Aristotle (2009). *Prior Analytics Book I.* Translated with an introduction and commentary by Gisela Striker. Clarendon Press, Oxford.

Avicenna (1984). *Remarks and Admonitions [= Pointers and Reminders].* Translated from the original Arabic with an introduction and notes by Shams Constantine Inati. Pontifical Institute of Mediaeval Studies, Toronto.

Malink, M. (2006). A reconstruction of Aristotle's modal syllogistic. *History and Philosophy of Logic,* 27:95–141.

Street, T. (2002). An outline of Avicenna's syllogistic. *Archiv für Geschichte der Philosophie,* 84(2):129–160.

Street, T. (2012). Medieval and modern interpretations of Avicenna's modal syllogistic. In Opwis, F. and Reisman, D., editors, *Islamic Philosophy, Science, Culture, and Religion,* pages 233–255. Brill, Leiden.

Thom, P. (2003). *Medieval Modal Systems: Problems and Concepts.* Ashgate Publishing, Aldershot.

Thom, P. (2008a). Al-Fārābī on indefinite and privative names. *Arabic Sciences and Philosophy,* 18:193–209.

Thom, P. (2008b). Logic and metaphysics in Avicenna's modal syllogistic. In Rahman, S., Street, T., and Tahiri, H., editors, *The Unity of Science in the Arabic Tradition,* pages 361–376. Springer Publishing Company, New York.

Thom, P. (2010). Abhari on the logic of conjunctive terms. *Arabic Sciences and Philosophy,* 20:105–117.

Varzi, A. (2011). Mereology. In Zalta, E., editor, *The Stanford Encyclopedia of Philosophy.* The Metaphysics Research Lab, spring 2011 edition.

---

[6]For the mereological principles on which these assumptions are modelled (see Varzi, 2011).

[7]I thank Tony Street and Riccardo Strobino for their kind help in clarifying my thoughts on this topic.

# Truth Preservation in Context and in Its Place

ELIA ZARDINI[†] [‡]

ABSTRACT. I show that context dependence generates dramatic failures of necessitation and transparency that in turn bring about substantial failures of the principle according to which logical consequence requires metaphysically necessary truth preservation. To accommodate for the failures of necessitation, I recommend as an alternative modally strong principle one according to which logical consequence requires semantically necessary truth preservation, and I note in passing an important anti-deflationist consequence of preferring the latter principle to the former. I stress however that even the latter principle has a range of application limited by the failures of transparency. Against a deeply entrenched assumption, consideration of context dependence and other vagaries of our uses of language thus brings a sobering appreciation of substantial gaps between logical consequence and the preservation of truth.

[†]LOGOS, Logic, Language and Cognition Research Group, Department of Logic, History and Philosophy of Science, University of Barcelona, Spain. Email: elia.zardini@ub.edu.

[‡]Earlier versions of the material in this paper have been presented in 2006 at the Friday Seminar (University of St Andrews), where Sujan Riyadh gave a valuable response; in 2008, at the Arché Philosophy of Logic Seminar (University of St Andrews); in 2010, at the 3rd Arché Foundations of Logical Consequence Workshop on *Propositions, Context and Consequence* (University of St Andrews); in 2011, at the PETAF Mid-Term Conference (University of Aberdeen) and at the COGITO Philosophy of Language Seminar (University of Bologna). I'd like to thank all these audiences for very stimulating comments and discussions (and Stephen Read for heroically attending on all these occasions save for the last one). Special thanks go to Dan López de Sa, Sebastiano Moruzzi, Julien Murzi, Eugenio Orlandelli, Peter Pagin, Jim Pryor, François Recanati, Sven Rosenkranz, Marcus Rossberg, Isidora Stojanović and Crispin Wright. I'm also grateful to the editors Catarina Dutilh Novaes and Ole Hjortland for conceiving this volume, inviting me to contribute to it and seeing through its production. Most importantly, I'd like to acknowledge here a very special debt to Stephen Read which goes far beyond his help with this paper. With his teaching, mentoring and research, Steve has had a major influence on my formation in philosophy of logic during my doctoral and postdoctoral work in St Andrews. His philosophical acumen, passion, thoroughness and honesty—as all these struck me most especially during the memorable seminars in medieval logic on St Andrews' *rive gauche*, sometimes leading in my imagination to a merge of Steve's figure with that of his beloved *doctor profundus*—have been a constant source of inspiration throughout the years. In writing the paper, I have benefitted, at different stages, from a RIP Jacobsen Fellowship, an AHRC Postdoctoral Research Fellowship and the FP7 Marie Curie Intra-European Fellowship 301493 with project on *A Non-Contractive Theory of Naive Semantic Properties: Logical Developments and Metaphysical Foundations* (NTNSP), as well as from partial funds from the project FFI2008-06153 of the Spanish Ministry of Science and Innovation on *Vagueness and Physics, Metaphysics, and Metametaphysics*, from the project FFI2011-25626 of the Spanish Ministry of Science and Innovation on *Reference, Self-Reference and Empirical Data*, from the project CONSOLIDER-INGENIO 2010 CSD2009-00056 of the Spanish Ministry of Science and Innovation on *Philosophy of Perspectival Thoughts and Facts* (PERSP) and from the FP7 Marie Curie Initial Training Network 238128 on *Perspectival Thoughts and Facts* (PETAF).

# 1  The Traditional Link between Logical Consequence and Necessary Truth Preservation

Patently, certain conclusions can logically follow[1] from certain premises even if some or all of the premises are false, and even if some or all of the conclusions are false. However, can it ever be that certain conclusions logically follow from certain premises whilst all of the premises are true and all of the conclusions false? In other (possibly non-equivalent) words, is it always the case that the fact that certain conclusions logically follow from certain premises implies that, if all of the premises are true, then some of the conclusions are also true? What is, more generally, the relation between logical consequence and the *preservation of truth*?

It is fair to say that it is a well-worn philosophical idea that logical consequence is indeed *intimately linked* with necessary truth preservation. In fact, necessary truth preservation is quite often assumed to be what logical consequence *consists in*. In one of the most influential papers in 20th-century logic and philosophy, Alfred Tarski identified in necessary truth preservation one of the central features of the notion of logical consequence. He set up his model-theoretic account of logical consequence in order to come as close as possible to capturing this feature in the systematic framework of his theory of truth:

> Consider any class $K$ of sentences and a sentence $X$ which follows from the sentences of this class. From an intuitive standpoint it can never happen that both the class $K$ consists only of true sentences and the sentence $X$ is false [...] It seems to me that everyone who understands the content of the above definition [the definition of logical consequence in terms of truth preservation in every model, EZ] must admit that it agrees quite well with common usage. This becomes still clearer from its various consequences. In particular, it can be proved, on the basis of this definition, that every consequence of true sentences must be true [...] (Tarski, 1936, pp. 414, 417).

More than half a century later, the assumption that necessary truth preservation is what logical consequence consists in has become part of the philosophical lore, so much so that it is freely used to force controversial philosophical moves. Here is Timothy Williamson using the slogan that logical consequence is necessary truth preservation to force supervaluationist approaches to vagueness to adopt (what is in certain respects) a non-classical logic:

> The problem for supervaluationists is that supertruth plays no role in the definition of local validity. Yet they identify truth with supertruth; since validity is necessary preservation of truth, they should identify it with necessary preservation of supertruth (Williamson, 1994, p. 148).

---

[1] Throughout, I use '*logically follow from*' and its relatives to denote the relation of logical consequence, '*entail*' and its relatives to denote the converse relation and '*implication*' and its relatives to denote the operation expressed by an ordinary conditional. '*Equivalence*' and its relatives denote two-way entailment.

The deep entrenchment of the assumption is also signaled by its being presented as one of the (few) uncontroversial starting points in contemporary surveys of philosophy of logic. This is witnessed for example by the following passage of Susan Haack's:

> What is going on, though, when one judges an informal argument to be valid? One is claiming, I take it, that its conclusion *follows from* its premises, that *its premises couldn't be true and its conclusion false* (Haack, 1978, p. 14).

Thus, Stephen Read is connecting to a solid tradition when, in an illuminating article on material consequence, he states:

> An argument is valid if and only if there is no possible situation where the premises are true and the conclusion false (Read, 1994, p. 256).[2]

In this paper, I'd like to cast some doubts on this traditional wisdom. As Read's quoted statement makes clear, the assumption that necessary truth preservation is what logical consequence consists in at least implies a *two-way link* that can in turn naturally be split into *two complementary claims*:

(SUFF) Necessary truth preservation *implies* logical consequence;

(NEC) Necessary truth preservation *is implied by* logical consequence,

on which we'll henceforth focus. I'm actually sympathetic to the *spirit* of both (SUFF) and (NEC), but also happen to think that, in both cases, such spirit, when properly understood, does not licence anything close to such *unrestricted* claims as (SUFF) and (NEC) implicitly are. In this paper, I'd like to exemplify this overall stance of mine with respect to (NEC), arguing that, in the presence of *context dependence*, (NEC) *requires some substantial qualifications*. Between (SUFF) and (NEC), it is rather the former that has sometimes been explicitly put into question (for example, because of certain concerns about relevance, to which Read, 2003, offers an interesting reply). Focussing on (NEC), I'm thus going to attack the traditional link between logical consequence and necessary truth preservation where it has usually been taken to be at its strongest.

## 2  Necessary Truth Preservation and the Naive Argument

Let's first get a bit clearer about what necessary truth preservation exactly amounts to. Arguably, several interestingly different notions have some claim to spell out at least *a* notion of "necessary truth preservation", but for our purposes it'll be best to say that an argument from $\varphi_0$, $\varphi_1$, $\varphi_2$... to $\psi_0$, $\psi_1$, $\psi_2$... preserves truth iff the *material conditional* 'If all of '$\varphi_0$', '$\varphi_1$', '$\varphi_2$'... are

---

[2]The linguistic succinctness of this statement should not obscure its conceptual richness: see for example Read (2003) for an insightful discussion of an important dimension of complexity concealed in the statement.

true, then some of '$\psi_0$', '$\psi_1$', '$\psi_2$'... are true' holds, and then focus on *necessary* truth preservation, where in turn, until section 8, the operative notion of necessity will be the very natural and usual one of *metaphysical* necessity: the necessity that concerns the ways *things could not have failed to be*. We thus obtain the following (provisional) sharpening of (NEC):

(MNEC⁻) If $\varphi_0$, $\varphi_1$, $\varphi_2$... entail $\psi_0$, $\psi_1$, $\psi_2$..., then, metaphysically necessarily, if all of $\varphi_0$, $\varphi_1$, $\varphi_2$... are true, then some of $\psi_0$, $\psi_1$, $\psi_2$... are true.[3]

Now, one gets easily tempted into (MNEC⁻) and, more generally, (NEC) by the following abstract argument (which I'll henceforth call 'the *Naive Argument*'; see Field, 2008, pp. 42–43 for a very similar argument). Suppose that $\varphi$ entails $\psi$.[4] Then, by the *deduction theorem*, the conditional 'If $\varphi$, then $\psi$' is valid. Hence, by *necessitation*, 'Metaphysically necessarily, if $\varphi$, then $\psi$' is valid too. By the *transparency* principle according to which $\varphi$ is fully intersubstitutable with ''$\varphi$' is true', that implies that 'Metaphysically necessarily, if ''$\varphi$' is true, then '$\psi$' is true' is also valid, and so, descending from '$P$''s being valid to its being the case that $P$, that, metaphysically necessarily, if $\varphi$ is true, then $\psi$ is true. (MNEC⁻) follows.

Since the Naive Argument relies on the deduction theorem, necessitation and transparency (the last one coupled with the related principle of descent from '$P$''s being valid to its being the case that $P$, see fn 26), it is only as plausible as the conjunction of these is. In this paper, the deduction theorem will be taken for granted[5] and the focus will be on how the vagaries of context dependence generate dramatic failures of necessitation (section 5) and transparency

---

[3]For all their vagueness, while (MNEC⁻) is more naturally understood as being a *schema* (NEC) is more naturally understood as being a full-blooded *universal generalisation*. However, important as it may be in other contexts, this difference is completely immaterial for our purposes, and so will henceforth be ignored.

[4]Our discussion does cover *multiple-premise* and *multiple-conclusion* arguments. However, in some cases it'll make for a more compact and less distracting presentation to focus on *single-premise* and *single-conclusion* arguments, as happens in the text. In all such cases, the discussion is meant to extend in the natural way to multiple-premise and multiple-conclusion arguments.

[5]As it should, I think. Recent discussions on the semantic paradoxes have focussed a lot on the fact that, in some prominent non-classical theories of truth (roughly, *naive non-substructural* theories), the deduction theorem fails and (NEC) is actually inconsistent (see Field, 2006). Puzzlingly enough, I've sometimes heard in conversation people hijacking this fact in order to argue that (NEC) fails, rather than—more correctly, it seems to me—taking the fact to point to the inadequacy of those non-classical theories. (A *naive substructural* theory that validates both the deduction theorem and a version of (NEC) without 'necessary' is variously developed in Zardini, 2011; Zardini, 2012c,d,e,f,g). Of course, I myself am going to argue that (NEC) and, in particular, (MNEC⁻) fail. However, the extent of failure that I envisage for (NEC) is importantly *smaller* than the one envisaged by the non-classical theories in question. Some of my points against (NEC) and, in particular, (MNEC⁻) (in section 5) will rely on certain valid arguments that crucially involve *intensional context-dependent* expressions and that fail *metaphysically necessarily* to preserve truth while still preserving truth *in the actual world at the present time*, whereas those non-classical theories are committed to there being valid arguments that only involve *extensional non-context-dependent* expressions and that nevertheless even fail to preserve truth *in the actual world at the present time*. My other points against (NEC) (in sections 6 and 7) will rely on valid arguments that crucially involve *context-dependent* expressions (or crucially involve sentences *utterances of which do not express propositions*) and that fail to preserve truth in the actual world at the present time, whereas those non-classical theories are committed to there being valid arguments that

(sections 6 and 7) that in turn bring about substantial failures of (MNEC$^-$) and, more generally, (NEC).

## 3  Context Dependence

Before moving on to substantiating that claim, it'll be helpful to have some background on context dependence, although for lack of space I'll have to presuppose some minimal familiarity with *two-dimensional semantics* and its applications in philosophy of language and linguistics, including some of its recent relativistic extensions (see Kaplan, 1989, for a standard reference on two-dimensional semantics and MacFarlane, 2003, for a seminal paper on its relativistic extensions). Say that a (syntactically individuated) expression $\varepsilon$ is *context dependent* iff, for some contexts $C_0$, $C_1$, $C_2$ and $C_3$, the *extension* of $\varepsilon$ as uttered with $C_0$ is *correctly assessed at $C_1$ to be $X$* while the extension of $\varepsilon$ as uttered with $C_2$ is correctly assessed at $C_3$ not to be $X$. I'll assume a standard view of circumstances of evaluation and contexts as *sequences* of objects. A *circumstance of evaluation* comprises a world, and maybe more (a time, an agent, a place etc.). A *context* contains everything a circumstance of evaluation contains, and maybe more (a time, an agent, a place, some *demonstrata* etc.). Each context $C$ thus determines a circumstance of evaluation $E_C$. I don't always assume that the context an utterance *has* or is *with* (*i.e.* the one that is *semantically relevant* for interpreting it) is the one *in* which the utterance *is made* (this last issue will become relevant in section 6).

Contemporary wisdom in philosophy of language distinguishes *at least* four ways in which the extension of an expression $\varepsilon$ may vary across contexts. Suppose that it is in fact the case that, for some contexts $C_0$, $C_1$, $C_2$ and $C_3$, the extension of $\varepsilon$ as uttered with $C_0$ is correctly assessed at $C_1$ to be $X$ while the extension of $\varepsilon$ as uttered with $C_2$ is correctly assessed at $C_3$ not to be $X$. There are at least four views about how that fact is best understood:

(SC)  For the *standard contextualist*, that fact holds in virtue of $\varepsilon$ as uttered with $C_0$ expressing a content different from that expressed by $\varepsilon$ as uttered with $C_2$;

(NC)  For the *non-indexical contextualist*, that fact holds rather in virtue of $\varepsilon$ as uttered with $C_0$ and as uttered with $C_2$ expressing a single content that $\varepsilon$ as uttered with $C_0$ brings to bear on a circumstance of evaluation different from that on which $\varepsilon$ as uttered with $C_2$ brings it to bear;

(TR)  For the *truth relativist*, that fact holds rather in virtue of $\varepsilon$ as uttered with $C_0$ and as uttered with $C_2$ expressing a single content that is correctly assessed at $C_1$ to determine $X$ as extension and correctly assessed at $C_3$ not to determine $X$ as extension;

(CR)  For the *content relativist*, that fact holds rather in virtue of $\varepsilon$ as uttered with $C_0$ and as uttered with $C_2$ being correctly assessed at $C_1$ to express

only involve *non-context-dependent* expressions (or only involve sentences *utterances of which express propositions*) and that nevertheless fail to preserve truth in the actual world at the present time.

a single content different from the single content which they are correctly assessed at $C_3$ to express.

In some of the arguments to follow, I'll have to make some (plausible) assumptions about this debate with respect to certain context-dependent expressions (see fns 13, 14, 19 and 23).[6]

## 4   Necessary Truth Preservation and Context Dependence

Until section 9, relying on work done in Zardini (2012a) I'm assuming that both logical-consequence bearers and truth bearers are *linguistic* entities. Moreover, again relying on work done in Zardini (2012a), I'm taking *sentences* to be the linguistic *logical-consequence bearers*. However, with a context-dependent language, it is widely acknowledged that the linguistic *truth bearers* are *utterances* (see Zardini, 2008, pp. 545–546; the alert reader will have noticed that something like that view was already being implicitly presupposed in the last section). There are very different ways of understanding what utterances exactly are: under one understanding, they are *concrete speech acts* (see Zardini, 2012i for a defence of the claim that utterances should be so understood if they are to serve as absolute truth bearers for a context-dependent language); under another understanding, they are *concrete sentence tokens*; under yet another understanding, they are *abstract sentence-context pairs*. Fortunately, all the arguments to follow will ultimately be neutral on exactly what to understand utterances to be, although, for reasons that will become clear shortly (see especially fn 9), in the presentation I'll assume them to be abstract sentence-context pairs (even if this is probably a simplification, see fn 25). I sometimes refer to utterances more neutrally with such phrases as 'utterance $u$ with context $C$' and 'sentence '$\varphi$' as uttered with context $C$'. I'll briefly comment in section 9 on how the arguments in this paper pan out if we consider instead *non-linguistic* logical-consequence bearers and truth bearers (such as propositions).

Thus, while sentences are the logical-consequence bearers, it is utterances that are the truth bearers. This fundamental metaphysical difference creates an initial problem for (NEC), since it is sentences that logically follow from sentences, but it is utterances that necessarily preserve the truth of utterances. In other words, (NEC) (as well as (SUFF)) suffers from an important *mismatch* between the kind of entity over which *logical consequence* operates and the kind of entity over which *necessary truth preservation* operates. This is an early and perhaps surprising indication that, in the presence of context dependence, contrary to the traditional wisdom there is no straightforward link between logical consequence and necessary truth preservation.

Still, there are some natural proposals for bridging the metaphysical gap between the logical-consequence bearers and the truth bearers. Notice that utterances are very similar to sentences, the only relevant difference being that utterances *have a particular context* (this is made vivid especially by the un-

---

[6]I should note that, while the inclusion of some relativistic extensions of two-dimensional semantics is useful in order to place our discussion in the right perspective, it'll turn out that the assumptions I'll have to make do not require relativism in the sense of (TR) or (CR).

derstanding of utterances that identifies them with sentence-context pairs). So we would be able to go from sentences (the realm of logical consequence) to utterances (the realm of necessary truth preservation) if only we could associate sentences with a particular context. But which one?

Here the Naive Argument, and in particular its reliance on transparency, gives us an important clue. It is a familiar point that, in the presence of context dependence, neither utterance truth nor sentential truth are in any way transparent. For example, if I am hungry, it does not follow that your *utterance* of the sentence 'I am hungry' is true—you might well not be hungry, in which case your utterance would be false. It is not even clear whether and in what sense it follows that the *sentence* 'I am hungry' is true—if I am hungry and you are not hungry why should the sentence 'I am hungry' give more weight to my hunger than to your satiety (see Zardini, 2008, pp. 545–561; Zardini, 2012h,i)? Since the Naive Argument relies on transparency, in its original version it simply breaks down in the presence of context dependence.

However, even in the presence of context dependence, utterance truth seems[7] to remain transparent for utterances *with this very same context* (*i.e.*, roughly, the context of my writing this paper, which I'll henceforth refer to with '$I$'). At least, this seems to be the case if—as is natural and as we'll do throughout—one understands the *relativised* notion of *utterance truth at a circumstance of evaluation* as:

($T_{at}^{E}$)  An utterance $\langle \varphi, C \rangle$ is true at a circumstance of evaluation $E$ iff the proposition expressed by $\varphi$ at $C$ holds at $E$

and if—as is fairly natural and as we'll do throughout—one then understands the *relativised* notion of *utterance truth in a circumstance of evaluation* as:

($T_{in}^{E}$)  An utterance $\langle \varphi, C \rangle$ is true in a circumstance of evaluation $E$ iff $\langle \varphi, C \rangle$ is true at $E$ and $\langle \varphi, C \rangle$ exists in $E$[8]

(it is the latter notion that expresses the idea of the relevant utterance falling in the extension of 'true' at the relevant circumstance of evaluation, and that is the notion we need in order to understand embeddings of 'true' under *metaphysically* modal operators). For example, quite generally, it seems to be the case that, under this understanding, metaphysically necessarily, $P$ iff $\langle 'P', I \rangle$ is true.

---

[7] The reason for the several 'seems'-hedges interspersed in this and the next two paragraphs will become clear in sections 6 and 7.

[8] An alternative understanding would have it that an utterance $\langle \varphi, C \rangle$ is true in a circumstance of evaluation $E$ iff the proposition expressed by $\varphi$ at $C$ holds at $E_C$ and $\langle \varphi, C \rangle$ exists in $E$. Useful as it may be for other purposes, this understanding is not suitable for ours, since, assuming that utterances as sentence-context pairs metaphysically necessarily exist (see fn 9), it does not allow for non-trivial embeddings under metaphysically modal operators (it's easy to see that, under this understanding, metaphysically necessarily, an utterance is true iff it is metaphysically necessarily true). And that in turn implies that, under this understanding, utterance truth is not transparent even restricting to utterances with $I$ (for example, metaphysically possibly, snow is black, but, under this understanding, it is not the case that, metaphysically possibly, $\langle$'Snow is black', $I \rangle$ is true, since in the world of $I$ snow is not black).

Thus, there is some hope of reviving the Naive Argument by sharpening further (MNEC⁻) so that it only concerns utterances with $I$:

(MNEC) If $\varphi_0$, $\varphi_1$, $\varphi_2 \ldots$ entail $\psi_0$, $\psi_1$, $\psi_2 \ldots$, then, metaphysically necessarily, if all of $\langle \varphi_0, I \rangle$, $\langle \varphi_1, I \rangle$, $\langle \varphi_2, I \rangle \ldots$ are true, then some of $\langle \psi_0, I \rangle$, $\langle \psi_1, I \rangle$, $\langle \psi_2, I \rangle \ldots$ are true.

For utterances with $I$ seem to respect transparency, and so the Naive Argument (in which transparency occurs as a key step) seems at least to establish (MNEC).[9] And, since the Naive Argument seems in turn one of the main reasons supporting (NEC), that speaks in favour of plumping for (MNEC) as a sharpening of (NEC).

## 5   Non-Normality

Unfortunately, although the utterances referred to in (MNEC) may seem to respect transparency (which was a key step in the Naive Argument), context-dependent languages have other features that make (MNEC) extremely problematic. In particular, certain context-dependent expressions licence arguably valid arguments that force the modal logic of natural language to be *non-normal*, and in particular to be such that the metarule of *necessitation* fails. For example, 'If snow is black, then, actually, snow is black' is arguably a validity in the logic of actuality. Yet, necessitation on that validity fails: 'Metaphysically necessarily, if snow is black, then, actually, snow is black', far from being another validity of the logic of actuality, embodies a misunderstanding of the workings of 'actually'. Necessitation was another key step in the Naive Argument, and so

---

[9]These considerations also point to the reasons for why, in this dialectic, it is better to understand utterances as abstract sentence-context pairs. Since there is no guarantee that the actual world @ contains a concrete speech act involving $\varphi$ or a token of $\varphi$, if we understood utterances as concrete entities of some kind or other transparency would straightforwardly fail even in the version that restricts to utterances with $I$: $\varphi$ would no longer entail 'An utterance of '$\varphi$' with $I$ is true', for, contrary to the abstract sentence-context pair $\langle \varphi, I \rangle$, the concrete entity that would now be required may not exist. And, for precisely this reason, (MNEC) would fail in a rather boring way: if $\varphi$ entails $\psi$ but @ only contains a speech act involving $\varphi$ or a token of $\varphi$, then, while it is the case that $\varphi$ as uttered with $I$ is true, it is not the case that $\psi$ as uttered with $I$ is true (for no utterance of $\psi$ would exist in @ in the first place). Relatedly, since there is no guarantee that a metaphysically possible world $w$ contains a concrete speech act involving $\varphi$ or a token of $\varphi$, if we understood utterances as concrete entities of some kind or other transparency would straightforwardly fail even in the version that restricts to utterances with $I$: 'Metaphysically possibly, $\varphi$' would no longer entail 'Metaphysically possibly, an utterance of '$\varphi$' with $I$ is true', for, contrary to the abstract sentence-context pair $\langle \varphi, I \rangle$, the concrete entity that would now be required may not exist in $w$. And, for precisely this reason, (MNEC) would again fail in a rather boring way: if $\varphi$ entails $\psi$ but $w$ only contains a speech act involving $\varphi$ or a token of $\varphi$, then, while it is the case that $\varphi$ as uttered with $I$ is true in $w$, it is not the case that $\psi$ as uttered with $I$ is true in $w$ (for no utterance of $\psi$ would exist in $w$ in the first place). I should perhaps stress that, since there is no guarantee that a metaphysically possible world $w$ contains the objects (world, time, agent, place, *demonstrata* etc.) involved in $I$, even if we understand utterances as abstract sentence-context pairs transparency may still fail even in the version that restricts to utterances with $I$ *if the existence of a sequence depends on the existence of the objects involved in the sequence* (in which case there would also be a problem for (MNEC), assuming that its spirit requires that, if $\varphi$ is valid, then, metaphysically necessarily, $\langle \varphi, I \rangle$ is true). I'll henceforth ignore this last issue.

it should come as no surprise that such failures of necessitation provide counterexamples to (MNEC). Arguably, in the logic of actuality, 'Actually, snow is black' logically follows from 'Snow is black'. Given this, (MNEC) requires that, metaphysically necessarily, if ⟨'Snow is black', $I$⟩ is true, then ⟨'Actually, snow is black', $I$⟩ is true. Consider however a world $w$ in which snow is black. By $(\mathrm{T}_{\mathrm{in}}^{E})$, ⟨'Snow is black', $I$⟩ is true in $w$ (since ⟨'Snow is black', $I$⟩ exists in $w$, says [that snow is black][10] and snow is indeed black in $w$), but ⟨'Actually, snow is black', $I$⟩ is not true in $w$ (since ⟨'Actually, snow is black', $I$⟩ says [that, actually (*i.e.* in @),[11] snow is black], and not even in $w$ is snow black in @). $w$ is thus a counterexample to the metaphysically strict implication required by (MNEC).

In fact, the failure of necessitation for context-dependent languages has even more disruptive effects, forcefully suggesting that no *modally strong* principle linking logical consequence with preservation of truth as uttered with $I$ is forthcoming. For not only does the *metaphysically strict implication* required by (MNEC) fail; in the example above, also the weaker *counterfactual implication* to the effect that, [if ⟨'Snow is black', $I$⟩ were true, then ⟨'Actually, snow is black', $I$⟩ would be true] fails (since the closest worlds in which ⟨'Snow is black', $I$⟩ is true—*i.e.* the closest worlds in which snow is black—are not worlds in which ⟨'Actually, snow is black', $I$⟩ is true—not even in those worlds is snow black in @).

An analogous structural flaw emerges if one is tempted by a retreat to actuality, claiming that, if logical consequence does not require *metaphysically necessary* truth preservation, it at least requires *eternal* truth preservation. In particular, certain context-dependent expressions licence arguably valid arguments that force the tense logic of natural language to be non-normal, and in particular to be such that the metarule of "*eternalisation*" (if $\varphi$ is valid, then 'Always, $\varphi$' is valid) fails. For example, 'If Hadrian rules Britannia, then, now, Hadrian rules Britannia' is arguably a validity of the logic of the present. Yet, eternalisation on that validity fails: 'Always, if Hadrian rules Britannia, then, now, Hadrian rules Britannia', far from being another validity of the logic of the present, embodies a misunderstanding of the workings of 'now'. Now, arguably, in the logic of the present 'Now, Hadrian rules Britannia' logically follows from 'Hadrian rules Britannia'. Consider however time 120 at which Hadrian ruled Britannia. By $(\mathrm{T}_{\mathrm{in}}^{E})$, ⟨'Hadrian rules Britannia', $I$⟩ is true in 120 (since ⟨'Hadrian rules Britannia', $I$⟩ exists in 120, says [that Hadrian rules Britannia] and Hadrian did rule Britannia in 120),[12] but ⟨'Now, Hadrian rules Britannia', $I$⟩ is not true in 120 (since ⟨'Now, Hadrian rules Britannia', $I$⟩ says [that, now (*i.e.* in 2012), Hadrian rules Britannia], and not even in 120 did

---

[10]Throughout, I use square brackets to disambiguate constituent structure in English.

[11]For the rest of this section, I'm assuming that the world and time of $I$ are @ and 2012 respectively.

[12]The last sentence should really read in tense-logical perspicuity 'In 120, Hadrian rules Britannia'. However, English syntax usually requires that a simple-present sentence modified by a past temporal adverb such as 'in 120' be transformed into the corresponding simple-past sentence, and for this reason the text has 'Hadrian did rule Britannia in 120'.

Hadrian rule Britannia in 2012). 120 is thus a counterexample to the idea that logical consequence requires eternal truth preservation.[13]

Sometimes, the arguments from $\varphi$ to 'Actually, $\varphi$' or to 'Now, $\varphi$' are resisted, mainly because of the question-begging reason that they generate non-normality in the logic. However, if anything like modal logic or tense logic make sense (and they do), it's hard to find fault with such arguments: there would seem to be no reason to think that 'actually'—contrary, say, to 'necessarily'—does not enjoy its own interesting modal logic, and no reason to think that 'now'—contrary, say, to 'always'—does not enjoy its own interesting tense logic; yet, if those expressions do have their own interesting logics, the arguments in question would seem to be absolutely central to them.

In any event, the counterexamples from non-normality need not rely on the peculiar logic of 'actually' and 'now'. Failures of necessitation and eternalisation occur at an even more fundamental level. For example, 'If everything

---

[13]The counterexample assumes—in my view plausibly—that the context dependence introduced by tense is of the (NC)-kind. The view is usually known as '*temporalism*', and the opposite view according to which the context dependence introduced by tense is of the (SC)-kind is usually known as '*eternalism*' (views according to which the context dependence introduced by tense is of either the (TR)- or the (CR)-kind seem rather hopeless). Under eternalism, the counterexample fails since, under eternalism, $\langle$'Hadrian rules Britannia', $C\rangle$ says [that Hadrian rules Britannia at the time of $C$], so that $\langle$'Hadrian rules Britannia', $I\rangle$ is not true in 120 (since, under eternalism, $\langle$'Hadrian rules Britannia', $I\rangle$ says [that Hadrian rules Britannia in 2012], and not even in 120 did Hadrian rule Britannia in 2012). Richard (1981) is an early—in my view inconclusive—criticism of temporalism. An analogous—in my view even more plausible—assumption was needed in the counterexamples involving the logic of actuality in the last two paragraphs (as well for some claims made in the last section), to the effect that the context dependence introduced by the indicative mood (and some other moods) is of the (NC)-kind. The view is sometimes known as '*contingentism*', and the opposite view according to which the context dependence introduced by the indicative mood (and some other moods) is of the (SC)-kind is sometimes known as '*necessitarianism*' (views according to which the context dependence introduced by the indicative mood (and some other moods) is of either the (TR)- or the (CR)-kind seem again rather hopeless). Schaffer (2012) is a recent—in my view inconclusive—criticism of contingentism. Having said this about the assumptions of the counterexamples, I hasten to add that the adoption of either eternalism or necessitarianism does little to ameliorate (MNEC)'s overall position. Let's focus, without loss of generality, on necessitarianism. Firstly, under necessitarianism, transparency straightforwardly fails even in the version that restricts to utterances with $I$. For example, while it is metaphysically necessary that [snow is black iff snow is black], under necessitarianism it is not metaphysically necessary that [snow is black iff $\langle$'Snow is black', $I\rangle$ is true]. For consider a world $w$ in which snow is black. Snow is black in $w$, but, under necessitarianism, $\langle$'Snow is black', $I\rangle$ is not true in $w$ (since, under necessitarianism, $\langle$'Snow is black', $I\rangle$ says [that snow is black in @], and not even in $w$ is snow black in @). Thus, under necessitarianism, the Naive Argument still fails to establish (MNEC), since it breaks down at the transparency step. Secondly, not only, under necessitarianism, is the Naive Argument blocked; (MNEC) itself is stripped of its intended force. For, under necessitarianism, '$\langle\varphi, C\rangle$ is true' does not have non-trivial embeddings under metaphysically modal operators (it's easy to see that, under necessitarianism, metaphysically necessarily, $\langle\varphi, C\rangle$ is true iff it is metaphysically necessarily true, see also fn 8). Thus, under necessitarianism, (MNEC) adds no real modal force to a requirement of merely actual truth preservation, and so, contrary to its own spirit, it places no constraint on logical consequence that is not met, say, by the silly argument from 'Snow is black' to 'Snow is black and grass is green'. Thirdly, under necessitarianism, principles very similar in spirit to (MNEC) fail. For example, under necessitarianism the principle that, if $\varphi$ entails $\psi$, then, metaphysically necessarily, $\varphi$ implies the truth of $\langle\psi, I\rangle$ fails (for 'Snow is black' entails itself, but, as noticed above, under necessitarianism it is not metaphysically necessary that, if snow is black, then $\langle$'Snow is black', $I\rangle$ is true).

is loved by God, then $x$ is loved by God' is a validity of standard non-free and free first-order logics. Yet, necessitation on that validity fails: 'Metaphysically necessarily, if everything is loved by God, then, $x$ is loved by God', far from being another validity, embodies a misunderstanding of the workings of free variables (assign Saul to $x$, and consider any world in which everything is loved by God but, *pace* Linsky and Zalta, 1994; Williamson, 1998, Saul does not exist). Now, in standard non-free and free first-order logics, '$x$ is loved by God' logically follows from 'Everything is loved by God'. Given this, (MNEC) requires that, metaphysically necessarily, if ⟨'Everything is loved by God', $I$⟩ is true, then ⟨'$x$ is loved by God', $I$⟩ is true. However, let $I$ assign Saul to '$x$', and consider a world $w$ in which everything is loved by God but Saul does not exist. By (T$_{\text{in}}^{E}$), ⟨'Everything is loved by God', $I$⟩ is true in $w$ (since ⟨'Everything is loved by God', $I$⟩ exists in $w$, says [that everything is loved by God] and everything is indeed loved by God in $w$), but ⟨'$x$ is loved by God', $I$⟩ is not true in $w$ (since ⟨'$x$ is loved by God', $I$⟩ says [that Saul is loved by God], and Saul is not loved by God in $w$, as he does not even exist in $w$). $w$ is thus a counterexample to the metaphysically strict implication required by (MNEC) that only relies on standard non-free or free first-order logics. (Analogous points apply of course to counterfactual and eternal truth preservation.)

Of course, in light of these counterexamples, one may retreat even further and claim that, if logical consequence requires neither metaphysically necessary nor eternal truth preservation, it at least requires actual, present truth preservation. However, it is not even clear that no analogous structural flaw would again emerge. For, in addition to *contingency* and *temporality*, it might be that truth values can change also because of *egocentricity*. For example, on an influential theory (see Lewis, 1979), when at least thinking "from the first-person perspective" *agents self-attribute properties*, which may be exemplified by some agents and fail to be exemplified by others. On this view, when John (a Californian), as the folk say, "believes that he lives in California", what he really does is to self-attribute the property $\lambda x(x$ lives in California$)$.[14] If that's correct, we should certainly model the rationality of agents' first-personal thought by having a logic of properties, according to which, for example, '$\lambda x(x$ lives in California$)$' entails '$\lambda x(x$ lives in California or $x$ lives in Alaska$)$'. 'Everyone' and 'I' would then be intensional operators in such *"personal"* logic, playing the same roles played in modal logic by 'necessarily' and 'actually' respectively (or in tense logic by 'always' and 'now' respectively).

In particular, 'I' would licence arguably valid arguments that force the personal logic of natural language to be non-normal, and in particular to be such that the metarule of *"generalisation"* (if '$\lambda x(\varphi)$' is valid, then '$\lambda x$(Everyone is such that $\varphi_{\text{they}/x}$)'[15] is valid) fails. For example, '$\lambda x$(If $x$ lives in California, then I live in California)' is arguably a validity of the logic of the first person. Yet, generalisation on that validity fails: '$\lambda x$(Everyone is such that, if they

---

[14]Such a theory can be interpreted as holding that the context dependence introduced by first-person pronouns, adjectives and similar devices is of the (NC)-kind. Stalnaker (1981) is an early—in my view inconclusive—criticism of the theory.

[15]Throughout, $\varphi_{\text{they}/\xi}$ is the result of substituting the impersonal 'they' (anaphoric on 'everyone') for the free occurrences of $\xi$ in $\varphi$ (making the adjustments required either by English morphology or by "clashes of pronouns").

live in California, then I live in California)', far from being another validity
of the logic of the first person, embodies a misunderstanding of the workings
of 'I'. Now, arguably, in the logic of the first person '$\lambda x$(I live in California)'
logically follows from '$\lambda x$($x$ lives in California)'. Consider however John. By
($\mathrm{T_{in}^{E}}$), $\langle$'$\lambda x$($x$ lives in California)', $I\rangle$ is true[16] for John (since $\langle$'$\lambda x$($x$ lives in
California)', $I\rangle$ exists for John, expresses the property of living in California
and John does live in California), but $\langle$'$\lambda x$(I live in California)', $I\rangle$ is not true
for John (since $\langle$'$\lambda x$(I live in California)', $I\rangle$ expresses the property of being
such that I (*i.e.* EZ) live in California, and not even John is such that EZ lives
in California). John would thus be a counterexample to the idea that logical
consequence requires actual, present (but impersonal) truth preservation.

Be that as it may with personal logic, actual, present truth preservation is
not a very interesting property—what is so special about 5.55pm of 15/05/2012
in @ (the time and world of $I$)? Nothing really. In other worlds and times, I'll
truly and justifiedly think that logical consequence requires *another*, similar
but different, property (preservation of truth in the world and at the time of
*that context* rather than preservation of truth in @ at 5.55pm of 15/05/2012).
In fact, although (MNEC) may initially have struck us as a plausible *univocal*
principle, *it in fact conveys at each new time a slightly different theory*, since
each new time will impose a slightly different understanding of the phrase 'this
very same context' which is the *definiens* of '$I$'. Thus, even if we endorsed a
watered down version of (MNEC) restricted to actual, present truth preservation, we would really be endorsing at each new time a slightly different theory.
Could it be that our theorizing about logical consequence and truth preservation is condemned to such an embarrassing level of *ephemerality*? This train of
thought actually suggests a sharpening of (NEC) alternative to (MNEC⁻) and
(MNEC), a sharpening which I'll explore in section 8. But before investigating
that alternative sharpening, it'll be helpful to observe how, beyond the dramatic
failures of necessitation and its like observed in this section, other vagaries of
context dependence generate equally dramatic failures of transparency which
make even actual, present truth preservation bound to fail.

# 6   Doubly Improper Utterances

As I've already mentioned in section 3, I don't always assume that the context
that an utterance has is the one in which the utterance is made—the world,
time, agent etc. in or by which an utterance happens to be uttered need not be
the world, time, agent etc. figuring in the context that is semantically relevant
for interpreting it (I'll call utterances exhibiting this divergence '*improper*').
For example, if $u$ is an utterance of a sentence belonging to a *mythological*
discourse, the pertinent world of the context that is semantically relevant for

---

[16]It is not clear that utterances of $\lambda$-expressions and other linguistic constructions expressing properties are properly evaluated in terms of truth and falsity (including truth and falsity
in a circumstance of evaluation). I'm assuming for the sake of argument, and for the time
being, that they are. Obviously, if they aren't, since a logic of properties is a perfectly fine
logic this will bring about substantial failures of (MNEC) and, more generally, (NEC). I'll articulate this point in section 7 with respect to clearer-cut cases of logical-consequence bearers
whose utterances are not properly evaluated in terms of truth and falsity (including truth
and falsity in a circumstance of evaluation).

interpreting $u$ may not be the world in which $u$ is made, but a world at which the mythology in question is true.[17] However, and most interestingly for our purposes, 'actual' and its like may in the same context be used to refer back to the world in which $u$ is made (I'll call improper utterances exhibiting this further kind of divergence *doubly improper*). Let's consider an example. An utterance $a_0$ of 'Achilles and Patroclus were in a romantic relationship' made in @ during a discussion of Greek mythology might well count as true. The context $M$ that is semantically relevant for interpreting $a_0$ has as world entering into the circumstance of evaluation $E_M$ a world at which Greek mythology is true. However, and most interestingly for our purposes, the speech can be truly expanded with an utterance $a_1$ of 'Achilles and Patroclus, whose actual existence is doubtful, were in a romantic relationship', presumably keeping the context fixed. Thus, although $M$ is such as to have as world entering into $E_M$ a world at which Greek mythology is true, it is also such as to assign @ to 'actual' and its like.

Moreover, $M$ might well be $I$. If so, by $(T_{in}^E)$, ⟨'Achilles and Patroclus were in a romantic relationship', $I$⟩ is true (that is, true in $E_I$: for ⟨'Achilles and Patroclus were in a romantic relationship', $I$⟩ exists, says [that Achilles and Patroclus were in a romantic relationship], the world $w$ entering into $E_I$ is a world at which Greek mythology is true and so Achilles and Patroclus were in a romantic relationship in $w$), but ⟨'Actually, Achilles and Patroclus were in a romantic relationship', $I$⟩ is not true (that is, not true in $E_I$: for ⟨'Actually, Achilles and Patroclus were in a romantic relationship', $I$⟩ says [that Achilles and Patroclus were in a romantic relationship in @] (for $I$ assigns @ to 'actually' and its like), the world $w$ entering into $E_I$ is a world at which Greek mythology is true but not even in $w$ were Achilles and Patroclus in a romantic relationship in @, as they did not even exist in @).[18]

Or, if $u$ is an utterance of a sentence belonging to a *historiographical* discourse, the pertinent time of the context that is semantically relevant for interpreting $u$ may not be the time at which $u$ is made, but the time at which the bit of history in question occurs. However, and most interestingly for our purposes, 'now' and its like may in the same context be used to refer back to the time at which $u$ is made. Let's consider an example. An utterance $b_0$ of 'Bradwardine is in Oxford' made in 2012 during a discussion of which logician is where in the 1320s might well count as true. The context $H$ that is semantically relevant for interpreting $b_0$ has as time entering into the circumstance of evaluation $E_H$ the 1320s. However, and most interestingly for our purposes, the speech can be truly expanded with an utterance $b_1$ of 'Bradwardine, who is now a highly regarded logician, is in Oxford', presumably keeping the context

---

[17]Realistically, in most situations of this kind no *single world* can be selected as the world that $u$ talks about, and it'd be more sensible to think of $u$ as talking about a *range of worlds*. However, since taking this point into account would require a lot of changes in the presentation of the argument without any change in its substance, I'll continue to talk under the useful pretence that there is a single world that $u$ talks about.

[18]Predelli (2005, pp. 40–75) provides a persuasive defence of the possibility and theoretical significance of *improper* utterances. However, he does not seem to contemplate the possibility of *doubly improper* utterances, as $a_1$ patently is. It is this possibility that belies his claim that every instance of 'If $\varphi$, then, actually, $\varphi$' is, for absolutely every context $C$, true at $C$ and $E_C$: the relevant instances of that schema are false at $M$ and $E_M$.

fixed. Thus, although $H$ is such as to have as time entering into $E_H$ the 1320s, it is also such as to assign 2012 to 'now' and its like.

Moreover, $H$ might well be $I$. If so, by $(T^E_{in})$, $\langle$'Bradwardine is in Oxford', $I\rangle$ is true (that is, true in $E_I$: for $\langle$'Bradwardine is in Oxford', $I\rangle$ exists, says [that Bradwardine is in Oxford], the time entering into $E_I$ is the 1320s and Bradwardine was indeed in Oxford in the 1320s), but $\langle$'Now, Bradwardine is in Oxford', $I\rangle$ is not true (that is, not true in $E_I$: for $\langle$'Now, Bradwardine is in Oxford', $I\rangle$ says [that Bradwardine is in Oxford in 2012] (for $I$ assigns 2012 to 'now' and its like), the time entering into $E_I$ is the 1320s but not even in the 1320s was Bradwardine in Oxford in 2012, as he does not even exist in 2012).[19]

Since, for example, assuming that $M$ is $I$ $\langle$'Achilles and Patroclus were in a romantic relationship', $I\rangle$ is true but $\langle$'Actually, Achilles and Patroclus were in a romantic relationship', $I\rangle$ is not true even if 'Achilles and Patroclus were in a romantic relationship' entails 'Actually, Achilles and Patroclus were in a romantic relationship', even a watered down version of (MNEC) restricted to actual, present truth preservation fails, and so even a watered down version of the Naive Argument which avoids the necessitation step and restricts itself to utterances with $I$ must break down. But where does that version of the Naive Argument exactly break down? It unsurprisingly breaks down at the *transparency* step from 'If $\varphi$, then $\psi$' being valid to 'If $\langle\varphi, I\rangle$ is true, then $\langle\psi, I\rangle$ is true' being valid (or being true). In particular, although the *non-semantic* sentence 'If Achilles and Patroclus were in a romantic relationship, then, actually, Achilles and Patroclus were in a romantic relationship' is valid, the *semantic* sentence 'If $\langle$'Achilles and Patroclus were in a romantic relationship', $I\rangle$ is true, then $\langle$'Actually, Achilles and Patroclus were in a romantic relationship', $I\rangle$ is true', far from being valid, is false. Contrary to transparency even as restricted to utterances with $I$ (see section 4), $\varphi$ is not always intersubstitutable with '$\langle\varphi, I\rangle$ is true'.

The examples considered in this section may seem baffling: how can one truly assert 'Achilles and Patroclus were in a romantic relationship' and, with the same context, truly deny 'Actually, Achilles and Patroclus were in a romantic relationship', if the former entails the latter? What emerges here is *how loose the relation is between logical consequence and the extreme variety of our uses of language.* To a very rough first approximation, rather unsurprisingly logical consequence is more tightly connected with uses of language exhibiting *full-fledged acceptance* (and expressing *belief*) rather than with uses of language only exhibiting *assertion*. It still seems plausible that, if one truly and full-fledgedly accepts 'Achilles and Patroclus were in a romantic relationship' (and so believes that Achilles and Patroclus were in a romantic relationship), then, in the same context, one can truly and full-fledgedly accept 'Actually, Achilles and Patroclus were in a romantic relationship' (and so believe that, in one's world, Achilles and Patroclus were in a romantic relationship). But some uses of

---

[19]I've put the point assuming, again, that the context dependence introduced by tense is of the (NC)-kind (see fn 13). But the point can equally well be put in a standard eternalist framework, in which the example I've offered would be interpreted as one where the implicit time variable introduced by the present tense is assigned a different value from the value assigned to 'now' and its like. An analogous comment holds for the example involving 'actually' in the third and second last paragraphs.

language, as exemplified by the mythological and historiographical discourses discussed above,[20] do not exhibit full-fledged acceptance, although they do exhibit assertion (and truth).[21] It should thus actually come as no surprise that (MNEC) fails for such uses.

## 7  Multiply Referring Utterances

In the limit case in which $\varphi$ logically follows "from nothing" (*i.e.* $\varphi$ is valid), we may assume that (MNEC) requires that, metaphysically necessarily, $\langle \varphi, I \rangle$ be true, and that a watered down version of (MNEC) restricted to actual, present truth preservation requires that $\langle \varphi, I \rangle$ be true. Even the last claim is however subject to well-known counterexamples of an even simpler character than those discussed in the last section. For example, 'If Dave is here, then Dave is here' is valid in sentential logic. But that sentence is uttered falsely in a context $D$ in which two different places $p_0$ and $p_1$ are successively demonstrated, with Dave being at $p_0$ but not at $p_1$ (I'll call utterances exhibiting this divergence '*multiply referring*').[22] Moreover, $D$ might well be $I$. If so, $\langle$'If Dave is here, then Dave is here', $I\rangle$ is not true (that is, not true in $E_I$).[23]

Since, assuming that $D$ is $I$, $\langle$'If Dave is here, then Dave is here', $I\rangle$ is not true even if 'If Dave is here, then Dave is here' is valid, even a watered down version of (MNEC) restricted to actual, present truth preservation (and to no-

---

[20] And arguably by other ones too. For instance, if $u$ is an utterance of a sentence belonging to a *suppositional* discourse, the pertinent world of the context that is semantically relevant for interpreting $u$ may not be the world in which $u$ is made, but a world at which the suppositions in question are true. However, and most interestingly for our purposes, 'actually' and its like may with the same context be used to refer back to the world in which $u$ is made. Let's consider an example. An utterance $c_0$ of 'Daugapils is the capital of Latvia' made in @ during a discussion of what follows under the supposition that the official and operative site of the Latvian Parliament, Prime Minister, President etc. is Daugapils rather than Riga might well count as true. The context $S$ that is semantically relevant for interpreting $c_0$ has as world entering into the circumstance of evaluation $E_S$ a world at which that supposition about Latvia is true. However, and most interestingly for our purposes, the speech can be truly expanded with an utterance $c_1$ of 'Daugapils, whose actual importance is less than Riga's, is the capital of Latvia', presumably keeping the context fixed. Thus, although $S$ is such as to have as world entering into $E_S$ a world at which that supposition about Latvia is true, it is also such as to assign @ to 'actual' and its like. And this opens the way to failures of even a watered down version of (MNEC) restricted to actual, present truth preservation which are analogous to those from mythological discourse detailed in the text.

[21] Also in the case of the historiographical discourse discussed in the text such full-fledged acceptance seems to be missing. Although in that case one does intend to connect with real facts of the matter, intuitively there is nevertheless a certain feeling of pretence when one so connects by uttering 'Bradwardine is in Oxford' in that situation (and, intuitively, in uttering that sentence in that situation one does not express any belief to the effect that Bradwardine is in Oxford).

[22] Someone may consider the hypothesis that the sentences that are uttered in cases of multiply referring utterances really have a *form* along the lines of that of 'If Dave is here$_i$, then Dave is here$_j$', which is uncontroversially invalid. I take such hypothesis to be unmotivated on empirical linguistic grounds (contrary to an analogous hypothesis for other context-dependent expressions like English personal pronouns). Thanks to Jim Pryor and François Recanati for discussions of this point.

[23] The particular counterexample is most plausibly interpreted as exploiting an (SC)-kind of context dependence. Yet, similar counterexamples are available which exploit other kinds of context dependence. For instance, under temporalism (see fn 13), we would still have the same problem for 'If Dave is sitting, then Dave is sitting'.

premise arguments)[24] fails,[25] and so even a watered down version of the Naive Argument which avoids the necessitation step and restricts itself to utterances with $I$ (and to no-premise arguments) must break down. But where does that version of the Naive Argument exactly break down? Again, it unsurprisingly breaks down at the *transparency* step from $\varphi$ being valid to '$\langle\varphi, I\rangle$ is true' being valid (or being true). In particular, although the *non-semantic* sentence 'If Dave is here, then Dave is here' is valid, the *semantic* sentence '$\langle$'If Dave is here, then Dave is here', $I\rangle$ is true', far from being valid, is false. Again, contrary to transparency even as restricted to utterances with $I$ (see section 4), $\varphi$ is not always intersubstitutable with '$\langle\varphi, I\rangle$ is true'.[26] Stephen Read, among many others, has rightly warned us that, in the presence of context dependence, for essentially the reasons mentioned in section 4 transparency fails (see, *e.g.*, Read, 2008, p. 4). What the last section and this section bring out is that, in the presence of context dependence, transparency fails *also for other reasons*, and that the full extent to which it fails is also such as to bring about substantial failures of (MNEC) and, more generally, (NEC)—principles that, as we've seen in section 1, are otherwise dear to Read and to many other theorists.

In a fallacy of *equivocation*, glorious failures of truth preservation are usually attributed to a failure of keeping the *meaning* of an expression fixed across an

---

[24]This parenthetical strengthening could already have been established by means of the examples discussed in the last section. For instance, because of the reasons given in that section, assuming that $M$ is $I$ $\langle$'If Achilles and Patroclus were in a romantic relationship', then, actually, Achilles and Patroclus were in a romantic relationship', $I\rangle$ is not true (that is, not true in $E_I$).

[25]Someone may consider the hypothesis that multiply referring utterances do not really have any *single* context, but rather span across *different* contexts. Then, it would be literally wrong to say that the relevant utterance of 'If Dave is here, then Dave is here' has $I$ as "its" context (plus, the representation of that utterance as $\langle$'If Dave is here, then Dave is here', $I\rangle$ would become at best inappropriate). And, since (MNEC) only talks about utterances with $I$, that utterance would now be irrelevant for the question whether (MNEC) holds. In reply, I of course have no in-principle objection to using the word 'context' so that multiply referring utterances count as not having a single "context"—certainly, one is free to individuate contexts with different levels of fineness of grain for different purposes! What I do object to is to use this freedom to stipulate away the counterexamples to (MNEC). Multiply referring utterances are perfectly legitimate, natural and useful utterances. They offer a potential touchstone for assessing generalisations no less than other utterances do. In particular, although in section 4 consideration of the Naive Argument did lead to a restriction to utterances with $I$, the reasons for that restriction by no means support a restriction to utterances that are not multiply referring: for those reasons concern how to block the illicit transition from my hunger to the truth of certain unrelated utterances and sentences (or *vice versa*), but multiple reference licences no additional such transition (what we're focussing on in the text is how it licences an illicit transition from a non-semantic sentence being valid to certain semantic sentences being valid). It may well be (and I'm actually very sympathetic to the idea) that multiply referring utterances require a revision of the nowadays standard semantic framework that interprets sentences at (single) contexts (and thus a revision of the representation of utterances as sentence-context pairs). But, if such revision is indeed needed, that should also lead to a revised formulation of (MNEC) that still encompasses multiply referring utterances. I try to make a start on a suitable non-standard semantic framework in Zardini (2012b).

[26]If one modified the Naive Argument by swapping the transparency step with the descent step from '$P$''s being valid to its being the case that $P$, then, although the problems discussed in the last section and in this section would no longer affect the transparency step, they would simply have been relocated at the descent step.

argument. For example, although the argument from 'Barclays is a bank' to 'Barclays is a bank or a charity' may at first be thought to be valid as it stands, its premise may be true (if 'bank' as it occurs there is understood as meaning money bank) while its conclusion false (if 'bank' as it occurs there is understood as meaning river bank). *That* failure of truth preservation is indeed plausibly reflected in a failure of logical consequence. For an *ambiguous* expression in natural language is plausibly taken to correspond, at the level of representation relevant for logical evaluation, to distinct lexical items, and, after such disambiguation has taken place, the equivocating argument is exposed as invalid. For example, the above argument, under the equivocating reading, is disambiguated as having as premise something like 'Barclays is a bank$_{MONEY}$' and as conclusion something like 'Barclays is a bank$_{RIVER}$ or a charity', and that argument is straightforwardly invalid.

However, we now see that the trouble emerging in a fallacy of equivocation is merely a *special* case of a *more general* trouble that has its ultimate root not so much in a difference in *meaning*, but in a more general difference in *extension*. For example, 'here' as it is used in $D$ has the same meaning but different referents as it occurs in the antecedent and as it occurs in the consequent, and that is sufficient for bringing about a failure of truth preservation. And, in that example as well as in many others, the difference in extension is *not* plausibly taken to correspond, at the level of representation relevant for logical evaluation, to distinct lexical items (see fn 22), and so such difference is not reflected in a failure of logical consequence, contrary to what happens in a fallacy of equivocation.

I should like to note that an appealing hypothesis is that doubly improper utterances and multiply referring utterances *are at root the same phenomenon*, in the sense that doubly improper utterances *are really just a special case* of multiply referring utterances. For multiple reference can be exhibited not only by two occurrences of the *same* expression, but also by two occurrences of two *different* but nevertheless *completely synonymous* expressions. For instance, an example very much analogous to the one given in this section involves an utterance of the sentence 'If Dave is here, then Dave is in this place'.[27] That is also an example in which a valid (or at least analytic) sentence is uttered falsely because occurrences of expressions which *logical evaluation* treats alike are *in context used* to latch onto different extensions. And one might think that something like the latter kind of multiple reference is also exhibited in the case of $a_1$ of the last section, on the grounds that the indicative mood and 'actual' are synonymous expressions (or at least morphemes) whose occurrences are treated alike by *logical evaluation* (at least at $C$ and $E_C$) by assigning to them the same possible world (the world entering into $E_C$), but are *in the context of $a_1$ used* to latch onto different possible worlds. Appealing as this line of thought may be in providing a *unified* diagnosis of the most dramatic failures of (MNEC), its pursuit is better left for another occasion.

I should also like to mention briefly a different series of considerations, which, although strictly speaking not concerning context dependence, vividly illustrate

---

[27]The example would be even nicer in some Romance languages (think for example of Italian 'Se Davide è qui, allora Davide è qua').

another dimension in which the extreme variety of our uses of language outstrips the narrow-mindedness embodied by (MNEC) and, more generally, (NEC). For among such uses, there are also the fundamentally *non-assertive* ones of giving *commands* and asking *questions*. We should certainly model the rationality of agents' giving commands and asking questions by having a logic of commands and questions (see Vranas, 2010, for a defence of the logic of commands and Groenendijk and Stokhof, 1984, for a defence of the logic of questions). Such logics typically have valid sentences like 'Bring it about that either there is a slab or not!' and 'Is it the case that either there is a slab or not?', which are usually judged to be valid because they express either a command that is satisfied by satisfying any command or a question that is settled by settling any question. Although such sentences are valid, utterances of them are arguably not true (and not false either), since they express commands or questions.[28]

# 8   Semantically Necessary Truth Preservation and Its Limits

Especially the dialectic of section 5 forcefully suggests that (MNEC) as a sharpening of (NEC) is on the wrong track. My own view is that we get a more interesting sharpening of (NEC) by shifting our focus from *metaphysical* necessity to some kind of *semantic* necessity: the necessity that concerns the ways *words could not have failed to be used*. That is the kind of meaning that is attached to 'necessarily' and its like when locutions like 'Necessarily, I am here now' sound true, and which is often heard as being "covertly metalinguistic".[29] Consequently, since, at least for a context-dependent language, semantic necessity can usefully be understood as somehow involving an implicit *universal quantification over contexts* (rather than over metaphysically possible worlds), I think that we should abandon the (egocentric) fixation on $I$ required by the Naive Argument and let instead the contexts associated with the relevant sentences be the contexts that are somehow implicitly quantified over by the operator of semantic necessity as well as be the contexts that provide the circumstance of evaluation for the relativised notion of utterance truth at a circumstance of evaluation (which is the notion that is most naturally used in order to understand embeddings of 'true' under *semantically* modal operators). The joint net effect of these changes is the following sharpening of (NEC):

---

[28]Similar cases could even come from *assertive* uses of language in which, once again, context dependence is typically involved. '$x$ is either prime or not' is valid, but it's very doubtful that an utterance of it anaphoric on the discourse-initial 'Suppose that $x$ is a natural number' is true (since it's very doubtful that such utterance expresses a proposition in the first place). 'If that dagger is covered with blood, that dagger is covered with blood' is valid, but it's very doubtful that an utterance of it with a context in which there is no dagger is true (since it's very doubtful that such utterance expresses a proposition in the first place).

[29]For an example of a contrast between metaphysical and semantic modality that plausibly does not involve context dependence, consider the falsity of 'Possibly, Hesperus is not Phosphorus' under the metaphysical-possibility reading and its truth under the semantic-possibility reading. This second example also indicates that *semantic* modality cannot be explained away in terms of *epistemic* modality—we know full well that Hesperus is Phosphorus.

(SNEC) If $\varphi_0$, $\varphi_1$, $\varphi_2$... entail $\psi_0$, $\psi_1$, $\psi_2$..., then, for every context $C$, if all of $\langle\varphi_0, C\rangle$, $\langle\varphi_1, C\rangle$, $\langle\varphi_2, C\rangle$... are true at $E_C$, then some of $\langle\psi_0, C\rangle$, $\langle\psi_1, C\rangle$, $\langle\psi_2, C\rangle$... are true at $E_C$.

In my view, (SNEC) is a considerable improvement over (MNEC), at least in the sense that it completely avoids the embarrassing dialectic that, in section 5, we observed (MNEC) to be exposed to. For example, the standard semantic clause for 'actually' is:

(@) For every context $C$ and circumstance of evaluation $E$, 'Actually, $\varphi$' is true at $C$ and $E$ iff $\varphi$ is true at $C$ and at the circumstance of evaluation that is just like $E$ save for having as world the world of $E_C$

(for simplicity, I'm setting aside for the time being the possibility of doubly improper utterances). Suppose that $\langle\varphi, C\rangle$ is true at $E_C$. Then, by $(\mathrm{T}_{at}^E)$, the proposition expressed by $\varphi$ at $C$ holds at $E_C$, which, in a standard two-dimensional semantic framework, is tantamount to saying that $\varphi$ is true at $C$ and $E_C$. Thus, by (@), 'Actually, $\varphi$' is true at $C$ and $E_C$, which again, in a standard two-dimensional semantic framework, is tantamount to saying that the proposition expressed by 'Actually, $\varphi$' at $C$ holds at $E_C$. Thus, by $(\mathrm{T}_{at}^E)$, $\langle$'Actually, $\varphi$', $C\rangle$ is true at $E_C$. And, since $\varphi$ and $C$ were arbitrary, this argument shows that (SNEC)—contrary to (MNEC)—is satisfied in the case of the valid argument schema from $\varphi$ to 'Actually, $\varphi$'. In the peculiar, semantic sense of (SNEC), that argument schema does necessarily preserve truth.[30]

Before proceeding further, it'll be worthwhile to record explicitly an important, *anti-deflationist* upshot of our discussion so far. According to deflationism, and a little roughly, transparency is the fundamental and unique principle on whose basis every other truth-theoretic principle can be accounted for (see, e.g., Horwich, 1998). Since (NEC) is a very salient truth-theoretic principle, short of rejecting it the deflationist will have to maintain that it too can be explained in terms of transparency. However, the only remotely *prima facie* natural account of (NEC) in terms of transparency that I can think of is something along the lines of the Naive Argument (and something along the lines of the Naive Argument is in effect quickly run by Horwich, 1998, p. 75). And, as I've already observed in section 4, by its very structure the Naive Argument can only hope to vindicate (MNEC) rather than (SNEC). Unfortunately, since (MNEC) has performed so poorly in the dialectic of section 5, the result is bad news for deflationism. It is instructive here to go back to how, in the last paragraph, I argued that (SNEC) is satisfied in the case of the valid argument schema from $\varphi$ to 'Actually, $\varphi$'. The argument relied on $(\mathrm{T}_{at}^E)$ and (@) (and on some basic features of a standard two-dimensional semantic framework), but nowhere on transparency: it relied on *deep, semantic* principles rather than

---

[30]While *weaker* than (MNEC) in not requiring *metaphysically* necessary truth preservation, (SNEC) is also *stronger* than (MNEC) in requiring *semantically* necessary truth preservation. And the fact that (SNEC) is in this sense more exacting than (MNEC) is welcome, as it weeds out arguments whose manifest invalidity is not detected by (MNEC). For example, since it is metaphysically necessary that $\langle$'It is 2012', $I\rangle$, $\langle$'Actually, snow is not black', $I\rangle$ and $\langle$'Hesperus is Phosphorus', $I\rangle$ are true, the manifest invalidity of the corresponding sentences is not detected by (MNEC), but such sentences are nevertheless weeded out by (SNEC).

on the *shallow, broadly logical* principle of intersubstitutability between $\varphi$ and '$\varphi$' is true'.[31]

Having said this much in favour of (SNEC) (and against deflationism), I should dampen the enthusiasm that this might have created by explicitly adding that the further problems discussed in sections 6 and 7 affect (SNEC) just as well as (MNEC). Indeed, with its implicit quantification over *absolutely all contexts*, in that respect (SNEC) makes things even worse than (MNEC): while, at least to some extent, I could watchfully try to police $I$ so that it does not give rise to doubly improper or multiply referring utterances (and, more generally, to untrue utterances of valid sentences), I have no such power over many other contexts that (SNEC), but not (MNEC), talks about. Still, having duly recognized the substantial limits to (SNEC) and, more generally, to (NEC) that are still placed by the extreme variety of our uses of language, I think that the considerable extent to which, *within those limits*, (SNEC) outperforms (MNEC) demonstrates that it is a better sharpening of (NEC) than (MNEC) is (and that we thus have a truth-theoretic principle—with an admittedly restricted range of application—that deflationism cannot account for).

# 9   Logical Consequence and Truth beyond Language

With both (MNEC) and (SNEC) on the table, we can briefly extend the scope of our discussion so far. Back in section 4, I've assumed that both logical-consequence bearers and truth bearers are *linguistic* entities, and have identified these with sentences and utterances respectively. However, it is widely assumed in contemporary philosophy of logic and language that there are also *non-linguistic* logical-consequence bearers and truth bearers: *propositions*.

There are two most salient variants of (MNEC) and (SNEC) in which propositions play a role. On the first variant, *sentences* are kept fixed as *logical-consequence bearers* and *propositions* are taken only as *truth bearers*:

(MNEC$^{SP}$)  If $\varphi_0$, $\varphi_1$, $\varphi_2$... entail $\psi_0$, $\psi_1$, $\psi_2$..., then, metaphysically necessarily, if all of $\ulcorner\varphi_0, I\urcorner$, $\ulcorner\varphi_1, I\urcorner$, $\ulcorner\varphi_2, I\urcorner$... are true, then some of $\ulcorner\psi_0, I\urcorner$, $\ulcorner\psi_1, I\urcorner$, $\ulcorner\psi_2, I\urcorner$... are true;

(SNEC$^{SP}$)  If $\varphi_0$, $\varphi_1$, $\varphi_2$... entail $\psi_0$, $\psi_1$, $\psi_2$..., then, for every context $C$, if all of $\ulcorner\varphi_0, C\urcorner$, $\ulcorner\varphi_1, C\urcorner$, $\ulcorner\varphi_2, C\urcorner$... are true at $E_C$, then some of $\ulcorner\psi_0, C\urcorner$, $\ulcorner\psi_1, C\urcorner$, $\ulcorner\psi_2, C\urcorner$... are true at $E_C$

---

[31] The only kind of broadly logical argument I can think of with respect to which (MNEC) does clearly better than (SNEC) concerns *transparency itself* (and, as will become apparent, the kind of argument in question can be said to be "broadly logical" only, at best, in a very stretched sense). As I've observed in section 4, in the presence of context dependence transparency truth fails. For example, I am Italian, but Stephen's utterance of 'I am Italian' is not true; conversely, Stephen's utterance of 'I am British' is true, but I am not British. Yet, even if transparency fails for some utterances, as I've also observed in section 4 a version restricted to utterances with $I$ still seems to hold. Let $i_0$ be $\langle$'I am British', $I\rangle$ and $i_1$ be $\langle$'I am Italian', $I\rangle$. Then, let's assume that, in some very stretched sense, the arguments from 'I am British' to '$i_0$ is true' and from '$i_1$ is true' to 'I am Italian' are valid. Let finally $S$ be Stephen's context (as opposed to $I$). It follows that $\langle$'I am British', $S\rangle$ is true at $E_S$ even though $\langle$'$i_0$ is true', $S\rangle$ is not true at $E_S$ (and so (SNEC), but not (MNEC), fails for the argument from 'I am British' to '$i_0$ is true'), and it follows that $\langle$'$i_1$ is true', $S\rangle$ is true at $E_S$ even though $\langle$'I am Italian', $S\rangle$ is not true at $E_S$ (and so (SNEC), but not (MNEC), fails for the argument from '$i_1$ is true' to 'I am Italian').

(where $\ulcorner \varphi, C \urcorner$ is the proposition expressed by $\varphi$ at $C$). On the second variant, *propositions* are taken *both as logical-consequence bearers and as truth bearers*:

($\textsc{mnec}^{\text{PP}}$) If $\mathcal{P}_0$, $\mathcal{P}_1$, $\mathcal{P}_2$... entail $\mathcal{Q}_0$, $\mathcal{Q}_1$, $\mathcal{Q}_2$..., then, metaphysically necessarily, if all of $\mathcal{P}_0$, $\mathcal{P}_1$, $\mathcal{P}_2$... are true, then some of $\mathcal{Q}_0$, $\mathcal{Q}_1$, $\mathcal{Q}_2$... are true;

($\textsc{snec}^{\text{PP}}$) If $\mathcal{P}_0$, $\mathcal{P}_1$, $\mathcal{P}_2$... entail $\mathcal{Q}_0$, $\mathcal{Q}_1$, $\mathcal{Q}_2$..., then, for every context $C$, if all of $\mathcal{P}_0$, $\mathcal{P}_1$, $\mathcal{P}_2$... are true at $E_C$, then some of $\mathcal{Q}_0$, $\mathcal{Q}_1$, $\mathcal{Q}_2$... are true at $E_C$.

(where $\mathcal{P}_0$, $\mathcal{Q}_0$ and their like range over propositions).

The dialectics to which both ($\textsc{mnec}$) and ($\textsc{snec}$) have been subjected do not essentially change in the case of ($\textsc{mnec}^{\text{SP}}$) and ($\textsc{snec}^{\text{SP}}$) (basically, throughout these dialectics, we simply need to replace talk of $\langle \varphi, C \rangle$ being true in or at $E$ with talk of $\ulcorner \varphi, C \urcorner$ being true in or at $E$). The situation is more interesting in the case of ($\textsc{mnec}^{\text{PP}}$) and ($\textsc{snec}^{\text{PP}}$). Notice that, given our liberal conception of contexts and assuming the metaphysically necessary existence of propositions, the main consequent of ($\textsc{snec}^{\text{PP}}$) now *entails* the main consequent of ($\textsc{mnec}^{\text{PP}}$), and so ($\textsc{snec}^{\text{PP}}$) itself now entails ($\textsc{mnec}^{\text{PP}}$) itself. It is for this reason that, while the dialectics to which both ($\textsc{mnec}$) and ($\textsc{snec}$) have been subjected in sections 6 and 7 also do not essentially change in the case of ($\textsc{mnec}^{\text{PP}}$) and ($\textsc{snec}^{\text{PP}}$) (for the dialectic of section 7, we need to focus on the kind of counterexample mentioned in fn 23), the dialectic in section 5 is in fact exacerbated. For example, the proposition that snow is black entails the proposition that, actually, snow is black, but it is metaphysically possible that the former proposition is true and the latter false. Hence, ($\textsc{mnec}^{\text{PP}}$) fails. Moreover, in this new setting, *the move from metaphysical modality to semantic modality can do nothing to ameliorate the situation*, since, given the entailment from ($\textsc{snec}^{\text{PP}}$) to ($\textsc{mnec}^{\text{PP}}$), ($\textsc{snec}^{\text{PP}}$) fails just as well as ($\textsc{mnec}^{\text{PP}}$) does. In my view, the fact that, in this new setting (in which propositions are taken as logical-consequence bearers), even *within the limits* placed by the problems discussed in sections 6 and 7 there is no *modally strong* principle linking logical consequence with truth preservation is yet another reason (in addition to those adduced in Zardini, 2012a) for taking sentences rather than propositions as the (primary) logical-consequence bearers (since doing so at least affords us ($\textsc{snec}$) or ($\textsc{snec}^{\text{SP}}$), which, within the limits placed by the problems discussed in sections 6 and 7, do provide modally strong principles linking logical consequence with truth preservation). Be that as it may, clearly the shift from sentences and utterances to propositions does nothing to protect the traditional link between logical consequence and necessary truth preservation from the attacks of this paper.

# 10  Logical Consequence and Truth

Non-normality shows that a modally strong principle linking logical consequence with truth preservation needs to be understood in terms of a modality concerning the ways *words could have been used* rather than the ways *things could have been* (and that such link cannot be accounted for by deflationisti-cally acceptable means). Moreover, doubly improper utterances and multiply referring utterances show how the extreme variety of our uses of language mani-fested in context dependence allows utterances *to have semantic properties that lie out with the purview of logic.* In those cases, there are more ways of referring and being true than logical consequence ever dreamt of. Somehow conversely, valid sentences utterances of which do not express propositions show how the extreme variety of our uses of language manifested in both its assertive (typi-cally context dependent) and non-assertive uses allows sentences *to have logical properties even if utterances of them lack the semantic properties required for being in the game for truth or falsity.* In those other cases, there are more ways of being valid and logically following-from than truth ever dreamt of. In all these kinds of cases, careful consideration of context dependence and other vagaries of our uses of language brings a sobering appreciation of substantial gaps between logical consequence and the preservation of truth.

# BIBLIOGRAPHY

Field, H. (2006). Truth and the unprovability of consistency. *Mind*, 115:567–606.

Field, H. (2008). *Saving Truth from Paradox*. Oxford University Press, Oxford.

Groenendijk, J. and Stokhof, M. (1984). *Studies on the Semantics of Questions and the Pragmatics of Answers*. PhD Thesis, University of Amsterdam, Amsterdam.

Haack, S. (1978). *Philosophy of Logics*. Cambridge University Press, Cambridge.

Horwich, P. (1998). *Truth*. Clarendon Press, Oxford, 2nd edition.

Kaplan, D. (1989). Demonstratives. In Almog, J., Perry, J., and Wettstein, H., editors, *Themes from Kaplan*, pages 481–563. Oxford University Press, Oxford.

Lewis, D. (1979). Attitudes *De Dicto* and *De Se. The Philosophical Review*, 88:513–543.

Linsky, B. and Zalta, E. (1994). In defense of the simplest quantified modal logic. *Philosophical Perspectives*, 8:431–458.

MacFarlane, J. (2003). Future contingents and relative truth. *The Philosophical Quarterly*, 53:321–336.

Predelli, S. (2005). *Contexts*. Oxford University Press, Oxford.

Read, S. (1994). Formal and material consequence. *Journal of Philosophical Logic*, 23:247–265.

Read, S. (2003). Logical consequence as truth-preservation. *Logique et Analyse*, 183:479–493.

Read, S. (2008). The truth schema and the liar. In Rahman, S., Tulenheimo, T., and Genot, E., editors, *Unity, Truth and the Liar: The Modern Relevance of Medieval Solutions to the Liar Paradox*, pages 3–17. Springer, New York.

Richard, M. (1981). Temporalism and eternalism. *Philosophical Studies*, 39:1–13.

Schaffer, J. (2012). Necessitarian propositions. *Synthese*. Forthcoming.

Stalnaker, R. (1981). Indexical belief. *Synthese*, 49:129–151.

Tarski, A. (1936). On the concept of logical consequence. In *Logic, Semantics, Metamathematics*, pages 409–420. Hackett, Indianapolis, 1983. 2nd edition by J. Corcoran.

Vranas, P. (2010). In defence of imperative inference. *Journal of Philosophical Logic*, 39:59–71.

Williamson, T. (1994). *Vagueness*. Routledge, London.

Williamson, T. (1998). Bare possibilia. *Erkenntnis*, 48:257–273.

Zardini, E. (2008). Truth and what is said. *Philosophical Perspectives*, 22:545–574.

Zardini, E. (2011). Truth without contra(di)ction. *The Review of Symbolic Logic*, 4:498–535.

Zardini, E. (2012a). The bearers of logical consequence. Unpublished manuscript.

Zardini, E. (2012b). Context and consequence. An intercontextual substructural logic. Unpublished manuscript.

Zardini, E. (2012c). Getting one for two, or the contractors' bad deal. Towards a unified solution to the semantic paradoxes. In Achourioti, T., Fujimoto, K., Galinon, H., and Martínez, J., editors, volume on truth. Springer, New York.

Zardini, E. (2012d). It is not the case that [$P$ and 'It is not the case that $P$' is true]. Unpublished manuscript.

Zardini, E. (2012e). Naive logical properties and structural properties. *The Journal of Philosophy*. Forthcoming.

Zardini, E. (2012f). Naive restricted quantification. Unpublished manuscript.

Zardini, E. (2012g). Naive truth and naive logical properties. Unpublished manuscript.

Zardini, E. (2012h). The opacity of truth. Unpublished manuscript.

Zardini, E. (2012i). The role of utterances in Bradwardine's theory of truth. *Recherches de Théologie et Philosophie Médiévales*. Forthcoming.

Printed by BoD™in Norderstedt, Germany

9 781848 900868